The Culture of English Puritanism, 1560–1700

THEMES IN FOCUS

Published titles

Jonathan Barry and Christopher Brooks
THE MIDDLING SORT OF PEOPLE
Culture, Society and Politics in England, 1550–1800

Christopher Durston and Jacqueline Eales
THE CULTURE OF ENGLISH PURITANISM, 1560–1700

Tim Harris
POPULAR CULTURE IN ENGLAND, *c.* 1500–1850

R.W. Scribner and Trevor Johnson
POPULAR RELIGION IN GERMANY AND
CENTRAL EUROPE, 1400–1800

Forthcoming titles

Patrick Collinson and John Craig
THE REFORMATION IN ENGLISH TOWNS, 1500–1640

Paul Griffiths, Adam Fox and Steven Hindle
THE EXPERIENCE OF AUTHORITY IN EARLY
MODERN ENGLAND

Roy Porter and Marie Mulvey Roberts
PLEASURE IN THE EIGHTEENTH CENTURY

Series Standing Order

If you would like to receive future titles in this series as they are published, you can make use of our standing order facility. To place a standing order please contact your bookseller or, in case of difficulty, write to us at the address below with your name and address and the name of the series. Please state with which title you wish to begin your standing order. (If you live outside the United Kingdom we may not have the rights for your area, in which case we will forward your order to the publisher concerned.)

Customer Services Department, Macmillan Distribution Ltd
Houndmills, Basingstoke, Hampshire, RG21 6XS, England.

The Culture of English Puritanism, 1560–1700

Edited by

CHRISTOPHER DURSTON *and* JACQUELINE EALES

First published 1996 by
MACMILLAN PRESS LTD
Houndmills, Basingstoke, Hampshire RG21 6XS
and London
Companies and representatives
throughout the world

ISBN 0-333-59745-1 hardcover
ISBN 0-333-59746-X paperback

A catalogue record for this book is available
from the British Library.

10 9 8 7 6 5 4 3 2 1
05 04 03 02 01 00 99 98 97 96

Printed in Malaysia

For Robin Briggs and Penelope Corfield

Contents

Contents

Introduction: The Puritan Ethos, 1560–1700

CHRISTOPHER DURSTON and JACQUELINE EALES

I

Attempts to define early-modern English 'puritanism' and to agree on a common usage for the noun and adjective 'puritan' have been going on for well over 400 years. Contemporaries set about the task almost as soon as the religious phenomenon made its appearance in the wake of the sixteenth-century Reformation crisis, and historians and other scholars have continued their efforts, generating a lively academic controversy which shows no sign of abating. The central reason why the debate has gone on for so long is that it has proved exceptionally difficult to reach any common ground. Tudor and Stuart commentators frequently engaged in bitter and unresolved disputes about who or what should be labelled puritan, and historians from Clarendon onwards often seem only to have emulated them. As a consequence, for all the impressive scholarly attention directed to the question since the late sixteenth century, the meaning of the word 'puritan' remains unclear and the precise nature of early-modern 'puritanism' continues to evade analysis. In a colourful acknowledgement of the confusion and sterility which has marked much of the historiography of puritanism, Patrick Collinson has likened it to 'a debate conducted among a group of blindfolded scholars in a darkened room about the shape and other attributes of the elephant sharing the room with them'.[1]

The persistence and apparent intractability of the problems surrounding the terms 'puritan' and 'puritanism' have led some participants in the debate to argue that they should be banished altogether from the historians' dictionary. Some contemporaries certainly believed them to be unhelpful: Giles Widdowes, an anti-puritan cleric, argued in 1630 that the term 'puritan' was 'ambiguous' and thus

1

'fallacious'; Henry Parker, a puritan lawyer, commented in 1641 that: 'by its confused application it deceives invisibly'; and Thomas Fuller, a moderate royalist clergyman and church historian, wanted to ban it from 'common discourse', on the grounds that it was 'so various in the acceptions thereof'.[2] A number of modern historians have expressed similar reservations. Christopher Hill commented in the 1950s that the word was 'a dragon in the path of every student of this period', and a few years later he described it as 'an admirable refuge from clarity of thought'.[3] Geoffrey Elton also argued that it has little practical value, and Basil Hall remarked that it was 'originally a useful coin of some value' which had 'become over-minted and ended in headlong inflation'.[4] C. H. George was even more blunt, declaring that:

> an analytical concept which obscures the realities and significance of differences of ideas, ideals, programmes and class affinities is a bad concept. Puritanism is such a concept and should be abandoned.[5]

Others, however, have been equally insistent that the term does have real meaning and value and should be retained. William Hunt, for example, the historian of Essex puritanism in the period preceding the English Civil War, has argued that it would be 'a serious error' to dispense with a label which is in his view 'indispensable to . . . description and analysis'.[6]

Several reasons can be put forward in an attempt to explain this controversy and confusion. The first is that very early on in their linguistic careers the words 'puritan' and 'puritanism' became loose and indiscriminate terms of abuse; indeed, one of the very first people to employ the word seems to have been the Catholic exile, Thomas Stapleton, who used it in a publication of 1565 to attack his English Protestant enemies.[7] As a direct result, in the period before 1640 only a few Tudor and Stuart men or women were prepared openly to associate themselves with these terms. One exception was Samuel Ward, town preacher of Ipswich from 1603 until his suspension in 1635, who declared in a sermon printed in 1615 that he desired to worship God 'with that which most call puritanism' and that he believed 'none shall ever please Christ till they appear odd, strange and precise men to the common sort; and yet need not be over just'.[8] Another was the lawyer William Prynne who, in a contribution to the altar controversy published in 1637, described 'we poor puritans' as the only men who kept both 'crown and religion safe'.[9] In addition to such rare public pronouncements, a few individuals also accepted the name puritan in private, as did the Herefordshire gentleman Sir Robert Harley in 1621 when he composed a highly positive 'Character' of a puritan as a response to a debate in the House of Commons.[10]

Many others, however, whom later historians have categorised as puritans shunned this term and preferred to label themselves 'the godly', 'professors', 'true gospellers' or 'the elect'. As a consequence, it was usually not they themselves who outlined the characteristics of the 'puritan' movement, but their enemies; and these witnesses for the prosecution were not primarily concerned with presenting accurate accounts, but instead drew crude caricatures which only reinforced their own and their readers' prejudices. This point was succinctly underlined in a sermon delivered in St Margaret's Church, Canterbury, in 1630 by Francis Rogers who argued 'there are many that speak much against puritants . . . but I am verily persuaded that none make more puritants in the Church and Commonwealth than they that most speak against them.'[11] As Patrick Collinson has more recently put it, puritanism was 'a term of art and stigmatization, which became a weapon of some verbal finesse but no philosophical precision'.[12] Among the charges which appeared most frequently in hostile accounts were the suggestions that puritanism was rebellious and schismatic in nature and that the vast majority of puritans were merely hypocrites. As Peter Lake reveals later, puritanism's identity was largely shaped by the dialectic interplay of opposing puritan and anti-puritan images of the movement; but to accept the hostile testimony of puritanism's enemies uncritically, as some have done in the past, is no more sensible than to leave the definition of modern socialism to a Conservative cabinet minister.

A second reason for the definitional inexactitudes which have plagued the study of puritanism is that the movement never really existed as an independent, free-standing entity. For much of its history it was an oppositional, agitatory movement, frequently in conflict with the secular and ecclesiastical authorities or with those many sections of local society which did not share its ideals. As such, it was only one component of a set of fluid and dynamic polarities, a fact which has prompted Patrick Collinson to warn that 'there is little point in constructing elaborate statements defining what in ontological terms Puritanism was and was not, when it was not a thing definable in itself but only one half of a stressful relationship.'[13] In the course of the century and a half which separated the accession of Elizabeth I from that of Queen Anne, the political, religious and social environment in England changed repeatedly and sometimes dramatically, and what was implied by the labels 'puritan' and 'puritanism' inevitably altered to reflect the evolving priorities and preoccupations of church, state and people. To a-very large degree, therefore, both the nature and extent of puritanism were determined by the changing environment within which it existed, so that, as Patrick Collinson has once again pointed out: 'No laboratory-bench taxonomy of religious types and tendencies in pre-revolutionary England will serve if it sticks labels on isolated and inert specimens and fails to appreciate that the very terms themselves are evidence of an unstable and dynamic situation.'[14]

The confusing effects of the interplay of these factors can be appreciated from even a short chronological account of the fortunes of early-modern puritanism. During the first 30 years of Elizabeth I's reign puritans were commonly identified as those most actively involved in the vigorous political campaign being waged in pulpit, press and parliament to bring about a further reformation of both the organisational structure and the liturgy of the newly established English Protestant church. In the forefront of such demands were a number of prominent radicals, such as the presbyterians Thomas Cartwright, Walter Travers and John Field, and the early separatists John Penry, Robert Browne and Henry Barrow. By the 1590s Elizabeth's secular and ecclesiastical advisers had silenced these men and destroyed their hopes of bringing about any immediate alteration in the governmental structure of the church, but puritan pressure for ceremonial and liturgical change continued on into the next century.

On his arrival in England in 1603 James I was faced with a well-orchestrated puritan call for reform of the church, and he responded by calling the Hampton Court Conference of 1604. In the event, the conference failed to deliver any major ecclesiastical change, and the subsequent appointment of Richard Bancroft as archbishop of Canterbury further dashed puritan hopes of support from the new monarch. In 1611, however, Bancroft was succeeded by George Abbot, a prelate who was much more sympathetic to the aspirations of the moderate puritan reformers, and throughout the remainder of James's reign a more relaxed, conciliatory approach was adopted towards those who refused to accept all of the ceremonial and liturgical elements of the Elizabethan Settlement. As a result, although they continued to call for a more thoroughly Protestant foreign policy, most Jacobean puritans saw little reason to engage in sustained agitation against James's church or government.

Following the rise of anti-Calvinistic English Arminianism in the mid 1620s, however, subversive political connotations were once more firmly attached to the word puritan. In the hands of Charles I, William Laud, and the other Laudian bishops who controlled the English church during the 1630s it became a highly convenient pejorative label, under which the many and varied groups and individuals who opposed or resisted them could be lumped together and denounced. As redefined by the Arminians, puritanism's boundaries were extended to encompass large numbers of moderate men and women whose religious views had hitherto been considered entirely orthodox, and once again it was perceived as a revolutionary movement bent on the destruction of both the English monarchy and the established episcopalian church. A great many of those whom Laud and his colleagues tarred with the puritan brush during the 1630s reacted with amazement, outrage and alarm to their altered religious status. In 1640 one of their number, Sir Benjamin Rudyerd, gave vent to their anger in parliament, complaining bitterly in the House of Commons that the Arminians and their allies had 'brought it to pass that under the name of puritans all our religion is branded . . . Their great work, their masterpiece now, is to make all those of the religion the suspected party of the kingdom.'[15] The following year another of Laud's critics, Henry Parker, echoed Rudyerd's comments in print, declaring in *A Discourse Concerning Puritans*:

> Thus far it appears what a vast circumference this word *puritan* has, and how by its large acception it is suited to cast dirt in the face of all goodness, Theological, Civil or Moral: so that scarce any man can avoid its imputation . . . if the confused misapplication of this foul word Puritan be not reformed in England, and that with speed, we can expect nothing but a sudden universal downfall of all goodness whatsoever.[16]

In 1642 many of these newly branded puritans protested in the most vigorous way possible by taking up arms against Charles and Laud in the English Civil War. Following the parliamentary victory in that conflict, puritanism temporarily lost its oppositional character and became instead the ideological underpinning of the successive political and religious establishments of Interregnum England. The return of Charles II in 1660, however, abruptly ended puritanism's brief identification with the ecclesiastical and secular authorities. During the 1660s it was violently expelled both from the political arena and from the confines of the national church itself. As John Spurr shows in the final chapter of this book, the next generation of puritans gradually abandoned the campaign to reform the English church from within, and embarked on a 30-year struggle for the right to worship outside it.

II

These factors, then, have done much to muddy the waters of puritan historiography, and to leave puritanism resembling not so much Hill's dragon or Collinson's elephant but, to use W. J. Sheils's phrase, a much more elusive 'Protean beast'.[17] Our own attempt to define this slippery creature must begin with a brief consideration of several features of the religious landscape of early-modern England which were *not* exclusively or incontrovertibly puritan. During the course of Elizabeth I's reign English Protestantism developed an ever-deepening hostility towards the Roman Catholic church and its head, the pope. By the early seventeenth century anti-Catholicism and anti-papalism had become core elements of the English people's political and religious heritage, and individuals from right across the conformist religious spectrum had come to regard the pope as the Antichrist – the arch-enemy of Christ and epitome of all that was evil. Over the same period, growing numbers of English Protestants had become convinced that they were members of a chosen people with a special relationship with their God, and that events on both a personal and national scale were governed by a divine Providence to which they should submit unquestioningly. While puritans were likely to subscribe to these ideas more readily, intensively and wholeheartedly than their less zealous neighbours, their near universal acceptance by 1625 prevents them from being seen as clear defining marks of puritanism.

Nor is it possible to draw a straight and unbroken line between puritans and non-puritans on the basis of theological belief. While some historians have argued that puritanism can be equated with a belief in the doctrine of predestination, others have expressed serious reservations about this view, and the dispute has generated a great deal of complex argument and debate. The doctrine of double predestination, which was implicit in the theology of Martin Luther but later elaborated by, and more closely associated with John Calvin and his followers, asserted that God had divided humankind into two immutable groups: the elect (or saved) who were destined for heaven, and the reprobate (or damned) who were destined for hell. In stark contrast to the Roman Catholic church's belief in free will and salvation through works, this predestinarian theology emphasised that the individual could never merit salvation nor exercise any control over his or her fate after death.

Scholars such as J. F. H. New, J. Sears McGee, Richard Greaves and Peter White have suggested that a ready acceptance of this austere doctrine was one of the defining features of English puritanism, and that during the period from 1560 to 1640 puritans were clearly separated from a mainstream which was much more cautious and ambivalent in its approach to predestination.[18] Other historians, however, in particular Nicholas Tyacke, R. T. Kendall and Peter Lake, have taken issue with aspects of this analysis and have shown that it needs substantial modification and refinement. They have argued convincingly that there was in fact a broad 'Calvinist consensus' within the Elizabethan and Jacobean church, and that between 1560 and 1625 the doctrine of predestination was accepted without question by virtually all of the most influential clergymen in England, puritan and non-puritan alike.[19] There is a great deal of persuasive evidence to support this view. In 1595, for example, an assault on the doctrine by William Barrett, a Cambridge University chaplain, was ultimately quashed by the drawing up of the unequivocally predestinarian Lambeth Articles which were endorsed by churchmen from right across the religious spectrum, including the bishop of London, Richard Fletcher, and the conservative archbishop of Canterbury, John Whitgift, who had been spearheading the campaign to root out Elizabethan puritanism. A few years later the puritan minister Josias Nichols of Eastwell in Kent claimed in print that, as well as sharing an aversion to idolatry and superstition and a firm commitment to royal authority, puritans and their opponents both preached 'one Faith and Substance of doctrine'.[20]

At the same time, however, there were within this predestinarian consensus many subtle shades of emphasis and interpretation, and puritans were criticised by their opponents for being overinclined to interpret the doctrine too literally and delve into its mysteries too deeply. At the Hampton Court Conference of 1604, Bishop Richard Bancroft was reported to have complained that 'very many in these days . . . presumed too much of persisting in grace, laying all their religion upon predestination.'[21] His comment suggests that it was a difference of degree of belief rather than a doctrinal disagreement which divided puritans from bishops. For many puritans a deep attachment to predestination was undoubtedly a central and commanding influence, and one which was revealed in a constant stress on the maintenance of godly behaviour and a search for assurance of salvation. Yet it is notable that when Sir Robert Harley penned his short manuscript profile of the typical puritan the doctrine of predestination was conspicuous by its absence from his list of defining attributes.[22]

Harley drew up this list of puritan attributes in 1621, when differing interpretations of the doctrine of predestination remained largely an area of rarified academic debate. Three years later, however, the publication of Richard Montagu's *A Gagg for the New Gospel? No: A New Gagg for an Old Goose . . .* presented the minority anti-Calvinist position to a wider lay audience and led to furious debates in successive parliamentary sessions between 1624 and 1629. Harley was one of those MPs who were most sensitive to this Arminian attack on predestination, and he spoke passionately on the issue in the House of Commons along with John Pym, Christopher Sherland, Francis Rous and others.[23] These debates make clear that from the mid 1620s onwards there was an increasingly close identification of puritanism with predestinarian beliefs, but this was a link that only really became meaningful once the Arminians had set about their attempt to destroy the pre-existing consensus. Before the mid 1620s it was nuances of interpretation rather than distinctive doctrinal position that distinguished puritans from their contemporaries.

It should also be remembered that the puritans themselves were often deeply divided. As Basil Hall has pointed out, individuals such as William Perkins, Thomas Helwys, Richard Baxter and John Bunyan – all men who have been described as puritans – possessed widely differing views on a range of doctrinal, organisational and liturgical issues.[24] But while it is undoubtedly true that much separated these men, they nonetheless shared something very important that justifies grouping them together under the label puritan, namely a common spiritual and cultural outlook. Above all else, puritanism was a movement grounded in a highly distinctive cast of mind – or to use a more fashionable term, *mentalité* – which displayed itself in the individual puritan as a peculiarly severe yet vibrant spirituality, and within groups of puritans as a unique and dynamic religious culture. For this reason, we would argue that it is through the study of this culture that puritanism is most fruitfully approached, and that it is around those who shared in it that the boundaries of the movement should be drawn.

III

Any attempt to define puritanism as a culture must, of course, begin with an explanation of what is meant by that concept. We will take as our working definition that employed by Peter Burke in his seminal study, *Popular Culture in Early Modern Europe*. According to Burke, culture is 'a system of shared meanings, attitudes and values, and the symbolic forms . . . in which they are expressed or embodied'.[25] Social and cultural historians and their anthropologist colleagues have debated at length whether an individual acquires his or her religious culture in early life through family and social influences, only later ascribing emotional content to its various rites and ceremonies; or whether conversely culture is primarily a vehicle for emotional need-fulfilment and as such is created by the psychology of the individual.[26] In our view, these approaches should not be considered as mutually exclusive, for the psyche gives rise to culture, and culture shapes the psyche in an on-going dialectic spiral.

Undoubtedly much of what was distinctive about the behaviour of early-modern puritans was the product of their very particular view of human nature and humanity's relationship with its Maker. Throughout his theological writings the founding father of puritanism, John Calvin, had argued that an enormous gulf separated a fallen and utterly evil humankind from an omnipotent, punitive and sometimes vengeful deity. He had missed no opportunity to ram home the message that 'there is more worth in all the vermin of the world than there is in man' and that the human mind was 'a sink and lurking place for every sort of filth'; and he had been careful never to allow his readers to forget that they were 'nothing but a worm of the earth, nothing but dust, ashes and rotting flesh'.[27] This extremely negative view of human nature had helped Calvin to explain why it was impossible for the individual ever to merit salvation, but as an almost inevitable by-product it created in those who took it most to heart a deep sense of their own unworthiness, allied to a constant preoccupation with the need to assuage God's wrath. These psychological concerns were at the root of the puritan insistence on the need for constant and vigilant self-examination by the individual, and for order, discipline and frequent collective 'humiliation' by the community.

When balanced out by a belief in Christ's saving grace and by some degree of confidence that one would obtain the salvation which was guaranteed to God's elect, such a mentality could manifest itself in great energy, productivity and material gain; and any resultant worldly success might well in its turn reinforce the individual puritan's assurance that he or she walked in God's favour. The puritan merchant Ignatius Jordan, for example, who served as mayor and MP for Exeter in the early seventeenth century, was described after his death as attaining 'a very great measure of assurance' by reason of 'his diligent attending upon and careful applying the means of grace, and God's blessing upon them'.[28] The fact that such puritan attitudes and patterns of behaviour could sometimes facilitate worldly advancement and financial gain has led some historians, notably Richard Tawney and Christopher Hill, to link the emergence of puritanism with the early growth of capitalism and to argue that the movement acquired most of its adherents from amongst the industrious 'better sort' within English society.[29] While a number of pre-Civil War communities were certainly dominated by a social elite of powerful and wealthy puritans, puritanism won converts from right across the social spectrum, including within its ranks aristocrats, gentlemen, clothworkers and cobblers. For this reason, few historians would now argue that it was a movement which reflected the economic interests of one particular socio-economic group. Moreover, although Tawney and Hill's thesis has generated a great deal of lively historical debate, it has not proved a route to a deeper appreciation of the puritan experience. For, as Geoffrey Dickens has emphasised, puritanism was always 'an obstinately religious phenomenon',[30] at the core of which remained an intense preoccupation with individual spiritual welfare and the highly personalised relationship with a stern and demanding Maker.

In some cases there occurred a precise defining moment which the individual puritan later considered to be crucial in his or her spiritual development. This was often experienced in young adulthood and was couched in terms of a sudden conversion experience which imparted for the first time a sense of assurance of salvation. Ignatius Jordan, for example, was sent to the Isle of Guernsey at the age of 15 where 'God . . . did by his grace effectually call and convert him'.[31] At the age of 17 or 18 Margaret Charlton, the future wife of Richard Baxter, was so moved by a sermon on Isaiah 27: 11 that 'the doctrine of conversion . . . was received on her heart as the seal on wax. Whereupon she presently fell to self-judging, and to frequent prayer, and reading, and serious thoughts of her present state, and her salvation.'[32]

A great many puritans, however, struggled for years before they could finally convince themselves that they were saved, and large numbers were never able to rid themselves entirely of lingering, nagging doubts about their elect status. In the case of some of these individuals, Calvin's emphasis on human unworthiness and divine justice appears to have created or – in those with a predisposition towards it – intensified tendencies towards an obsessive and psychologically damaging introspection, and to have produced the depressions and extremes of self-loathing which afflicted many individual English puritans. Among those who suffered in this way were the young Oliver Cromwell and, less famously, one of Lady Brilliana Harley's maids, who was described in 1640 as 'in grievous agony of conscience and despair; she says she shall be damned'.[33] It was also common for such doubts to be experienced by those approaching death. The authors of funeral sermons and godly lives were at pains to demonstrate that the faith of their puritan subjects had helped them to overcome their death-bed fears, but, as Ralph Houlbrooke shows later in this volume, some suffered considerable anguish before doing so. Several contemporaries clearly regarded such anxieties as a central feature of the puritan mentality. Early in James I's reign Richard Butler, an ecclesiastical official, was reported to have described a puritan as a Protestant 'frayed out of his wits'; and a few years later in 1615 Sir John Harington reiterated the point, defining puritans as 'Protestants scared out of their wits'.[34]

Detailed evidence both of the existence of this mentality and of the way in which it displayed itself in behaviour is provided in the private writings of substantial numbers of early-modern puritans. Two particularly well-researched examples are the London wood-turner, Nehemiah Wallington, and the Essex clergyman, Ralph Josselin. Wallington grew up in one of the capital's many puritan families during the reign of James I. His adolescent years were marked by a deep spiritual crisis during which he was consumed by intense feelings of shame and despair over what he called his 'most vile and sinful corruption'. These difficulties centred on a growing conviction that he was destined for hell, a belief which appears to have been fuelled by his inability to come to terms with his emerging sexuality. Successive bouts of depression and anxiety brought him to the verge of a complete mental breakdown and to several attempts at suicide. After 1618 he found some relief from his psychological torment by dedicating his life to God, and thereafter he was driven by a compulsive urge to record in writing the details of what remained an often agonised pilgrim's progress.

Between 1618 and 1654 he penned no fewer than 50 volumes of personal religious writings, amounting in all to around 20,000 pages. Included in this extraordinary spiritual record were accounts of his own religious experiences, transcripts of sermons and psalms, descriptions of divine judgements on sinners and mercies towards the just, and commentaries on God's involvement in contemporary political and religious events. As Wallington himself made clear, the motivation behind all this obsessive writing was the pressing need for self-examination and for acknowledgement of his own failures and sinfulness. Determined to remember that he had a 'filthy, odious and polluted heart' and that there was 'a sty of filthiness' within him, he summed up his remarkable literary efforts in the comment: 'I glorify God by self-examination and judgement of myself'.[35]

Ralph Josselin shared with Wallington both a preoccupation with the need for constant self-examination and vigilance against sin and temptation, and a deep sense of personal unworthiness. His long diary, which covers the greater part of his adult life from the 1640s to the 1680s, is liberally peppered with comments such as: 'the Lord affect me with the vileness of my nature'; 'I stick in the mire, Oh Lord pull me out'; 'my heart is still clogged with old corruptions'; and 'I have Lord my bitter roots of mind, vanity and pollution, which thou knowest, make me watchful and jealous that I be not overcome with them'.[36] What is also made clear in the diary is that Josselin struggled for long periods to square the dictates of his persecutory puritan conscience with a conflicting, residual instinct to think well of himself – a psychological dilemma he on one occasion neatly encapsulated in the comment: 'I desire to loathe myself, but yet I attain not to an inward spiritual frame.'[37]

Detailed consideration of the writings of Wallington and Josselin can tempt one to suggest that puritanism should be seen as one response to the Protestant abolition of the Catholic sacrament of auricular confession, since for many individuals this had proved a very effective safety-valve for precisely the feelings of guilt and fear which oppressed these men for so long. By no means all of the contemporaries who shared Wallington and Josselin's obsessive indulgence in self-scrutiny and self-abasement were to be found within the puritan camp; nor did all puritans suffer the same degree of mental strife as these two. There is, nonetheless, a sufficient correlation between puritanism and these psychological traits for us to regard them as an important mental seam running through most of the movement's spiritual and cultural manifestations.

IV

We shall begin our delineation of puritan culture by considering the views of three seventeenth-century commentators, Josias Nichols, Henry Parker and John Geree, all of whom wrote from within the puritan fold. These witnesses for the defence clearly believed that their movement was a spiritual and cultural force and should be defined as such. Josias Nichols, puritan minister of Eastwell in Kent during Elizabeth I's reign, commented on the nature of puritanism in his work *The Plea of the Innocent* published in 1602. After suggesting that clergymen were often denounced as puritans because of their 'seeking for reformation of some ceremonies and of some part of the ecclesiastical discipline', he went on to characterise lay puritans as 'the people [who] do hear sermons, talk of the Scriptures, [and] sing Psalms together in private houses etc.'[38]

Henry Parker was a godly lawyer and the nephew of the staunchly puritan nobleman, William Fiennes, Lord Saye and Sele. During the early 1640s he supported the resurgent prebyterians and later in the decade he was identified with Independency. In his *A Discourse Concerning Puritans* published in 1641, he identified four categories which had been employed to classify puritans during the period from 1560 to 1640. The first three of these were ecclesiastical puritans, who wished to purge the church of what they regarded as its popish ritual; puritans in religion, who were noted for their hatred of popery; and state or political puritans who had opposed the policies of Charles I's government during the late 1620s and 1630s. In his view, however, by far the most important group was the fourth. This contained those whom he labelled 'ethical puritans' or puritans in morality, who were distinguished 'by their remarkable and singular zeal to God and the Truth'. Parker claimed that during the early decades of Elizabeth's reign all those in the movement had been ecclesiastical puritans, but that by 1600 it was the ethical puritans who had come to dominate it and that subsequently the term puritan was most frequently used to denote a characteristic moral and ethical standpoint. Thus he defined his fellow puritans as 'men of strict life and precise opinions which cannot be hated for any thing but their zeal and piety', and declared that 'the most ordinary badge of puritans is their more religious and conscionable conversation than that which is seen in other men'.[39]

Five years later in 1646 John Geree published *The Character of an Old English Puritane or Non-Conformist*. Geree had been the minister of Tewkesbury in Gloucestershire until his suspension in the mid 1620s. He had been restored to the living in 1641 by the Long Parliament's Committee for Plundered Ministers, by which time he had fully embraced the presbyterian position. He wrote *The Character* at a time when the structure of the nation's religious life appeared to be breaking down and many presbyterians were becoming increasingly alarmed by the proliferation of radical sects in London and elsewhere. Perhaps as a result, the tract contains a highly nostalgic picture of pre-Civil War puritanism, and one which lays great stress on the movement's orderliness and acceptance of secular and ecclesiastical authority.

Geree's archetypal (male) puritan was 'such a one that honoured God above all, and under God gave every one his due, making the

Word of God the rule of his worship'. He adopted a lifestyle distinguished above all by prayer, Bible-reading, and frequent resort to sermons and lectures. When he prayed he would sometimes employ the set forms laid down in the less corrupt parts of the Prayer Book, but he much preferred extempore prayers, 'where, by the gift of God, expressions were varied according to present wants and occasions'. He regarded both the private and public reading of scripture and attendance at sermons as indispensable and complementary activities, believing that, while the Word read had more 'authority', the Word preached often had more 'efficacy'. It was on Sunday that this distinctive spiritual approach was most visible. Having made his preparations on Saturday evening and 'redeemed' Sunday morning from 'superfluous sleep', Geree's puritan devoted virtually the whole of the Christian sabbath to religious exercises. As a man of 'good spiritual appetite', he was not satisfied with one meal of preaching, but sought out a second sermon in the afternoon, sometimes travelling outside his parish to attend one. He augmented these sermons with private Bible-study and informal meetings for religious instruction at home or in church. While he was prepared to accept that Sunday could also be a time for 'needful refreshing', he nonetheless considered lawful recreations to be 'unseasonable' on that day, and unlawful ones 'abominable'.

For Geree's puritan the Lord's Supper was 'part of his soul's food', and he considered it important both to partake of it himself and to 'have the scandalous cast out of communion'. While he was scathing about the 'mock-fasts' of the papists, he 'neglected not an occasion to humble his soul by right fasting'. He was opposed to any church music which 'moved sensual delight and was a hindrance to spiritual enlargements', but he enjoyed the singing of metrical psalms, 'wherein though he neglected not the melody of the voice yet he chiefly looked after that of the heart'. His daily life was marked by gravity, sobriety and asceticism, and he was careful to avoid any excess or vanity, 'rather beating down the body than pampering it'. Finally, he took great pains to turn his family and household into a puritan church in miniature, 'admitting none to it but such as feared God and labouring that those who were born in it might be born again to God'. Thus he strove to bring up his children 'in nurture and admonition of the Lord', and 'commanded his servants to keep the way of the Lord'. Geree concluded by declaring of his puritan: 'His whole life he accounted a warfare, wherein Christ was his Captain;

his arms, prayers and tears; the Cross his banner, and his word *vincit qui patitur* [he conquers who suffers].'[40]

V

This helpful testimony takes us some considerable way towards an understanding of puritan culture. To obtain a fuller picture we must now flesh it out with the comments of other contemporaries and the findings of some of the modern scholars who have studied the movement.

At the level of personal spirituality, puritanism was above all else a movement predicated upon the revealed Word of God as transmitted through the scriptures. While all Protestants stressed the importance of the individual acquiring a working knowledge of scripture, for the puritan the Bible was elevated to the status of the sole and complete repository of doctrinal and moral truth. In his *English Puritanisme* published in 1605, the non-conformist cleric William Bradshaw claimed that the Word of God contained in the Bible was 'of absolute perfection' and 'the sole canon and rule of all matters'; and a few years later Sir Robert Harley described a puritan as 'one that dares do nothing in the worship of God or course of his life but what God's word warrants him, and dares not leave undone anything that the word commands him'.[41]

Most puritans either owned a Bible or had easy access to one. A great many of them were able to read its contents for themselves, and those who could not were eager to take every opportunity to have it read to them. Their preferred version was the Geneva Bible which appeared in 1560 and included extensive Calvinist notes in the margin. They devoted considerable time and effort, both privately and collectively, to Bible-reading and interpretation and in many cases acquired as a consequence an impressive scriptural knowledge. Their ability to refer to, and quote at length, obscure Old and New Testament texts in defence of their views and actions was legendary, and was frequently remarked upon derisively by their critics; in 1628, for example, John Earle wrote of a she-puritan: 'She overflows so much with the Bible that she spills it upon every occasion, and will not cudgel her maids without Scripture.'[42] Some puritans took a particular interest in the law-giving books of the Old Testament and attempted to construct their personal and communal morality upon a strict and literal interpretation of the Ten Commandments and the other injunctions of the Mosaic Law. Many were also given to drawing close parallels between the events described in the Bible and developments occurring in their own lifetimes. Thus during the Interregnum Oliver Cromwell increasingly came to see himself as a second Joshua or Moses leading God's chosen English people out of the Egyptian slavery of Charles I's reign and through the political wilderness of the 1650s towards a distant Promised Land.

Furthermore, while other English Protestants were prepared to accept as legitimate a number of beliefs and practices which their church had adopted despite the fact that they had no specific biblical sanction, the puritans' extreme reliance on scripture led them both to reject these accretions and to denounce the whole idea that certain religious observances were *'adiaphora'* – 'things indifferent' – and that the leaders of the church and government had the right to decide whether they were valid and binding. Sir Robert Harley commented that 'to Things Indifferent' the puritan 'thinks himself not born a bondsman'; and William Bradshaw went much further, arguing that 'anything that cannot be justified by scripture is unlawful in worship', and that it was positively sinful 'to perform any other worship to God, whether external or internal, moral or ceremonial, in whole or in part, than that which God himself requires in his word'.[43] Patrick Collinson has suggested that this issue of *adiaphora* was of such importance that it should be seen as the point 'where the geological fault-line between Anglicanism and Nonconformity, Church and Chapel, began'.[44]

It was this same emphasis on the Bible and rejection of *adiaphora* which led puritans to denounce much of what they saw as the ritualistic and formulaic liturgy of the Elizabethan church and to seek to replace it with their own simpler and more attenuated forms of worship. While a few of them rejected the 1559 Book of Common Prayer in its entirety, most were prepared to use it selectively, avoiding those parts which they found most offensive. Thus, they spurned many of the set prayers in the book, preferring instead to compose their own improvised, extempore prayers. They also had grave doubts about a number of its ceremonies. Those which appear to have caused the most friction were the ones associated with the important personal milestones of birth, marriage and death; for most puritans were reluctant to let these events pass unmarked, yet at the same time deeply resented having to solemnise them using the objectionable rites contained in the Prayer Book.

The main religious rites connected with birth were baptism and churching. While most puritans accepted the validity and importance of infant baptism, they objected to several features of the Prayer Book baptismal service. They argued that baptism should take place at the front of the church before the whole congregation rather than more privately at the font. Many of them also opposed the practice of choosing godparents – or 'gossips' – for the child and allowing them to present it to the minister for baptism, on the grounds that this implied a dilution of parental responsibility for the child's subsequent spiritual welfare. They also objected strongly to the signing of the cross on the child's forehead, regarding this as a relic of popery. The churching ceremony, which marked the public re-entry into the church of women who had recently given birth, consisted of the reciting of a number of set prayers over the mother on her first appearance at the parish church following her confinement. While most Tudor and Stuart mothers undoubtedly regarded this service primarily as a welcome opportunity to give thanks for their safe delivery, many puritans rejected it as another 'heretical, blasphemous and popish foolery', and a few were also worried that it appeared to contain suggestions of ritual purification. Their objections increased during the 1630s when the Laudian authorities attempted to force women to wear veils and kneel while being churched.[45]

Puritans were similarly affronted by many of the English church's procedures for the solemnising of marriages. They were appalled by the endemic confusion surrounding matrimonial canon law, and found it offensive that couples who purchased a special marriage licence could avoid the reading of their banns in church prior to their wedding. With regard to the marriage service itself, they took exception to the use of the ring and the husband's promise to worship his wife with his body, both of which features appeared to them an encouragement to idolatry. During the 1630s some puritans also resisted Laudian efforts to encourage couples to receive communion during the wedding service.

Although the Elizabethan church had dispensed with many of the Roman Catholic ceremonies associated with death, it had not gone far enough for most puritans, who continued to regard the Prayer Book burial service as uncomfortably close to popery and wished to simplify drastically this and the other rituals that surrounded the dying. As Ralph Houlbrooke's contribution to this volume illustrates, puritans considered the Prayer Book rituals to be unnecessary and superstitious, and believed that they should seek from within themselves the resources which would allow them to approach death with patience, dignity and assurance of salvation. They hoped that their deaths would vindicate their puritan lifestyles and provide a potent source of inspiration for their families, friends and any others who either witnessed them or read reports of them. The depth of puritan hostility to all these rites of passage ceremonies was made clear during the 1640s and 1650s when, as Christopher Durston shows later in this volume, post-Civil War puritan regimes radically simplified the baptismal service, abolished churching, and attempted to banish the church from any involvement at weddings and burials.

Another popular feature of more mainstream worship which was rejected by puritans was church music. They outlawed the use of all musical instruments in church, and the only singing they were prepared to countenance was the slow and somewhat monotonous chanting of metrical psalms. This one musical concession was, however, one to which some of them appear to have become inordinately attached. Puritan psalms were regularly sung not only during services but also on the journeys to and from the local parish church, as well as on fast-days and trips outside the parish to hear other preachers. Indeed, Patrick Collinson suggests later in this volume that there is a good case for arguing that, like eighteenth-century Methodism, seventeenth-century puritanism was 'born in song' – albeit not the sort of song that would appeal to many modern ears!

It was also of great importance to puritans that their pared-down liturgy should be conducted in appropriate buildings. They wished to worship in sparsely furnished and plainly decorated churches, laid out primarily as arenas for the hearing of God's Word rather than for the dispensing of sacraments. They favoured churches which possessed prominent pulpits and lecterns, but modest and unadorned wooden communion tables. When in the 1630s the Laudian authorities mounted a campaign for the replacement of such movable communion tables with permanent altars positioned in the chancel and separated from the body of the church by rails, many puritans were outraged and some resisted fiercely. Nor was puritan 'iconophobia' directed only at altars and their 'clothes, tapers, basins and other Romish furniture'.[46] Rather it extended to cover all church paintings, sculptures and stained glass, and, as Margaret Aston shows in her contribution to this volume, on a number of occasions between 1560 and 1640, and increasingly frequently during the 1640s, it exploded into violent bouts of image-breaking.

VI

While iconoclasm could be the work of a lone individual, it was more often a social activity. Scholars of puritanism have only relatively recently come to realise that in its active expression puritanism was a social experience which placed great emphasis on 'the communal aspects of the Christian experience'.[47] The main vehicles for puritan socialisation were sermons and fasts. It was of vital importance to puritans that they should have frequent access to 'painful' preachers whose sermons could provide them with the encouragement, admonition and edification which they regarded as the essential elements of a healthy spiritual diet. They considered preaching to be an indispensable ingredient of Sunday worship, and many of them also regularly attended four or five weekday sermons; on one occasion Nehemiah Wallington notched up the impressive total of no fewer than nineteen in seven days![48] In the first instance, they looked to find such suitable sermons in their local parishes, but if their minister proved 'a dumb dog' who neglected preaching, they were prepared to travel considerable distances to attend them elsewhere. Over time, this travelling – or 'gadding' – became an important spiritual activity in its own right. Groups of travelling puritans often walked together for several hours on their way to and from worship, discussing sermons, singing psalms, and cementing the ties that linked them together as 'friends in the Lord'. As a result, gadding played an important part in fostering the social cohesion of local puritan networks and providing them with opportunities for the defiant flaunting of their lifestyles before their ungodly neighbours. Patrick Collinson elaborates on this theme of the social dimension of attendance at sermons in his later contribution.

Communal public fasting was another extremely important aspect of puritan sociability; indeed Collinson claims in this volume that 'an anthropologist wanting to describe puritan culture . . . should be led without further delay to the puritan fast'. The practice of public fasting had been inherited by Christianity from Judaism and had been a conspicuous feature of its worship from its earliest years. Throughout the medieval period, Roman Catholics had fasted or abstained from meat at designated times in the week and the year, in particular on Fridays and throughout Lent. The Protestant reformers of the sixteenth century had objected to the routinised nature of these Catholic fasts, but had nonetheless continued to regard fast-days organised for specific purposes as legitimate and valuable. The Elizabethan church settlement, therefore, made provision for the holding of occasional public fast-days at times of particular crisis, and a number of such days were called by the authorities during Elizabeth I's reign, for example during the serious plague visitations of 1563 and 1593 and the Armada crisis of 1588.[49]

It was the puritan movement, however, which showed the most enthusiasm for public fasting and indulged in the practice most frequently, by supplementing the rare opportunities for government-sponsored fasting with their own unauthorised days. During Elizabeth's reign the holding of such unsanctioned fast-days became an important feature of religious life in many puritan communities. They normally took the form of a day devoted entirely to a round of sermons, prayers and psalm-singing, often concluding with a simple, shared meal. They also frequently involved the collecting of money from the participants, either for the poor or for some other godly cause. Elizabeth and her government became increasingly alarmed by these occurrences and in 1604 Archbishop Bancroft specifically banned them in his ecclesiastical canons. Nonetheless, puritans continued to hold regular fasts throughout the period from 1604 to 1629. When William Laud came to power in the 1630s he tried hard to stamp out what he called this 'ill-custom', and several puritan ministers found themselves in serious trouble for organising illegal fast-days. Charles Chauncey, for example, was summoned to appear before the Court of High Commission in 1637 for presiding at a fast at Marston St Lawrence in Northamptonshire, at which he had preached for six hours to an audience of 60 local puritans, including Lord Saye and Sele.[50] The strength of puritan commitment to fasting was illustrated during the Civil War years when the parliamentary authorities tried to enforce the observation of a day of 'fasting and humiliation' on the last Wednesday of every month. This regular day was abandoned in the early months of 1649, but further occasional fast-days were held at intervals throughout the Interregnum.[51]

One of the primary purposes of these days was to inculcate an individual and collective sense of 'humiliation' by providing puritans with an ideal opportunity for lengthy meditation upon the insignificance and depravity of humankind and the power and justice of God – perspectives which, as we have seen, were at the very core of the puritan mental outlook. Puritans also saw fasting as a particularly effective means of assuaging or diverting God's wrath, in that it could make reparations for past sins and remove these obstacles to the advancement of the godly cause. The puritan fast-day was also, however, an important social occasion – perhaps even, as Collinson suggests in his chapter, the 'exact counterpart, antitype, and even parody of the festive day, and particularly of the wake, or church ale'. Certainly, many puritans regarded regular attendance at fast-days as an important way to maintain contacts and mutually to foster the inner resources needed to persevere along the difficult spiritual road they had chosen for themselves. Ralph Josselin's diary, for example, reveals that over a period of many years he derived great support and comfort from joining with his godly friends and neighbours in the observing of small-scale local fasts.[52]

The most regular and frequent expression of social puritanism, however, occurred on Sunday, the puritan 'mart-day of the soul'.[53] Having carefully prepared on Saturday evening, puritans devoted the whole of the Christian sabbath to a continual round of public and household religious exercises, shunning all temptation to relax or indulge in alternative, non-religious leisure pursuits. During the early part of Elizabeth I's reign there had been some disagreement within the puritan movement over whether such a rigorous observance of Sunday was required by God's law or was merely an option available to the most dedicated. By the end of the sixteenth century those who considered it to be obligatory had begun to win the argument, and the years from 1595 to the middle of James I's reign saw the publication of a spate of influential puritan treatises in support of sabbatarianism. As a result, from the early seventeenth century onwards it became one of the most visible defining features of puritanism.

In 1618 James I deeply offended puritans by issuing a 'Book of Sports' which gave official sanction and encouragement to participation in 'harmless recreations' after Sunday worship. Thereafter the question of how Sunday should be observed became a hotly debated issue which sharply divided puritans from their less zealous contemporaries. Following the Laudian take-over of the church and the reissuing of the 'Book of Sports' by Charles I in 1633, the controversy deepened and became still more bitter. Neglect of the sabbath was thus one of the earliest abuses addressed by the puritan MPs of the Long Parliament in the early 1640s.[54]

In his book *The English Sabbath* Kenneth Parker has disputed this analysis, claiming instead that sabbatarianism was a mainstream principle of the Elizabethan and Jacobean church and was never espoused solely by the puritan movement. According to Parker, it only became associated with puritanism because the Arminian apologist, Peter Heylyn, was successful in smearing it as puritan during the 1630s.[55] There are, however, a number of problems with this interpretation, not the least of which is Parker's serious underestimation of the significance of the puritan sabbatarian movement which emerged in the 1590s.

VII

We come now to the vexed questions of how puritans related to their neighbours and to what extent they attempted to change and control the behaviour of those they tended to regard as the ungodly multitude. Most puritans were very conscious of the need to preserve their religious identities and to distinguish themselves clearly from the unregenerate. Some indeed went to bizarre lengths to achieve these ends. Numbers of puritans had been giving their children biblical Christian names from the 1560s onwards, but during the 1580s some of them abandoned these and began using their own invented names with strong didactic overtones. This practice probably started in Cranbrook in Kent, where one father called his children born between 1589 and 1600, Comfort, No-strength, More-Gift, Mercy, Sure-Trust and Stand-Well. It then spread out to other parts of Kent and across the border into East Sussex, from where the famous puritan brothers Praise-God and Fear-God Barebone originated. It subsequently began to be adopted in a few areas of Northamptonshire, too.[56] Although it failed to catch on in a big way outside the south-eastern corner of the country, where it was adopted it proved a particularly striking means of proclaiming a puritan identity.

In most cases, however, the desire to be marked out from those less zealous than themselves did not lead puritans into complete separation from the ungodly, but into what one might rather call a semi-detached relationship with the remainder of the parochial community. Before 1640 most puritans realised that it was impractical to seek to restrict membership of the state church to the godly alone, and argued instead that the sanction of excommunication should be invoked only against the most persistent and scandalous sinners. Similarly, they did not wish to bar from communion all those within their communities whose religious standards fell short of their own, although they did believe that potential communicants should be examined and instructed each time they wished to receive the sacrament.

Social and religious historians have spent much time investigating the links between puritanism and social control, and a number of differing approaches have emerged from their studies. One well-established school of thought has suggested that puritanism was the key driving force behind attempts to control the more unruly behaviour of the English people during the early-modern period, and that the primary reason why periodic attacks were launched against irreligion, drunkenness, sexual immorality and popular festivities was that these phenomena were deeply offensive to influential puritans on religious grounds. Keith Wrightson and David Levine, for example, discovered that during the early seventeenth century the Essex village of Terling was dominated by a group of puritan laymen who had acquired considerable influence within the local administration and collaborated in a concerted effort to control unruly and immoral behaviour.[57] Another historian of pre-Civil War Essex, William Hunt, has also argued that puritanism was behind attempts in that county to reform moral standards and that it provided the 'theological legitimation for a cultural revolution which contemporaries called "the reformation of manners" '.[58]

This direct equation of attempts to control disorderly behaviour with puritanism has been challenged by a number of other historians. Some of these have objected to the idea that a desire to reform society should be seen as exclusively puritan. After pointing out that vigorous attempts to control popular behaviour occurred both in pre-Reformation England and Counter-Reformation Europe, Margaret Spufford concluded:

I do not for one instant dispute that in any period, people of strong religious convictions will express these in rigidly held moral attitudes and actions . . . I do dispute that this situation was in any way peculiar to puritanism.[59]

Others have suggested that the motivation behind attempts to change certain types of immoral activity in early-modern England may have been economic as much as religious. In support of this theory they have revealed that campaigns to control illicit sexual behaviour can be found within areas without any strong puritan influence, and that they tended to become most vigorous during periods when economic conditions were particularly unfavourable. Martin Ingram's researches into the situation in several communities in Wiltshire, for example, have revealed that the same concern to prevent fornication and pre-nuptial pregnancy that Wrightson and Levine observed in Terling was also evident in villages like Keevil where puritans did not enjoy the same local dominance.[60] This finding might indicate that hostility to sexual transgression was driven not solely by religious scruples but also by more pragmatic worries that it would produce a spate of bastard children who would become a charge upon the parish poor-rate.

Establishing the relative importance of the various motivating impulses behind attempts to reform behaviour is a far from simple task for the historian. There was no such thing as a typical man or woman or a typical community in early-modern England, and motivation differed greatly from individual to individual and from location to location. In addition, most of those who became involved in efforts to achieve a 'reformation of manners' were motivated by a *mélange* of considerations, and only rarely have they left the first-hand testimony which would reveal which of these were the more compelling. Nonetheless, there may be sufficient evidence to allow us to argue that, while some aspects of the drive to reform moral behaviour were not distinctively puritan, other components – in particular opposition to drunkenness and the traditional festivities of the ritual year – probably were. Although Martin Ingram observed in Keevil the same strong hostility to any illicit sexual activity which might produce more mouths for the parish to feed as Wrightson and Levine had in Terling, what may be of equal significance is that he did not find there the same intense preoccupation with the need to eradicate alehouses and popular revelry as was evident in the puritan village.[61]

In his recent study of popular festivities in early-modern England, Ronald Hutton concedes that social and economic anxieties did play some part in attacks on rural pastimes; he is nonetheless clearly of the opinion that 'religion was the most potent source of attitudes to traditional festivity', and that opposition to festive culture 'was much more marked at the radical end of the English Protestant spectrum'.[62]

Although the picture is a complicated one, there can be little real doubt that many puritans were deeply scandalised by what they saw as the disorderly and immoral lifestyles of their ungodly contemporaries. Further, as they believed that the bad example of the ungodly might tempt them into sinning and thus weaken their own sense of assurance of salvation, they were loathe to turn a blind eye to moral transgressions, and, where and when they could, took action against them. As William Hunt has again commented:

> *Puritan* . . . implies a will to impose certain standards upon society as a whole. *Puritanism* entails hostility to the traditional culture . . . A man of irreproachable personal piety who nevertheless has no objection to his neighbours' boozing on the Sabbath or fornicating in haylofts is not a Puritan. A Puritan who minds his business is a contradiction in terms.[63]

For this reason, during the 80-year period that preceded the English Civil War it was those towns and villages with a strong puritan presence which were most likely to experience tensions and divisions, and to end up polarised between 'those who gadded to sermons and those who gadded to dances, sports and other pastimes'.[64] In addition, as Jacqueline Eales shows later in this volume, beyond the confines of the local community, many individual puritans who had acquired office as justices of the peace, members of parliament and courtiers attempted to use their political influence to further puritan reform ideals. Victory in the Civil War gave puritans the ideal opportunity to perfect this work of national moral reformation and, as Christopher Durston's later contribution to this volume reveals, they spared no pains in an attempt to impose their own godly culture upon an unwilling English people.

In his contribution to this volume, Martin Ingram charts the evolution of the relationship between Elizabethan and early-Stuart puritans and the ecclesiastical courts, the established church's prin-

cipal agent of clerical discipline and social control. During Elizabeth
I's reign there was much hostility; some puritan writers were
extremely critical of the courts, and numbers of puritan clergy were
reported to them by parishioners who accused them of refusing to
use sections of the Prayer Book, excluding the ungodly from communion, or victimising individual parishioners in their sermons. Following James I's accession the relationship improved somewhat and
Ingram argues that 'it is probably true to say that for two decades
after 1605 puritan clergy were less likely to be in trouble with the
church courts . . . than to co-operate with them in the punishment of
sin'. Tensions remained, however, and following the Arminian
take-over of the church in the late 1620s the old animosities
resurfaced, as both lay and clerical puritans fell foul of court officials
intent on imposing the new Laudian liturgical injunctions.

VIII

Examples of this puritan culture in action can be found at the
individual, family and community level. We have already discussed
how Nehemiah Wallington and Ralph Josselin's puritanism was both
productive and reflective of their inner mental worlds, but their
diaries and other spiritual writings also provide ample evidence of
the ways in which their puritanism was expressed in a daily round of
Bible-study, prayer, fasting, and attendance at sermons.[65] They
further reveal that both men shared in a widespread puritan aspira-
tion to turn their families into little churches. This process, which
some historians have labelled 'the spiritualization of the household',
involved the locating of worship within the home as well as the
church, and the exercising of a strict discipline over household
members by the puritan *paterfamilias*. As Jacqueline Eales has shown
elsewhere in her detailed study of the Harley family, Sir Robert
Harley exercised a firm puritan discipline over all his relatives and
servants at Brampton Bryan in Herefordshire and frequently involved them in his own strenuous spiritual labours by holding private
household fasts and prayer-meetings.[66] This and other work by Eales
has also, however, made clear that while the husband and father
theoretically exercised an absolute power within the puritan family a
number of puritan women also exercised real influence through their

roles as wives and mothers. Lady Brilliana Harley was able to discuss spiritual issues on equal terms with her husband, and took much of the responsibility for the religious education of her children. While her son Edward was away studying at Oxford she wrote to him regularly, often expressing her concern that his spiritual welfare might be threatened by the ungodly environment of the university.[67] Other notable puritan women, such as Jane Ratcliffe, Lady Mary Vere, Margaret Baxter and Katherine Clarke, won wide praise from godly male commentators for their personal piety, their influence over their relatives, and their patronage of struggling puritan clergy.[68]

It was also common for important puritan families within the ranks of the gentry and aristocracy to intermarry and to maintain close links with a wide circle of extended kin. Jacqueline Eales's contribution to this volume examines the crucial role played by family traditions and kinship networks, as well as lay patronage and clerical influence, in sustaining puritanism in the period from the Elizabethan Settlement to the outbreak of the Civil War. Eales also stresses the importance of the book trade in the expansion and dissemination of puritan culture during these years. During the half-century which preceded the Civil War, a number of noted puritan authors, such as William Perkins, Thomas Gataker, John Dod, William Gouge, and William Whately, published a series of domestic conduct books in which they outlined in great detail the way the ideal puritan household should be organised.[69] These titles sold in great quantities and were extensively consulted by those striving to turn their families into model puritan communities in miniature.

Beyond the confines of such godly families, what puritans saw as the English religious desert also contained a number of conspicuous oases of regional and municipal puritanism. These were grouped mainly in London, Essex, East Anglia, and parts of Kent, East Sussex, the Midlands and the West Country, and they included nationally renowned puritan towns like Colchester, Banbury and Dorchester. In such communities cliques of lay puritans gained control of the reins of power and, usually in conjunction with an actively puritan parochial ministry, laboured with varying degrees of success to create their own English Genevas. The self-conscious sense of separation and godliness which this could engender is strongly reflected in William Gouge's description of the London parish of St Anne's, where he was lecturer, as 'our little state in the Blackfriars'.[70]

Colchester had been a conspicuous centre of Protestant support from very early on in the English Reformation, and during the reigns of Elizabeth I and the first two Stuarts it was dominated by a group of rich puritan merchants who worked closely with municipal officials, such as the Elizabethan recorder, Sir Francis Walsingham, to secure the town for the godly cause. They appointed the two noted puritans, George Northey and William Ames, to the town lectureship, and repeatedly clashed with the ecclesiastical authorities for their 'neglect of the more learned clergy'. During the 1630s several Colchester men, including John Bastwick and Thomas Cotton, set out to undermine the impact of the Laudian religious innovations, winning much support for their activities from the 'zealants' of the town who gathered to hear them 'as people use when ballads are sung'.[71]

Banbury meanwhile became the epicentre of a cluster of puritan communities in north Oxfordshire and south Northamptonshire. Through the patronage of a number of influential local puritan families, including the Copes, the Fiennes and the Knollys, puritan preachers were appointed both to the borough and to a number of the surrounding villages during the 1580s. Banbury itself was served by Thomas Brasbridge until his deprivation in 1590, and then from 1610 to 1638 by the redoubtable William Whately. By the beginning of James's reign, it was notorious for its godliness, and the terms 'Banbury man' and 'Banbury brother' were employed by, amongst others, Ben Jonson as synonyms for puritan. The antiquary William Camden joked that the town was chiefly famous for 'cakes and zeal', and a popular doggerel rhyme described how a Banbury puritan had hanged his cat on Monday for killing a mouse on a Sunday.[72]

As David Underdown has recently shown, the catalyst for the puritan rise to power in Dorchester was a fire that destroyed a large part of the town in 1613. In the aftermath of this 'fire from heaven', the formidable puritan preacher, John White, forged a close alliance with a number of influential lay puritans and together they set about the task of reshaping the life of the community and turning it into a Calvinist 'city on a hill'. Over the next 30 years, they achieved an enormous amount in the areas of education, poor relief and the care of the sick and elderly; and through their ceaseless hounding of drunkards, fornicators and sabbath-breakers they also made some real progress towards the creation of a more sober and disciplined population. According to Underdown, by the eve of the Civil War they had turned Dorchester into 'the most puritan place in England'. Their success was never, however, total. Many of the town's inhabitants conformed to the ideals of the municipal elite more from a desire for a quiet life than out of any genuine puritan commitment, and some others fought the reformers every inch of the way. While Dorchester retained its puritan character during the 1640s and 1650s, after the Restoration its religious fervour faded away, destroyed to a large degree by the 'chorus of mocking laughter' from an ungodly element which the puritans had never been able to eradicate.[73] Attempts to establish similar puritan 'New Jerusalems' occurred in a number of other English towns, including Cranbrook, Lewes, Rye, Gloucester, Coventry, Newbury, and Northampton; while they too achieved some degree of short-term success, they also invariably proved deeply divisive and met with determined and persistent opposition.

While it was these urban communities which were most notorious amongst contemporaries for their adherence to godly values, puritanism also flourished in a number of the rural locations identified above. From his researches into the social and political culture of the south-western counties of Somerset, Wiltshire and Devon during the seventeenth century, David Underdown found that puritanism was concentrated within woodland and pasture areas, and that it was largely absent from the 'champion' arable-farming regions. He attempted to explain this distribution by suggesting that the prevailing economic and cultural ethos of the cornlands was collectivist, whilst that of the wood-pasture areas was necessarily more individualistic and thus more likely to foster Protestant nonconformity. The wood-pasture regions did contain many of those centres of cloth trade and manufacture which are well known to have been fertile seed-beds for puritan ideas, but beyond this Underdown's thesis is seriously weakened by the large number of communities which fail to conform to his pattern.[74]

IX

To define puritanism according to the cultural criteria outlined above is to suggest that the boundaries of the movement were very wide and that a range of individuals from moderate puritans through presbyterians to radical sectaries can justifiably and usefully be identified with the label puritan. A number of contemporary commentators and later scholars have rejected such an inclusive definition and claimed that separatists should be clearly distinguished from puritans as a result of their renunciation of the national church. We would argue against this approach and agree instead with Geoffrey Nuttall that 'the final step of Separatism left undestroyed the greater part of those ideas and ideals which still, as hitherto, they [the separatists] had in common with the more conservative puritans from among whom they came.'[75] Because separatists shared with other puritans a common culture, what divided them from each other was of far less practical significance than what cut them off from the religious mainstream. This shared ground was emphasised in the Instrument of Government of 1653, the constitutional basis for the rule of Cromwell and his fellow puritan generals in the mid 1650s; this denied toleration to Roman Catholics and episcopalians but extended it to 'such as profess faith in God by Jesus Christ (though differing in judgement from the doctrine, worship or discipline publicly held forth)'.[76] Moderate puritans, presbyterians and separatists were all deeply committed to Bible-reading and Bible-study, sermon-attendance and sermon-gadding, fasting and whole-day sabbatarianism; and all of them eagerly participated in a ceaseless round of such spiritual activities. It was this behaviour which more than anything else marked out a man or woman as a puritan. In essence then, as William Haller commented more than 50 years ago, early-modern English puritanism was a 'spiritual outlook, way of life, and mode of expression'.[77]

1. Elizabethan and Jacobean Puritanism as Forms of Popular Religious Culture

PATRICK COLLINSON

Traditionally, puritanism and culture have been seen as polar opposites, so that an essay on puritan culture might seem to merit no more space than the topic of snakes in that book on Iceland which, according to Dr Samuel Johnson, contained a chapter consisting of the single sentence: 'There are no snakes to be found anywhere in the island.' Puritanism, it is assumed, had to do not with culture but with sermons and the sabbath, a bleak day of unalleviated religion, punctuating a week otherwise filled by unrelenting toil. On the subject of holy days, or holidays, where Elizabethan culture is mostly to be sought, the puritan 'Book of Discipline' of the 1580s did indeed include a chapter of one sentence: 'Holidays are conveniently to be abolished.'

But if man shall not live by bread alone, he must have bread, and perhaps some butter and even jam to spread on it; and it is not likely that puritans found all their needs supplied by 'every word that proceedeth out of the mouth of God' (Matthew 4.4). For puritans too were men and women, and even children, creatures of flesh and blood. And if we include in 'culture' not only the high culture nowadays categorised as 'the arts', and that problematical substance 'popular culture', but those man-spun webs of meaning which anthropologists define as culture,[1] then it is certain that puritans, even puritans, must have had a culture. What that culture may have consisted of, and how far it constituted a distinctive subculture in Elizabethan and Jacobean England is the subject to be explored in this essay.

I

Puritanism was, to a considerable extent, a negative culture, or culture of negation, and so not easily discussable. Most Elizabethans were still uninhibited in their use of the old Catholic oaths, there being no Protestant, still less puritan, oaths with which to fortify one's speech. We may say that puritans did not swear, that that was not part of their cultural repertoire. But having said so much, what else do we say? – although very much could be said in an essay (a different essay from this one) on that fundamental constituent of any culture which is language. When Jacobean playwrights pilloried puritans, it was their peculiar language which they selected for satirical treatment.

And then there is gesture. When the anthropologist Clifford Geertz attended the cockfights of twentieth-century Bali, he observed the shrugs, winks and not-quite winks of the actively participating, wagering crowd: all precious particles of culture, according to his definition of it. We cannot travel to that other country which was the English puritan equivalent of the Balinese cockfight: a world of gratuitously pious gestures, and especially of the uplifted white of the eye. Consequently the argument of this essay will focus on that space which is spare time, where culture in the conventional and vulgar sense was fitted.

And first we may address puritanism as an anti-cultural force, asserting itself in those vicious conflicts between the cultural forms of Elizabethan and Jacobean England which we assume to have been popular and their 'censorious', 'precise' critics, struggles which came to full fruition in numerous local communities in the early decades of the seventeenth century.[2] For it was those local teacup storms which gave substance, a cultural or counter-cultural substance, to the very concept of 'puritan'. Commenting on the royal Book of Sports (to which we shall return), which James I targeted at 'Puritans and precise people', Kenneth Parker insists that it is more to the point to determine when and how the sabbatarianism which the king scouted became identified with 'puritanism' than to search for the supposed 'puritan' origins of the sabbatarian principle.[3]

The word puritan was not employed in the Elizabethan period as routinely as historians have tended to use it. In so far as it does appear in the record, it usually signifies religious nonconformity. Thus, in 1575, an ecclesiastical commission meeting in Gloucester complained of a Cirencester man, who had rejected the ministry of his conformist vicar, that upon his release from prison, 'he hath used himself like a puritan as heretofore he had done in absenting him self from church'.[4] But Mark Byford, in his account of reformation and religious and political conflict in Elizabethan Colchester, makes no use of the 'p' word, since it never once occurs in the copious local records on which his dissertation is based.[5]

Philip Stubbes is normally referred to as a 'puritan',[6] on the basis of his comprehensive diatribe called *The Anatomie of Abuses* (1583). But Stubbes devoted much of *The second part of the Anatomie of Abuses*, called *The Display of Corruptions* (a text generically closer to estates satire than to complaint literature) to a trenchant denunciation of the principles of ecclesiastical puritanism.[7] The only justification for calling Stubbes a puritan is that, a generation later, that was the label often attached to those who held his 'stoical' views on plays, sports and pastimes, especially when conducted on the sabbath.[8] That 'puritan' was a stigma increasingly deployed in the street wars and cultural contentions of Jacobean England owed a good deal to the satirical and theatrical anti-puritan backlash provoked, initially, by 'Martin Marprelate' and his anti-episcopal pamphlets (1588–9).[9]

That is not to say that the thing identified as 'puritanism' had no real or prior existence, any more than the large quadruped which Sir Harry Johnston 'discovered' in the Ituri rainforests in 1900 had no existence until Johnston gave it a name, 'okapi'. But the question 'what's in a name?' should never be regarded as merely rhetorical. The initially unfriendly attachment of the name doubtless reinforced that process of self-recognition among godly Protestants, those denounced as puritans, in which the real substance of Jacobean puritanism came to consist. There was that much difference between puritans and okapis.

In what follows we shall largely ignore 'puritan' anti-theatricality, a heavily traversed and complex topic, and will exclude altogether the attack on the public, metropolitan theatres, concentrating rather on the popular culture of rural and provincial urban England. This is a scene now brightly illuminated by the ever-extending arc-lights of the Toronto series, *Records of Early English Drama* (*REED*).[10] But the 'complaint literature' of the 1570s and 1580s, for all its well-worn familiarity, still provides a useful map of what to look for in the volumes of *REED*.

The obscure Humphrey Roberts, 'minister of the Church in Kings Langley', wrote his *An earnest complaint of divers vain, wicked and abused exercises practised on the Sabbath day* in 1572, before the advent of the London theatres, which may explain his preoccupation with such country customs as 'silver games', 'commonly used in the country, where the people are most ignorant'. Roberts describes the licensing of these games (which seem to have been athletic contests for silver prizes, with the profit going to charity), and the calling of banns advertising them, 'at which time they carry their Banners hanged upon Poles, with drums and instruments played before them, proclaiming this their vanities to be holden upon Sunday at such a time'.[11]

Roberts, in common with his fellow complaint writers,[12] denounced country dancing as a means to draw the youth away from preaching and prayer, writing darkly of dancing maids who 'do return home to their friends sometime with more than they carried forth'.[13] While Stubbes lashed out casually at dancing's 'macho' counterpart, football, 'a friendly kind of fight', 'this murthering play',[14] he dealt at greater length with that 'introit to all kind of lewdness', dancing.[15] The Bristol preacher John Northbrooke indicted dancing as 'the vilest vice of all', with its 'disordinate gestures', 'monstrous thumping of the feet', 'wanton songs to dishonest verses', both maidens and matrons groped, kissed, and 'dishonestly embraced'.[16] These complaints of the 1570s and early 1580s accurately reflect the popularity of the minstrels and Sunday dancing in, for example, Kent; and their unpopularity with the authorities.[17]

Against the warp of their generalised and sabbatarian complaints (the better the day the worse the deed), these writers worked the woof of their attack on the succession of seasonal episodes in the traditional festive calendar: football on Shrove Tuesday, the jollity of the maypole or 'summer pole' from May Day to midsummer, the excesses of the parish festivals known as wakes, with the more occasional church ales. Stubbes's account of 'the order of Maygames' is justly famous: shenanigans in the woods overnight, with their gravid consequences, the pole brought back in triumph (perhaps stolen from the next village), painted and 'covered all over with flowers', its erection 'with handkerchiefs and flags hovering on the top', summer houses and arbours, a floor of straw to dance on. In this rich detail Stubbes inadvertently supplied us with the most vivid of all evocations of Merry England. In Lancashire, the eve of May Day was called 'Mischief Night'.[18] Presently the embattled Protestant preachers of that county drew up their own litany of pastimes which commonly defiled the sabbath: 'Wakes, Ales, Greens, May-games, Rushbearings, Bearbaits, Doveales, Bonfires, all manner unlawful Gaming, Piping and Dancing, and such like.' These were the pleasures, especially in the north-west of England, of the cultur-ally and morally contested months, May to July.

It was not until James I's extraordinary intervention in the cultural life of Lancashire in 1617 that this militant antipathy to traditional rural pastimes, implying a particularly implacable sabbatarianism, became attached to puritanism rather than to more broadly based establishment concern for good order and the reformation of man-ners. The circumstances are well known. Lancashire was a county deeply divided in religion. Among Protestants, and even in the perception of the privy council in the south, it was a commonplace that papists exploited the attractions of the village green 'purposely by these means to draw the People from the service of God and to disturb the same'.[20] A fiercely Protestant element of the local bench took a particularly hard line on the people's sports. In 1616, the assize judge Edward Bromley was induced by this local pressure to put his name to orders forbidding piping and dancing (as well as a number of 'unlawful' pastimes) on the Sabbath Day, 'in any part of the day'. The underlying issue here was one of abusing the sabbath, whereas earlier orders had been designed to ensure a proper division of the day between religion and sport. This was to go beyond the law in terms which had been inconclusively debated in parliament as recently as 1614, although the Devon bench had taken a similarly hard line as early as 1595, and would stick to it for the next 36 years.[21]

But when the king passed through Lancashire on his return from Scotland in 1617, Catholic or crypto-Catholic opponents of sabbatar-ian absolutism persuaded him that it was a policy sure to alienate papists and confirm them in their recusancy. With the assistance of the bishop of the diocese, Thomas Morton, James proceeded to promulgate his own code of practice, the Book of Sports, which allowed 'harmless Recreation' (specifically, mixed dancing, may-games, Whitsun ales and morris dances, as well as strenuous sports), so that they be 'without impediment or neglect of Divine Service', a 'benefit and liberty' specifically denied to recusants. James prefaced this declaration with a preamble characteristic in its even-handed censure of both 'papists' and 'puritans', but particularly and omin-ously critical of those puritans and precise people who had unlawfully prevented 'our good people' from using their 'lawful recreations' after evening prayer.[22] Although the national promulgation of these orders was at the time blurred and blunted by bishops and magistrates, their revival in the altered circumstances of 1633, together with Charles I's demand that they be read from all pulpits, served to equate strict sabbatarianism with 'puritans' as redefined by Archbishop Laud and his colleagues, with momentous consequences for English politics and even (or so it was later alleged) the outflow of conscientious emigrants to New England.[23]

Before, and to a considerable extent after, 1618, the position of authority on what might be called whole-day sabbatarianism was confused, and consequently it is not as clear as it might be that this really was an exclusively puritan stand. The Northamptonshire magnate Sir Edward Mountagu promoted a strict sabbath bill in the 1614 Parliament, while it was opposed by his brother, Bishop James Mountagu, significantly the Dean of the Chapel Royal and editor of James I's published works. When Edward Mountagu attempted to interfere with the annual wake in the Northamptonshire parish of John Williams, a future bishop of Lincoln and Lord Keeper, Williams said that he would not tolerate the interference of a 'precise Justice', perhaps a conscious reference to the character of Justice Overdo in Ben Jonson's *Bartholomew Fair*.[24]

But the king himself, in 1603, had issued a vaguely worded proclamation which outlawed a number of pastimes 'at any time' on the sabbath. In 1579, Bishop Cox of Ely, specifying wanton dancing and maygames, had insisted: 'No such disorders to be kept upon the Sabbath day'; while Bishop John Coldwell of Salisbury had spoken in orders of 1595 of the Lord's Day as 'consecrated wholly to his service'. However, no extant Jacobean ecclesiastical injunctions entertain the concept of profaning the sabbath, as such. Following the lead of Archbishop Bancroft's articles for ten dioceses and the influential London articles of Bishop Richard Vaughan, both of 1605, there was something like an absolute prohibition on the use of church property and premises for profane purposes, such as the invasion of the church by maygames and morris dancers. This prohibition was itself a departure from pre-Reformation cultural practice and was liable to be denounced as 'precise' at a local level. The Jacobean episcopate also ruled against 'unlawful' games on Sundays, which included, besides bear- and bull-baiting and stageplays, bowls for the lower classes, a pastime restricted by a statute of

1541. But no articles absolutely prohibit such lawful pastimes as dancing at any time on the sabbath. However, Bishop Francis Godwin of Hereford seems to have been the only Jacobean bishop to have explicitly enforced the royal Book of Sports, enquiring: 'Whether the minister do not defer the afternoon service unseasonably for the debarring or hindering of fit recreation?'[25]

That that should have been the policy of a bishop of Hereford may have been significant. Lancashire was not an isolated or unique case. Even before the royal declaration of 1618, there is evidence that the sporting and festive life was not only fighting back, but was developing new and more sophisticated and politically resistant forms. This is apparent in Herefordshire, Worcestershire and neighbouring parts of Gloucestershire: which is to say, the broad valleys of Avon, Severn and Wye, from the western slopes of the Cotswolds in the east to the Malvern Hills, Black Mountains and Forest of Dean in the west. Here the traditional calendrical rhythm of sports and pastimes may have been only a little less closely intertwined with the old religion, or with reconstructed versions of it, than in Lancashire. In the 1620s and 1630s, Herefordshire's solitary godly gentleman and precise magistrate, Sir Robert Harley, sat out on a limb in the extreme north-west of the otherwise conservative county and diocese, at Brampton Bryan.[26]

At Hereford in 1609, the May games took the form of a notable horse-race, which drew 'knights, esquires and gallants (of the best sort)' from the whole region, including Lord Herbert of Raglan. Bath itself was emptied by the event at faraway Hereford, where 'the streets swarmed with people, the people staring and joyfully welcoming whole bevies of gallants'. The gathering of quality at 'this Olympic race' was indicative of a new disposition towards popular pastimes, even their appropriation, as well as articulating distinctly anti-puritanical values.[27]

In the context of the Hereford race meeting, the assembled gentry promoted a remarkable morris dance consisting entirely of aged persons, all allegedly approaching or exceeding 100 years of age, all born within ten miles of Hereford. This great event was recorded in print as *Old Meg of Herefordshire*.[28] Will Kemp's nine-day wonder of dancing the morris from London to Norwich in 1600, a media event which had drawn huge crowds in East Anglia,[29] was quite put in the shade. Meg herself, who played the Maid Marion, claimed to have been present when Prince Arthur died at Ludlow, which was in

1502. At the other end of the seventeenth century, the deprived Archbishop William Sancroft, awaiting eviction from Lambeth Palace, warmed to this nostalgic emblem of the good old days, as he copied *Old Meg* into one of his notebooks.[30]

The author of *Old Meg* claimed that Herefordshire was top of the morris-dancing league: 'Herefordshire for a Morris-dance.' The ecclesiastical court records bear him out. From a belt of parishes just to the north of Hereford, the minstrels and morris men were regularly presented, invariably for performing during service time. At Woolhope in 1620, the vicar was himself 'a spectator of such as danced before evening prayer on sabbath days'.[31] Sometimes the courts were reacting to friction within the dancing communities themselves. From the Worcestershire village of Longdon, the parish constable complained that the summertime 'maygames, Morrises and dancings' attracted 'rude Ruffians and drunken Companions' from neighbouring parishes, leading to quarrels and affrays.[32] A more serious disturbance upset the Whit Monday dancing in the Herefordshire village of Goodrich in 1609, defying the ostensible purpose of the event 'to make peace and love between all neighbours if any debate were'. The Goodrich riot, which came to the attention of Star Chamber, was evidently a settling of old scores, but it contained an element of cultural and religious conflict. At the centre of the affray was the village constable, William Philpot, who was said to have detested and disparaged 'ministers and professors of the Word of God', specifically the vicar of the parish, interrupting and profaning the exercise of the Word with dancing, drinking 'and other idle maygames'. One of Philpot's opponents spoke of the Whitsun games as 'not only a ridiculous but an ungodly custom'.[33]

Presently, in Gloucester gaol, a bankrupt but erudite clergyman called Christopher Windle penned an anti-puritan diatribe in the form of a Latin commentary on the Book of Sports explaining that he was himself Lancashire born. This was a learned treatise, which connected legitimate pastimes to the doctrine of the incarnation, since Christ himself was fully human. Windle tells us that the prisoners in Gloucester castle were allowed their own 'summer pole', so why should it be denied to those at liberty? He also writes of 'those peevish brethren in whose parishes crowds gather as soon as the poles are raised, more to oppose the clamouring minister than to give themselves pleasure.'[34] These were highly inflamed, thoroughly political issues.

Not far from Gloucester, on the western escarpment of the Cotswolds, these same years witnessed a more notable defiance of the enemies of Merry England in the shape of Robert Dover's Cotswold Games.[35] Dover was a Norfolk man, significantly a Catholic recusant by upbringing, who with other members of his extended family pulled up his roots and resettled in Gloucestershire. There, in the neighbourhood of Saintbury and Chipping Camden, he seems to have taken over and formalised the age-old midsummer games, which the poet Michael Drayton had already celebrated in the pastoral verse of his great chorographical poem, *Poly-Olbion*, an evocation of bagpipes, swains, sillabubs and nosegays.[36] This world belonged to its shepherds, whose difference from the cloth-workers of the neighbouring plain was self-evident to contemporaries. Dover's games, after a mid-seventeenth-century interruption, continued until 1852, and the Ordnance Survey map still marks 'Dover's Hill'. Since the Second World War, Dover's games have revived and to this day flourish, headed by a local Roman Catholic priest, on horseback and in Dover's costume.

From the collection of verses congratulating Dover later printed by Drayton, Ben Jonson and other poets as *Annalia Dubrensia* (1636), we learn many details about 'Mr Robert Dover's Olympic Games', and can infer more about their cultural and political significance. They consisted of the traditional country pursuits of wrestling, leaping, dancing and running races, but with an added 'civility' which was imparted by Dover's organisation, the self-conscious neo-classicism implied in the 'Olympic' title, with a harpist dressed up as Homer, and the presence of large numbers of the gentry, together with provision for their tastes, hunting, coursing, horse-racing. Proceedings were controlled by guns fired from a wooden castle, and by Dover, riding a white horse, dressed in elaborate courtly costume. Chess was provided in tents, 'for Politicians'. Here were some of the roots of a Cavalier culture.

Thomas Whichcote, in his *View of Devonshire MDCXXX*[37] spoke of the old rural pastimes as 'by zeal discommended and discountenanced and so utterly out of use'. As we have seen, such things had been 'discountenanced' in Devon since at least 1595. But we ought not to make a simple 'whiggish' assessment of the festive culture of Jacobean England as old-fashioned and decadent. We have seen that the Hereford horse-races, too, were described as 'Olympic'. And, on the other side of England, just to the south of Cambridge, the summer games on the Gogmagog Hills (which were strenuously opposed by university, county and even royal authority[38]) were also designated 'Olympic games', 'such exercises as bowling, running, jumping, shooting and wrestling', but including some more dubious amusements.[39]

From *Annalia Dubrensia*, the anti-puritan, proto-royalist significance of this small renaissance of Merry England is evident. John Trussell (an indifferent poet!) wrote:

> The countrie wakes and whirlings have appeared
> Of late like forraine pastimes. Carnivals,
> Palme and rush-bearing, harmlesse Whitson-ales
> Running at quintain May-games, general playes,
> By some more nice than wise, of latter dayes,
> Have in their standings, lectures, exercises,
> Beene so reproved, traduced, condemned for vices,
> Profane and heathenish that now few dare
> Set them afoote.[40]

But 'well-minded jovialists' would tell how by Dover's industry 'a second birth is given to honest Pastime, harmless mirth'. Ben Jonson wrote:

> Here they advance true love and neighbourhood,
> And doe both Church and Common-wealth the Good,
> In spite of Hipocrites, who are the worst
> Of subjects. Let such envie till they burst!'[41]

The writer of the poem *Pasquils Palinodia* (1619), (who may have been William Fennor and who tells us that his 'native town' was 'Leede', which may or may not have been Leeds) wrote with nostalgic regret about a world he reckoned to have lost. But no doubt the active, politically charged nostalgia was some guarantee that it was not lost at all:

> Happy the age and harmlesse were the dayes,
> (For then true love and amity was found,)
> When every village did a May-pole raise,
> And *Whitson-ales*, and *May-games* did abound:

And all the lusty Yonkers in a rout
With merry Lasses daunc'd the rod about,
Then friendship to their banquets bid the guests,
And poore men far'd the better for their feasts . . .

Then Lords of Castles Mannor, Townes and Towers,
Reioyc'd when they beheld the Farmers flourish,
And would come downe, unto the Sommer-Bower
To see the country gallants daunce the Morris . . .

But since the Sommer-poles were overthrowne,
And all good sports and merryments decayed,
How times and men are chang'd . . .[42]

At Bolsover Castle in Derbyshire, high on a ridge above the
redundant coalmine and the constituency of Dennis Skinner MP,
stands the most striking of all memorials to these cultural, political,
and even religious values. The painted ceiling of the small antecham-
ber called 'Heaven' in Sir Charles Cavendish's poetic dream castle,
dated 1619, two years after Sir William Cavendish, later the first
duke of Newcastle, had inherited the property, is crowded with
chubby cherubs, all with 'mechanical' Derbyshire faces, celebrating
the ascension of Christ into the firmament. The rusticity of this
religious scene, which is unique for its period, was evidently intended
and not (as Pevsner seems to suggest) a matter of the artist's limited
talent. The cherubs are playing a variety of musical instruments,
from lutes to sackbuts, and at each corner there is an open leaf of
Thomas Ravenscroft's *Musicall phansies, fitting the court, citie and countrey
humours* (1611). Everyone is dancing, even the ascending Christ, who
is spinning to the music.[43]

II

In the evolving culture of the late Elizabethan and Jacobean provincial town, we can detect some parallel developments, but also
significant differences, and some intimations of values and politics
differing from Dover's proto-royalism; and a cultural agenda which
might have been better served by that reign which was not to be, the
reign of Henry IX, than by Charles I. But how far we should

attribute these distinctive features to 'puritanism' is, as ever, problematical.

In all the provincial cities and towns so far included in *Records of Early English Drama*, the story is more or less consistent.[44] The native mimetic tradition in the shape of the religious drama was suppressed or allowed to die, a process almost complete by 1580.[45] Thereafter, the urban magistracy became increasingly resistant to the visits of the licensed travelling companies, more often than not finding some reason for paying the players to go away. At Barnstaple and Plymouth, the phrases used were 'to rid the Town of them', 'to rid them out of Town'.[46] At Chester in 1596 the authorities responded to criticism from the pulpit by not only banning plays and bear-baiting within the city, but forbidding any citizen to seek out such entertainments elsewhere, on pain of 'punishment and fine'.[47] One senses an ingrained antipathy to any leisure pursuit threatening libidinous disorder. At Norwich in May 1629, the town assembly moved to suppress the Sunday recreation of rowing down the river for country picnics, as well as 'may meetings' for dancing and cudgel play at the Market Cross, 'by Troops and multitudes'.[48]

Reports that the 'multitude' resented interference of this kind with traditional patterns of leisure and sociability, as well as with Sunday trading, coupled with evidence that these were often the policies of small and unrepresentative factions on the make, has created the impression among some social historians of top-down 'social control', as much political and economic in motivation as religious and moral. The sabbatarian efforts of the austere Ignatius Jordan as mayor of Exeter were met with 'much reluctancy', 'commotions and tumults'.[49] Opponents of a puritan regime in Stratford-upon-Avon in the 1620s used the common device of a rhyming and libellous ballad to attack 'the Chief Rulers in the Synagogue of Stratford' as 'but a few': 'I think they are but seven.'[50]

Yet there is contrary evidence that in the Elizabethan and Jacobean town, the enforcement of strict but consensual moral codes enjoyed widespread support, and that the machinery employed itself amounted to a kind of popular culture, at once traditional and Protestant. In Colchester, this took the form of carting adulterers and fornicators around the town in a tumbrel with placards hung around their necks, a kind of parodic wedding ceremony closely related to the public shaming ritual of the skimmington or 'rough riding'. The people of Colchester approved of this punishment and perhaps enjoyed it, if not on the receiving end; only taking exception when it was imposed by some magistrates and preachers with uncharitable excess and in dubious circumstances. Mark Byford comments: 'Given the right conditions, Protestantism could flourish because of, rather than in spite of, popular values.'[51] We are beginning to acknowledge a comparable approximation of 'puritan' moralistic concern to the stock-in-trade of Elizabethan pulp literature, the so-called 'popular' quasi-journalism of murder pamphlets and other accounts of wonders and monsters: 'providentialism' colonising the sensational press, or coexisting with it in a kind of symbiosis.[52]

Out of the detritus of remnants of the old pastimes, there emerged in the towns a new slimmed-down, secular and increasingly civic-cum-martial festive culture. In Norwich, the powerful St George's gild discontinued its traditional St George's Day pageant, and as early as 1559. No more 'George nor Margaret'. 'But for pastime the dragon to come in and show him self as in other years.' The concession to popular taste which was 'Old Snap' would endure for three centuries.[53] In late-Elizabethan Chester, the aptly named Mayor Henry Hardware cleaned up the annual midsummer parade, all that was left after the suppression of the Whitsun mystery plays. The giants (the Gog and Magog of many urban pageants, 'Hogmagog' in Newcastle),[54] the devils with cups and cans enticing men dressed in women's clothing, the naked boys: all were replaced with a man on horseback, clad in white armour. Already, as early as 1539, the violence of Shrove Tuesday football had been converted into foot-races and horse-races for silver prizes. In 1609, a new horse-race for gentlemen was introduced on St George's Day, an event marked by a book of verses presented to Prince Henry. One local chronicler called Hardware 'over-zealous', but another, while admitting that his reforms had aroused some popular opposition, defended what he called 'the Decency of the midsummer show as it is now yearly used'.[55]

In early seventeenth-century Carlisle, there was horse-racing on the King's Moor with a silver bowl given outright to the victor, and further silver prizes for running races and other Shrove Tuesday exercises.[56] In Elizabethan Plymouth, May Day had been marked by expenditure on a maypole and morris dances. But soon after 1600, the occasion called not for summer poles and dancing but drums and gunpowder, and in the 1620s, May Day disappears from the Plymouth calendar altogether; whereas the civic ceremony of 'Freedom

Day', with small boys crossing Plymouth Sound in boats to confirm the city limits over against the great private estate of Mount Edgcumbe was kept with due solemnity, the boys being rewarded with nuts and fruit.[57] When Princess Elizabeth visited Coventry in 1604, she heard a sermon and was given a dinner. But the only other entertainment offered was the sober sight of the mayor and other magistrates and members of the city companies lining the streets, 'standing' in their gowns and hoods.[58] In Salisbury, the traditional Whitsun games were first reduced to 'children's dances', and then abandoned altogether.[59]

At York, the fun, festivity and dramatic performances proper to Whitsuntide were progressively replaced by the annual 'Show of Armour' on 'midsummer eve' (or on St Peter's Eve, June 28th), every citizen being obliged to attend, 'with their best Armour and furniture'. This was not merely a muster but a 'show' in the sense of a parade, the company assembling on the Knavesmire at 9 o'clock and processing into the city with fife and drums, discharging their handguns, led by the sheriffs on horseback, in red gowns.[60] As with the man at arms at Chester, replacing naked boys in nets and devils tempting transvestites, the new urban culture was secular (but with undertones of godliness), civic-minded, patriotic, and martial. In Banbury, the 'precise' justices pulled down the 'superstitious' market crosses for which the town was (and is) famous, but purchased a new and splendid silver mace, as the symbol of their enhanced dignity.[61]

David Cressy has described the 'distinctively Protestant national culture' of seventeenth-century England, and he has drawn attention to a 'new national, secular and dynastic calendar', superimposing itself on the traditional Christian (and ultimately pre-Christian) festive calendar, 'an annual symphony of loyal celebration'.[62] The new red-letter days, marked by Protestant thankfulness, watchfulness and commemoration, celebrated Queen Elizabeth's 'crownation' (or, more properly, accession) day, November 17th, the defeat of the Spanish Armada, the abortive Gunpowder Plot of November 5th, the return of a still unmarried Prince Charles from Spain in October 1623, and, later in the same month, the Blackfriars disaster in which 100 papists and their sympathisers attending a Jesuit sermon died when the building collapsed, an event which occurred providentially on November 5th, according to the pope's own calendar.[63] What Cressy calls the 'vocabulary of celebration' consisted of the ringing of bells and lighting of bonfires. On the prince's return from Spain, one observer counted as many as 300 bonfires between Whitechapel and Temple Bar.[64] It is remarkable how all these commemorative occasions, later to be joined by the anniversary of the landing of William of Orange at Torbay, occurred in the back end of the year, a time traditionally almost bereft of festivity. It has been said that by the late seventeenth century 'the Spring belonged to the Tories and the autumn to the Whigs'.[65]

III

This was Protestant culture, and the best evidence we have that by the early decades of the seventeenth century England was a Protestant nation, not merely officially but in the sentiments and gut-reactions of the masses; if not quite, suggests Dr Christopher Haigh in a subtle distinction, a nation of Protestants.[66]

But bonfires and bells were not the essence of puritan culture, a substance which has so far eluded us in our pursuit of puritanism as an anti-cultural force and which, to my certain knowledge, no previous historian has troubled to look for. This Snark must now be hunted.

We have no reason to suppose that those super-Protestants who often went by the name of puritans were excluded, still less excluded themselves, from the celebratory culture of bonfires and bells. Preachers in the 'godly' puritan vein regularly used their sermons, especially on the appropriate calendrical occasions, to conduct their hearers past the successive milestones in post-Reformation national memory.[67] It was no accident that the first of the many Fast Sermons delivered before the Long Parliament was preached on 17 November 1640. Yet preachers in this tradition often employed such occasions to complain in the manner of Old Testament prophecy of the sin of the nation in its ingratitude and shameful disregard of so many mercies and 'national blessings', a pulpit rhetoric which was potentially divisive and sectarian and, in the later years of James I's pacific and inappropriately Hispanophilic foreign policy and under his successor, pregnant with the religious politics of opposition.[68] If the Jews told Pontius Pilate that they had no king but Caesar, there was a real sense in which puritans acknowledged the rule of God alone and thus respected and obeyed earthly rulers only in so far as they were godly instruments of the divine will and purpose. Richard Rich, the bastard uncle of the Elizabethan Lord Rich and a member of a family famous in three generations for its godly religion and politics,[69] was charged in 1582 with having 'sharply reprehended' a preacher for exhorting his people to solemnise the queen's accession day. 'Such as do celebrate the same day do make of the queen's Majesty an idol.'[70]

Any attempt to decipher and characterise puritanism as a culture must begin, and probably end, with the sermon and its various concomitants. But the sermon must be properly appreciated, not as some kind of text once read to an audience, all content and no style or delivery, but as performance, a performance which necessarily eludes us when we encounter, as we must, that same sermon, or rather something like it, in written and, as often as not, printed form.[71] Recent historians of the Reformation have been sadly mistaken in considering the sermon as nothing more than a means of communicating certain religious information, technically demanding and unwelcome information at that, and they have been over-pessimistic in their assumptions about the difficulty, even the impossibility, of instilling that information into hearts and minds not well disposed to receive it.[72]

Some sermons were more of a performance than others. Not all preachers possessed the fiery, histrionic talents of John Rogers of Dedham, to whom the people of Ipswich flocked from a dozen miles away 'to get a little fire'; nor did all covet those pulpit skills, which had more in common with the pre-Reformation delivery of the friars than with the Reformed Protestant tradition, which favoured a certain gravity and the economical use of body language. However, when the hearers spoke of their preference for an 'edifying' ministry, it may well have been the capacity to stir the heart and emotions which they had in mind.[73] Yet, all sermons, however staid, were performances of a kind: otherwise the demand for a godly and lively preaching ministry as distinct from a bare and dead reading ministry, a puritan commonplace, would have been meaningless.[74] Thomas Wilson in his *Arte of Rhetorique* (editions 1553, 1560, 1562, 1563, 1567, 1580, 1584, 1585) advocated a judicious measure of the histrionic in pulpit rhetoric. 'Except men find delight, they will not long abide: delight them, and win them; weary them, and you will lose them for ever . . . Therefore, even these ancient preachers must now and then play the fools in the pulpit, to serve to tickle the ears of their fleeting audience, or else they are like some time to preach to the bare walls . . .'[75]

That preachers were performers, comparable to and in competition with other performers (and players in some sense preachers), was no less apparent to contemporary observers of Elizabethan and Jacobean England than to modern students of the competitive and adversarial relations of theatre and pulpit.[76] The Gloucestershire cleric Christopher Windle, in his commentary on the king's Book of Sports, compared those who gathered as spectators around the maypole to church-goers who 'gaze at the pulpits, the Bible, the preachers; they are awed and wonder at their sermons and their chanting, customs, positions and gestures.'[77] Richard Corbet, in some satirical verses addressed to a puritan minister of Worcestershire, a redoubtable feller of maypoles, wrote:

> When in our Sinagogue wee rayle at sinne,
> And tell men of the faults which they are in,
> With hand and voice so following on theames,
> That wee put out the side-men from their dreames,
> Sounds not the Pulpett, which wee then belabour,
> Better, and holyer, than the Tabor?[78]

It has to be said that none of us has been privileged to hear an Elizabethan or Jacobean sermon, still less to share the experience of those who did. Few, if any, of the accounts of audience reception, such as the Essex preacher George Gifford's 'in at the one ear and out at the other',[79] were recorded for the purpose of assisting twentieth-century historians in their perfectly disinterested enquiries. The anthropological observer of Balinese cockfights has the advantage over us.

What I have called the 'concomitants' of preaching may, in the experience of sermon-goers, have been more memorably important than the contents of the sermon itself. These included attendance at the sermon, the going to and the coming away from it, a deliberate, formalised act, social rather than solitary, and anti-social too in the hostile perception of the onlookers who were not themselves willing sermon-goers.[80] In Colchester, an innkeeper complained to two of his customers about the sermon-going habits of the good wives of the town:

There be a sort of women of this town that go to the Sermons with the books under their arms ... & when they come there the whores must be pewed & there they set & sleep & what they do we cannot see & then they come home to their husbands & say he made a good & godly Sermon, & yet they play the Whores before they come home ...[81]

Strip away the innkeeper's anti-puritan sexism and we can find some valuable clues as to the nature of 'puritan culture' in the testimony of this vicious vignette: the freedom of wives to go to (probably afternoon) sermons, their Bibles under their arms, their presence more important than anything they may have learned. 'He made a good and godly Sermon.'[82]

The 'concomitants' also included psalm-singing on the way to church and in church, sermon 'repetition' shared with other sermon-goers after the sermon, in meetings which in the perception of often hostile authorities were construed as 'conventicles';[83] and above all, the thick fabric of sociability with other, like-minded sermon-goers, not necessarily kindred, not 'natural' associates and often not neighbours, but what a puritan would call 'friends in the Lord'. The popular authors John Dod and Robert Cleaver advised their readers not to rely upon 'carnal friends' but on godly men, 'for they will prove our surest friends. Vicinity and neighbourhood will fail, and alliance and kindred will fail, but grace and religion will never fail.'[84] The biographer Samuel Clarke described how those who followed his own preaching in the Wirral of Cheshire, 'though living ten or twelve miles asunder, were as intimate and familiar as if they had all been of one household.'[85] In many parts of early-Stuart England, and perhaps especially in the north country, with its greater distances to travel and lingering traditions of late-medieval open house-keeping, to be drawn into this spiritual kindred was to enjoy the generous hospitality of the more 'eminent Christians', on days of preaching and conference, or at the dinners punctuating the two sermons which were standard fare at northern funerals.[86] This is the world of farms, inns and meeting houses richly evoked in the later seventeenth century in the diaries and 'event books' of the dissenting minister Oliver Heywood, whose own funeral in 1702 was accompanied by a 'treat of cold posset, stewed prunes and cheese'. The living Heywood wrote with a kind of routinised enthusiasm about the meetings which connected his Pennine itineraries: 'Oh what a heart melting day was it'; 'It was a good day, blessed be God.'[87] If preaching was the magnetic pole of puritan culture, those attracted to it by these patterns of sociability, constituting a society within society, were its content.

We have written so far of sermon-goers. 'Sermon-gadders' was the contemporary phrase, indicating a considerable journey out of the parish to hear a sermon elsewhere, either for lack of any provision at home, or in response to the reputation of some more 'edifying' preacher, or to attend some notable 'exercise', perhaps the combination lecture in the local market town or a weekday lecture at a famous preaching centre, like Rogers's Dedham. The character writer John Earle wrote of the 'She-Puritan' that she would rather share an uncomfortable ride with her husband to a 'coughing' minister than hear a perfectly good sermon at home.[88]

David Cressy has remarked that 'the geography of popular festivity still needs to be worked out on a national as well as regional level.'[89] The same is true of puritan culture, and the first desideratum is to plot the patterns of sermon gadding. John Fielding has done this for Jacobean Northamptonshire, with a map which traces the gadders as they moved across country to some 35 parishes identified as preaching centres, to seven combination lectures and five other lectures.[90] The antagonistic, mutually exclusive reciprocity of popular and puritan culture is very neat. The writers of complaint literature objected to the unrestrained 'swarming' of young people, and especially young women, to dances and other sports. Anti-puritans shook their heads over the equally disorderly traipsing to sermons, especially on working days.[91]

IV

All that has so far been said about the puritan sermon and its constituencies applies with particular force to the extraordinary occasions for preaching and other, related, exercises known as fasts. With the puritan fast we have finally reached our destination and tracked down our quarry. An anthropologist, wanting to describe puritan culture with the Clifford Geertzian technique of 'thick' description, should be led without further delay to the puritan fast.

The fast was part of the shared religious economy of the Reformed communities of western Europe. It differed from Catholic (or Anglican) fasting in that its occurrence conformed to no regular ecclesiastical calendar, but was organised for a particular purpose, as occasion demanded, typically some calamitous event, experienced or anticipated, and interpreted as a sign of divine displeasure. In 1580, the occasion was an earthquake. But it could be almost anything, from the death of Sir Philip Sidney to the imprisonment in the Tower of William Davison, the secretary of state, for his part in the execution of Mary Queen of Scots.[92]

As the word implies, a fast entailed, as with the Catholics, abstention from food and, for that matter, sexual intercourse. But for Protestants, there was no intrinsic merit in these austerities, and the main business of the day, normally the entire day, was a shared participation in the ministry of the word, provided on an unusually lavish scale and intended to arouse a mood or state of shared repentance which might fend off God's heavy judgements or 'obtain some special grace at the hand of the Lord'.[93]

Public authority announced a fast from time to time, and promulgated special liturgies for the purpose. The parliaments of the 1620s opened with fast sermons (something Queen Elizabeth had refused to countenance in 1581), and the famous Fast Sermons of the Long Parliament were not a novelty. What was 'puritan' about the puritan fast was that some ministers took it upon themselves, as individuals or as groups organised in conference, to announce a fast, to define its intention, and to make their own arrangements. Thus in the bestdocumented case, that of Stamford in the aftermath of the 1580 earthquake, the ministers with the backing of local magistrates and other gentry, flagrantly disregarded the orders which the bishop and Lord Burghley, the lord of the town, had made a condition for allowing this locally organised event to proceed; particularly by turning it into a great religious rally for the entire region.[94]

In Norfolk, the nonconformist minister Samuel Greenway was said to have neglected the fasts announced by authority; 'but himself . . . appointed solemn fasts for reformation to be had etc., and gathered money of such as came to the sermons of other towns, which he bestowed as pleased himself . . .'[95] As this account suggests, a fast was evidently not a fast without a collection of money (an unauthorised and even illegal collection, which was designated for the poor or, as it might be, the relief of foreign Protestants.[96] In late-

Elizabethan Southwark, a preacher took it upon himself to proclaim a fast to be held on the secular feast day of Twelfth Night, instructing the people to give what they would normally have spent on themselves in celebration of the holiday.[97] What was 'puritan' about these fasts was also the prodigiousness of the proceedings; as the archbishop of York complained in 1581, 'all the day preaching and praying . . . The young ministers of these our times grow mad'.[98] At Southill in Bedfordshire in 1603, the event lasted for eight hours, from 9 to 5, with six hours of sermons from five preachers, the rest of the time presumably reserved for meditation and prayer.[99] At St Albans a few years earlier, Erasmus Cooke handled the preaching single-handed, holding forth for six-and-a-half hours.[100]

Around 1600, fasts were held in several parts of England for the novel and sensational purpose of exorcising demons, usually in young adolescent persons, and this too was a puritan peculiarity. It was the speciality of the virtually professional puritan exorcist, John Darrell, who operated in the east Midlands and in Lancashire.[101] In 1600 the godly in London harnessed their spiritual energies to the cause of relieving the young, bewitched and possessed Mary Glover of her 'vexations'.[102] For this reason, the canons of 1604, in forbidding unauthorised fasts, linked them for all time to come with the issue of exorcism.[103]

Erasmus Cooke's self-appointed fast took place at Whitsuntide, and attracted an influx from 'other and foreign parishes'. Evidently, the puritan fast day was a rather exact counterpart, antitype, and even parody of the festive day, and particularly of the wake, or church ale. Let us exercise our imaginations. People set out in groups early in the morning to travel as many as 10 or 12 miles, disorderly groups in that they consisted indiscriminately of both sexes and all ages and they returned, exhausted, late in the evening. At St Albans it was noted that 'this gadding people came from far and went home late, both young men and young women together'.[104] A shared meal before the homeward journey must have been a necessity. The end-product, at one level, as with a church ale, was a sum of money collected for a charitable purpose. We should not assume that everyone present was engaged for all the long hours of the fast in spiritual exercises. There may have been some foundation to the anti-puritan slander that there were some sexual shenanigans on the side. More legitimately, the godly sometimes found their spouses in these circumstances, just as defenders of country dances justified them for the same reason.

So the puritan fast had its collateral, horizontal connections with the general patterns and rhythms of leisure activity in Elizabethan and Jacobean England. There may also have been some vertical connections, with the religious practice of the past, and in particular with pilgrimage, another form of 'gadding'. The Devon shrine of Our Lady of Pilton had been one of the main centres of pilgrimage in the West Country.[105] In 1586, the town clerk of Barnstaple recorded that on St Luke's Day (October 18th), there was

> a trental of sermons at Pilton, so that divers as well men and women rode and went thither. They called it an exercise or holy fast, and there some offered [money] as they did when they went on pilgrimage. And the like was kept at Shirwell, to the admiration of all Protestants.[106]

What we have so far learned is reminiscent of the great open-air communion services which were a feature of the Scottish presbyterian culture of the early seventeenth century, and which were later exported to both Ulster and the American colonies, a piece of religious phenomenology recently investigated by Leigh Eric Schmidt.[107] These 'holy fairs', as the poet Robert Burns famously described them in 1785, formed the crucible for seventeenth-century covenanting and eighteenth-century religious revival, as in the extraordinary events at Cambuslang, outside Glasgow, in 1742, and in Kentucky between 1790 and 1810.

These great occasions not only brought the gadders from afar and sent them home late but kept them for several days, lodging with the locals and sleeping in their barns, or, as later in America, camping (hence 'camp meetings'). At their heart, the climax of much fervent prayer and preaching, was that often underestimated religious institution, the awesome solemnity of the sacrament of the Lord's Supper performed according to the Reformed rite, sternly 'fenced' against known sinners, and administered at long tables, laid out with white cloths, in the open air, the faithful in their best clothes with (unusually in Scotland) shoes and stockings on their feet. Leigh Eric Schmidt remarks, as the historian of English puritanism might remark, on the obvious continuity with the festal rituals of the old religion, and on the cultural value of these extraordinary gatherings, as varying and punctuating a calendar consisting otherwise of the unrelieved succession of weekly sabbaths.

In England too, days of fasting and humiliation were sometimes merely preparations for a celebration of the sacrament which was unusual in that it embraced communicants from many parishes. In Leicestershire in 1579 a communion at Market Bosworth was widely publicised, to be preceded by a 'preparation' in the form of several sermons, the occasion being the 'sin abounding in all places', and 'the cruel assaults of our great enemies'.[108] At about the same time in neighbouring Northamptonshire, the godly were making their way in numbers to the communions held in the house of the puritan entrepreneur and parliamentarian George Carleton at Overston, and to Peter Wentworth's home over the Oxfordshire border at Lillingston Lovell.[109]

The only account we have of a 'holy fair' in Elizabethan England which approaches in detail the sources exploited by Schmidt for seventeenth-century Scotland and eighteenth-century America comes down to us courtesy of William Weston, a Jesuit priest imprisoned at Wisbech Castle, where the custodian was none other than George Carleton. To see what he described, Weston only had to look out of his window, although he naturally peppered his account with mordant religious prejudice. 'They used to come in crowds, flocking from all quarters to be present at their exercises.' First, three or four sermons, preached one after another. 'Then they went to communion, not receiving it either on their knees or standing, but moving by, so that it might be called a Passover in very truth.' Everyone had his or her Bible, searched for the texts, and subsequently disputed their meaning, 'all of them, men and women, boys and girls, labourers, workmen and simpletons; and these discussions were often wont, as it was said, to produce quarrels and fights.' (Evidently Weston did not witness any fights himself.) Finally everyone 'ended the farce with a plentiful supper'.[110]

Schmidt describes the religious fairs of presbyterian Scotland, Ulster and America as consisting of a series of concentric circles of religious intensity, hot at the centre, cooler at the periphery, where the main business of the day may not have been religious at all. Rabbie Burns made the same point, in verse:

> On this hand sits a Chosen swatch,
> Wi' screwed-up, race-proud faces;
> On that, a set o' chaps at watch,
> Thrang winken on the lasses.

On the edge, there could be drinking, courting, even some fighting. 'People ate, drank, conversed, and courted, but they also prayed, meditated, and covenanted.'[111] One is reminded of the disorders associated in the nineteenth century with pilgrimage to Glendalough, in the Wicklow Mountains, which worried the Irish hierarchy.

That almost unique seventeenth-century English source, the diary of the Lancashire apprentice and burgeoning entrepreneur, Roger Lowe, is entirely consistent with the scenario which Schmidt, with the assistance of Burns, has painted. Lowe seems to have divided his waking hours into three more or less equal portions: his work, his regular attendance at sermons and other religious exercises, and his constant presence in the alehouse, where he and his friends drank a bit too much, and courted and chased the girls, 'the Lord forgive us'; but also debated the relative merits of episcopacy and presbytery. Lowe was for the presbytery.[112]

Schmidt also writes of a series of 'thresholds' of experience associated with religious gatherings of this kind, including the thresholds of emergence from childhood through adolescence to adulthood. The religious thresholds entailed a series of converting and committing experiences of progressive intensity. For someone not disposed to be religious, it was a risky thing to find oneself on the edge of this magnetic field, no less dangerous than for the moth which is irresistibly drawn to the candle flame. For in these 'fair-days of the gospel', 'religion and culture, communion and community, piety and sociability commingled'.[113] And so they did in that holistically realistic account of the culture of 'puritan' New England, as 'superstitious' as it was 'religious', recently achieved by David Hall.[114]

Unfortunately, the English evidence will not allow us to attribute to the puritans and their culture the full intensity and exuberance of the phenomena studied by Schmidt. But we may note that redhot Rogers of Dedham much resembled his exact contemporary, the Scottish preacher Robert Bruce, who 'made always an earthquake upon his hearers and rarely preached but to a weeping auditory'. (When Bruce's disciple John Livingston preached at a communion in 1630, many fell to the ground, 'as if they had been dead'. This was already 'revival'.)[115] At Dedham, too, Rogers's hearers were moved to something more than the sighs, tears and stern clearings of the throat which may have been the conventional responses of the auditory of an 'edifying' preacher (another almost inaccessible facet of puritan culture).[116] Even a wedding sermon, as handled by Rogers, could become an occasion for mourning, 'so that all the Ministers that were at the Marriage were employed in comforting, or advising, consciences awakened by that Sermon.'[117] Poor moths!

We may be sure that psalm-singing, in transit and at the sermons and fasts, was an essential element in the proceedings, as it was in Scotland, where 'singing was perhaps the most all-embracing activity of the communion rituals'. All could sing, if all were not fit for the sacrament.[118] At Southill in Bedfordshire in 1603 there was psalm-singing before the five sermons, 'and between every sermon was one psalm'.[119] It is a cliché that the Methodism of the eighteenth century was 'born in song', since the fact is announced on the first page of the *Methodist Hymn-Book*. But this was no less true of the Calvinism and puritanism of the seventeenth-century generations even if, to our ears and musical sensibilities, metrical psalms sung to painfully slow tunes have little of the uplifting charm of 'Amazing Grace'.

If more could be said about the culture of psalm-singing, a whole book . could be devoted to the distinctive culture of the godly household: and has been in the pioneering German work, *The Puritan Family*.[120] But perhaps we have now discovered and said enough to establish with confidence that puritanism was a potent, catching culture, or counter-culture, no less than it was a doctrine, an ideology, and a discipline.

Appendix

This essay was completed and submitted to the editors for publication before the appearance of Ronald Hutton's ambitious *The Rise and Fall of Merry England: the Ritual Year 1400–1700* (Oxford, 1994), a study as conversant with the literary evidence of Jonson, Drayton and Herrick as with inexhaustible folkloristic materials, as well as with his principal source, churchwardens' accounts, all of which surviving from before 1690 he claims not only to have consulted but to have *read*. The subjects of this formidable book and my modest essay are not the same. Dr Hutton has no interest in puritan sermon-gadding and all-day fasts as a restructuring of the ritual year and forms of culture in their own right. I refer to no churchwardens' accounts. But in other respects (the negative aspect of my subject) we cover similar ground, although the scope of Hutton's research renders much of my essay redundant, except for the purpose of the student who prefers 30 pages on a subject to 300. Here too he encounters Old Meg of Hereford, 'Old Snap' of Norwich, Captain Robert Dover and his Cotswold Games (a matter greatly overrated according to Hutton, thanks to the literary hype of *Annalia Dubrensia*), and Christopher Windle the bankrupt, fun-loving cleric with a view of the world from Gloucester gaol. More than earlier accounts, and against the grain of some, Hutton finds in 'evangelical Protestantism' the principal reason for the decline in traditional festivals and seasonal rituals under Elizabeth, and for the revival and intensification of the campaign later, in the seventeenth century. But while he rarely uses the problematical word 'puritan' in this connection, he still renders rather too simple, and simply antagonistic, the relation between the moral concerns and utterances of the complaint writers and Elizabethan and Jacobean society more generally, and especially its book trade. It is most unfortunate that he perpetuates the mistaken impression that Philip Stubbes was a censorious puritan who favoured further reformation of the church on a presbyterian basis (pp. 131–2). In fact, Stubbes devoted the largest section of *The second part of the Anatomie of Abuses* to a denunciation of the presbyterian would-be reformers. Stubbes was the closest approximation to a professional writer that the middle years of Elizabeth produced, and he had links with the more ephemeral and sensational end of the book trade which suggest that his motivation was not all that it may seem to have been.

2. Puritans and the Church Courts, 1560–1640

MARTIN INGRAM

John Field and Thomas Wilcox's *Admonition to the Parliament* of 1572 denounced the courts of the archbishop of Canterbury as 'the filthy quagmire, and poisoned plash of all the abominations that do infect the whole realm', and hence attacked the lower jurisdiction of the 'commissary's court' as

> but a petty little stinking ditch, that floweth out of that former great puddle . . . In this court, for non payment of two pence, a man shall be excommunicated if he appear not when he is sent for . . . And, as it is lightly granted and given forth, so if the money be paid, and the court discharged, it is as quickly called in again. This court . . . punisheth whoredoms and adulteries with toyish censures, remitteth without satisfying the congregation, . . . giveth out dispensations for unlawful marriages, and committeth a thousand such like abominations. God deliver all Christians out of this anti-christian tyranny, where the judges, advocates and proctors for the most part are papists, and as for the scribes and notaries as greedy as cormorants . . .

Among the most interesting things about this passage is its intemperate language, the 'bitterness of the style' that Field admitted, and this characteristic of certain puritan utterances will be among the objects of attention in the later parts of this chapter.[1] More generally the *Admonition* is important because it was one among a number of texts which, whatever its impact on contemporaries, served to fix in the minds of generations of historians an adverse if not outright hostile view of the ecclesiastical courts in Elizabethan and early-Stuart England, and a particular set of ideas about the relations

between these courts and the puritan exponents of further reformation in the English church.[2] The research of the last generation into
both the phenomenon of puritanism and the workings of ecclesiastical justice has, however, greatly modified these older views. The
church courts emerge in a much more favourable light, both as a
system of justice and as an agent of religious reformation, while the
relationship between the courts and puritan ministers and lay people
is seen to have been more complex and less thoroughly negative than
used to be thought. Nonetheless, there were profound differences of
ethos between the bureaucrats who mostly ran the courts and
committed puritans, which ensured that the latter could never rest
entirely satisfied with them. Moreover, there was just sufficient
substance in charges of corruption and inefficiency to give colour to
demands for their abolition. Such demands were given greater urgency
by the aggressive manner in which Laudian policies were promoted
during Charles I's personal rule, which ensured that the courts fell
victim with the bishops to the political crisis of the early 1640s.

This chapter will attempt to cover, albeit cursorily, several different aspects of the topic: puritan criticisms of the courts and how far
they were justified; complaints about puritan ministers and lay
people relayed to the courts, and what underlay them; and how the
courts themselves dealt with puritan activities. It will not confine
itself simply to relations between church courts and puritans, but set
these in the wider context of the business of the courts. On the other
hand, it does not pretend to provide more than a partial view of
puritanism. Plainly many aspects of puritan theology, piety, sociability and mentality cannot be adequately viewed through the optic
of ecclesiastical justice, nor can the vitally important activities of
gentry and noble patrons who rarely made an appearance before the
ordinary church courts.

The survey is informed by evidence derived from both secondary
works and published and unpublished primary sources, relating to a
wide range of English dioceses. A full study would explore differences
between the northern province, where puritans were comparatively
unmolested by the authorities before about 1620, and the province
of Canterbury, which witnessed conflict from early in Elizabeth's
reign; and would further chart contrasts within the southern province
– between, for example, the diocese of Peterborough, where puritans
were numerous and the authorities aggressive, and the diocese of
Salisbury, where the conflicts were much more muted. But for

brevity's sake the focus is on some broad, central themes which could (with variations) be illustrated from almost any area where puritans formed a significant presence.[3] To give some sense of locality and individual personality, however, the detailed examples have mostly been drawn from the 80 or so parishes scattered across Berkshire, Wiltshire, Dorset and Devon that were subject to the jurisdiction of the dean of Salisbury. This 'peculiar' – that is, an area exempt from normal episcopal control – is of special interest for several reasons. Reports of puritan activities came repeatedly from a number of its parishes, including populous market towns and small country villages. The list – figures in brackets offer some indication of size by citing, when this information is available, the number of communicants reported in 1603 – included Beaminster (600), Mapperton (50), Lyme Regis (1100), Fordington (360), Bloxworth, Stratton and Sherborne in Dorset; Calne (1300), Ogbourne St Andrew (260), Ramsbury, Baydon and Shalbourne in Wiltshire; and Faringdon and Hungerford in Berkshire. The dean who held office between 1577 and 1604 was none other than Dr John Bridges, author of the 1400-page *Defence of the Government Established in the Church of Englande for Ecclesiasticall Matters* (1587) and butt of the merciless Martin Marprelate. Later deans included John Gordon (1605–19), the Scottish courtier and scholar; John Williams (1619–20) and John Bowle (1620–30), who became respectively bishop of Lincoln and of Rochester; and, during the personal rule, Edmund Mason (1630–5), tutor to Prince Charles, and Richard Bailey (1635–67), a kinsman of Laud. A variety of styles of churchmanship can thus be illustrated from this peculiar. Moreover the archive of the jurisdiction is particularly rich. As well as the formal court proceedings, many of the original churchwardens' presentments survive intact and are supplemented by notes and letters; these illuminate the local situation and provide insights into the culture not only of puritanism itself, but also of the local society of which it formed part and of the church court establishment.[4]

I

The ecclesiastical courts had gradually developed during the middle ages as the key institutions in the administrative and judicial aspects of the church's activities. Having survived the Reformation virtually intact, by the late sixteenth century they formed an elaborate hierarchy. At the apex were the appeal courts and other tribunals of the two English provinces of Canterbury and York; at the base were the courts of the archdeacons, typically covering the area of a small county. In between, representing what was in practice the most important level of ecclesiastical justice, were the episcopal courts of the 27 English and Welsh dioceses. (The dean of Salisbury's peculiar, which exercised quasi-episcopal authority, was in effect a miniature version of such a jurisdiction.) These institutions were supplemented by the Courts of High Commission based at London, York and Durham, and also by various local commissions that existed from time to time in the reign of Elizabeth and during the early years of James I; their special powers, resting on parliamentary sanction and the royal prerogative, were designed to strengthen the normal system of ecclesiastical justice.

Together these various courts supervised the clergy, oversaw the upkeep of churches and the provision of church services, and also enforced the payment of tithes to support the ministry. In addition they exercised discipline over the faith and morals of the laity, enforcing religious observances such as church attendance, and punishing adultery, fornication and other sins. They also had jurisdiction over probate and testamentary disputes, certain forms of defamation, and marriage, separation and annulment. Some of these matters were dealt with as suits between parties, much like modern civil litigation. Many were dealt with '*ex officio*', as 'criminal' or disciplinary cases; and there was an elaborate visitation system whereby officers of the courts periodically went on tour to gather 'presentments' or 'detections' of offences from the churchwardens and sidesmen who represented the individual parishes. The ultimate sanction of the courts was excommunication, involving the exclusion of the offender from the services of the church and a variety of legal disabilities, but in practice it was mostly used to punish contumacy – that is, failure to appear or otherwise obey the mandates of the court. For people who did turn up to answer disciplinary charges, the most common outcome in lesser cases was some form of 'admonition' or telling off from the judge, while the characteristic ecclesiastical punishments for more serious offences were various forms of public confession or 'penance'.[5]

Many features of this system of justice appear bizarre to modern eyes. But in this period ordinary people took for granted the public regulation of many forms of personal behaviour, including religious beliefs and observances and sexual morality. On the other hand, people were used to conducting an extraordinarily wide range of business through courts of law, and coping with a bewildering tangle of jurisdictions. As to the actual workings of the church courts, the tendency of recent work has been to rescue their reputation from at least the more extreme of their critics. The law which the courts administered was a well established and sophisticated system. Rooted in the canon law of the western church, it had been modified over the centuries by local custom and was further adapted in the sixteenth and seventeenth centuries by means of a series of parliamentary statutes and ecclesiastical canons. Following Henry VIII's abolition of the study of canon law at the universities, the courts were mostly staffed by civil lawyers. But their headquarters at Doctors' Commons provided the forum for the continuing study of ecclesiastical law, which persisted not as a moribund relic but as a vibrant and evolving tradition.[6]

Some of the criticisms levelled against the church courts in this period were essentially partisan, reflecting the bitterness experienced by puritan ministers or laypeople who felt victimised by the courts, or deriving from common-law rivals of the spiritual jurisdiction. A more dispassionate view suggests that, in terms of rationality and fairness to litigants, the principles and procedures of the courts often had much to recommend them. This is true even of the notorious *ex officio* oath, which was administered to defendants in serious disciplinary cases and could, so puritan critics and their common-law allies claimed, force individuals of tender conscience to incriminate themselves. It is now known that the issues were far more complex than appears at first sight, since the privilege against self-incrimination itself had strong roots in Roman canon law. In any case the *ex officio* oath was generally used scrupulously, and it is doubtful how far it really disadvantaged defendants.[7]

The Millenary Petition presented to James I in 1603 complained of 'the longsomeness of suits . . . which hang sometimes two, three, four, five, six, or seven years', but again the charge tends to evaporate when closely examined. The summary procedures used in disciplinary cases were often very swift, and judges could similarly offer an express service in some party-and-party suits. The speed with which other forms of litigation were conducted depended very much on the assiduity of the litigants and their legal representatives, whose role it was to take the initiative in prosecuting suits. For technical reasons, comparisons with the secular courts are hard to make; but there is little real evidence of excessive delay.[8] Contemporary accusations of corruption also seem grossly exaggerated, though here the evidence is more mixed. An exceptionally scandalous situation existed at Gloucester under the weak rule of Bishop Cheyney (1562–79) and his notoriously corrupt chancellor Thomas Powell, and remained unsatisfactory even into the next century. More typical was the low-level venality which affected various dioceses from time to time, involving payments of 'a quart of wine' or small sums to the summoners of the courts, or *douceurs* offered to the judge in the hope of securing favourable treatment. 'Corruption' of this sort, while hardly edifying, was probably typical of most courts of law in this period.[9] The further puritan charge, that ecclesiastical officials exacted extortionate fees, has even less substance. Certainly church court litigation was financed by fees, which were allocated to the judges and the various officials according to set formulae, while defendants in disciplinary cases, guilty and innocent alike, were likewise liable to pay the charges of the courts. But this was common practice in all tribunals in the period. Strict comparisons with the secular courts are again not easy, but it does not appear that ecclesiastical justice was particularly burdensome or expensive. In order to forestall criticisms, the level of fees in church courts was officially pegged by Archbishop Whitgift in 1597, and although this standard was not universally applied it was certainly influential. This meant that, in a period of continuing inflation, the courts were offering a cheaper and cheaper service as time went on. In any case fees were often reduced or waived for poor defendants, while some courts deliberately minimised their fees in disciplinary cases.[10]

But none of these defences, which measure ecclesiastical justice by the standards of the legal establishment generally, really met the most fundamental and heartfelt of puritan objections. At base the godly disliked the spiritual courts because, along with the use of the surplice, the ring in marriage, the sign of the cross in baptism, and a variety of other puritan shibboleths, they were seen as 'popish abuses yet remaining in the English church', 'corruptions' that persisted 'to the hindrance of the gospel, to the joy of the wicked, and to the grief and dismay of all those that profess Christ's religion, and labour to attain Christian reformation'. The *Admonition*'s claim that the judges, registrars and other court officers were actually 'papists' was an obvious exaggeration, but it is the case that at the beginning of Elizabeth's reign many were of deeply conservative hue and liable to obstruct the propagation of protestantism, and it took time to replace them with more committed individuals. In any case puritans were apt to believe that the personnel who ran the courts did so essentially for their own profit, without a true vocation to pastoral duty and godly reformation. Again this was a calumny: detailed studies have revealed plenty of dedicated professionals who did their best according to their lights, taking (as the civilian Thomas Wilson insisted) 'great pains for small gains'. But certainly there could be a certain tension between the financial interests of the administrators and the pastoral mission of the church.[11] Recognising that there were deep differences of ethos between church court administrators and puritan zealots, it is easy to see how the latter could view ecclesiastical justice as a travesty of discipline which required, not simply overhaul, but radical reform. The more extreme puritan (or 'presbyterian') solution was to root out the old system entirely, and in its place 'to plant in every congregation a lawful and godly seignorie' consisting of the minister acting in association with lay elders or magistrates: that is, a form of 'discipline' supposedly congruent with apostolic models and with the 'best reformed churches' of continental Europe.[12]

Both to moderates and to extremists, what appeared most scandalous among existing arrangements was the practice of excommunication. In the early days of Christianity, according to the *Admonition*, it had been 'the last censure of the church, and never went forth but for notorious crimes... Then excommunication was greatly regarded and feared'. In point of fact, even within living memory the full rigour of the sentence had been used relatively rarely, for the pre-Reformation courts had generally employed the simpler form of 'suspension' or 'lesser excommunication' (exclusion from the church building) as the first line of defence against contumacy. However, this sanction had proved increasingly ineffective during the disruptions of the Reformation years, and the authorities had been panicked into substituting the sentence of 'greater excommunication' (which theoretically entailed social ostracism and legal as well as merely religious disabilities) in the hope – soon dashed – that it would command more respect. The causes of this apparent failure are complex, and recent research suggests that the sanction was not as futile as historians have often supposed. Many sexual offenders were young and mobile, and had moved on before excommunication could directly affect them; but from a local point of view the sentence did aptly symbolise their riddance from the parish. In some other cases apparent ineffectiveness was the result of administrative inertia, not of self-conscious defiance of the church on the part of delinquents. On the other hand, when excommunication was directed against settled householders it was by no means without force and throughout this period was still a sanction to be feared. Nonetheless puritan critics were right to complain that excommunication had become a routine matter, in effect 'pronounced for every light trifle' but easily redeemed on payment of a fee. The bishops' stock defence, that contumacy amounted to contempt of the church and so justified the use of this extreme sanction, was weak and flawed. Even such stalwart defenders of the Elizabethan settlement as Archbishops Whitgift and Bancroft recognised that the situation was a scandal and sought vainly for a remedy.[13]

Complaints about penance were less convincing. It was claimed that current practice was a mere perversion of the laudable discipline of the early church, and that the punishment 'is so light that they esteem not of it; they fear it not, they make but a jest of it'. In reality, the penances imposed by the church courts could involve real humiliation. Characteristically culprits were ordered to confess their offence publicly in church, dressed in a white sheet and carrying a white rod; sometimes they had to go bare-legged for greater shame, or wear 'papers' setting forth their offence in large letters. They often had to stand before the congregation during the whole service, which not uncommonly included a sermon or homily on an appropriately edifying subject (the sinfulness of adultery, for example). To conclude the proceedings, culprits asked God, and sometimes also their neighbours, for forgiveness, and joined with the congregation in saying the Lord's Prayer in what was intended to be a ritual of reconciliation. In very serious cases, penances were performed in the market place. For all but the most shameless, and certainly for anyone of local standing and credit, such penances surely bore hard, and it is scarcely surprising that some people broke down and wept as they performed them. Why then did these penalties fail to meet with the approval of puritans? Firstly they were imposed by a remote ecclesiastical official, not by local representatives who, it was claimed, alone could judge what was required to 'satisfy' the congregation. Secondly (a related point) it was supposed that many penances were actually commuted into a money payment, though in point of fact such commutations were very sparingly used in most dioceses. Finally the most zealous did not in any case believe that what they contemptuously referred to as 'pricking in blanket, or pinning in a sheet', however harsh they may appear today, were sufficient penalties for such heinous sins as 'adultery, whoredom, drunkenness, etc.'. They had in mind the rigorous standard of biblical law, and some wished that the most serious offences should incur the death penalty or other draconian punishments.[14]

Puritan demands for the remodelling of ecclesiastical discipline were in the early years of Elizabeth's reign spiced not only by an urgent desire for reformation but also by the belief that they were eminently attainable. Since the reign of Henry VIII it had been widely accepted among reformers that the English church required a revised body of ecclesiastical law, and in Edward VI's reign a new *corpus* had actually been drafted by a team of civil and canon lawyers headed by Archbishop Cranmer. This revised system, though not wholly congruent with what Elizabethan puritans wanted, certainly went some way to meet their demands; hence its publication by John Foxe in time for the parliament of 1571, under the title of *Reformatio Legum Ecclesiasticarum*, helped to nourish expectations of change – though predictably Elizabeth refused to countenance it, as Edward's minister the duke of Northumberland had likewise done in 1552–3. Irrespective of the fate of the *Reformatio Legum*, there was undoubtedly widespread clerical support in the early years of Elizabeth's reign for stricter and surer penalties against sin and irreligion. Thus proposals drafted for the Convocation of 1563 desired

> that such as do not communicate thrice a year at the least, be severely punished; and such as have not, nor will not communicate at all, to be as in case of heresy; or else some grievous fine to be set upon them . . . That adulterers and fornicators may be punished by strait imprisonment and open shame, if the offender be vile and stubborn, etc., as carting by the civil magistrate, etc. Some think banishment and perpetual prison to be meet for adulterers.[15]

Puritan demands that discipline be exercised *locally* were in some respects more problematic. Apart from the implications for the church hierarchy, it was naïve to demand that 'a fit minister and elder of the congregation . . . ought to determine of the degrees prohibited in marriage, of cases and just causes of divorce'; in a dynastic society in which marital legitimacy and due descent of property were of immense importance, especially in the higher ranks, such a decentralised free-for-all was for most people completely unthinkable. Some versions of the puritans' plans recognised this by providing that cases concerning marriage, testaments and tithes should be dealt with by some species of secular court, but nonetheless the issues remained problematic.[16] However, simpler matters of religious and moral discipline could well be conducted locally, and to some extent the structures already existed. Ordinary householders of the middling sort regularly served – often by house-row or some other system of rotation – as churchwardens, tithingmen, constables and collectors for (later overseers of) the poor, and in these roles they exercised a good deal of discretionary authority. Indeed the existing system of ecclesiastical justice clearly assumed that local officers would cajole and warn offenders before presenting the obdurate, and in that sense the work of the church courts was rooted in a system of local discipline. Householders without local office in any case exercised a degree of formal authority over their children, apprentices and household servants; slipping easily into quasi-legal forms of expression, they were wont to 'examine' them about their behaviour and 'admonish' or 'chastise' them if anything were amiss. Even women (largely excluded from positions of public authority) played a role in this local discipline: mistresses were often thought the best persons to deal with errant female servants, while it was common practice for the midwife and other 'honest women' to interrogate unmarried mothers in childbed, to extort from them (often under threat of withholding help during the delivery) the name of the men who had gotten them with child. Sometimes the leading householders would act together to exclude an undesirable from the community. Thus a declaration drawn up at Highworth in 1598 announced

> To all to whom these presents shall come, we whose names are here subscribed send greeting. Know ye that we do testify of matters of truth by these presents that John Temple . . . butcher is a man not of good behaviour nor of good fame or name but a whoremaster, a drunkard, a liar and a common quarreller, a brawler, fighter and a disturbator of his honest neighbours in so much that he is utterly unworthy to live in a commonwealth . . .

Among the signatories to this declaration were the minister, bailiff, constable and churchwardens; and in this it was typical of most of these various mechanisms of parochial discipline, which characteristically involved such local authority figures as senior yeomen, gentlemen, justices of the peace, and clergymen.[17] Herein might be discerned the raw materials for local consistories. Against this background it is hardly surprising that some ministers who were dissatisfied with the existing state of the church courts began to move towards independence. Around 1592 the vicar of Sherborne was accused of announcing publicly in church that

> I understand that in my absence divers of my parish have been excommunicated for not receiving the communion, which I know have all received except two or three of them; it is not for that cause but for not paying two shillings apiece to the apparitor, which is contrary to law and equity; wherefore I would wish you should not refrain their company but to account of them as good neighbours and Christians; and it were to be wished that such matters might be ended by the worshipful men hereby, and not to vex them to that bribing court of Sarum.[18]

Such a development could be facilitated by the tradition of jurisdictional independence that certain communities enjoyed. Some country villages – for a variety of legal and geographical reasons – were effectively in this position,[19] but it was far more common among cities and boroughs. In London and Westminster, and in provincial towns such as Norwich, Exeter, Colchester and Devizes, there was a well-established tradition of civic regulation of moral conduct, one feature of which was the infliction on sexual offenders of a range of customary punishments – carting round the town, imprisonment, whipping, branding, banishment, or any combination of these – which in their severity came close to what puritans desired.[20] This background helps to explain how in the earlier part of Elizabeth's reign it was possible in some towns for puritan clergy, urban magistrates and county justices to combine forces to promote the Gospel and combat irreligion and vice, in some instances creating novel forms of tribunal that had more than a smack of presbytery about them. However, no sooner were these experiments underway than they fell foul of the existing hierarchy. The 'order of Northampton' (1571) initially attracted the support of the bishop of

Peterborough, but he swiftly suppressed it when the implications for ecclesiastical jurisdiction became apparent; a somewhat similar project at Bury St Edmunds (Suffolk) in 1579, whose draconian penalties against 'suspected papists' and sundry sinners more obviously exceeded the law of the land, immediately aroused the opposition of Bishop Freke of Norwich.[21] These reactions were straws in the wind. The same decade witnessed Queen Elizabeth's decision to suppress the prophesyings and the consequent suspension of Archbishop Grindal. The door was thus firmly closed against any kind of far-reaching reform of the church courts or local experiments in congregational discipline.

II

Moderate, officially inspired reform of church courts procedures did continue, as many of the canons of 1571, 1575, 1585, 1597 and 1604 bear witness, but the basic structures remained unchanged.[22] In retrospect it is clear that, contrary to puritan complaints, these courts proved to be by no means ineffective agents of further reformation in England. Their role cannot be easily disentangled from the work of the church as a whole, including the activities of bishops, clergy and innumerable lay people. But much of that broader picture can usefully be constructed round the institutional structure of the church courts, simply because the latter served as the hub of diocesan and archidiaconal administration, and impinged so often on the life of the parish. In other words the ecclesiastical jurisdiction was not divorced from the pastoral mission of the church but part and parcel of it. Visitations were a means whereby bishops could become acquainted with their dioceses and with the people under their charge. The episcopate could thus express their concerns in visitation sermons and charges; meet with their clergy to cajole and encourage; get a sense of the temper of lay people; and take the opportunity to conduct what seems to have been the very popular rite of confirmation or 'bishopping'. The diocesan legal administration was the focus for a wide range of pastoral functions, notably the institution of clergymen and the licensing of preachers, curates and schoolmasters. It was also the prime means for the regulation of the ministry; while the proceedings of the courts were integral to the church's task of inculcating the reformed religion among the laity and raising popular standards of religious observance and moral conduct – an indispensable complement to the work of the parish clergy. Small wonder that bishops and archdeacons commonly gave a great deal of attention to the operation of their courts (especially the disciplinary side), whether by personal attendance or by working through trusted deputies.[23]

There are obvious difficulties in assessing the achievements of the official church in this period, but it is possible to chart a number of developments which may plausibly be seen as the fruits of successful mission and which to a greater or lesser extent depended on the work of the church courts. One was an improvement in the quality of the parish clergy. In the early years of Elizabeth's reign the ministry was at a very low ebb. There was a shortage of priests of any sort, a severe shortage of committed Protestant ministers, and an absolute dearth of educated and skilful preachers. To this extent puritan criticisms of 'dumb dogs' and other unsatisfactory features of the ministry were well founded. But 50 years later the situation had changed markedly. Kenneth Fincham is no doubt right to warn historians against *exaggerating* this shift. In various parts of the country, including the northern and western Midlands and above all in Lancashire and some other northern shires, the improvement in clerical standards was patchy and limited; and everywhere there remained many poor, relatively ill-educated ministers and some scandalous cases of individual neglect. But in much of lowland England a very marked change did take place, to the extent that the ideal of a well-educated, committed, preaching ministry was by the death of James I much closer to being realised. Of course this development owed much to broader social changes, such as the expansion of educational opportunities and more favourable economic conditions for some clergy. But, as numerous diocesan studies testify, it did owe something to personal initiatives on the part of the episcopate and to the routine work of the church courts. Not only were the latter the means whereby scandalous and inadequate ministers were brought to book, but the courts also exerted the constant and routine pressure that was needed to ensure the satisfactory performance of clerical duties, particularly the more troublesome and difficult tasks such as catechising.[24]

The ecclesiastical courts played an even more important role in helping to inculcate the reformed religion among the laity. Again the legacy that Elizabethan churchmen inherited was a difficult one. In 1559 committed Protestants formed only a tiny minority in most areas; religious conservatism was strong, and in some regions (particularly parts of the north) it was almost overwhelming. On the other hand, the religious turmoil of the previous generation had dislocated established beliefs and observances in ways which were probably highly destructive, and conducive not to zealous commitment but to bitterness, religious apathy, and even recourse to witchcraft and magic. Just how 'Protestant' England had become by the 1620s or 1630s is a question that turns as much on definitions as on evidence; and historians who insist that the internalisation of strict doctrines of justification by faith alone is the key criterion, are bound to take a pessimistic view. However, it can hardly be denied that by this time there had occurred massive shifts in beliefs and attitudes which – whether or not they are thought to be 'Protestant' – were distinctively *post-Reformation*, not least in being decidedly anti-Catholic. The records of the church courts reflect how this change occurred. The precise pattern naturally varied from diocese to diocese, area to area, and indeed parish to parish; but a number of major stages may be identified which, at the cost of some simplification, give some sense of this crucial evolution.[25]

The first decade or so of the Elizabethan regime concentrated above all on the dismantling of the apparatus of Catholic worship, the provision of what was required for the new Protestant services, and the enforcement of the changed arrangements. Out went images, altar-stones, crosses, mass vestments, and such personal aids to piety as rosaries; in came communion tables, prayer books, the Ten Commandments and other sentences of scripture painted round the walls of the church, and similar innovations. These material changes of course took time and money. But they were largely complete by 1575, and any further activities on this front were in the nature of mopping-up campaigns. Meanwhile the focus of attention had shifted to the identification of stubborn Catholics or 'recusants'. Purely spiritual sanctions were obviously of limited use against a section of society that categorically denied the authority of the church that issued them, and much of the most effective action against recusancy was taken by the secular courts or by the High Commission. But the ordinary church courts did play a significant role that continued through Elizabeth's reign into that of James I and his son: they marginalised notorious recusants by keeping them in a

state of permanent excommunication, and compiled registers of
'offenders' which they turned over as required to the secular authorities. The result of all these activities was that before the turn of
the century – except in parts of the north and in a few pockets in the
south – committed Catholics had been reduced to a tiny and
embattled minority.[26]

Meanwhile the church courts directed their energies towards
raising standards of religious observance among lay people, the great
majority of whom were at least nominal conformists. A major focus
of attention was the communion. The canons envisaged that the
people should receive at least three times a year, but for enforcement
purposes the courts settled for the lower standard of at least annual
reception at Easter. The admittedly imperfect evidence suggests that
the church had gone far towards achieving this aim by the early
seventeenth century, while in many parishes more frequent communions were commonplace. Correspondingly the ecclesiastical courts
in many areas gradually put more emphasis on enforcing regular
attendance at the ordinary Sunday services of morning and evening
prayer, and again there is evidence of some success. By the 1620s
and 1630s, defaulters were often presented for absence on specified
days or from particular services, suggesting careful monitoring and
even the use of attendance registers in some places. A related
development was increasing action against the profanation of holy
days and, more particularly, the Christian sabbath. The timing and
incidence of prosecutions for these offences were particularly vari-
able, and the complexity and ambiguity of popular responses defy
easy generalisation; moreover the issue became complicated by the
controversies over the Book of Sports, which will feature later in the
chapter. But it is safe to conclude that by the 1620s and 1630s the
ban on Sunday work was much more consistently enforced, and
respected by the people, than it had been a generation or so earlier.
By the same token some other forms of profanation of the sabbath,
such as victualling and alehouse-haunting, were increasingly discountenanced both by the courts and by local society.[27]

The church courts' success was by no means confined to the
sphere of religious observances and the establishment of Protestantism. Despite the strictures of puritan critics, they also had an impact
in the broader field of personal morality, especially the regulation of
marriage and the punishment of sexual misdoings. The matrimonial
law which the courts had inherited from the middle ages was shot

through with complexities and ambiguities, and the resulting uncertainties in popular practice were compounded by the debates and dislocations associated with the Reformation. Under Elizabeth and the early Stuarts, however, ecclesiastical judges interpreted the laws conscientiously in ways which reaffirmed the importance of marriage in church as the only sure guarantee of a legally and socially acceptable union, while at the same time restricting the availability of annulment and separation. In short, the courts did much to buttress the state of marriage after a period of uncertainty. They also continued, and in some ways intensified, their traditional attack on fornication and adultery. Bastard-bearing – resented by most people in this period not merely on moral grounds but also because the support of poor illegitimate children imposed burdens on parish poor rates – was prosecuted with particular rigour, while the courts also stepped up prosecutions for pre-nuptial fornication or bridal pregnancy. Human nature, combined with social customs that took for granted a good deal of familiarity between courting couples, inevitably set limits on the courts' success in these areas. But detailed studies both of the working of ecclesiastical justice and of demographic behaviour in the parishes indicate a discernible if not dramatic shift in the moral climate between the 1580s and the 1630s; and while this change certainly cannot be attributed *wholly* to the work of the church courts, the latter undoubtedly played a significant part in bringing it about.[28]

Armed only with the 'rusty sword' of excommunication and the supposedly 'toyish censures' of penance, the church courts were thus able to achieve a good measure of success. Their great advantage was their ability to exert sustained pressure. In visitation after visitation, year after year, decade after decade, they upheld the standards of Protestant religion and Christian morality; and this was so despite the fact that numerous *individual* offenders escaped the net or set the courts at defiance. The approach of the judges may be described as broadly consensual, marching slightly in advance of popular attitudes to effect steady if unspectacular improvement. However, this cautious approach was not dictated solely by the weakness of court procedures or the pusillanimity of the judges, as puritan criticisms might lead us to expect. Rather it derived from the traditional ethos of canon law, which emphasised the medicinal rather than retributive purposes of ecclesiastical discipline, and was inclined to leniency over strict justice. In other words the courts believed that people could be induced to behave better, and tried to achieve this by moderate treatment before they resorted to the strictest penalties. Closely related was the principle of maintaining peace and harmony. This was part of the rationale even for the courts' jurisdiction over adultery and similar heinous sins, for such offences were supposed to be a grievous affront not only to God but also to the Christian community, and had to be restrained lest they provoke bitterness and strife between husband and wife and neighbour and neighbour. The duty of peace-making also underlay the church courts' adjudication of party-and-party suits. Indeed it was a basic principle of ecclesiastical law that the parties should be encouraged to settle the matters at issue by mediation and compromise, and apparitors, proctors and judges can often be seen facilitating such informal settlements with the help of parish ministers, local notables, and the friends and neighbours of the litigants.[29]

This eirenic emphasis was not, of course, peculiar to the church courts themselves. Among the traditional duties of the parish clergy was to act as peacemakers among their parishioners. To support them in this role, the church courts offered a special remedy for 'opprobrious words against the clergy', while contentious ministers were themselves subject to disciplinary action. The church and churchyard were specially protected areas, in which any form of quarrelling or brawling was, irrespective of the rights and wrongs of the matter, liable to punishment.[30] Exactly the same principle underpinned the use of the Book of Common Prayer. A proclamation of September 1548 had looked forward to the establishment shortly of 'one uniform order . . . to put an end of all controversies in religion', while the liturgy and regulations concerning worship that eventually emerged in the reign of Elizabeth laid considerable emphasis on peace and harmony. 'Because in all alterations, and specially in rites and ceremonies', affirmed the Royal Injunctions of 1559, 'there happeneth discord amongst the people and thereupon slanderous words and railings whereby charity, the knot of all Christian society, is loosed: the Queen's majesty being most desirous of all other earthly things that her people should live in charity both towards God and man . . . willeth and straightly commandeth all manner her subjects to forbear all vain and contentious disputations in matters of religion, and not to use in despite or rebuke of any person . . . contentious words.' Likewise the rubrics of the Book of Common Prayer instructed the minister to reject from the sacrament of Holy Communion not only notorious sinners but also 'those betwixt whom he perceiveth malice and hatred to reign, not suffering them to be partakers of the Lord's Table until he know them to be reconciled'.[31]

III

It is against this background that puritan protests against the Prayer Book, and the church courts' response to them, must in part be understood. The stock view, that sees the intermittent prosecutions, suspensions and deprivations as heavy-handed aggression on the part of the crown and ecclesiastical hierarchy, partly reflects the opinion of contemporary puritans. The ministers who spearheaded the campaign for further reformation in the reign of Elizabeth appealed to 'the honour of God and the holy peace of this church' and called for toleration of their scruples in the name of Christian charity; on the other hand they accused the church authorities of obduracy, harsh dealing in the courts, and recourse to 'reproachful names' such as 'fool, dolt, boy, knave and arrant knave' as well as 'precisians' and 'puritans'. However, their opponents accused them with equal vigour of disrupting the church over 'matters indifferent', of wilful disobedience if they persisted in their objections, and of bringing contention to their parishes. The charges of disruption were indignantly denied, and are of course not easy to evaluate.[32] But certain it is that many known puritan ministers in Elizabeth's reign are found at the epicentre of parochial convulsions, and some were repeatedly in trouble in different places; and this offers a suggestive angle for understanding what from a local viewpoint underlay prosecutions.[33]

The puritan activities that caused complaint – or rather such activities as they were perceived by churchwardens and questmen – may be reconstructed from parochial 'detections' or reports to the authorities. Prominent among them was the minister's refusal to use the sign of the cross in baptism. In puritan eyes this part of the rite was a superstitious survival; but the parents of new-born children were not unnaturally concerned that the ceremony should be duly performed, to the extent that at Ogbourne St Andrew in 1604 one woman challenged the minister, 'Sir, shall we not have our child christened? If you will not cross it we will carry it where we shall have it', and only 'with much ado' was she induced to keep silence. Scruples over burial could also lead to strife, as at Beaminster around 1592, when a man was reported for 'abusing of the minister at a funeral, swearing that he would lay the spade about his ears because he did not take the spade and say earth to earth, etc.' The abbreviation, omission, or rearrangement of prayers and other material in the regular Prayer Book services also caused concern. Thus at Sherborne in 1582 it was reported that the vicar, David Dee, left out large sections of common prayer, 'in place of which he useth his preachings, far from the edifying of the congregation', while he likewise 'leaveth out the exhortation and confession in the time of the communion and useth such as himself instantly deviseth to the mislike of the communicants'.

The activities of the same man illustrate several other causes of resentment. One was the rejection of parishioners from the communion for reasons other than those laid down in the Prayer Book: usually the minister claimed that the people concerned were ignorant of basic Christian principles, but some cases raise suspicions that he was restricting participation in the communion to those whom he considered to be among the elect, and excluding the unregenerate multitude. Another cause of dissension was 'particular' preaching, aimed at specific members of the congregation: thus it was said of David Dee that 'if any secret admonition be given him by a secret friend [concerning the behaviour of parishioners], he maketh public declamations upon the same, freighting his sermons therewith to the offence of many'. A related problem was the preaching of what seemed like hard and uncharitable doctrines: the churchwardens of Mapperton complained in 1598 that their rector, George Bowden, taught that 'the best works that we do is sin and abomination and filthiness before God, moreover . . . that a child when that he is born be [ap]pointed to be damned or saved'. Additional complaints concerned failure to observe holy days, inveighing against standing up at the reading of the Gospel, refusal to bow at the name of Jesus, and – the most characteristic mark of puritan nonconformity – refusing to wear the surplice.[34]

Historians have interpreted complaints of this sort as evidence of popular attachment to Prayer Book services. One variant of this view, promoted by Christopher Haigh, sees the phenomenon as a species of 'parish anglicanism' based on a deeply conservative attachment to ritual, a kind of second best to the old Catholic ways; and when, as at Mapperton, a puritan minister had replaced an aged clerical survivor from the reign of Mary, such an interpretation has obvious plausibility. Yet Judith Maltby's alternative view, which sees the phenomenon rather in terms of positive commitment to the liturgy of the Elizabethan and Jacobean church, may well be equally valid in other cases.[35] However, it must be emphasised that in either circumstance there were often other considerations at work. Indeed it is plain that many of the cases that were brought before the courts involved not merely neglect or rejection of the official forms but ministerial behaviour that appeared in some more positive sense reprehensible: it was the *manner* of the neglect that was equally at issue. Some of the ministers involved were accused of flagrant defiance of authority. Thus George Bowden of Mapperton, reluctantly complying with an order to wear the surplice in 1598, allegedly said that 'the wicked had caused him now to put on the badge of superstition'. 'Whether he meant our sovereign lady the Queen . . .,' observed the churchwardens circumspectly, 'or by whom else he spoke it, we know not.' Similarly at Sherborne in 1591 it was said that 'our vicar [Francis Scarlett] coming to the place in the church where Mr Dean's book [presumably Bridges' *Defence*] is tied, used these words, viz. "Here is Mr Dean's book tied in a chain", and contemptuously took the book and threw him down and said, "Now Mr Dean may see how long his chain is" '. Such hostile accounts must obviously be viewed with caution, but they appear plausible in the light of the fact that some extremists were prepared to voice similar sentiments actually in court. 'I speak to your conscience, if you have a conscience', ranted the radical Salisbury preacher, Matthew Fenton, in the bishop's consistory in 1598; 'I mean not to answer you, you show your own impudency.' Being asked by one of the court officials 'whether he were not ashamed to use such speeches', he replied 'No, I am not ashamed'.[36]

Instead of or in addition to such expressions of defiance, some ministers apparently indulged in words and gestures which – in a society in which, as we have seen, the clergy were supposed to be peacemakers, church and churchyard were protected against strife, and slanderous words (especially sexual defamation) were a common cause of litigation – must have appeared at best unseemly, at worst deeply shocking to many of their parishioners. Of George Bowden it was said that 'as soon as he hath ended the gospel he plucketh . . . [the surplice] off most vehemently and down he throweth it', preaching of conformist ministers that 'men comes [*sic*] in black apparel and white toys [i.e. fripperies, meaning the surplice] upon their backs, and yet they are ravening wolves'; his schoolmaster colleague 'doth speak hard against the surplice and saith he that standeth in the church in his surplice doth stand as though he did bear penance in a white sheet'. Such invective with sexual or scatological associations was not unusual, and it was commonplace to denounce the surplice in terms such as 'popish rag', 'mass smock' or 'smell smock'.[37]

How are these forms of puritan behaviour to be explained? For the ministers concerned, the surplice and the other ornaments and ceremonies were indeed abominations which defiled the church and represented a stumbling block to the unconverted; while some of the sexual and similarly 'offensive' language and metaphor had a close affinity with some contemporary religious polemic, including the *Admonition to the Parliament* and the Martin Marprelate tracts.[38] Some preachers cast themselves in the role of Old Testament patriarchs and prophets: thus Matthew Fenton of Salisbury proudly proclaimed that 'as God sent Moses unto Pharaoh, and hardened Pharaoh's heart, so God sent him . . . to preach His gospel unto this city'. As an element in preaching, dramatic denunciations and theatrical gestures may be seen as deliberate contrivances, designed to startle passive conformists from their complacency and to induce conversion through shock. (Later Quaker practices, such as 'going naked as a sign', were more extreme versions of the same technique.) With the same end in view ministers might vigorously interrogate their congregations from the pulpit: thus George Bowden 'did demand a question in his sermon, "Who commands you to keep holy the Apostles' days, Our Lady days, festival days (and to fast the evening), and the holy time of Lent? It is not commanded by God" '. Sometimes they actually ridiculed their flocks for their lack of understanding or attachment to 'outward show and old ceremonies'. Unfortunately these sallies were apt to be resented, and might even provoke in retaliation a species of charivari. Thus in 1607 a woman of Castleton was reported for going 'in derision' to meet the minister and a newly married couple 'with a surplice on her back and a pair of spectacles on her nose and a book in her hands, saying . . . "I cannot endure this papistical book!" '.[39]

Some of the cases of vociferous complaint against puritan ministers were complicated by disputes over non-doctrinal matters of contention. It was said that David Dee of Sherborne 'preacheth his own griefs and quarrels', and that he had rejected various people from the communion 'for not paying tithes such as he demandeth' and for other 'private occasions of offence'; in general he 'dealeth rather contentiously than lovingly with his parishioners'. Similarly Thomas Hickman, parson of Upton Scudamore, was at law with his parishioners, allegedly kept sheep in the churchyard so that the church and church porch became filled with dung, and overall was said to be 'so envious and brabbling that the . . . parishioners are weary of him'. But it would be wrong to see disputes over tithes and the like as the 'real' cause of dispute, and the charges of distinctively puritan activities as merely a ploy to vex an unpopular minister. Rather, in the eyes of parishioners the puritan zeal and combative evangelical style seemed to be of a piece with uncharitable dealing; and even in cases where extraneous disputes were not apparently at issue, puritan ministers were accused of contravening the fundamental duty of promoting peace. Thus the churchwardens and other leading inhabitants of Mapperton requested that the parish might be served by

> an honest and quiet godly man, such a one as may settle and frame together that which this hath dispersed; for now we live a most tormentable and miserable and ungodly life and it will never be amended so long as this continue in that place; for before this came to dwell amongst us we lived quietly in love and in charity one with another, but now we live as ungodly, one despiting a[nother] . . .[40]

Disgruntled parishioners looked to the ecclesiastical authorities for redress, sometimes recalling them to their duties in a tone of self-righteous injury. 'Mr Dean hath spoken and written against the puritans before this time', growled the Mapperton churchwardens in 1598, patently referring to Bridges' *Defence*, 'but now your peculiars are full, and none worse than in our own parish . . .' However, the courts were not, as supine as this might imply; as the puritans themselves complained bitterly, the authorities could on occasion show their teeth by resorting to the suspension or even deprivation of recalcitrant ministers. How far the courts employed such draconian measures varied from region to region and time to time, depending on central government policy and the vagaries of personality and local circumstance. There were no deprivations in the dean of Salisbury's peculiar in 1604–5, but all suspect clergy were summoned to court and virtually all of them were persuaded or browbeaten into making at least a partial submission. The court under Dean Bridges had already shown that it was not afraid to take exemplary action: Thomas Charleton, vicar of Faringdon, for example, was deprived in 1588 for not merely failing to observe the Book of Common Prayer (in particular for baptising in a basin without the sign of the cross), but also expressing doubts whether it was founded on the word of God.[41]

Such severity should not obscure the fact that the church courts proceeded as far as they could in a spirit of moderation and accommodation. In the case of Charleton, Bridges laboured long to persuade him to submit, and only resorted to deprivation when he judged him to be 'refractory' and 'incorrigible'. Similarly, when David Dee of Sherborne was inhibited from preaching in 1584, it was only after protracted proceedings extending over several years, and at the earnest petition of the inhabitants who had simply had enough. Indeed it may be said that, outside the periods of official crackdown (as in 1583–4, 1588–90 and 1604–5), the church courts' main concern was not so much to achieve absolute conformity as to damp down excessive puritan enthusiasm and to secure an accommodation between the ministers concerned and their parishioners. Thus in 1582 David Dee had been admonished 'in the exposition of scripture not to use more vehement zeal than was fitting' and to behave himself discreetly; while in proceedings against George Bowden of Mapperton, instigated by the churchwardens and parishioners in 1598, the matters at issue were referred to commissioners and settled by concord between the parties. In proceedings of this nature, the observance of the Book of Common Prayer served, as had originally been intended, as a means of promoting religious harmony, and therein lay the basis of church courts' insistence on it.[42]

IV

As has often been observed, the 1604–5 campaign against puritan ministers was succeeded by a long period of relative calm in most dioceses. Having broken the recalcitrant and secured at least token submission from the rest of the clergy, the authorities were hardly inclined to push the matter further. On the other hand, ministers who were still troubled by scruples found solace in occasional conformity or discreet forms of nonconformism. The report of the churchwardens of Ogbourne St Andrew in 1613 is revealing. Earlier, as we have already seen, the local minister's scruples had caused uproar; now it was merely stated that 'sometimes Mr Sedgewick doth sign children with the cross and sometimes omit the sign of the cross, and he doth [seldom *struck through*] [never *interlineated*] wear the surplice, and the surplice is insufficient'. By 1622 the wardens were able to report positively that 'baptism is observed and cross without intermission', and that 'our minister doth observe the Book of Common Prayer in every point, weareth the surplice and observeth all other rites'. To take another example, in Mapperton the vociferous complaints of the 1590s died away completely, though the same minister continued to serve the cure throughout the reign of James I and beyond.[43] It would, however, be wrong to think of ministers as simply cowed into submission. They must themselves have become aware that a combative style was not the best way to win over their flocks, and were perhaps inclined to try other forms of pastoral mission. Moderation was also encouraged by the need to avoid schism in the church (the few ministers who came to view the national church as irredeemably corrupt and hence chose to separate aroused immense anger and bitterness), and by concern about religious radicalism among lay people, of the kind that will shortly be discussed. In the case of some ministers, the discretion that comes with advancing years probably also had a part to play.

This change of attitude made possible a rather different relationship between puritan ministers and the church courts. To be sure, some of these clergy probably kept their distance from the official 'courts of reformation' and relied on their own powers of preaching and exhortation, and on the assistance of puritan magistrates, to combat godlessness and vice. But others were perfectly willing to make use of the machinery of ecclesiastical justice; and it is probably true to say that for two decades after 1605 puritan clergy were less likely to be in trouble with the church courts, or to voice criticisms of the spiritual jurisdiction, than to co-operate with them in the punishment of sin. However such activities were not necessarily very visible at the time, and are often difficult for modern historians to discern, simply because they blended in with the wider pattern of the courts' disciplinary action. It was not merely puritans but respectable people more generally who were concerned to punish fornication, adultery, breaches of the sabbath, and other lapses of personal morality and religious observance. It is true that godly ministers, in alliance with churchwardens and local magistrates, did sometimes spearhead moral campaigns which multiplied the number of prosecutions or targeted particular groups of offenders such as drunkards or people who worked or played games on the sabbath. The case of Terling in Essex is a well-known example of such processes. But initiatives of this nature were always hard to sustain, not least because they tended to arouse opposition from less zealous parishioners, and if the puritan presence in a community was weak they might never make much headway.[44] The records of the dean of Salisbury's peculiar reveal ample evidence of the efforts of the godly preaching minister, John Geare, to combat irreligion and vice in Lyme Regis, and in particular to control the excesses of the 'Cobb ale'; but even he had only partial success, and overall it emerges that parishes with a puritan tradition did not produce markedly more prosecutions for immorality and lax religious observance than other communities.[45]

Nonetheless a connection did establish itself in the popular mind between moral activism and the godly, to the extent that advocates of firm discipline were, whatever their brand of churchmanship, apt to be labelled 'puritans'. In Wylye in 1624, the daughter of one of the churchwardens inveighed against the newly appointed minister who, though apparently a complete conformist in matters of ceremony and church government, had tried to mount a campaign against drunkenness, sexual immorality, and games and dancing:

> we had a good parson here before but now we have a puritan . . .
> a pox in him that ever he did come hither . . . these proud
> puritans are up at the top now but I hope they will have a time
> to come as fast down as ever they come up.

Such utterances reflect how far issues such as the wearing of the surplice and the role of the church courts, central to the controversies reviewed earlier, had now receded from view. The case also illustrates how skirmishings between the godly and their fellow parishioners sometimes degenerated into protracted feuds and often led to spates of prosecutions initiated by both sides, sometimes involving the secular courts as well as the church. In such cases ecclesiastical judges did not necessarily side either with the precisians or with their detractors, but generally tried to administer the law impartially and, as always, did what they could to restore peace in the parish.[46]

But the situation should not be idealised. Letters and presentments from authoritarian ministers – whether or not they held puritan positions on ceremonies and the Prayer Book – sometimes complained of inadequate support from the courts, or urged them to take firmer action. When, as was inevitably sometimes the case, judges or court officials were actually guilty of venality or slackness – or even when they were *thought* to be so – such protests could acquire a bitter edge reminiscent of earlier puritan diatribes against the 'bawdy courts'.[47] In other respects, too, the theme of harmony between puritans and church courts should not be exaggerated. The issue of ceremonial conformity still lurked in the background, its relative invisibility depending on something of a stand-off between courts and clergy. Periodically ministers were still charged with the usual offences: failing to wear the surplice, abbreviating or rearranging the Prayer Book services, baptising from a bowl or from a basin or bucket set in the font, neglecting the sign of the cross, and so forth. Sometimes these cases came to light because the minister concerned was indiscreet or deliberately defiant; sometimes they were reported by unusually conscientious churchwardens; on occasion they were stirred up by individuals or parish factions at odds with a particular minister, who exploited charges of nonconformity for essentially malicious ends. Thus John Gibson, the minister of Ruscombe and Sandhurst (Berkshire), was in 1608 charged with not wearing the surplice in the course of a complex dispute over his right to the living; 20 years later Richard Gillingham, rector of Lillington (Dorset), found himself likewise accused when he reported the churchwardens for neglect of their duties. But only rarely did these cases of ceremonial nonconformity involve the fierce controversies so characteristic of the late-Elizabethan period; and in the dean of Salisbury's jurisdiction, as in most parts of England at this time, they were generally dealt with leniently by the courts.[48]

A more general phenomenon was the slowly growing incidence of prosecutions for nonconformity among lay people. Patrick Collinson has suggested that the scandal of the 'popish rag' was often felt less strongly by Elizabethan ministers than by their godly congregations, who in effect forced them to make a stand.[49] Quite how common this was may be doubted, since the bulk of cases of puritan nonconformity which came before the church courts in Elizabeth's reign and the early years of James I centred on the clergy, and they are much more often found at odds with their parishioners than championing the cause of puritan lay people. Yet such zealots did exist and occasionally came to the attention of the courts. Some were in fact so radical that they teetered on the brink of sectarianism, or even made the break entirely; such extreme courses were partly stimulated by clerical debates about separation. In Salisbury diocese a group of Brownists was active in and around the remote cloth-weaving parish of Slaughterford at the beginning of James I's reign, with connections with exiled congregations in Amsterdam. Meeting at the houses of a certain Thomas Cullimer and a fuller named William Hore, it centred on Thomas White, formerly curate of the parish, and Thomas Powell, 'late preacher of Slaughterford'; and it included various lay people, including a weaver who affirmed that he 'resorteth to the church of God, but for the temple made with hands he alloweth it not for a church'. Their assemblies may on occasion have numbered 'above thirty' or even 'three score persons', and although the group probably did not survive long as a coherent entity, members of the Cullimer family were still being prosecuted for non-attendance at church in the 1620s.[50] At Bere Regis around 1617, one Robert Gatherill was presented for neglecting his parish church, going to services elsewhere, receiving the communion from other ministers, and also for admitting into his house 'one Mrs Slowe of Sarum who did preach' to a group of neighbours; Joan Slowe, the wife of Richard Slowe, was (with others) repeatedly detected in Salisbury in the 1620s and 1630s as an anabaptist and for teaching school without a licence. A less edifying case of sectarianism was reported in 1622 from Melksham, where Henry Cheevers and Mary Banfield had made a written covenant to forsake their present spouses and live as man and wife or 'David and Jonathan'. Cheevers claimed that if she refused him her body she was not doing the duty of a wife, and the couple called their legitimate children bastards because their legal spouses were not 'converted to the faith and were not in the state of regeneration'. Cheevers planned that 'if this country would not suffer them so to live together' he would sell his goods, put fifty pounds in his purse and make a fresh start elsewhere, leaving 'his own wife a base scab as he found her'.[51]

These relatively extreme cases may at first sight appear remote from mainstream puritanism. But there were connections. The Millenary Petition of 1603 was in itself a moderate document that centred on the provision of able, resident, preaching ministers and some limited reforms in discipline and ceremonies. Yet it was powered by the euphoria of the expectant puritan ministry, which in turn generated some barely controllable lay excitement. At Easter 1603 there was a disturbance at the church of Box when a weaver and a roughmason 'denied the Book of Common Prayer and the Book of Homilies, saying that there could be no edification for the people by them, and that the unpreaching minister could not rightly nor had no power to administer the sacraments'. A few days later in the churchyard there was an attack on the vicar, John Coren, whose scandalous life was notorious and who was at odds with most of his parishioners. The protesters generalised ominously from his case, 'utterly denying the ministry for the most part to have no lawful calling and withall threatening in general terms that the said John Coren, with a thousand of like insufficiency, should sooner than he was aware of be thrown out of their places by the heels'. Among the protesters, it should be noted, was one of the men who the next year would be examined for attending the separatist meetings at Slaughterford.[52]

Such cases help to explain why the authorities were so concerned about nonconformism of any kind: they saw it as the thin end of an uncomfortably thick wedge. Those fears inclined them – and some local officers when they were called upon to make detections – to suspect any form of private religious gathering of being a 'conventicle'. Reported cases (which were not numerous) are in fact hard to evaluate. Some, especially in the 1580s and 1590s when ceremonies and ornaments were such an issue, centred on attempts to procure a 'pure' form of baptism; such cases were the counterpart of demands by conformist parishioners *for* signing with a cross, and were a worry to the authorities not least because they might involve silenced or deprived ministers or other clergy who had been in trouble for nonconformity. Thus in 1598 James Frend of Hungerford had his child baptised in his house by 'a minister . . . dwelling in Sarum'; it was done in 'a basin of water' with 'an exhortation out of the tenth of Mark' in the presence of another man and half a dozen women. The officiant was in fact Matthew Fenton, the radical preacher whose activities have already been noted.[53] More often supposed conventicles involved prayer, Bible-reading or exhortation; and most of these charges seem to have arisen either from the activities of schoolmasters whose teaching veered close to preaching, or from meetings of godly lay people for Bible-reading, 'repetitions' of sermons, or other forms of mutual edification which did not necessarily imply dissatisfaction with the church. Thus at Fordington in 1600, Luke Bower was said to be 'one that doth often times draw young people unto him and in his house doth privately interpret and expound unto them the holy scriptures after his own weak sense and learning'; at Calne around 1616, it was reported that Mr Owen 'teacheth school . . . without any licence . . . [and] that divers have resorted unto . . . [him] privately to hear either lectures, readings or exposition in divinity, who were none of his own family as we have heard'. From Sherborne in 1625 came an alarmist report that 'there are private meetings and conventicles divers times at the houses of John Okely and John Wakefordes and John Raymentes, where much company doth resort, and confer of the scriptures and expound the scriptures as the report goeth, where they stay oftentimes till twelve of the clock at night as the fame goeth'. The narrow interrogation of the supposed culprits revealed a rather less threatening reality. John Raymond, for example, admitted that one Wednesday some two months before, he 'had some of his friends which came to visit him from Milborne Port, and he being at a sermon in the forenoon, and taking notes of the sermon, did after dinner repeat the same unto his family in the hearing of them, and as he remembreth John Wayford alias Wakeford came in the interim'. There had been other meetings, some involving John Okely as well, but hardly more seditious; so the judge dismissed the people concerned with a simple admonition. Such activities reflected the growing attraction of some species of 'puritan' piety among a section of lay people – a development which was of course fostered, at least in part, by the pastoral endeavours of the erstwhile puritan firebrands or of their more circumspect colleagues and successors.[54]

A variety of other lay puritan activities came before the courts. There were occasional objections to the 'churching' of women after childbirth, which some dismissed as 'a Jewish ceremony'.[55] A few people were presented for impugning other aspects of the Prayer Book and ceremonies, often in terms similar to those used by zealous ministers. At Stratton in 1613, a certain Thomasine Cooper was in trouble 'for reporting the procession in the Book of Common Prayer is a rag of Rome, and it is good it were ripped out of the book'; while in 1617 Thomas Gill of Sherborne denounced the Book in 'a scorning manner' as 'popery, popery!' Gill was also charged with railing against the rites of the church and, more particularly, with refusing to kneel at communion; such refusal was in fact rarely reported in the dean's peculiar, though in some other areas of England it was a common point of principle among the godly.[56]

However, by the early seventeenth century, certainly the most characteristic offence of puritan lay people was what the authorities reprovingly called 'gadding', that is going to other parishes to hear sermons. At a basic level this merely reflected a laudable desire to gain access to spiritually nourishing preaching when sermons in the home parish were lacking or of poor quality. 'We have no sermons at home', pleaded one of the churchwardens of Stratton in 1614, 'therefore I hope my lord will give me leave to go where there is one.'[57] Nonetheless the church courts were inclined to be wary. 'Gadding' was sometimes associated with the belief that the services of a non-preaching minister or 'dumb dog' were invalid, a doctrine that the courts simply could not entertain; with the equally unacceptable opinion that there was no merit in the official 'homilies' prescribed for use when there was no sermon; or with abuse of the parish minister. Moreover, many people went 'gadding', not because there was no sermon in their parish church, but in order to hear a well-known preacher or to secure sermons of the kind they wanted, and the practice was often linked with complex patterns of puritan piety and sociability. Gadding to sermons also overlapped with the practice of going to another church to receive communion from a particular minister, a phenomenon which cut across the parish-centred worship of the Book of Common Prayer and raised the spectre of congregationalism.[58] In view of these complexities the Jacobean church courts adopted a flexible response, mostly dismissing cases with an admonition but on occasion imposing stricter punishments; and similar policies were followed in the case of the other manifestations of puritan fervour reviewed here. Two considerations which weighed with the courts, as in cases involving puritan ministers, were the degree of local disruption occasioned by these activities and the extent to which they expressed real defiance of authority. As always the courts strove to quieten controversy among neighbours and to cow the recalcitrant. In King James's reign, at least, they were inclined to take a lenient view of non-threatening expressions of lay piety.

V

The Jacobean church thus seemed to have reached a reasonable compromise between the interests of puritan ministers, godly lay people, and other members of the church. It was based on a degree of give-and-take on all sides. Puritan clergy had learnt the virtues of discretion – not least because it facilitated their pastoral ministry – and most were prepared to practise at least occasional conformity in matters of ceremonies; godly layfolk found ways of practising their piety within the structures of the official church; while the ecclesiastical courts, for their part, enforced the rules with sense and moderation, dealing as best they might with the parochial squabbles that occasionally came to light. This admittedly fragile peace began to crumble under the pressure of new policies associated with Archbishops Laud and Neile and their circles. The problems were prefigured by James I's Declaration of Sports of 1618, which stirred up profound issues of sabbatarian doctrine and put a severe strain on the consciences of both clerical and lay puritans. In a telling case from Peterborough diocese, a Northampton woman found herself confronted by a maidservant who claimed that 'she must play upon the Sabbath days and holidays and obey the king's laws in that point or else be hanged', to which she replied that 'she hoped there was no such law, but if there were . . . whether hadst thou rather the king should hang thee, or the devil burn thee'. Brought into court and questioned whether she accepted the lawfulness of recreations on Sunday, she insisted that 'for her part she doth not think it lawful, let others do what they list'. Similarly the minister of St Mary's in Marlborough was told by midsummer merrymakers that 'the king did allow of it by his book', to which he replied that 'he was king of the earth, but there was a king above him that must be served, and that they served the devil by it and not god, and [referring to a morris dancer] it was an idol which they served'.[59]

The issue of authority became even more pressing when Charles I reissued the Book of Sports in 1633, and it is significant that this matter proved capable of provoking some ministers into ill-advised outbursts of the kind that had been so common in the 1580s and 1590s but had since been eschewed. Even so, the number of cases was fewer than might perhaps have been expected, while the tone of ministerial comment was somewhat more restrained than of yore. The curate of Beaminster, Thomas Spratt, soberly read the 1633 Declaration, but in conclusion pointed out that 'there is no one commanded to use these recreations . . . but these laws are left to every one's choice . . . therefore I do advise you rather to obey God's laws' (though a hostile witness claimed that he added 'rather than the laws of the king'). His moderation contrasts with, for example, the sexually charged metaphors of the curate of Bodicote (Oxfordshire), who outraged his parishioners when he allegedly preached 'against the king's declaration or book, . . . [saying] that the garland was brought into the church under pretence of adorning the same therewith, but that it did deflower the said church . . . [and] that by keeping of Whitsun ales the people did make the church of God an alehouse'.[60] In general, ministers were able to combine their scruples with circumspection through a variety of expedients (such as publishing the Declaration in a near-empty church or having it read by a neighbouring minister), and in many areas the church courts proved willing to connive at these practices.[61]

This moderation was more apparent than real, however. The episode left many wounded consciences, both clerical and lay; moreover the sabbatarian issues and questions of public order raised by the Book of Sports undoubtedly aroused disquiet far beyond the ranks of puritans narrowly defined. The same was true of the policy of railing-in communion tables and setting them altar-wise at the east end of the church: not only did this affront the godly and raise in some minds suspicions of popish innovation, but at a basic level it represented a disruption of long-standing liturgical arrangements and entailed substantial costs, both administrative and financial, for the majority of parishes. Making pews uniform in height was another burden. Other aspects of what for convenience may be termed Laudian policies likewise had an uncomfortably wide impact. In many areas the courts stepped up prosecutions for 'gadding', and dealt with some of them with an unusual severity which verged, at times, on vindictiveness. Thus a group of people from Aldbourne were prosecuted in 1638–9 for going to the neighbouring church of Baydon to hear the preaching of Mr John Wilde (who in the early years of the century had been one of the most recalcitrant ministers

in the Wiltshire part of the dean's jurisdiction). One woman explained that once a month she visited her father in that parish and
took the opportunity to hear the sermon; but the judge insisted that,
while she could visit her father, it must be on a Sunday when Mr
Wilde did *not* preach. An increased emphasis on the sanctity of holy
days apart from Sunday led to more prosecutions for not abstaining
from buying, selling and other work on these days, issues that had
never aroused much enthusiasm among ordinary parishioners. The
novel insistence on doing 'lowly reverence' at the name of Jesus and
standing for the Gospel, Creed and *Gloria* – matters on which there
was much diversity of practice before the 1630s – had an even
greater impact, in effect turning whole congregations into delinquents, and indignant ones at that. At Fordington in 1635, it was
reported that a churchwarden, a sidesman and the parish clerk
usually sat during the Gospel, as a result of which 'many of the
parishioners are carried away to the same irreverent gesture, either
of sitting or leaning unseemly on their seats and pew doors . . .
accounting standing but superstition'. At Beaminster in 1634, a
presentment signed by only one of the churchwardens offered an
enormous list of specific offenders and explained that neither the
minister 'nor any in the parish doth bow, or use lowly reverence (in
time of divine service) when the blessed name of the Lord Jesus is
mentioned (other than himself [i.e. the writer]); therefore I pray you
let not me be laughed at or had in derision because I do it, and none
besides myself'. That the courts had to be informed by such an
isolated individual reflects the fact that they were becoming partisan.[62]

In other respects, too, the favourable symbiosis between church
courts and the wider society which had been achieved in the reigns
of Elizabeth and James I was by the 1630s beginning to weaken. In
a sense the courts were the victim of their own success. Around 1600
they could, despite their manifold weaknesses and limitations, be
plausibly seen as an indispensable bulwark against a rising tide of
bastardy and other social ills, and as such they commanded a
considerable measure of local support. But a generation later bastardy rates had fallen markedly, and in other respects the work of
the courts appeared less vital; they were hence more vulnerable to
criticism of their other activities, especially when they impinged (as
did Laudian policies) on a wide range of parochial interests. On the
other hand, the decline in some traditional forms of business – with
a concomitant loss of fee income – may have been among the factors

which inclined church court administrators to support such policies, since they generated new forms of business on a considerable scale. An alternative response, seen in Salisbury diocese, was a slide towards administrative slackness and petty venality. Neither approach was likely to produce a satisfied public. As the interests of church courts and many parishioners drew apart, the battery of puritan charges against ecclesiastical justice – criticisms that had never been wholly dispelled – were revived and reinvigorated. In 1641 the minister of Stockton wrote to the diocesan chancellor to complain of the immorality of certain women, adding urgently:

> I pray for example sake do something . . . Here we have had many . . . without any or very small exemplary punishment . . . The world saith ye of spiritual courts care not for punishment of sin for example and discipline in beggars who are able to pay no fees.

He went on to describe the bishop's consistory as 'your despised court' – ominous words when the House of Commons was debating the Root and Branch bill for ecclesiastical reform.[63]

In short, in the overturning days of 1640–2, the church courts found that the dirt thrown by the *Admonition to the Parliament* and similar puritan diatribes still stuck to them; indeed many of the old accusations were in effect simply repeated in the Root and Branch Petition. Implicated in the fate of the Laudian episcopate, with few friends and many enemies, they collapsed with startling rapidity. So swiftly did they fall, indeed, that no proper plans were made for their replacement; and in any case the courts had dominated the scene for so long and performed such complex functions that an adequate substitute was hard to find. Only when they had gone did it become apparent what an important role they had, for all their imperfections, managed to play. In the next 20 years a dismayed clergy, puritan and otherwise, was to discover what it was to exercise their ministry without the aid of a system of public discipline.[64]

3. Puritans and Iconoclasm, 1560–1660

MARGARET ASTON

What do the following have in common: a surplice, a maypole, a depiction of God the Father, a churchyard cross, bowing at the name of Jesus, and the man's words to the woman in the marriage service? The question would have been no parlour game to the men and women who are the topic of this chapter. It could almost have formed part of one of the countless catechisms and books of spiritual edification that were daily meat and drink to the godly – those whose days began and ended with private prayer and meditation. The answer was a matter of eternal verities, affecting the highest of all concerns in this life: how to serve God in spirit and in truth. Divine law as laid down in Scripture, above all in the Ten Commandments, prohibited false worship, everything that represented or smacked of idols, and the idol-service of banned or banished images. Objects and forms of behaviour that contravened the Decalogue prohibitions against serving other gods or worshipping images, must be done away. A cross on a church steeple, as much as a husband telling his wife 'I thee worship', both came to seem, to the purest of the purifiers, contraventions of that law.

Ben Jonson's *Bartholomew Fair* gives us an idea of what this trait looked like in 1614 to those who did not share it. Zeal-of-the-land Busy, one of the characters in the play, was 'a Banbury man' – hailing from one of the recognised centres of puritanism. Busy, 'moved in spirit' on behalf of 'afflicted saints' against the 'peeping of popery' in the fair's 'merchandise of Babylon', tries to seize the toys on one of the stalls. The proctor John Littlewit protests. 'Pray you forbear, I am put in trust with them.' Busy is unstoppable. 'And this idolatrous grove of images, this flasket of idols, which I will pull down', and he throws down the gingerbread basket, to the dismay of Joan Trash, the gingerbread woman. 'O my ware, my ware, God bless it!' But the breaker, divinely superior and satisfied in his self-appointed task, carries on oblivious 'In my zeal, and glory to be thus exercised'. With his head lost in clouds of biblical utterance, the 'Bedlam purity' of this pedantic busybody cuts him off from the fun of the fair, the normal realities of daily experience. For him, the danger outweighed all worldly judgements; the idols that he saw threatened everyone and had to be pulled down.[1]

As their dubbing itself indicates, puritans were to some degree always outsiders. However people accept, or adapt to their own nicknames, abusive tags of this kind inevitably tend to formalise ways of seeing and being. Puritans, no more than Lollards or Quakers, may not have become what they were thought to be, but they could not avoid reacting in some way to the stereotypes that were foisted on them. Maybe this applies somewhat less to iconoclasm than to some other forms of behaviour, since pen-portrait 'characters' of puritans found plenty of features to focus on, apart from image-breaking. Nevertheless activities like those of Zeal-of-the-land Busy did become significant among those whom we (like contemporaries) can recognise as puritan. A series of spontaneous initiatives to destroy perceived idols characterised puritan activity during the decades after 1560, and, after 80 years of testing and stretching Elizabethan orthodoxies, the legality of images and image-breaking proved critical in attacks on the church. Perceptions of puritanism altered between 1560 and 1660, but actions comparable to that lampooned in *Bartholomew Fair* remained characteristic of a spiritual zeal that had political, as well as personal dimensions.

There is no doubt that puritans were responsible for the most egregious acts of image-breaking in this period, and that this played a significant part in the build-up to the Civil War. But not all who opposed church images were puritans, nor did all puritans who believed that any religious image might become an idol feel impelled to destroy. As the Church of England itself changed though the course of this century, so did the nature of iconoclasm. We have to consider the legal or official position of the church and the circumstances of the destruction, as well as the kind of imagery it was directed against. Since the church had itself so whole-heartedly undertaken the reform of its own imagery, the emergence of the puritan case calls for elucidation.

As an integral part of the reforming process endorsed in England, the case against the 'idolatry' of traditional religion had already gone far by 1560. The amount of destruction that had taken place under Edward VI in 1547–8, and again, after Mary's reign, under Elizabeth in 1558–9, shows that the battle against papal idolatry had achieved a great deal – as least as far as physical objects were concerned. Pilgrimage shrines, reredoses, statues of saints and carved rood figures, along with great numbers of service books, vestments and vessels had all been removed from churches, sold, secreted, broken or burnt; church paintings had been whitewashed over and scriptural texts were taking their place on the walls. Was not the English Church showing itself a true daughter of Zwingli and Calvin, in accepting the premise that conversion must include outer as well as inner purification – the physical erasure of past error must accompany the inculcation of the Word? Cranmer in his Catechism of 1548, and the Book of Homilies of 1563, both endorsed the principle that English believers lived by the Scriptures and had no imagery in their places of worship.

The Royal Injunctions issued in 1559 for 'the suppression of superstition' and to implant true religion, remained the ecclesiastical law thereafter. Injunction 23 ordered the clergy to

> take away, utterly extinct and destroy all shrines, covering of shrines, all tables, candlesticks, trindals, and rolls of wax, pictures, paintings, and all other monuments of feigned miracles, pilgrimages, idolatry and superstition, so that there remain no memory of the same in walls, glasses, windows, or elsewhere within their churches and houses, *preserving nevertheless or repairing both the walls and glass windows.* And they shall exhort all their parishioners to do the like within their several houses.[2]

Repeating as it did an earlier injunction of Edward VI, this was a truly radical measure, seemingly setting within its sights imagery of all kinds that could be construed as idolatrous inside churches, and extending the proscription to domestic dwellings. But Elizabeth added the clause in italics – a proviso that, as we shall see, was to stir many a puritan conscience.

How clear was it what constituted 'monuments of superstition', and how important were distinctions of place in defining them? Was the crucifix, with its image of Christ crucified, or the bare cross itself to be accounted such? The cross was the central symbol of the Christian faith and (until the recent changes) the great rood that towered from the rood loft over the nave made the crucifix the central image in all English churches. Queen Elizabeth herself – the Supreme Governor of the Church – was not prepared to endorse reformers' proscription of cross and crucifix, though in the end her defence of them was pushed back into the confines of her own chapel and free-standing monuments in open secular places. And neither of these remained immune from the sniping of freelance purifying iconoclasts.

The cross was central to the problem of image-reform, in large part because it had occupied a central and peculiar place in medieval image-theory. The greatest scholastic pundit, St Thomas Aquinas, had propounded the view that the cross was owed the highest form of worship – that *latria* which to Protestant reformers could not be other than idolatry. Those who believed that Christians must be preserved from every danger of superstitious worship had undertaken the destruction of crosses long before 1560, and in 1609 James I (unable to resist a punch at any inviting theological target) published his scorn for those 'that worship a piece of a stick'.[3] James however, like his predecessor, distinguished use from worship, and the many crosses and crucifixes that were still to be seen in and after 1560, remained not only because no purifier had yet got round to removing them, but because it still seemed reasonable to suppose and defensible to argue that in secular places and out of harm's way a religious image would not automatically be idolised.

Some puritans made no bones about domestic imagery of cross or crucifix – witness the earl of Leicester's picture in the Great Gallery at Wanstead in 1588 of 'Christ taken from the Cross'. Diehards on the contrary were convinced that not only the 'cross material', but even the 'sign aerial' was the 'principal badge of popery', and as such must be eradicated. This view was propounded at length by Robert Parker in 1607 in his *Scholasticall Discourse against Symbolizing with Antichrist in Ceremonies: Especially in the Signe of the Crosse,* a work which, bringing the threat of prosecution by the High Commission, forced the author into exile in Holland, where he died in 1614. Yet Parker's belief that 'the cross cannot but admonish the mind of popery', was seemingly endorsed at this very time by the statute passed in 1606 after the Gunpowder Plot, which declared crucifixes to be among the 'relics of popery' which JPs, searching houses of popish recusants, should see defaced and burned. Fear of popery proved a movable goalpost for Church of England orthodoxy. Parker's view that the cross, trespassing against every one of the Ten Commandments 'will never go from the possession of private houses until the public house of God do spew it out', could be read with a different intensity a generation after his death, when the English Church itself seemed in danger of joining hands with popery.[4]

On the other hand there was unanimous agreement about another kind of image, that of the Trinity, with the depiction of God the Father as an old man. Cranmer had pointed out the dangers of such representations, which caused people to think that God had physical properties, whereas scripture made plain that no man could see God and live, and that Moses himself had only heard, not seen the Lord in Mount Horeb. God could not be imaged. The principle was enshrined in Calvin's *Institutes*: 'We believe it wrong that God should be represented by a visible appearance, because he himself has forbidden it and it cannot be done without some defacing of his glory.' William Perkins followed suit, for all believers must know that to represent God in an image, even those 'shapes in which God himself hath heretofore testified his presence', was to diminish his glory, circumscribing it with finite bodily majesty. Trinity imagery was therefore illicit, regardless of whether or not it was worshipped. 'Yea, the image of God himself is not only expressly forbidden to be worshipped, but even to be made', as King James put it, defending his position as 'a Catholic Christian' against Cardinal Bellarmine. To set eyes on such an image was accordingly, as we shall see, a source of acute anxiety to those of puritan temperament, whose whole being was structured by the line and rule of scripture.[5]

The image was ousted by the word. Visual depictions were to have no place in worship or belief; they could not teach the faith nor, given the danger of their mere presence in churches, could they be thought of as ornament. 'Images, which cannot be without lies', as the Homily against Peril of Idolatry put it in 1563, 'ought not to be made, or put to any use of religion, or to be placed in churches and temples', where they 'cannot possibly be without danger of worshipping and idolatry'. The centuries-old defence of images as 'books' for lay people, alternatives to or routes towards the instruction of the page, had become anathema: 'either they be no books, or, if they be, they be false and lying books, the teachers of all error.' Yet the Homily, while pursuing this adamant line, proscribing all ecclesiastical imagery, implicitly admitted that there was still a certain distance to go. This long three-part sermon ended with a prayer or call for action (addressed to the ears of responsible listeners): 'Wherefore God's horrible wrath, and our most dreadful danger cannot be avoided, without the destruction and utter abolishing of all such images and idols out of the church and temple of God, which to accomplish, God put in the minds of all Christian princes.' In a sense all the iconoclastic acts of the ensuing 70 or so years amounted to such a 'putting in mind' – though that was not how the authorities perceived them. Perhaps it is significant that these radical ('puritan' in later terminology) passages appeared in the third part of the Homily, which was not intended for uncontrolled general reading.[6]

The discrepancy between theory and practice, thus acknowledged in the Second Book of Homilies in 1563, continued thereafter, and one of the facets of the 'precise' was their unreadiness to accept this state of imperfection. Essentially, those who from the 1560s earned for themselves the name of puritan believed the reformation process in England to be seriously incomplete. Many churchmen themselves had to agree with this viewpoint. The great question was, how to achieve the necessary shove forwards.

Official iconoclasm continued in Elizabeth's reign – where the diocesan shared the godly intention of the homilist. The thorough enquiry conducted in the diocese of Lincoln in 1566 into 'monuments of superstition' and 'popish ornaments' remaining since Queen Mary's reign, yielded a large harvest of objects for defacing and burning. And when Edmund Grindal became archbishop of York in 1570 after a decade as bishop of London, he was shocked to find the north resembling another church, and proceeded to take firm remedial action. In 1571 a special commission was appointed to discover and demolish rood-lofts and to see to the necessary defacing. Grindal also took steps to demolish churchyard crosses, and other bishops were actively engaged on the same mission in the 1570s. Yet these iconoclastic moves, focused on churches and churchyards, did not go far enough for some. There still remained much to affront the godly, including contaminating 'pagan' survivals such as maypoles, which were a long-standing sore to the godly, finally condemned by parliament in 1644, but up again in 1660 (to the consternation of those like the Cheshire preacher Adam Martindale, whose wife translated his public reproof into action, and 'whipped it down in the night with a framing-saw').[7] Provocative medieval imagery was to be found, not only in secular hands and places, but even in church buildings. As it is not possible here to look closely at all varieties of puritan iconoclastic initiative, I shall put the focus on one particularly contentious class of imagery which illustrates the continuity of freelance destruction, and the head of steam that built up in the seventeenth century.

In the 1560s the place where most medieval ecclesiastical imagery still survived in parish churches was in their windows. Official iconoclastic reform here hung fire for two reasons: policy and practicality. The policy was that of the Supreme Governor, Queen Elizabeth, whose reluctance to promote the full aniconic case of the Homilies was demonstrated both by her protection of cross and crucifix, and also by her orders against the alienation of church bells and the defacing of funeral monuments. The practicalities (also a matter of royal concern) involved the maintenance of church buildings in a condition not only of decency but sheer usability. Given the structural changes involved in altering rood-lofts and altars, this second consideration was to prove important. It particularly concerned church windows which occupied a central place in puritan worries.

Gashes on walls were one thing; holes in windows another. Parishioners might not take kindly either to the expense, or the draughty results, of knocking superstition out of the painted panes in their church. As Injunction 23 shows, the imagery in church glass was already a matter of concern at the start of Elizabeth's reign. A strong sense of the proprieties of places of worship, as well perhaps as an economic instinct for preservation, dictated the queen's addition to this clause. There was also the possibility of social disruption, and in September 1560 a royal proclamation added an important proviso to the injunction, forbidding anyone to break down or deface any image in glass windows in any church, without consent of the ordinary – the authority in ecclesiastical jurisdiction, which usually meant the bishop. 'Reforming' church windows by breaking offensive sections of imagery might be relatively easy in parish churches, but if the building was to remain usable it could also be expensive. For this reason alone alterations in church glass hung fire. It was most unusual for a bishop, like the troublesome Marmaduke Middleton at St David's in 1583, to order such defacing (in this case of the crucifix and two Marys in chancel windows) throughout his diocese. As William Harrison described English churches in 1577, window imagery remained a large exception to their otherwise reformed appearance. 'All images, shrines, tabernacles, rood lofts, and monuments of idolatry are removed, taken down, and defaced; only the stories in glass windows excepted, which, for want of sufficient store of new stuff and by reason of extreme charge that should grow by the alteration of the same into white panes throughout the realm, are not altogether abolished in most places at once but by little and little suffered to decay, that white glass may be provided and set up in their rooms.'[8]

Puritans were enraged by this lackadaisical attitude. Godliness to them was not a matter of convenience, economic or otherwise. Idols were as dangerous to souls in the sixteenth century as they had ever been in the Old Testament and 'God commandeth to root out the monuments of superstition and idolatry'. Anthony Gilby, who wrote these words, listed in 1566 a hundred 'points of popery, yet remaining, which deform the English Reformation'. These included, besides organs and bells, 'the images of the Trinity, and many other monuments of superstition, generally in all church windows'. A few years later, one Gilbert Alcock, supplicating convocation about the idolatrous ceremonies still upheld by law, feared for any individual who broke God's law and became a worshipper of images in his church, glass windows included. And in 1590 the anxious author of a work pointedly called *The Reformation of Religion by Josiah*, whose address to the prince blended admonition with threat like the Homily against Idolatry, drew attention again to the spiritual treason that might be committed through images set up in high streets and in glass windows. The idols that were seen to endanger souls were not only in church, and those that were could scarcely be called 'graven images'.[9]

This concern took effect in direct action. In 1565, George Withers, fellow-commoner of Corpus Christi College, Cambridge, a man of zealous enthusiasm (certainly quite a 'Busy'!), caused what Archbishop Parker referred to as a 'racket' in Cambridge 'for the reformation of the university windows'. He preached a sermon calling for the destruction of all superstitious painted glass in the university, and it is an interesting reflection of the relationship between official and do-it-yourself iconoclasm that Withers was prompted by the authorities' removal of stained glass from windows in the Schools. Withers himself apparently paid for a university grace for the destruction of superstitious inscriptions in glass windows in the university. The archbishop believed that zealots took this cue and destroyed a lot of glass. Certainly the following year Trinity College paid for repairs to windows in the chapel that had been 'broken forth' on account of 'superstition'. This is the more remarkable because the windows of this new building had only been glazed the previous year, mainly with plain or heraldic glass.[10]

In the 1570s, a fellow student at Oxford helped to inspire a Cheshire squire with 'zeal against that profane beast of Rome, and all popery, both persons and things, with all their monuments, rites, and ceremonies'. John Bruen (1560–1625) of Bruen Stapleford, near Chester, became the model of a reforming puritan gentleman, who, after experiencing an archetypal conversion about 1587, abandoned hunting and hawking, disparked his deerpark, and gave himself and his household over to prayer, psalm-singing, Bible-study and frugal living. William Perkins, no less, praised Bruen Stapelford as 'the very topsail of all England' for its religious example, and when Bruen died the parish clerk, in admiration for this man 'second to none in piety', entered an unusual epitaph in the burial record.

> An Israelite in whom no guile
> Or fraud was ever found;
> A Phoenix rare,
> Whose virtues fair
> Through all our coasts do sound.[11]

John Bruen's fame was promoted by a neighbouring puritan minister, William Hinde, curate of Bunbury, who wrote his life. Hinde died in 1629 but his *Faithfull Remonstrance of The Holy Life and Happy Death of John Bruen* remained in manuscript until – significantly – 1641. When we read what it has to say about Bruen's iconoclasm, this delay seems comprehensible.

> For finding in the church of Tarvin, in his own chapel, which of ancient right did appertain unto him and his family, many superstitious images, and idolatrous pictures in the painted windows, and they so thick, and dark that there was, as he himself saith, scarce the breadth of a groat of white glass amongst them: he knowing by the truth of God, that though the Papists will have images to be lay men's books, yet they teach no other lessons but of lies, nor any doctrine but of vanities to them that profess to learn by them; and considering that these dumb and dark images by their painted coats and colours, did both darken the light of

the church, and obscure the brightness of the Gospel: He presently took order, to pull down all these painted puppets, and popish
idols, in a warrantable and peaceable manner, and of his own cost
and charge, repaired the breaches, and beautified the windows
with white and bright glass again.[12]

Hinde went on to explain that Bruen was encouraged both by the
Elizabethan injunction cited above, and by a local commission that
had been appointed to deal with objects of superstition. He found
patterns in scripture and examples of other godly and holy men 'to
lead him, and countenance him in this act'. 'And so upon these, and
the like grounds, this gentleman went forwards from his chapel to
the rest of the church, defacing all the popish and superstitious
images, which he found dangerous, and offensive in any quarter, or
corner of it' – something which was clearly going to be censured by
all 'patrons of popery': 'to deal so rudely and contumeliously, with
the images of God, of Christ, and of his saints'.[13]

The emphases in this account are interestingly defensive. William
Hinde put the best face on actions that (when he wrote, as opposed
to when the world read his words) were as dubious legally as they
were, for purifiers, undoubtedly godly. First there was his stress on
Bruen's proprietary rights. When he 'took order' for this destruction,
he did so as one with hereditary rights over his parish church. The
Bruen family's connection with Tarvin went back two centuries, and
in 1580 the church of St Andrew had a number of stained glass
windows with the figures and coats of arms of the Bruens, not only
in the family's chapel at the east end of the south aisle, but also in a
four-light window in the north aisle. Bruen apparently started with
family memorials in a family chapel – objects over which he might
claim some personal right. It was in keeping with the puritan temper
to deplore the vanity of such worldly monuments, particularly when,
as here, they included 'superstitious' requests for prayer. John
Bruen's scrupulous conscience must surely have been embarrassed by
the inscription in one of his ancestor's windows: 'Orate pro bono
statu Johannis Bruyn . . .' – 'pray for the well-being of John Bruen'.[14]

Bruen's dismissal of 'laymen's books' suggests familiarity with the
arguments of the Homily, and his commonplace book (his 'Cards')
shows that readings of Calvin and Babington informed his views of
superstition.[15] His iconoclasm apparently included religious imagery,
but we know most about the destruction of the armorial glass that

was still in Tarvin church in 1580. For Bruen the darkness produced by idols was physical as well as spiritual; he was against the dim religious light by which papal 'books' obscured the light of the Gospel, obstructing the reading of proper books. It seemed to help to exonerate Bruen that he had paid for the reglazing, which beautified St Andrew's with the clarity of light-giving white glass. And last, not least, was the fact that this deed had not been socially disruptive; no riot or disorder here, but a local squire who did as godly magistrate should do; peacefully erasing ancient superstition and causes of idolatry. Tarvin was a model for the English church at large, and showed puritan sympathisers what zealous gentry could achieve.

Iconoclastic initiatives like those of Withers and Bruen arose from a sense of responsibility among the godly. Their burden of conscience for all 'afflicted saints' prompted them to act on behalf of defective magistrates, on whom fell the prime duty to abolish idolatry. Destruction was the task of the Supreme Governor. Jewel prescribed this obligation in his *Apology of the Church of England*: 'God by his prophets often and earnestly commandeth the king to cut down the groves, to break down the images and altars of idols.' Yet there were also plenty of hints in the all too copious instructions circulating on this subject, that dutiful believers could not sit on their hands when magistrates failed God's law. Thomas Rogers explained that God's censure of images was such that 'He commendeth greatly and praiseth such men as have destroyed images, and not bowed unto idols', and Jewel too agreed that breaking idols was far from being an offence against divine law. 'Neither doth God throughout all his holy scriptures any where condemn image-breakers; but expressly and every where he condemneth image-worshippers and image-makers.' Fidelity to biblical laws of destruction might seem to override human laws. 'Here note, what the people of God [the true Israelites] ought to do to images, where they find them', commented the homilist on Deuteronomy 7, with its injunction to break and burn graven images. Zeal-of-the-land's swipe had a good base in theology.[16]

John Bruen himself managed to escape legal proceedings. The case was different for a number of others (including some of his servants) who chanced their arm and destroyed, or tried to destroy, monuments of idolatry without proper sanction. This occurred when enthusiasts attacked several of England's famous free-standing crosses. Though cross and crucifix were officially swept out of church and churchyard, public monuments of this kind long remained in markets, streets and open spaces. To the purists it looked as if unforgivable *laissez-faire* had halted the progress of reform. Others, when pressed, could make out a case for the historical and civil use of such monuments, perhaps adding the argument that decreasing numbers of people were likely to worship a cross standing in the middle of street or market-place. Whatever the Edwardian and Elizabethan injunctions said about eliminating domestic images (and perhaps those most feared were secreted images that had once been in church), there was a school of thought that readily tolerated religious imagery in wholly secular settings.

Cross-breaking continued as a form of conscientious exploit throughout this period, and a number of cases ended up in courts of law. Churchyard crosses were, as we have seen, destroyed officially, but that did not prevent such demolition having an illicit face. We can see here, rather clearly, that potentially discordant counterpoint between the purifiers and the church. The cross-breakers who destroyed the churchyard cross of Springthorpe in Lincolnshire, in the night of 22 November 1563, probably escaped scot-free, unlike the seven men accused by the bishop of Chester 40 years later, who confessed to having one Sunday 'with their staves throw[n] down a stone cross standing in the churchyard of Wharton'. Two of these iconoclasts had gone on the same night to break imagery (including that of the church's patron, St Andrew) in the chancel window at Tarvin and, as servants of John Bruen, were strongly suspected of being inspired by their master.[17] Such initiatives by lay people, which reflect the impact of puritan example, were subject to the penalties of the law. But clandestine iconclasts of this kind seem often to have evaded prosecution, perhaps not surprisingly given the concurrent actions by members of the episcopal bench.

Some of the most famous monuments in the land were demolished in this way. At Durham the fourteenth-century stone cross erected to commemorate the victory over the Scots in 1346, was in 1589 (as recorded by a partial reporter) 'in the night time . . . broken down and defaced by some lewd and contemptuous wicked persons', who had been encouraged 'by some who love Christ the worse for the cross' sake'. The opponents of the famous cross at Banbury sent workmen to hew it down at sunrise on a summer morning in July 1600. Before the task was far advanced a crowd of objectors had gathered, who were unable to prevent the demolition but were ready to continue their fuss, and the case was taken to Star Chamber. Play was duly made with the argument that the cross (which, like Neville's Cross, bore carved scenes) had been venerated – witness the doffing of a hat by a passing parishioner – but this seemed a tenuous argument to the losers of a valued ancient monument. This determined opposition to iconoclasm in a town so notorious for puritan views, shows clearly that people of such persuasions were far from being at one on the having or destroying of images.[18] And in the case of England's premier civic cross, standing in the middle of Cheapside in London, this lack of unity (combined with interventions by the crown, civic and ecclesiastical authorities) helped the monument to survive, despite batteries of attacks by nameless iconoclasts, well into the 1640s.

The uneasy balance between toleration and proscription of religious imagery began to alter in the seventeenth century. Already in 1606 the anxiety to prevent further destruction of church art appeared in a long lament on the nearly lost art of glass painting, which Henry Peacham included in his *Art of Drawing*. Earlier donors of church windows would have spent their money elsewhere, he thought, could they have foreseen the fate of painted windows, deprived of whole panes that had borne the names or coats of arms of founders and benefactors, and 'for want of repair partly . . . beaten down by the weather, partly by over precise parsons and vicars, . . . and the windows stopped up with straw and sedge', if not completely blocked up. Peacham, capable of distinguishing art from religion, had 'pilgrimaged' in search of good specimens, and reported many good pieces to exist in various places, above all King's College Chapel in Cambridge, and Henry VII's Chapel at Westminster. Six years later, in his expanded work on *The Gentleman's Exercise* of drawing, Peacham signalled still more openly his view of this matter. It was wrong, of course, for pictures of Christ, Apostles or Martyrs to be set up in churches for worship, but 'that pictures of these kinds may be drawn and set up to draw the beholder *ad Historicum usum*, and not *ad cultum*, I hold them very lawful and tolerable in the windows of churches and the private houses, and deserving not to be beaten down with that violence and fury as they have been by our Puritans in many places.'[19]

Peacham was here propounding a view quite other than that of pundits such as William Perkins, whose guidance on the line between permissible and illicit imagery represented prevailing orthodoxy in late sixteenth-century England. 'We hold the historical use of images to be good and lawful . . . whether they be human, or divine.' So biblical stories could be painted 'in private places'. Churches, however, were different. 'And here it must be remembered that the painting of the history of the Bible, though otherwise lawful in itself, is not expedient in churches; because danger of idolatry may arise thence. And therefore commendable is the practice of the Church of England, that suffers not in places that serve for use of religion, images either carved or painted, no not the history of the Bible painted.'[20]

Articles for enquiry issued by bishops when visiting their dioceses reflect this changing outlook. Whereas early seventeenth-century bishops were worried about the harbouring of superstitious objects (mass books, vestments or ornaments), kept 'for a day', uncancelled or undefaced, a seemingly contrary concern was being sounded in the 1630s. 'Have any monuments or tombs of the dead in your church or churchyard been cast down, defaced, ruined? have any arms or pictures in glass-windows been taken down, especially of our Saviour hanging on the cross, in the great east window, and white glass or other set up in place thereof? have any leaden or brasen inscriptions upon grave-stones been defaced, purloined, sold? by whom?' Bishop Montagu's questions at Norwich in 1638 reflected the priorities of Archbishop Laud. But to those of puritan sympathy, ungodly idolaters seemed to be wrecking the godly achievement of a century of image-breaking.[21]

Purifiers who saw images going up instead of coming down feared the invasion of Antichrist. The idols of Rome, so long detested and feared, against which the Church of England seemed so wholly to have committed itself, were coming back into place, in the shape not only of crosses in public places but actually in imagery inside churches, in idolatrous acts of reverence towards the east end, where communion tables, railed and reverenced, were once again acquiring the attributes of altars of sacrifice. Those who argued in defence of imagery, claiming – as did Richard Montagu in his *Appello Caesarem* (1625) – that the Homily against Idolatry was not to be taken as dogmatic for all time, appeared to be participating in a con-certed move towards Rome. John Bruen was milder than many when he wrote in his Commonplace Book: 'The union or mixture of our religion with the popish religion is but a dream of unwise politiques'.[22]

James I dropped utterances into these dangerous waters. 'I am no *Iconomachus*' he told the world in 1609. The position that images must not be allowed any degree of holiness, but had a legitimate role in private decoration and public use, could then seem trite. Fifteen years later, it was otherwise. The king was effectively joining sides in a polarising world when he reportedly told his last parliament in 1624 'that as you have two hands you ought to use them both, that as with one hand you labour to suppress Papists, so with the other you be careful to sweep out the Puritans'. The godly who for so long regarded the improvement of the English Church as their *raison d'être* were being branded as an alien force. For his part the king would as soon 'lay down my crown to the Pope as to a popular part of Puritans'. Changing attitudes towards church images played their part in this, and helped to place a new premium on acts of iconoclasm. King James sounded a note of advice in his words to this parliament.

> I would not have you scared with a speculation they have given in against the bishop of Norwich, who if he be guilty must be punished. But I am very far grieved at this, gentle bishops, that you call the ornaments of the church idolatry, being nothing but the pictures of the Apostles and such like as I have in mine own chapel. I praise my lord of Norwich for thus ordering his churches, and I commend it in spite of all the Puritans, and I command you my lords bishops to do the like in your several dioceses.[23]

The grievances against Samuel Harsnett, bishop of Norwich, to which the king referred, had been brought up to this parliament from the citizens of Norwich, thanks to the support of the puritan mayor of the city. Since his arrival in the diocese in 1619 Harsnett had aroused considerable opposition, for putting down preaching and setting up images (including crucifixes and a high altar). Thanks to royal endorsement, this policy moved further during the reign of Charles I, when the spectre of 'popish' imagery, blatantly visible in Henrietta Maria's Catholic chapels, enhanced alarmist reactions to the idolatrous 'innovations' of bishops.

There were increasing numbers of places where people could see crosses and images being put back, inside and outside church. This was wormwood and gall to the purifiers such as William Prynne, who in his *Histriomastix* (1633) denounced those 'who now erect crucifixes and images in our churches contrary to our articles, injunctions, homilies, canons, statutes, and writers . . .'[24] Between 1610 and 1625 work was done on the market cross at Ipswich; at Gloucester Bishop Goodman collected funds for the high cross, but ran into trouble with his plans for a crucifix at Windsor, and chided the recalcitrant townsmen: 'Hath not the town of Windsor sometimes received a cheque for Puritanism?' At Bristol nearly £200 was spent on the high cross in 1633–4, the work including statues of both James I and Charles I, the latter of which was to fall victim to Commonwealth iconoclasm, when public images of the Stuart kings were officially demolished.[25]

New stained glass windows went up in cathedrals, chapels, and parish churches, thanks to lay as well as ecclesiastical patrons, and they portrayed scenes from both Old and New Testaments (including Nativity, Last Supper and Crucifixion). The work of Bernard and Abraham van Linge still to be seen in various chapels of Oxford colleges and at Lincoln's Inn, was sponsored by Bishops Laud and Williams; the Flemish glass in Peterhouse, Cambridge, by Matthew Wren; and both Chester and Durham cathedrals – thanks to John Bridgeman and John Cosin – gained new east windows glazed with scenes from the life of Christ. The Crucifixion hung in the new painted glass over the altar at Durham, as it did in Laud's chapel at Lambeth, where the extensive reglazing scheme was particularly provocative in view of the fact that these windows had long since been 'reformed' with clear glass. And in Oxford the new porch of St Mary's with its statue of Virgin and Child, was the work of Laud's chaplain, Dr Morgan Owen.[26]

It is no accident that the most notorious prosecution of a puritan for illegal iconoclasm concerned a Trinity image in a stained glass window. This was an egregiously unlawful image in the most lastingly contentious medium. Henry Sherfield, recorder of Salisbury and a man whose puritan credentials are well attested by his role in that city's attempts at social reform, was proceeded against in Star Chamber in 1633 for having broken a window in the church of St Edmund, Salisbury. The stained glass – said to be very 'ancient and fair' – depicted the story of Creation in a way which greatly offended Sherfield, who sat in church facing it for 20 years. Apart from lack of fidelity to Genesis, what particularly affronted him was 'this profane representation of God the Father' ('a little old man in a blue and red coat'). Most Protestants would have agreed that this was a forbidden image, and indeed Sherfield's prosecutors (Bishop Laud included) did so at his trial. Half a century earlier the neighbouring church of St Thomas in Salisbury had spent 4d, 'putting out the picture of the Father in the east window', on the order of the subdean, and in 1571 the zealous Bishop Robert Horne (who as dean of Durham had demolished the cloister glass of the life and miracles of St Cuthbert), ordered all images of the Trinity in the windows of his cathedral of Winchester, to be 'put out and extinguished'.[27]

Sherfield himself claimed the authority of the church vestry of St Edmund (of which he was a member) for 'picking out' with his staff the part of the window that represented the Deity. The church accounts record that on 16 January 1630 it was decided 'that Mr Recorder may, if it please him, take down the window wherein God is painted in many places, as if he were there creating the world: so as he do instead thereof make new the same window with white glass, for that the said window is somewhat decayed and broken, and is very darksome, whereby such as sit near to the same cannot see to read in their books.'[28] It was also maintained that the window imagery had been the object of idolatrous prayers and gestures.

Sherfield's action has similarities to John Bruen's, but the outcome is illuminatingly different. Zealous 'improvement' of his parish church was undertaken in both cases by an iconoclast of gentry standing and sufficient means to reglaze the window to give light to a book-reading congregation. But both men were acting unlawfully, for neither had obtained diocesan authorisation, and, whatever Sherfield's bishop thought of the matter, the work of the puritan magistracy in Salisbury was a source of deep anxiety to the recorder's prosecutors. For Laud and his fellow Arminian bishops, reform must on no account be carried out by private persons or parish vestries, and several members of the legal profession expressed like views in Sherfield's Star Chamber hearing. 'Zeal must not transport a man out of his calling, nor beyond his bounds': 'Reformation is, and always hath been a work of public authority.' The question which emerged as supremely important in this trial was 'whether a parishioner may of himself undertake to pull down . . . what he conceiveth to be idolatrous, and so take upon him to be a reformer?' To allow this, to let private men 'make batteries against glass windows in churches at their pleasure', seemed to open a door to chaos. 'If this, or such like things should be permitted in the church government, to be done upon private authority, why should not the like men do the like in the commonwealth? And then we should be at an evil pass' – prophetic words.[29]

Despite his claim that his window-breaking had been done alone and peacefully, Sherfield was regarded as having acted with great disobedience, in contempt of the bishops, thereby offending the king's regal power. The puritan iconoclast erred not in condemning the idol, nor in calling for its destruction, but in personally undertaking the destruction. His zeal appeared to threaten the social order. Sherfield's judges, who sentenced him to confess his offence and pay a £500 fine, had to bear in mind the possible repercussions of punishing too severely his offence in 'pulling that down which the church disalloweth'.[30]

Such was the ancient ambiguity of a situation in which images were simultaneously tolerated and proscribed, and in which the action of breaking them could be both legal and illegal. Sherfield's case marks some sort of watershed in the perception of this process. For by the 1630s the position of the church had changed, and puritans were increasingly being seen as acting against it. The reform of images, for many Laudian churchmen, had become a matter of repair and restoration, not removal, and to anxious purifiers it looked as if the entire process of reformation was being reversed. The return of imagery spelt the return of popery.

As 'innovations' in the shape of fresh images and fresh defenders of church pictures became more conspicuous in the 1630s, so puritan opposition widened. A paper war of argument and counter-argument grew into an iconoclastic offensive that took a revolutionary turn after the meeting of the Long Parliament in November 1640. The busiest of the zealous gentry were critical in these developments, and it is interesting to see how the godly formed nucleated groups from which charges of spiritual energy might be released in bursts of iconoclasm. John Bruen's household seems to have radiated in this way. Bruen himself was a correspondent of Sir Robert Harley during the 1620s, and Sir Robert's earnestness as an opponent of idolatry was proved not only by his speeches in parliament during this decade, but thereafter by his own undertakings in that cause, on which more shortly.[31] Bruen's son Calvin Bruen lived up to his name and his father's repute by his own readiness to battle against idolatry and superstition.

Calvin Bruen was a mercer (and in the 1630s high sheriff) of Chester. Together with a handful of other Chester citizens, he was in trouble with the ecclesiastical commissioners of the diocese of York in 1637 for his support for William Prynne. That summer Prynne was being moved to more isolated imprisonment at Caernarvon Castle, after his second trial and sentence (together with Henry Burton and John Bastwick) on charges related to the pamphlet *Newes from Ipswich*. The men of Chester had cheered him on his way, helping him on a shopping trip to equip his Welsh prison with bedding and furniture, and seeing him over the dangerous marshes when he departed. Bruen was accused of having taken this opportunity to meet up with the prisoner (whose escorts were evidently tolerant) 'for extemporary prayers and repetitions with Mr Prynne as also for procuring the picture of the said Mr Prynne to be drawn by a limner in Chester'. Though some details of the encounter were dropped from the final charge, the event was taken very seriously. Bishop Bridgeman was in close communication with Archbishop Laud, and Bruen, who was imprisoned and fined £800, only secured his release by making public confession in both the cathedral and Common Hall of Chester, of how 'audaciously and wickedly' he had 'countenanced the said Prynne'.[32]

In 1640–1 both Bruen (petitioning parliament), and Prynne (in more than one of his books) made known their versions of this affair. Whatever Prynne said, this was certainly no chance encounter. One of the Chester suspects, Peter Ince, was a stationer, said to have kept Chester well supplied with puritan books, and to have visited Prynne when he was in the Tower after his prosecution for *Histriomastix*. Calvin Bruen, who was reported to have obtained a copy of Alexander Leighton's *Sions plea against the prelacie* as soon as it came out, seems to have been a ringleader. He appears to have invited Prynne to stay at Bruen Stapelford (Prynne had the sense to decline), and also to have arranged for his portrait to be drawn by Thomas Pulford. Five copies of this likeness were made, and so keen were the authorities to put a stop to any hero-worship of the condemned author, that they went so far as to take a leaf out of the iconoclasts' own book. Initially ordering these pictures to be 'spoiled and defaced', they then decided to go one better. By then the Chester officials had already zealously burnt the portraits, so the word came from on high for public destruction of the frames that had contained them. This rather ludicrous ceremony duly took place at Chester High Cross on 12 December 1637, before (it was claimed) a large crowd shouting 'burn them, burn them'.[33]

If Calvin Bruen had read *Newes from Ipswich* before he met Prynne, he might well have wanted to join the condemned author in prayers for delivery from the gathering clouds of 'popish superstition and idolatry'. The pseudonymous pamphlet, 'discovering certain late detestable practices of some domineering Lordly Prelates', attacked the bishops – especially Bishop Wren of Norwich – for undermining the church and plunging it into retributive plague. It was a cry of despair against 'their Romish innovations, whereat the whole kingdom cry shame, which breed a general fear of a sudden alteration of our religion'. 'Wherefore O England, England, if ever thou wilt be free from pests and judgements, take notice of these thy Antichristian Prelates, desperate practices, innovations, and popish designs, to bewail, oppose, redress them with all thy force and power.' Chester itself gave cause for such anger. Bishop Bridgeman's remodelling of the east end of his cathedral appears to have included plans for a new stone altar in the Lady Chapel, reinstating the old stone slab of the high altar which had been removed in 1550. Such at least seems the likely interpretation of Prynne's 1641 accusation about Bridgeman's altars, including 'one in the Cathedral at Chester used in times of Popery, which he caused to be digged up out of the ground where it was formerly buried'. No wonder the innovators were regarded as responsible for religious regression.[34]

Whether or not Calvin Bruen kept Prynne informed of Chester affairs, he remained active in opposition to these iniquities. The destruction of altar rails and church windows seems to have been under way in Cheshire churches before April 1641, and Bruen played his part. He compiled a report of the state of churches in the city of Chester for the benefit of the mayor. The name of Bruen entered the public domain this year, with the publication of William Hinde's *Holy Life . . . of John Bruen* early in 1641, when the author's son rightly judged the times ripe enough to profit from this inspiring example. Puritan iconoclasts could afford to be bolder, with the 'manifest evils of prelates and the dangers of papists and Arminians' published in the Root and Branch Petition. The sense of division was growing. The sermon preached before Calvin Bruen's submission in Chester Cathedral on Sunday 17 December 1637 was on a text of Matthew which included the words 'if he neglect to hear the church, let him be unto thee as an heathen man and a publican'. 'Puritan' had entered a new phase of opprobium, on a par with Anabaptist, Brownist and Presbyterian, implying nonconformity that threatened the social equilibrium.[35]

Among those who were outstandingly devoted to the call to redress innovations and fight idolatry was Sir Robert Harley. His conviction was deep and profoundly scriptural (perhaps rather literally so), and his performance of iconoclastic duties was both private and public. Early in 1639 Harley's daughter Brilliana, aged about ten, wrote from their home at Brampton Bryan in Herefordshire to her brother Edward who, at fourteen, had recently started his studies at Oxford. 'My father had lately brought him', Brilliana wrote to Ned in her childish hand, 'a most horrible picture of the great God of heaven [and] earth the which he broke all to pieces.' She was evidently struck by the event, and a month later wrote again with more details.

> The image that I writ you word of, it was found in Buckton in one Robert Mathiss' house, he plucking up a plank in his stable, he found it there and did keep it a quarter of a year in his house, and it should abeen sold for 7 [?] pounds. Then somebody told my father of it and then my father sent for it and broke it in pieces and flung the dust of it upon the water.[36]

Well educated as she was in a pious puritan household, with a mother who read Calvin and Perkins, young Brilliana knew that any depiction of the 'great God of heaven' was itself a horrible offence against the majesty of the unseeable Deity. She must also have realised that her father, if not exactly another Moses, was acting strictly according to Old Testament prescription in his treatment of this shocking picture. The purer the iconclast the closer his imitation of scriptural models: that meant adding the various biblical admonitions as to how 'ye shall destroy . . .' to the decalogue 'thou shalt not worship . . .' The fate of the golden calf was a paradigm, and Moses in his fury 'burnt it in the fire, and ground it to powder, and strawed it upon the water, and made the children of Israel drink of it'.[37]

But if Brilliana was a little awestruck by her father's high-handed intervention, she was right to be. Although Harley was much less vulnerable than Henry Sherfield, since this image was not in a church (though it doubtless once had been), he was exploiting his local gentry influence. The best legal justification he could have claimed would have been the Elizabethan injunction cited above. The whole incident is very suggestive both of unexpected discoveries of long-secreted church images, and of the attitudes of finders – not to mention the continuing existence of domestic religious pictures.

Unlike the north-country clergyman in Elizabeth's reign, who, on digging up a cache of alabaster carvings in his garden, at once destroyed them, Harley's neighbours (making their find at a time when the artistic atmosphere was altering), were ready to keep their picture. The fact that it was about to change hands by sale (for a respectable sum) is no proof that the owners were ungodly in the eyes of those less censorious than Sir Robert.

Yet a century of reforming indoctrination and scriptural teaching and reading had implanted the rejection of idols as a parish commonplace. The vocabulary of literature and the phrases of local iconoclasts alike reflect a religious world that had earnestly taken to heart the prohibition of the second commandment. Old Testament priorities dictated rural destruction. In 1640 at Radwinter in Essex the soldiers who pulled down altar rails and images, lit the fire to burn them with words that echoed Isaiah and Baruch on their lips. The following year, when other rioters in the county broke and burnt altar rails at Latton, one of those responsible said these 'gave offence to his conscience, and the placing of them was against God's law and the king's, as appeareth by the twentieth chapter of Exodus and about the twentieth verse'.[38]

From the beginning of the Long Parliament the iconoclastic momentum grew and seemed unstoppable as the Scottish war and Scottish propaganda enhanced awareness of the dangers and vulnerability of the Arminian regime. The legislation on the question of images reflects a split between Commons and Lords (and there were differences in the House of Commons itself), but though this delayed the passage of bills it did not hold up the expectation and anticipatory actions in the country at large. Action was already under way in some areas when on 23 January 1641 the Commons referred to a conference with the Lords the plan to send commissioners into every county to deface, demolish and remove all images, altars, crucifixes, superstitious pictures and relics of idolatry from all churches or chapels. The pulling down and burning of altar rails, representing the heart of the much-hated Laudian innovations, spread rapidly, promoted by the publication on 1 September of the Commons' declaration that 'to make a picture for divine worship sake, either of God, or of Christ, or of the Virgin Mary, or the like, this is diabolical . . .'. The Lords, however, had made clear their opposition to any ceremonial change of this kind, and forbade the parish clergy to make alterations.[39]

Then, on 8 September 1641, by which time the authority of bishops and church courts had been whittled away, the House of Commons took a momentous decision. It decided to press ahead with unilateral action against the 'innovations in or about the worship of God', concerning which so many petitions had flowed in to Westminster since the opening of parliament. The churchwardens of every parish were 'forthwith' to see to the removal of communion rails and the levelling of chancel steps, and 'all crucifixes, scandalous pictures of any one or more persons of the Trinity, and all images of the Virgin Mary, shall be taken away and abolished', and all bowing at the name of Jesus or towards the east end was to stop. Brushing aside the Lords' reservations, the Commons resolved that this order 'shall be an order of itself without any addition for the present'. It was to be printed and published, and the knights, citizens and burgesses were to see to its publication in their various counties, cities and boroughs.[40]

This was indeed a radical decision. In one move the Commons jettisoned simultaneously parliamentary procedure and ecclesiastical authority. The long maintained episcopal control over alterations to parish churches was thrown to the winds, as the House of Commons asserted its own law over a matter that a century of Reformation had proved to be highly contentious. The iconoclasm so long regarded as essential to purify these places of worship, was put into the hands of the very people who had repeatedly displayed their vehemence on this issue: local laymen. The gentry church already foreshadowed by men like John Bruen, Henry Sherfield and Robert Harley had arrived.

One could hardly imagine a more complete switch of the priorities that had governed a century of physical changes in parish churches. By this step the House of Commons reversed the ruling so carefully applied since 1560, and which had been so rigorously upheld during the Arminian regime: the unlawfulness of purifying parish churches without diocesan consent. Destruction that had previously been illegal and challenging, and therefore often performed by subterfuge, under cover of darkness, was now above board, and under the supervision of knights and burgesses instead of bishops. The godly were now in the saddle, with no need to look over their shoulder. The old war against idolatry had climaxed in a dangerous challenge.

The radicalism of the Lower House in thus transferring the iconoclastic initiative into lay hands, overriding the caution of the

Upper House, helped to turn some religious reformers away from the camp of unwavering purifers like Harley. Sir Edward Dering, who had presented the case for root and branch abolition of the bishops to parliament in 1641, was anxious in 1642 to make clear how he differed from the 'rooters'. 'I have no bias but a conscience warmed with zeal' – warm but not fiery like the most fervent zealots. Dering was greatly concerned at the Commons' unilateral action, doubting both its legality and its wisdom. Could an order of the House be binding, he asked, when it ventured so far from existing law? – and this at 'a dangerous time to make any determinations in matter of religion'.

Dering stalled at the Commons' iconoclastic orders. The 'more severe reformation of our churchmen' that he wanted stopped well short of the extreme solutions of 1641. Had the opportunity offered, and the validity of the 8 September order been debated, he was ready 'to have unbosomed myself'. As it was, he explained himself in print. He was quite unable to accept the ultimate iconoclastic position – indeed it 'horrored' him – that made an idol of the name of Jesus. Dering for one was not going to be frightened off doing bodily reverence to his Saviour.

> Oh you make an idol of a name. I beseech you Sir, paint me a voice, make a sound visible if you can: when you have taught mine ears to see, and mine eyes to hear, I may then perhaps understand this subtle argument. In the mean time reduce this dainty species of new idolatry, under its proper head, (the second commandment) if you can.[41]

For 'unbosoming' himself of these and other speeches in print in 1642, Dering was imprisoned for ten days by the House of Commons who ordered his book to be burnt, after which he promoted a Kent petition to the House, which supported episcopacy and called for 'some severe law ... against laymen, for daring to arrogate to themselves and to exercise the holy function of the ministry'.[42]

The rift that Ben Jonson staged between Busy and the stall-keeper in *Bartholomew Fair* was becoming ever more serious. Dering was not alone in his worries as the parliamentary initiative immediately took effect in increased iconoclasm. There were plenty of individuals eager to jump into action the moment they learnt of the Commons' order – not for them scruples about the legitimacy of so godly a decision. A church in Nottinghamshire, two miles away from Colonel John Hutchinson's house, had a crucifix in the window over the altar and other 'superstitious paintings, of the priest's own ordering' on the walls. The incumbent, evidently in sympathy with Laudian 'beautifying', tried to conform with the new order by removing only the heads of offending images, which he carefully preserved in his closet. But the churchwardens consulted with Colonel Hutchinson, and he made sure that the glass was broken and all the superstitious paintings were 'blotted out'. Thanks to this zeal, Lucy Hutchinson recorded, her husband began to be branded 'with the name of Puritan'. A similar chain of events took place at Neston in Cheshire. Here both minister and churchwardens stood by the 'ancient imagery' in their glass, and it was Lady Brereton who insisted and whose man 'most zealously broke all the windows'. In Chelmsford the churchwardens thought they had complied with the law by removing images of Virgin and Crucifixion from the east window, and reglazing it with white glass. Others were not satisfied with this 'partial imperfect Reformation', and on 5 November – a signal day for such action – these 'sectaries' beat down the whole window with long poles and stones. The same treatment seems to have destroyed the glass of London's parish churches in October 1641.[43]

Sir Robert Harley was among those who were quick to exert their new powers. On 11 October 1641 he received certification from the rector and churchwardens of Kingsland (where he held land, a few miles from Brampton Bryan), that the communion table had been 'turned as it was in former times' and its rails taken down, and 'there is no other innovation in the memory of men'. Three days earlier, Harley had written to the churchwardens of Leominster, sending them a copy of the order of the House of Commons, and telling them to 'abolish' several crucifixes (both carved and in glass) which he had noticed in their church when returning from the quarter sessions at Hereford on 6 October. This new-style official iconoclast seems to have made a thorough inspection, and duly proscribed the crucifix carved on the 'great stone cross' in the churchyard, another over the porch, and those painted in the 'great windows' at the east and west ends, the latter of which also included 'scandalous pictures of the persons of the Trinity'. In churches of which he was patron Harley executed his duties in person, reducing the churchyard cross at Wigmore to dust with a sledgehammer, and at Leintwardine casting the shivered 'idols' he had hammered out of the church windows into the River Teme (patterning himself on Asa in the Book of Chronicles).[44]

Revolutionary though it was, the order of September 1641 did not go far enough for those of Harley's persuasion. For its sphere of application was still limited (like earlier Tudor directives) to ecclesiastical buildings: cathedrals, churches and chapels. Fierce puritans like the writer John Vicars hoped for more, and the latter published in 1641 his book on *The Sinfulness and Unlawfulness of having or making the Picture of Christ's Humanity* – even for civil or moral uses – calling for 'holy zeal, to destroy and utterly ruinate all the pictures or images of the Lord Christ'. This prayer was to be answered – even if not by Sir Edward Dering, one of two MPs to whom the book was dedicated.

The Long Parliament duly saw to it that legislation caught up with 'wider puritan objectives. On 28 August 1643 another great step forward was taken when both Houses passed an ordinance that extended the destruction to churchyards, places of public prayer, or 'any other open place'. At long last (a very long last as some saw it), great free-standing crosses like Paul's Cross, Cheapside and Charing Crosses in London (not to mention the 'innovatory' monuments that some Arminian bishops had been working on) became legitimate targets. In fact Cheapside Cross had already been downed to a considerable fanfare in the spring of 1643, by the committee appointed to deal with monuments of idolatry in the cities of London and Westminster. Then in May 1644, an ordinance designed 'the better to accomplish the blessed Reformation so happily begun', took in hand for the whole country, in addition to the clearance of churches, the destruction of all images of the persons of the Trinity, of saint or angel, 'in any open place within this kingdom'. The iconoclasts had reached their hour of triumph. Idolatry was to be erased from every quarter, the pollution of the image wiped out of every street or square. The purification of the precise was not bounded by church walls or ground deemed holy; it imposed itself on universal space.[45]

An enormous amount of destruction followed, and the cathedrals suffered conspicuously. This can be explained in part by their containing some of the more outstanding works of Laudian 'beautifying', and also by the animus against the bishops and prelatical dignity (Laud and Wren coming in for particular hostility). It is also possible to see in this culmination of a long ongoing puritan programme, the continuing initiative of the same dedicated (perhaps fanatical is the right word) individuals of gentry status, who had for decades been torch-bearers of this cause. William Dowsing, who was responsible for destroying so much church imagery in Cambridgeshire and Suffolk, and Richard Culmer, who undertook the same mission in Canterbury Cathedral, were both performing, under the new parliamentary dispensation, the purifying work that their predecessors had accomplished without authority from above. It may be that the commissions they secured were the result of their own manoeuvres and connections, which allowed them thus to carry forward officially the reformation of superstition and idolatry.[46]

Legislation thus at length proscribed the idols (crosses, Trinity images, saints in windows) that hot-headed puritans had been attacking for generations; the new order had finally arrived, the long-sought 'blessed Reformation'. Holy writ and worldly writ had at last come together, and Dowsing might well believe in his divine mission as godly magistrate of this new order as, with literal faithfulness to parliamentary orders, he levelled altars, removed crosses and images of Trinity, Virgin and saints, and prised from the ground brasses invoking prayers for the dead.

At the centre, as chairman of the committee set up in April 1643 to destroy monuments of idolatry and superstition in London and Westminster, Sir Robert Harley supervised the wiping out not only of the burgeoning new art in the queen's Catholic chapels, but also of much pre-Reformation glass, some of the highest quality. The detailed account of the work carried out under his direction reads as a depressing catalogue of large-scale defacing and destroying. Organs and windows were pulled down in the royal chapels at Greenwich, Hampton Court and Whitehall, and in the last pictures were defaced and the stone cross over the chapel cut down. The work in Westminster Abbey was very extensive, and included taking down angels and the 'cleansing out of pictures', among them those in the chapels of both Queen Elizabeth and the duke of Richmond. Some of this work necessitated the erection of scaffolding, both 'to cut out the Resurrection where the kings and queens stand', and 'to take down the statues of the Virgin Mary and other saints'. After Peacham's remarks, the saddest part of this record is that relating to the large sums spent in 1645 on the work in Henry VII's chapel, where hundreds of feet of glass were replaced at a cost of over £55. Harley's leadership in this iconoclastic campaign was clearly important, and once again we can see the godly co-operating in their mission. Richard Culmer described in his *Cathedrall Newes from Canterbury* (1644), the rich gold and silver embroidery called the Glory-cloth that had recently been made for the high altar of Canterbury Cathedral 'to usher in the breaden God of Rome, and idolatry'. He duly delivered this to Harley's committee, who took evidence from John Rowell, the embroiderer. Culmer was paid the sum of £8 11s 2d by Harley in June 1645, after the Glory-cloth had been burnt.[47]

Difficult though it may now be to grasp, such bonfires of idols marked the triumphant arrival of a new spiritual regime, representing for the godly a tremendous sense of achievement. This was the reformation the purifiers had so long and so earnestly awaited. Nehemiah Wallington, a London turner who recorded his joy in these momentous days, carefully set aside some fragments of stained glass from a destroyed church window 'to keep for a remembrance to show to the generation to come what God hath done for us, to give us such a reformation that our forefathers never saw the like'. The insistent priorities of decades of Busies, heightened by the anxieties of threatening popery, produced a sense of apocalyptic contest, a cosmic struggle of good and evil. The rector of All Hallows, Barking, condemned as black, spotted, and venomous toads all who spoke against the ceremonies of the church, and warned them they were in a state of damnation. As war became a present reality in the 1640s and increased the toll of destruction, the women of Middlesex expressed their view of the devilish evil of stained glass windows. 'We desire also, that profane glass windows, whose superstitious paint makes many idolaters, may be humbled and dashed in pieces against the ground; for our conscience tells us that they are diabolical, and the father of darkness was the inventor of them, being the chief patron to damnable pride.' The world could divide, cut light from darkness, split views of salvation and grace, over a painted window.[48]

An image might also separate neighbour from puritan neighbour. When Richard Culmer saw a window with a depiction of the *Salvator Mundi* in the vicarage-house at Minster, near Canterbury, he had no hesitation in breaking it to pieces. Equally merciless was the young Sir William Springate, who as deputy lieutenant for Kent in the 1640s encouraged his soldiers to break pictures and crosses, and handed out surplices to pregnant women. One day, on a visit to a co-parliamentarian who helped in search-and-destroy missions to 'popish' houses, and who had a firmly puritan wife, Springate caught sight of paintings of the Crucifixion and Resurrection hanging in the hall. He forthwith sliced the pictures out of their frames and presented them, spiked on his sword, to his host's unfortunate wife in the parlour, from where the paintings had been removed, 'to manifest a kind of neglect of them'. This was a case of puritan ticking off puritan. 'What a shame is it' (as Springate's widow recalled his rebuke, many years later) 'that thy husband should be so zealous a prosecutor of the papists, and spare such things in his own house.'[49]

Thanks to parliamentary legislation, a religious image was at risk of being 'purified' out of existence wherever it was. An altarpiece by Rubens in the queen's chapel at Somerset House was thrown into the Thames, and in 1645, when parliament was considering the fate of the duke of Buckingham's great collection at York House, it was resolved that all idolatrous paintings of the second person of the Trinity should be burnt forthwith. The conscientious found plenty to worry about. In the summer of 1644, a month after the ordinance extending iconoclasm to every place in the land, Colonel Herbert Morley wrote to Speaker Lenthall about a shocking painting that had been found on a ship from Dunkirk, driven ashore near Worthing. It depicted, besides 'monstrous shapes' of the Trinity and the Virgin 'sitting in heaven', a scene which he took to show Charles I with Henrietta Maria in the act of offering the royal sceptre to Pope Urban VIII. The colonel (who had in fact misread a painting of St Ursula) sent the picture up to London, recommending that it should be burnt by the common hangman as 'an hieroglyphic of the causes and intents of our present troubles'.[50]

This incident encapsulates the way in which fresh discontents were overtaking the old iconoclastic cause. New popery looked much more terrible than old; the idolaters of this age seemed to have gone beyond harbouring relics of Rome to become active agents of Rome. But it was by no means only continental Catholics who vied for possession of the king's 'superstitious' pictures in 1649. Colonel Hutchinson, who had earned the name of puritan for his iconoclastic role in 1641, spent over £1300 on works of art in the royal collection in 1649–50, and they were not all depictions of fruit and cheese or 'the dog called Mouse'. The bulk of this huge sum went on three Titians, including the Venus of the Pardo (sold on a few years later to Cardinal Mazarin), another Venus, and 'Mary, Christ, St Mark and a genious kneelinge' – not to mention minor purchases of a copper 'Lady and Joseph' and a silver Madonna. Robert Harley and John Hutchinson both laboured under what Edward Dering called 'the general obloquy of a Puritan', but we can be sure that the decoration of their houses was very different.[51]

We can see then that puritan commitment to the eradication of idolatry, starting in the 1560s with dissatisfaction at the state of Elizabethan churches, reached a climax in the 1640s. Increasingly it was puritans who gave a high profile to an objective which the English church had embraced, and increasingly it seemed natural to equate iconoclasts with puritans. Yet it would to rash to see all civil-war iconoclasts as puritan, or every puritan as a potential image-breaker. Taking up arms in defence of the true Protestant religion against papists and atheists, might appear to place the sword of Reformation in the soldier's hands, but transferring the magistrate's iconoclastic duty thus further down the line helped to link the cause more conspicuously than ever before with indiscriminate destruction. Sir Thomas Fairfax, who is said to have protected York's stained glass from 'the ungovernable fury of an enraged rabble', is not the only parliamentary general believed to have saved church windows through these years. The Civil War placed a durable distorting frame around both phenomena – puritanism and iconoclasm. There was no straightforward match between them.[52]

Although the purifying of puritans was always associated with cleansing the church from the corrupting relics of papal idolatry, the fight against Arminian 'innovations' as new popery both broadened and altered the iconoclastic agenda. Those who agreed on the imperative need to down altar rails and new altar imagery might differ as to whether the pure church they were working for had already existed, or was only now coming into being. To attack new popery did not mean one was a puritan. Nor did the features of the promised purified land please all the godly and pure in heart. The image-breaking that took place between 1560 and 1660 did not differ in essentials from that which had preceded it. But during this century iconoclasm played a critical role in helping to define not only the nature of a puritan, but also the chameleon-like nature of the Church of England.

4. The Puritan Death-bed, c.1560–c.1660

RALPH HOULBROOKE

'But the end is the crown of the whole work, and the last act (if any) carrieth away the applause.' Thus Charles Fitz-Geffrey, preacher and poet, adapted a Senecan aphorism and incorporated it into the sermon which he delivered in 1620 at the funeral of Lady Rous, mother of his 'most honoured friend', John Pym.[1] The notion that dying was the most important part of a person's life performance had a long history. It was in this supreme test that his or her true character revealed itself. As another preacher, George Ferebe, wrote in 1614, 'the end of a man perfectly trieth a man'.[2] The English puritans inherited these ideas, and they help to explain the pro-minence of death-beds in puritan biographical literature. Yet their practical application often gave rise to problems. How should one interpret the seemingly 'good' death of someone who had led a bad life? What was one to make of the deaths of 'good' people whose dying 'performance' was marred by the effects of a terminal illness, or cut short by the suddenness of their end? Puritans, along with other Christians, argued that behaviour in face of death must be read as part of the whole life's record. 'If the end be well, then all is well, true' Fitz-Geffrey continued, 'but this is most certain, that life shall end well, that is well led.' The 'last act' nevertheless bulked especially large in accounts of puritan lives. This was largely because the puritan way of dying assigned the individual's inner faith a particu-larly important role, and all but eliminated the supportive framework of liturgy and sacrament.

The ancient last rites of the Catholic Church helped the seriously ill and dying to prepare for their departure from the world. Remin-ders of the Christian duties of restitution, reconciliation and charit-able giving were included in the Order for the Visitation of the Sick. The invalid was enjoined to make a guided profession of faith and a

122

confession of sins. He or she received absolution and might then participate in the Holy Eucharist if physically able to do so. The sacrament of extreme unction was administered to the dying by means of anointing with oil of the eyes, ears, nose, lips, hands and feet. These rites were accompanied by psalms and collects. The priest sprinkled the sick person with holy water. The dying man was encouraged to focus his devotion on a crucifix placed near him in order to remind him of Christ's saving sacrifice on the cross. In practice these rites may have been drastically curtailed in individual cases, and many people probably died without receiving them all. Yet the priest's help at the death-bed was generally regarded as essential. As one Thomas Crabbe of Axminster in Devon remarked in about 1536, every man 'must needs have a priest at his coming into the world, and a priest at his departing'.[3]

From the early fifteenth century onwards, the church's liturgy was supplemented by works of guidance specifically devoted to the *ars moriendi* or 'Craft of Dying'. This literature represented the death-bed as a test which it was essential to pass. Confronted by the temptations of unbelief, despair, impatience, spiritual pride and avarice, the dying would find their chief resource in contemplating the redemptive power of Christ's death. They were encouraged to imitate his behaviour on the cross. They would receive assistance not only from the priest but also from lay carers and helpers who would read them appropriate texts and pray for them. The presence of large numbers of people at the death-bed was thought to be a good thing. They could not only help the dying, but also learn salutary lessons from the experience themselves.[4]

The Protestant Reformation in England drastically abbreviated and simplified the last rites. The dying person's confession of sins to the priest became optional, and extreme unction disappeared altogether from the 1552 Book of Common Prayer. The Communion of the Sick was normally to be shared by a 'good number' besides the sick man, and celebrated only after some hours' notice had been given, requirements which may have discouraged some people from seeking it.[5] Such helps as holy water, the crucifix and the invocation of saints vanished. The rejection of the doctrine of purgatory meant that the dying were now faced with only two possible destinations after death: heaven or hell. They were deprived of any prospect of assistance from the prayers of those they left behind them. If anything, the doctrinal and liturgical changes of the

Protestant Reformation enhanced the importance of the final drama of the death-bed. Yet they also left the dying person with diminished ritual support.

Ars moriendi writing was naturally influenced by the doctrinal changes. The first important English Protestant contribution to the genre was Thomas Becon's *The Sicke Mannes Salue*, composed before 1553, though its earliest surviving copy dates from 1561. Becon had been arrested for preaching Protestant doctrines as early as 1540. Later one of Cranmer's household chaplains, he had spent his exile during Mary's reign at Strassburg, Frankfurt and Marburg. His *Salue* has the flavour of Reformed Protestantism. It was among the best selling Elizabethan devotional works, tedious though it may seem to the modern reader. It is cast in the form of a dialogue between the sick man Epaphroditus and four friends who come to comfort and encourage him. One of them, Philemon, who takes the most prominent and authoritative role in the conversations, is clearly a minister, but his clerical character is not emphasised. No Holy Communion takes place. The leading actor is the dying man himself, who holds centre stage for much of the time. He dictates his will, delivers a lengthy declaration of his faith, and says farewell to his family. He acknowledges and bewails his sins, though without specific details. Philemon tells the sick man that his genuine repentance is a sure sign of his salvation. So Epaphroditus receives powerful comfort and support from his friends, especially when he falters. But he lacks any kind of sacramental assistance, and the lengthy speeches put into his mouth create a daunting impression of the knowledge and faith expected of the dying Protestant.[6]

Over 30 years later, in 1595, appeared *A Salve for a Sicke Man*, written by William Perkins, the most widely read and influential puritan theologian. Perkins's title was perhaps a gesture of respect towards Becon's well known treatise, but his own book is pithier and more forcefully written than Becon's. In his discussion of particular preparations for death, the doctrine of the papists is set out as the yardstick of what must be avoided. They require (he claims) a comprehensive confession, reception of the Eucharist, and extreme unction. But there is no scriptural warrant for any of these. The minister may declare that God pardons a man's sins without knowing the details of all of them. 'For he which soundly and truly repents of one or some few sins, repents of all.' The Supper of the Lord should only be celebrated in the assembly of God's people.

Perkins was thus far less permissive on this point than the Book of Common Prayer.[7]

The sick person's affliction comes from God, says Perkins. The *right* response to it is to seek reconciliation with God by means of fresh examination of heart and life, a confession to him of recent and serious sins, and renewed prayer. If the sick man is unable to renew his faith and repentance on his own, he must (as St James recommended) seek the help of the elders of the church. By this phrase he did *not* mean ministers alone, but also other men who have knowledge of God's Word and the gift of prayer. Every Christian has a responsibility to comfort his brother in sickness. The sick man may make a confession of any sins which lie particularly heavily on his conscience. But it need not be comprehensive, or made to a minister. His own foremost duties towards other people are to forgive and seek forgiveness where appropriate, and to leave his family well provided for not only materially, but (by means of religious exhortations) spiritually also.[8]

Three things are expected of the Christian as he finally draws close to death. First, that he die in faith, placing his whole reliance on God's special love and mercy, focusing his inward eye on Christ crucified. This inner faith is to be expressed by the outward signs of prayer or thanksgiving. In the pangs of death, it may be impossible to utter prayers. But the sighs, sobs and groans of a repentant and believing heart are prayers before God, as effectual as if expressed by the best voice in the world. Last words may proclaim faith with especial power. The second duty is to die readily, in submission to God's will, and the third to render his soul into the hands of God as the most faithful keeper of all. As the result of an afterthought, Perkins added a sort of appendix in which he pointed out that the last combat with the devil in the pangs of death is often the most dangerous of all. 'When thou art tempted of *Satan* and seest no way to escape', Perkins advised, 'even plainly close up thine eyes, and answer nothing, but commend thy cause to God.'[9]

If there is a single work whose stamp upon subsequent accounts of puritan deaths can be discerned more readily than all others, it is *A Salve for a Sicke Man*. One is repeatedly reminded of it both by the overall shape of these accounts and by the details of the narrative. It seems very likely that its clear and forceful recommendations did also influence the attitudes and comportment of the dying. Some of the advice read by the godly differed from Perkins's in important respects. Lewis Bayly's *The Practice of Piety* (1612), for instance, was popular among puritans. Yet Bayly recommended the dying man to make his confession to a godly pastor if he had difficulty in completing his repentance, and then to receive the sacrament of the Lord's Supper.[10] But surviving descriptions of godly dying show that the mainstream of puritan practice followed Becon and Perkins rather than Bayly.

When at last their brief and partial triumph gave the puritans the opportunity of replacing the Book of Common Prayer with a pattern of their own devising in A Directory for the Publique Worship of God early in 1645, the Communion of the Sick disappeared. The section of the Directory concerned with the Visitation of the Sick takes the shape of a set of instructions or guidelines for the minister. He is to explain to the invalid that his affliction comes from God's hand, investigate his religious knowledge if he suspects him of ignorance, supply any necessary instruction, and exhort him to carry out a thorough self-examination. The pastor must on the one hand give comfort and support, especially to those broken in spirit, but on the other awaken the unrepentant to their danger, and warn the complacent not to rely on their own merits. There is a form of prayer confessing and bewailing sins in general terms and seeking God's mercy and help. Recommended as a suitable model, it was not intended to be followed exactly. As one might expect, there are no set prayers. Nor is there any suggestion that the dying person should make a confession of particular sins. Here, then, is some helpful pastoral advice for a minister who will have to attend the death-beds of all sorts and conditions of people. But it is no more than that. There is no longer any liturgical framework, and the pastor's task is by his advice and exhortation to encourage and focus the sick person's own spiritual efforts.[11]

Thus far we have been concerned with advice and prescription. But what of the *practice* of the puritan 'craft of dying'? A rich abundance of source materials is available for analysis. Most of them fall into one of four categories: funeral sermons, biographies, diaries and separate accounts of death-beds. Sermons probably make up the biggest category, though many of them give relatively few details. The account of the life and death of the deceased person usually took up no more than a quarter of the sermon. Preachers had patterns of Christian living and dying in mind, and to some extent selected their materials in order to illustrate them. But the formulaic character of funeral sermons must not be exaggerated. One cannot read large numbers of these sermons without enjoying the skill with which the most varied individual character traits and idiosyncrasies were accommodated within the flexible framework of the basic models. Funeral sermons had been preached long before the Reformation, but they were not published in large numbers before the seventeenth century. The numbers appearing in each decade then increased rapidly between the 1600s and the 1620s, when about 40 were printed. Almost every shade on the spectrum of churchmanship was represented in the list of authors of published sermons. The medium was never one exploited exclusively by puritans.

Especially full death-bed accounts were published in the biographies of such famous puritans as Katherine Stubbes (d. 1590) and John Bruen (d. 1625). These spiritual biographies, written soon after the deaths of their subjects, must be distinguished from the enormous collections of short lives assembled by the indefatigable biographer Samuel Clarke (1599–1682), who for the most part used funeral sermons and older biographies in his own compilations.[12] Both funeral sermons and biographies often incorporated the testimonies or memoranda of eye-witnesses. Many of these no longer survive in their original form. One example of such an account, never printed in early-modern times, Nathaniel Gilby's description of the death of the third earl of Huntingdon in 1595, was discovered only a few years ago. Finally, some vivid accounts of death-beds are also to be found in diaries or autobiographical annals. Among surviving diaries, the earliest reasonably full ones date from the second half of Elizabeth's reign.

All those who described death-beds had certain purposes in view. The most important of these were reassurance, encouragement and edification. The ability to show Christian faith and patience on the death-bed was a valuable indication of the likely destination of the dying. Some accounts were clearly written to dispel fears or malicious rumours of death-bed apathy, apostasy or despair. The dying could be well aware that their 'performance' would be weighed up by foes as well as friends. Mrs Mary Gunter remarked before her death in 1622 that she knew what the world would conclude if she said anything foolish through pain or lack of sleep: 'This is the end of all your precise Folks, they die mad, or not themselves, &c.'[13] The behaviour of those who had died well offered examples to fortify those who would come after them. Some of the published biographies were offered for the instruction of the larger community of godly people. Philip Stubbes channelled his grief at the loss of his young wife Katherine into making her life *A Christal Glasse for Christian Women* (1591). He published his account, he said, in order to glorify God and edify men.[14]

The circumstances which led to the production of one death-bed account are recorded unusually fully in some letters written by Sir Simonds D'Ewes, a puritan member of the Long Parliament. When he lost his wife through smallpox in 1641, he was especially distraught because he had left her while she was sick, convinced that the crisis was past. He had lost precious time in persuading her that she would live instead of helping to prepare her for heaven. He wrote to one of those who had attended her death-bed: '. . . I expect from you in a whole sheet of paper or two, for which I give you a week's time to pen it, a full discourse of all the passages of her sickness from the first to the last, excepting the three days I was there: but especially of that which happened those two dreadful days after my departure, of which the last was to her a day of rest and glory.' Having heard that she had complained of a lack of assurance of God's love during her illness, D'Ewes pressed for some evidence that those with her had encouraged and reassured her, and that before her death she had 'expressed some more comfort' than had already been described to him. 'Not', he wrote, 'that I think it can in any way conduce to strengthen my assurance that she is a glorious Saint in heaven; but that it might encourage us that are remaining to follow her godly example.' Had she not left some requests for him to perform, concerning her children or any of her friends? The answer to his anxious enquiries was evidently a reassuring one, but he responded by demanding yet further precise details.[15]

These letters cast a vivid light on puritan attitudes to death. We see the anxious husband seeking a minute account of his wife's end, pressing for reassuring details. We see him trying to come to terms with his own conscience, and his wife's imagined reproaches, while quelling fears that her end had not been a 'comfortable' one. The purposes of the death-bed narrative – assurance and encouragement – are clearly specified. D'Ewes said that he could not read the resulting account too often. Raw material was probably gathered for countless funeral sermons in a similar fashion. (In this case D'Ewes concluded that it was too late for a sermon, because his wife had already been buried.)

Earthly life was a long process of dying. Its most important aim should be to prepare oneself for the far more important life hereafter. The thought was expressed in countless pithy axioms and epigrams such as 'Live to die, and die to live eternally' or 'Death is the gateway of life'. These commonplaces were shared by writers of all religious persuasions. But in England it was among the puritans that the Protestant ideal of following one's vocation in the world without being wedded to worldly things was most widely pursued. When death summoned him, the individual had to be willing to obey the call. Ideally, he should be ready, his earthly affairs in order. The onset of illness served as a warning to make his will and pay his debts, if he had not already done so. Bulstrode Whitelocke, lawyer, politician and diarist, remembered that both his parents had been well prepared for death. His mother had been 'called by some a Puritan', and, he added 'if truely to fear God be so, she was so, (and) happy in being so'. Coming home with her son the day of her death in 1631, she insisted on going up to the house on foot, saying that she wanted to walk there for the last time. She was undaunted by the 'prophetic sense of her near approaching death'. The following year, Whitelocke's father, while maintaining a cheerful demeanour, often alluded to his forthcoming departure and reunion with his 'beloved Companion in heaven'. On leaving London for the last time, he bade his fellow lawyers farewell, telling them that he would never see them again.[16]

Yet even the godly were sometimes reluctant to accept the terminal character of the last illness, as the fullest accounts sometimes reveal. The death of the third earl of Huntingdon, in December 1595, was preceded by an illness of about a fortnight. Yet until shortly before the end he was hoping to set out from York to London, where he expected to be able to consult physicians more expert than those available in the northern capital. It was not until two days before his death, when Huntingdon could barely speak, that serious spiritual preparation began, at the instance of his household chaplain Nathaniel Gilby. Huntingdon died without making a will. Under these circumstances, it was hardly surprising that Gilby should have penned an exceptionally detailed account, showing that this authentically puritan nobleman had nevertheless died a good death.[17] But it was more satisfactory and more usual to report that the deceased had set his house in order in good time to allow him to concentrate his dying thoughts on the coming encounter with his Maker.

The participants in the death-bed drama – the dying person and his or her helpers – brought to the occasion their own resources of faith and experience, their expectations and the lessons they had learnt at previous death-beds. But however expertly they played their parts, the course of events was largely shaped by the nature of the fatal illness, something which lay outside their control. It might be short or long, terribly painful, or relatively easy to bear. The pious countess of Huntingdon, wife of the fifth earl, who died in 1634, had frequently prayed that when God called her, He would do so by a consumption. She thought that God was more likely to be in the 'still soft voice of consumption' than in the 'whirlwind of a convulsion' or the fire of a fever. Her wish was granted, and her mouth was full of thanks 'to that gracious hand which lay so light upon her, and made her suffer no more'. In her case, the terminal illness brought a change of gear in the process of preparation for death which (according to her funeral sermon) had already taken up most of her life, but no violent disruption of her devotional activity.[18]

The loss of control as a result of delirium during high fevers was a much feared prospect. Sleeplessness, and the 'malignant, and fiery working' of his smallpox made Edward Lewkenor fear 'lest any disorderly, impatient, or profane speeches should pass from him, to the dishonour of Almighty God, and grief, and sorrow of his friends about him: his request therefore was hourly to God, for Christ's sake, to set a watch before his mouth, and to keep the door of his lips.' He tearfully begged for pardon for those few lapses which occurred during his violent fits. Delirious ravings and other unseemly behaviour might be natural results of the terminal illness. William Perkins pointed this out in his *Salve*, and sensibly advised onlookers to take them in good part. But they were nevertheless difficult to reconcile with the ideal pattern of the good death. The effects of plague were especially dreaded. In 1645, the preacher at his funeral resolved to say nothing of the death of William Strode, one of the five members whom Charles I had tried to arrest in the House of Commons in January 1642, save to stop false and spiteful rumours. Strode, he insisted, had not died of the plague, and had not fallen into raging distempers. 'Some clouds indeed were cast upon his faculties by the violence of the disease, yet was his demeanour and his dissolution quiet.'[19]

Painful sickness was often regarded as a test of the individual's patience; impatience had been one of the five grievous temptations

of the death-bed against which the medieval *Craft of Dying* had
warned. The great danger was that the sufferer would repine not only
against the disease itself, but against its first cause, God's providence.
Patience and submission in suffering were frequently praised attributes of the good death. An outstanding example was furnished by
Katherine, wife of Philip Stubbes, who died in 1590. About a
fortnight after her safe delivery of a son, God suddenly visited her
with a burning quotidian ague which continued for six weeks. In all
this time she never slept an hour together, yet the Lord kept her in
perfect understanding throughout and she showed no signs of discon-
tent or impatience, remaining consistently faithful to God. Edward
Lewkenor was specially commended in 1636 for making 'no impatient
speeches, no murmuring and repining, no crying out upon the
disease: no accusing of secondary causes'. His patient silence had been
occasionally broken by short prayers in which he sought some
alleviation of his pain or increase in strength. But William Perkins,
dying in excruciating pain from the stone in 1602, refused to seek any
mitigation of his agony. 'Pray not for an ease of my torment', he told
a friend, 'but for an increase of my patience.' But not every good end
was preceded by arduous trials. Preachers and diarists readily accepted that some deaths were much easier than others. Barnaby
Potter described the last sickness of Sir Edward Seymour in 1613 as
short, and on the whole not very sharp. Seymour gave up his soul
without a struggle. Sir Anthony Rous was happy in the manner of his
death in 1622, 'a short sickness making way to a quiet and peaceable
dissolution'. His mortality had fallen from him like a cloak.[20]

Patience in suffering and submission to God's will were important
aspects of the craft of dying, but puritans were usually described as
playing a more active role in the drama of their own death-beds,
especially by means of good advice and exhortations, declarations of
faith, devout prayers, and the ready acceptance of death itself. Sir
James Whitelocke's death, succinctly described by his son Bulstrode,
was exemplary in all these respects. 'In the afternoon, he lay down
upon his bed, gave good counsel to those about him, expressed fully
his assurance of the love of God to him, & of his eternal happiness
through the merits of Christ, & so recommending his soul to God,
and fetching two or three little groans, his breath expired on the 22
day of June, 1632.'[21]

Valedictory exhortations to friends and family members occupied
a prominent place in many accounts of death-beds. John Bruen

(d. 1625), an outstanding example of the godly layman, gave his son 'many wholesome instructions, and gracious exhortations, praying for him, and blessing his children, encouraging him to be constant in religion, . . . exhorting him also, to uphold the worship, and service of God, both in the assembly, and in his family . . .'. John Preston testified in his sermon for Arthur Upton in 1619 that his 'talk for the most part in his sickness was of heavenly matters, and such as came to comfort him, might receive comfort from him'. As might be expected, the parting messages of godly ministers were amongst those most fully recorded. Thomas Gataker, a famous presbyterian pastor, addressed each member of his family in turn the day before his death in 1654. Each received advice appropriate to his or her character or responsibilities. He exhorted them all to live in concord. Another minister, Mr John Carter, most of whose children were not present at his death-bed in 1635, left for all the members of his family the simple message 'Stand fast in the faith, and love one another'. Ministers' responsibilities extended beyond their own families to the members of their congregations. William Whateley of Banbury (d. 1639) was one of those who gave 'heavenly and wholesome counsel' to their parishioners. He exhorted them to read, hear and meditate upon the Word of God, to pray, and to maintain brotherly love.[22]

Godly women, too, delivered exhortations and made their last requests. Katherine Stubbes and Lady Magdalen Hastings both entreated their husbands not to grieve or mourn for them. Some mothers showed a strong concern for the godly upbringing of their children and reminded those children of their duties. Elizabeth Whitelocke spent much of the last day of her life discoursing with her son Bulstrode against the fear of death. It was, she said, but a passage to a better life for those who trusted in God. They would meet again in heaven. Women's death-bed speeches were often heard with a special respect which reinforced their authority within the family. But sometimes their interests ranged outside the household. Lady Hastings urged Sir Francis to support the godly pastor of their parish, who had been treated disrespectfully by some of his flock.[23]

Puritans were expected to be strong in faith and to know what they believed. William Perkins made it clear in his *Salve* that the experienced Christian should not need 'catechising' (a tart reference, this, to the rehearsal of the articles of faith in the Order for the Visitation of the Sick). The lively faith of the dying puritan might be expected to manifest itself to those around the death-bed, not only in exhortation and prayer, but in some more explicit testimony concerning his own belief and assurance. The recorded utterances are often fairly concise: heartfelt extemporary statements rather than rehearsals of points of doctrine. They were especially important in giving spectators their most tangible evidence of the happy state of the dying person and examples to fortify them when they faced their own time of trial. Those of famous ministers were heard with particular eagerness. When Edward Dering lay dying, in 1576, it was his friends who prompted him to say something for their edification and comfort. The sun shining in his face gave added force to his assertion that there was but one righteousness in the world, one communion of saints. He insisted that all his hopes of salvation rested only on the righteousness of Jesus Christ. He blessed God for the fact that he felt 'so much inward joy and comfort' in his soul, that if put to a choice between death and life, he would a thousand times rather choose death, if it were consistent with God's will. In 1631, Robert Bolton's neighbours, who had heard him speak during his ministry of the exceeding comforts that were in Christ, wanted to know what he was now experiencing. He was too weak to manage more than a few words, but they were eloquent ones. He was, he told them, as full of comfort as his heart could hold, and felt nothing in his soul but Christ, with whom he heartily desired to be.[24]

Some pithy statements were also made by godly laypeople. In 1584, Sir Gawen Carew, a leading Devon Protestant, allegedly spoke of his creation, redemption, sanctification and justification as succinctly as the most expert divine could have done. The staunchly puritan third earl of Huntingdon was caught unawares by a sudden turn for the worse in his fatal illness three days before his death in 1595. Late the following day he was reminded by one of his chaplains of the duty of declaring his perseverance in the faith. Only after some time was he able to articulate, and then with difficulty, what his chaplain called a 'worthy, brief, pithy and well studied speech'. 'I profess Jesus Christ God and man to be my only saviour. And so must you do too: and if I should speak this twelvemonth I could say no more.' In the middle of his last night alive, when asked to give some sign of his continuing faith and the comfort he derived from it, he raised his hands three times.[25]

An exceptionally full confession of faith is to be found in Philip Stubbes's account of his wife Katherine's death. A girl of nineteen dying of fever could hardly have delivered a statement as fluent and coherent as the one which Stubbes wrote down. It is a long but vigorous declaration, which deals with a wide range of key doctrines concerning the resurrection of the body, the fate of the soul, justification by faith, the relationship between faith and works, predestination, the visible and invisible churches, and the nature of the sacraments. Yet a personal preoccupation is reflected in a lengthy passage on the grounds for believing in the mutual recognition of souls in heaven, where Katherine no doubt hoped to be reunited with her husband and her little son. Another pious woman, Rebecka Crispe, seems to have been less self-reliant and readier to seek advice. Around the beginning of her last sickness in 1620, she sent for the famous London preacher Thomas Gataker, the spiritual adviser with whom, because he was her kinsman, she felt most at ease. Before a few friends, she made a pithy profession of her faith, desiring to be better informed if necessary, or to have it further confirmed. She wanted to be continually engaged in this process of learning, 'forgetting her pains and weakness when she was about it, and neglecting her natural rest, to attend it'.[26]

Prayer – independent, varied, fervent, and often extemporary – occupies a prominent place in many accounts of puritan death-beds. The dying might use set forms. But they also sent up prayers of their own – praise for blessings bestowed, and a variety of petitions: for mercy, for a sense of God's love and forgiveness, for strength to bear the trials of the death-bed, and for help for those left behind. But the commonest, especially in the later stages, were such pleas as 'Lord Jesus come quickly, come quickly', or 'Come, oh come Lord Jesus the bright morning star; Come Lord Jesus; I desire to be dissolved, and to be with thee'. Katherine Stubbes could be heard voicing softly and insistently, over and over again, such prayers as 'Oh my good God, why not now? . . . I am ready for thee, I am prepared, oh receive me now for thy Christ his sake. Oh send thy messenger death to fetch me . . . oh send my gaoler to deliver my soul out of prison.' Committals of the soul into the hands of God were among the reported last words of many godly Christians. 'My heart fails, and my strength fails, but God is my fortress and the strong rock of my salvation', declared Thomas Gataker in 1654: 'Into thy hands therefore I commend my soul; for thou hast redeemed me oh God of truth.' Prayers often occupied the last moments of speech, and continued through the ensuing silence, uplifted hands their only outward signs.[27]

Compared with godly exhortations, firm and manifest faith, and devout prayers, certain other elements of the traditional craft of dying, such as the confession of sins, reconciliation, forgiveness and seeking forgiveness, play only a small part in the surviving narratives. As we have seen, Becon's *Salue* had encouraged only a general acknowledgement of sins rather than a specific account of them. The onset of sickness was described by Perkins as a cue for the renewed confession of the individual's sins before God. Their private journals suggest that some puritans were acutely conscious of personal failings. But the likelihood that they regarded them above all as matters for secret examination and things to be acknowledged to God alone helps to explain why the accounts of puritan death-beds say so little about confession. Some of the godly were described as repentant. 'In his sickness he was very penitent and sorrowful, confessed his sin, desiring God to forgive him', wrote John Preston of the Devon gentleman Arthur Upton, though he added that Upton assured himself that his sins had been forgiven him for Christ's sake. Upton also forgave and forgot all wrongs and injuries done him. The young Suffolk gentleman Edward Lewkenor was commended for the 'exact survey' which he took of his former life during his illness. He was much troubled by the sight of his former weaknesses and infirmities, even though they were not damnable sins; his repentance was true and hearty, and his prayers were delivered with contrition as well as faith and submission.[28]

The death-bed narratives suggest that a spiritual crisis during the last illness was a relatively rare experience. Katherine Brettergh, a Lancashire lady, and the sister of John Bruen, belonged to the minority of puritans who suffered such a crisis, or perhaps two crises, since there seem to have been two separate episodes in her case. Faced with the thought of the severity of God's justice and the greatness of her sins, she accused herself of pride in her own beauty. Then she began to think that she had no faith and that she was a hypocrite. Sometimes she would cast her Bible away from her, saying that it was indeed the Book of Life, but that she had read it unprofitably, and therefore feared that it had become the Book of Death to her. Sometimes she accused herself of impatience, bewailed her not feeling God's spirit, doubted of her election, and wished that she had never been born, or that she had been made any other creature but a woman. But eventually God sent her peace and comfort of conscience.[29]

Some of the sick had a vivid sense of the devil as the source of the temptations which they suffered. Katherine Brettergh was one of them. She felt that Satan was interfering with her prayers, and entreated her friends constantly to help her against the tempter with their own intercessions. Once, emerging from a great conflict with Satan, she told him not to reason with her, a weak woman, but with Christ her advocate. This was the sort of response to diabolical pressure which William Perkins had recommended. But Philip Stubbes included in his dramatic account of a 'most wonderful combat' between Satan and his wife Katherine's soul a lengthy tirade which she addressed to the devil, insisting that all her sins had been pardoned for Christ's sake. Scarcely had she finished her defiant address before she was able to announce with triumphant smiles that he had gone. Hadn't those around her seen him 'fly like a coward, and run away like a beaten cock'? On the day of her death in 1634, the countess of Huntingdon said that she saw Satan hovering over her, but like a bird in the air, unable to seize upon her. Although some men had a sense of diabolical presence, those who experienced it most acutely seem to have been women, perhaps because of the impression made on them by the story of Eve's fall.[30]

The dying sometimes felt ecstatic happiness. It could be particularly intense after periods of spiritual doubt or dullness. According to her husband's account, Katherine Stubbes saw, immediately after the successful outcome of her conflict with Satan, millions of angels with fiery chariots about her, ready to carry her soul into heaven. Then, after fervent prayers and exhortations, she seemed suddenly to rejoice, as though she had seen some still more glorious sight. Rising in her bed, she stretched forth her arms to embrace and welcome death, commending her soul into God's hands with her last breath. Perhaps the most extraordinary instance of this sort was the ecstatic happiness experienced in two generations of the Janeway family. William Janeway, minister of Kelshall (Herts), had dark fears about his state in the next world. In response to the prayers of his son John, God vouchsafed him a 'fit of overpowering Love and Joy' so great that he could not contain himself. He questioned whether he could have borne it had it been greater still. Now, he told John, he was ready to die. John in his turn had his soul filled with 'Joys unspeakable' before his death in 1657, and he cried out in his ecstasy, wishing that he could communicate his feelings to those around him.[31]

Puritans were usually perceived as passing their last moments in a state of readiness for death, submissive to God's will, and in confident hope of their salvation in Jesus Christ. The moment of death was described as quiet or peaceful, even in those cases where the previous illness had been painful and tedious. In his last throes, the earl of Huntingdon willingly yielded to death as God's messenger. He departed like a healthy man falling asleep after hard work or a tedious journey 'most sweetly, quietly and comfortably'. One woman's end 'was so quiet and peaceable, that her departure was scarce sensible to those that were nearest about her'.[32] It may be that in many of these cases the normal outcome of the terminal illness would have been a gradual loss of consciousness. What interests us here is not the physical reality, in so far as that might be separated from the individual's psychological and spiritual state, but the interpretation of what they saw by the observers of the death-bed.

So far we have been concerned with what death-bed narratives tell us of the attitudes and behaviour of the dying. But what of the parts played by those around them: pastors, friends and family? Ministers of God's Word had special expertise and responsibilities. The exceptionally full description of the death of the earl of Huntingdon in 1595 shows that the clergy attending upon him tried to help him above all by means of prayer with him and for him, and comfortable readings from scripture, especially on the great themes of forgiveness and remission of sins and justification by faith. Two of the ministers present exhorted him to continue in faith and to give some testimonial of his perseverance. When his death seemed imminent, his household chaplain tried to comfort him with the prospect of his being received into eternal life. These ministrations – especially prayer and encouraging words – are described in many other shorter accounts. One gentleman had with him during his last days 'diverse reverend Ministers, in whose godly speeches, and devout prayers, and good company he much rejoiced'. Another spent his sickness either talking to 'grave Divines' or in hearty prayers. The power of prayer is well conveyed in Sir Simonds D'Ewes's account of his mother's death. He remembered how the minister who attended her had knelt near her, very earnestly and audibly calling on God to strengthen and comfort her in her last agony, and to receive her into eternal blessedness. She had raised her right hand to show her joining in that petition especially, and fervently assented with her dying voice. During the last hours of his life in 1625, John Bruen was 'never at quiet, unless he were either meditating and praying himself, or had some godly man or good minister to pray with him, and for him'. The picture of the godly pastors' ministrations which the death-bed narratives give us is very much in line with William Perkins's suggestions. References to participation in Holy Communion are far less common. Attempts to elicit anything resembling a confession of sins seem to have been rare. Dr John Chadwich asked Sir George St Paul shortly before his death in 1613 whether he remembered dealing hardly with any man, and whether, if so, he had made restitution. But Chadwich may have been emboldened by an unusual readiness on Sir George's part to seek his spiritual advice or even direction. The scrupulous baronet had once asked him whether he might lawfully kneel on a cushion when making his private prayers.[33] The assistance of godly ministers at the death-bed could be valuable. But not all pious Protestant layfolk seem to have judged it necessary. Bulstrode Whitelocke's parents, both of whom foresaw their deaths, departed from the world without any recorded help from a minister.[34]

Several accounts of the death-beds of godly men and women make clear how crucial the supportive role of family and friends often was. Their prayers and readings gave spiritual sustenance to the dying. The spread of literacy and of knowledge of the scriptures among the pious laity all enabled friends and relatives to perform the 'ministerial' function to some extent. Perkins made explicit a point that was implicit in the *dramatis personae* of Becon's dialogue: it is not the duty of the ministers of the Word alone to visit and comfort the sick. Every Christian man (it seems clear that he meant women too) should be able to comfort his brother in sickness. In practice family members, where available, probably played the chief part. The death-bed narratives contain some striking examples of such help. When her illness took a turn for the worse 30 days before her death in 1622, Mary Gunter had a final hour-long talk with her husband about her desire for the things of this life. 'And now sweet-heart', she said after they had finished, 'no more words between you and me about any worldly thing, only let me earnestly request you, and charge you, that as you see my weaknesses to increase, you will not fail to assist me, and to call upon me, to follow the Lord with prayer and patience.' She knew, she continued, that Satan, seeing that his time was short, would try to take advantage of her weakness, and she therefore asked her husband now especially to help her with his 'counsel, comfort, and prayers'. We have already seen how John Janeway acted as his father's spiritual counsellor. It was after John had 'wrestled' with God for his father that William was filled with the joy for which his son had begged.[35]

But the presence of family and friends at the bedside could be distracting, either because their grief interfered with the process of relinquishing earthly ties and turning to God, or because they continued to will the recovery of the dying person at a stage when he or she was already trying to come to terms with death. The notion that attachment to one's family, and especially their presence at the death-bed, makes it more difficult to die, had already been well established in the medieval *ars moriendi*. Especially vivid testimony of one dying woman's sense of being actively held back from heaven by those to whom she was closest on earth comes from the description of the last days of Elizabeth, wife of John Angier, a famous Lancashire minister. Afraid that her strength and patience would fail during her long-drawn-out last illness in 1641, and longing for death, she asked her husband, 'Love, why will you not let me go?', and reproached the family round her bed with the words 'you know not what wrong you do me that you will not let me go to God . . .' The prospect of the distress which might be caused to the dying or to those around them sometimes made it seem preferable to die without the company of close relatives. John Foxe the martyrologist, foreseeing his death, sent his sons away beforehand because, although he loved them, he did not want them present when he died. Returning home from London in 1632, Sir James Whitelocke would not let his 26-year-old son Bulstrode come with him. He told his servants that he was not willing to let his son see him die 'lest it might make too much impression upon him'.[36]

Both men and women were well represented among the practitioners of the puritan 'craft of dying'. Furthermore, it gave each sex scope for the exercise of qualities more usually associated with the other. Men, normally expected to be active and dominant, were now called upon to be submissive, and to wait patiently for death, sometimes likened to a kiss from God's mouth. Women were better trained for this ordeal. Most of them had gone through the trials of childbirth, a sort of rehearsal for the last act, and many had done so several times. In the upper ranks of society in particular it was looked upon as a hazardous experience, and some pious women prepared themselves spiritually as for death itself. Elizabeth Jocelin was commended for secretly buying her winding sheet when she knew that she was pregnant. William Perkins grouped 'Women when they travail with child' along with mariners and soldiers as potential beneficiaries of his *Salve*, as well as the sick.[37]

If men were called upon to exhibit virtues in which women were better schooled, women for their part had certain exceptional opportunities on the death-bed. Forbidden to speak in church, they might now utter prayers, exhortations and statements of faith which were heard with a special respect. And whereas *all* Christian dying demanded patient submission to God's will, the puritan way of death, which particularly encouraged the outward manifestation of individual faith, allowed women a prominent role in the drama of their own death-beds. One example illustrates this in striking fashion. In May 1661, when approaching persecution cast its shadow before it, Elizabeth Heywood, wife and daughter of eminent ministers, lay dying of consumption in her father's house. After delivering exhortations to the children of the household, she turned to her father, John Angier, and her husband, Oliver Heywood. She made a long speech in which she admonished them to keep close to God and his truth, regardless of persecution, and to let God's church lie near their hearts. Then she prayed fervently for the preservation of the church and the restraint of the 'bitter-spirited' men who were bent on the punishment of the puritans. Shortly afterwards, Heywood mentioned what she had said. She replied 'that she wondered at herself how she [had] begun and proceeded in that discourse, and thought it strange that she had spoken such things, and so did others, since her modesty had formerly shut up her lips in silence: but her honoured father judged it some strange ecstasy wherein she was acted by a strong motion of the spirit, beyond her purpose, and above her present infirmity.'[38]

Even more remarkable than the way in which the puritan way of dying gave weight to the words of godly women were the opportunities it gave to some children. Only some: it seems unlikely that many children, even in puritan families, were fully capable of making a 'good death'. The idea that it gave children opportunities might seem absurd. It may appear more accurate to think in terms of pressures towards religious precocity. Yet what stands out from some life stories is the independence of the children concerned rather than the weight of parental authority. The largest collection of children's biographies, in which their 'Joyful Deaths' bulked large, was James Janeway's *A Token for Children*. Published in two parts in 1671 and 1673, the collection contains the lives of thirteen children, three of whom certainly died before 1660. Janeway's main message was the importance of timely religious instruction. Children were not too little to go to heaven or hell. The earliest of Janeway's examples, Charles Bridgeman (*c.*1620–32), prayed as soon as he could speak, was an assiduous reader of scripture, and ready to tell servants and his brothers their duties. During his lingering sickness he thought about heaven a great deal and asked serious questions about the nature of his soul. He was ready to give an account of his hope, wanted to die so as to go to his Saviour, and prophesied that he would die on a Sunday. On the appointed day he saw in a trance a sweet heavenly messenger who had come to take him away, fervently requested prayers, asked forgiveness of his family and all the world, and prayed Christ to receive his soul. Anne Lane (*c.*1630–*c.*1640) was already concerned about the fate of her soul when she was about five, and eager to know what she should do to be saved. Her questions prompted her father's conversion. She watched her parents carefully, was grieved if her father spent time in unprofitable company, and if she thought he was neglecting his shop would remind him how precious time was. She died before she was ten. Tabitha Alder (*c.*1636–44), the child of a minister in Kent, became afraid that she would go to hell when she fell sick at the age of seven. She explained that she found it hard to love God because she could not see him. But this changed when a friend spent a day in fasting and prayer for her. The prospect of her death was now comforting to her. She would soon be with Jesus as his bride. She continued in an ecstasy of joy and had a vision of approaching glory just before her death. Clearly these children were all exceptionally precocious, but what also stands out from the stories is adults' readiness to take them seriously, and even, in the extraordinary case of Anne Lane, to accept a partial reversal of the normal chain of authority. Various elements recur in several of Janeway's stories, including a strong concern with the afterlife and a readiness to die.[39]

Janeway seems to have regarded all his cases as exceptional, even though entirely credible. When one turns to the diary of the Essex minister Ralph Josselin, who between 1642 and 1663 fathered eight children who survived infancy, there are few signs of the intense religiosity which pervades Janeway's cases. His daughter Mary died in 1650, when she was eight, about the same age as Tabitha Alder. Josselin characterised her as a child of ten thousand, full of wisdom, woman-like gravity, knowledge and sweet expressions of God. But his account of her death-bed concentrates mainly on the progress of her disease. He described her as being thankful, mindful of God, and crying out 'Poor I, poor I'. But there is no mention of any fervent prayers, declarations of faith, or visions of heaven. We may be confident that he would have recorded such things, because he described in great detail a dream which his son Tom had four years later, at the age of ten, in which he met Mary in heaven.[40] It was probably not until adolescence, in the case of most puritans, that the requisite combination of mental and emotional development made the good death fully possible.

In England, interest in the comportment of the dying probably reached its highest level in the years between the Reformation and the Glorious Revolution. The last rites were curtailed during the Reformation, and the more thoroughgoing Protestants were reluctant to place much reliance upon them. The 'craft of dying' assumed a greater importance than it had ever possessed before. Many of those who died drew on their inner resources (or, as they saw it, the strength given them by God) in order to take the leading part in the drama of the death-bed. Large numbers of people were intensely interested in the performances of those who had gone before them, both as guides to how they themselves might behave and as sources of encouragement and reassurance. There was a large readership for works of counsel, especially those written by Becon and Perkins. There was no script for this last act, no prescriptive ritual framework, but rather various ingredients, which might be put together as circumstances and individual choice dictated. Of these, by far the most important was the testimony of saving faith. A large body of surviving evidence leaves no doubt that believers were buoyed up in the face of physical extinction, and supported through appalling pain, by the prospect of eternal life. The enormous early-modern interest in death-bed performances may seem morbid to us with our very different attitudes and perspective. But this interest had very little of the mawkish sentimentality which early twentieth-century sensibilities detected in Victorian death-bed literature. At issue were life and death: eternal life or the living death of the soul.

The puritans thought of the elect as a small number among the multitudes of the ungodly. This select band was of course scattered through every rank of society. But it is clear that its upper ranks, together with wealthier elements of the 'middling sort' were disproportionately well represented in the types of material which throw most light on the practice of good dying. So this analysis has necessarily drawn on the experience of a minority small in both religious and social terms. But the audience encouraged by such examples of godly dying was almost certainly far larger.

Many features of the puritans' ideal way of dying were ones shared with other Protestants. Some were indeed common to all Christians. But the classic puritan type of the *ars moriendi* made especially heavy demands of the individual at the heart of the death-bed drama. The requisite resources of faith and knowledge which fitted him or her for the role were often the fruits of long years of training. The great majority of the population were not spiritual athletes. The comfortable or warning words of the godly pastor may all too often have fallen on barren ground. 'I dealt as well as I could with him', wrote the Lancashire minister Henry Newcome in 1655, after visiting a 'poor ale man' in his sickness, 'but saw with him . . . how hard it is to *get within* poor persons at such a time, to fasten anything on them of their danger and concernment.'[41]

Within the Church of England, a growing number of influential clergymen saw the puritan way of dying as quite unsuitable for most Christians. Instead, they emphasised the need for repentance, confession of sins to a priest, and humility on the part of penitent sinners in need of mercy. They reasserted the value of Holy Communion as a pledge of Christ's love of the dying Christian. Already during the last decade of Elizabeth I's reign Lancelot Andrewes as a London vicar was using in his visitation of the sick a manual of prayers and sick-bed duties of his own devising which contained a systematic and detailed framework for the making of confessions.[42] But it was during the Interregnum and at the Restoration that 'Anglican' criticism of the puritan ministry to the dying was most strongly expressed. In 1651 was published the foremost work of the Anglican *ars moriendi*, Jeremy Taylor's *Holy Dying*. Taylor's minister, the 'holy man', is the 'physician of souls', who guides the dying in confession and administers the Holy Sacrament.[43] The most tangible consequence in this field of the Anglican triumph in 1662 was the alteration of the relevant Prayer Book rubric, which now required the minister to 'move' the sick person to make a confession of his sins, if he felt his conscience troubled. The extent to which practice actually changed within the church under the influence of these ideas is too big a question to broach here. The old puritan pattern certainly survived among the Protestant nonconformists after 1662. It is clear that no one dominant way of dying emerged in a divided England after the Reformation. It may be that the puritans, by diminishing the individual's dependence on the man of God, and by weakening the sacramental framework, indirectly and unintentionally helped open the way to the secularisation of the death-bed and, in the longer term, the rise of medical management.

5. 'A Charitable Christian Hatred': The Godly and their Enemies in the 1630s

PETER LAKE

I *A good death*

On July 14 1637, the people of Northampton were confronted with an extraordinary sight.[1] A man and two women were about to be executed for infanticide. The man was John Barker, vicar of Pitchley, and the two women his maidservant and his kinswoman. Barker was accused of fathering a child through his adulterous liaison with the maidservant and all three parties had been found guilty of doing away with the child. Executions, of course, attracted crowds and provided puritans with opportunities to display their evangelical skills on the gallows, converting and counselling felons in the last moments before death, eliciting from them those last dying speeches in which they confessed their sins, expressed their repentance and threw themselves on the mercy of God.[2] Here, however, was a rather different spectacle; the puritan minister was the felon and the obvious lesson to be learned was anything but the normal edifying confirmation of the power of puritan godliness in the face of sin, Satan and death.

Barker himself was well aware of the situation. 'I ... was a minister, a preacher, one that was noted all the country over, that the very king and court took notice, such a man as I, in an eminent calling that was taken for a sincere (as the world calls them) a puritan minister. I was taken for a strict godly man', lamented Barker, but now his public humiliation could only bring down trouble, contempt, even despair upon the heads of the godly. 'I have been ... a great

145

offence to true religion and to faithful ministers and to the holy profession of the gospel . . . my fall is that which many do rejoice in, that they may thereby take occasion to jeer, sing and rhyme of it.' 'The enemies of the truth' 'will say . . . I knew and saw one hanged as good as you' and conclude that 'all which profess religion are naught because I am'.

Barker, however, did his best to counteract such conclusions. There had been twelve apostles and only one of them had been 'a hypocrite, [an] atheist, a murderer'. Did that, then, make it sensible to conclude that 'all were hypocrites, all thieves, all murderers'? The blame for his sins should rest on him alone and not be used to taint the godly as a group. After all, as Barker pointed out, it had not been an excess of 'religion that caused me to sin but the want of it'. His fault was not that he had been a puritan but that his profession of religion had been 'a mere outside, nothing in truth'. Indeed, Barker begged the crowd in 'the words of a dying man' to remember that the 'falls of the faithful are the destruction of the wicked'. 'By our fall and miscarriage they take liberty to sin although thereby they destroy themselves. Now will such say come on, do not you know how such strict and dissembling puritans have lived themselves. Thus will they encourage themselves and others in all sorts of voluptuous ways.' But this, Barker told the crowd, was precisely the wrong lesson to draw from his fate.

> Know therefore thus much, that though holiness be scoffed at, without holiness you shall never be saved. You must abide in the truth and walk in that way which is called puritanism, or you shall never come to heaven. Those that are most religious and have most of the power of godliness in them, those and those only are the best Christians, those which you call puritans and except you become such as they are, ye shall certainly be damned for ever in hell.

The expostulations and laments quoted above were, in fact, all part of a belated attempt to turn the polemical and political tables, and through the public performance of Barker's conversion, sealed by a suitably good death on the gallows, to demonstrate again the truth and power of puritan religion. Barker was attended on the scaffold by a number of leading local ministers – Daniel Cawdray, Thomas Ball and Daniel Rogers. They are described acting out on the scaffold the series of dialectical exchanges between law and gospel, divine justice and mercy, humble repentance and hopeful assurance, that made up the elaborate choreography of the puritan conversion. As they have come down to us, the exchanges seem spontaneous but this was a script that all the parties knew intimately and we should probably view the resulting scene as a set of improvised variations on themes central to puritan soteriology. The result was a cross between a performed catechism and a dramatised and compressed version of the classic puritan conversion narrative, acted out on the scaffold in a series of call-and-response exchanges between Barker and the attendant ministers.

Barker admitted his adultery with the maid but denied any role in the murder of the child. While this may have served to mitigate his offence in the eyes of the people it certainly did not lead him to harp on his innocence or lament his fate. Rather he presented his current predicament as a just punishment for and merciful visitation upon his former rooted sins of adultery, 'incontinency' and 'uncleanness'. On his own account, Barker's had been a rooted sin from which he had been unable to wean himself.

> Although I preached the truth and against that sin and had many checks of conscience and reproofs by other sermons that I heard yet I lived in it and continued so to do and so I am persuaded I should have done till I had died and so I had been damned for that sin if God had not took this course to break that sin, that master sin, that bosom sin, that abominable sin for that which I now abhor myself.

Barker thus presented his impending execution for a crime of which, he claimed, he was not guilty, as a merciful exercise of God's providence, whereby a just but loving God had prised his servant away from a 'bosom sin', a sin that Barker would otherwise have taken to his grave and that would in turn have consigned Barker himself to hell.

In the conventional puritan theory of conversion the sinner was brought to a sense of his or her own corruption and impotence through the curse of the moral law. Convinced of the sheer impossibility of earning salvation through human obedience to God's will the sinner was forced to rely only on the divine gift of faith in Christ to achieve salvation. In Barker's case it had taken his public disgrace and condemnation to death to bring him to this state and convince him of the falsity and hypocrisy of his past profession of Christianity.

But having been broken by the law, Barker was now in desperate need of the salve of the gospel. He confronted death on the gallows a self-confessed sinner and hypocrite, stripped of his former pretensions to learning, godliness and that aura of power and holiness that attended the godly preaching minister.

> Throw away my self, all my Greek and Latin and learning is nothing. I must go the same way to heaven as the poorest Christian doth, if I should stand upon the same foundation I did before I should certainly be damned . . . I have nothing to trust unto no merit but free mercy which I humbly crave of almighty God.

Only the free grace of God could save him now and for this Barker turned in terror and despair to his fellow ministers and through them to Christ himself.

His gallows performance was studded with expressions of his despair before the magnitude of his own sins, his fear of death and petitions for divine mercy and ministerial intercession and reassurance. At times Barker seemed at his wits' end, searching in vain for a settled assurance of his stake in the mercy and merits of Christ. 'This foundation is but of two day's standing, it is very weak . . . I never had this work of truth but since yesterday.' Turning to the ministers on the gallows he implored their intercession with a God who seemed now to have turned his face against him:

> Oh beg, sirs, beg that God would show me one glimpse of his favour, a little of it, be it never so little; you can prevail with God; all God's people pray for me as for your own souls . . . Hath God forgotten to be gracious? Hath he shut up his tender mercies in displeasures? Will the Lord cast off forever and will he be merciful no more?

In reply the ministers sought to comfort him, steering him away from sheer despair and terror towards a properly fearful and yet assured sense of his stake in the free grace of God and the merits and intercession of Christ. It was, one minister told him, 'better to go to heaven from a gallows than from a down bed to hell'. His end might be shameful but not as shameful as that suffered for him by Christ. In reply to Barker's anguished claim that 'all the mercy in heaven is too little for me', Daniel Cawdray objected that that could not be so:

> 'it is infinite mercy and', said he [Barker], 'so are my sins. Ah, what shall I do, I shall be in hell anon. Ah, what is one drop of Christ's blood worth, what would I not give for it?' 'Why', said Mr Cawdray, 'you may have it for nothing, if you do but thirst, you may have it freely, without money or price. You are stung with your sins, the brazen serpent is set up, it is but looking and you shall be whole.'

Conversely, Thomas Ball explained that God's apparent indifference to his plight represented 'but fatherly chastisements and in the sharpest of them you may read father'.

While Barker might look ultimately to Christ for salvation he looked in the interim to his fellow ministers for consolation and encouragement. 'You have melted my heart', he told them at one point. 'It was like a stone before, before you came to me and now I cannot look upon any of you but it melts my heart.' Anxiously reviewing his chances of salvation, he asked them:

> 'Sirs, I pray you tell me, what what do you think of me?' They said 'we are well satisfied since we see your heart so wounded and broken for sin and you so wholly brought off of your self, and are very well persuaded of you.' 'May I take your words', saith he, they answer 'you may take God's word'. In reply to his hope that 'I might see your faces in heaven', they told him, they hoped he should though he went before them. 'Oh what a merry joyful meeting shall we have in heaven, then,' said they, 'this is a good argument that you are translated from death to life, because you love the brethren and wish their salvation.'

It was therefore through his reintegration into the community of the godly, through the dynamic interaction between the ministers' good opinion of him and his affection for them as both the initiating agents and confirming mirror of his conversion that Barker achieved a more settled sense that he was indeed going to heaven from the gallows. At the last, he was even able, in a breathtaking inversion of his status as a condemned felon and suppliant sinner, to reclaim his role as a minister and role model for the godly, using his own experience as an examplar for any and every poor sinner confronting death and judgement. There could scarcely be a clearer example of the collective nature of puritan piety and identity formation. The godly had reclaimed one of their own and almost literally pushed him up to heaven from the gallows.

Ultimately, however, the proof of this pudding was in the dying and the whole extraordinary performance was legitimated (and other critical, sceptical or derisive readings silenced) by the way Barker died. He embraced his fate, we are told, with equanimity and even joy. 'Oh now blessed be God, I have some peace, now I dare die, now will I hasten to the full fruition of glory which the Lord hath laid up for them that love him.' With that he descended to the ladder's foot, took his leave of the ministers, blessed them and the people and died with the words 'Come Lord Jesus, come quickly, come quickly, come quickly' on his lips.

II   *Puritanism from the inside out*

How would contemporaries have read this remarkable performance? Viewed from inside the puritan view of the world, Barker's dreadful disgrace and good death could be taken to encapsulate and confirm many of the central saving truths of true religion. Here was a tableau in which one could see the danger of hidden, unacknowledged sins, the dreadful consequences of a false and hypocritical profession of religion, the awesome providential punishment handed out by God to sinners, but also the merciful saving power of his free grace.[3] But Barker himself had hinted at another darker and more derisive reading, only too available to those who viewed the scene from outside the puritan position. This chapter attempts to take the inherent polyvalence, the multivocality, of Barker's end and to use it as a point of entry into that process of identity formation and labelling whereby the godly and their enemies looked at each other, and, not liking what they saw, decided what to say and do about it. This is a subject of some significance for it was, in large part, in such charged exchanges that puritanism, name and thing, was born and achieved its multiple meanings and ideological resonances.[4]

Northamptonshire is moreover the perfect locale for such an enquiry. The researches of John Fielding have revealed the county to have been intensely divided in religion. Godly ministers and laity confronted Catholic and crypto-Catholic neighbours and a stridently conformist clerical group who had seized control of the church courts from a remarkably early date. The result was a good deal of religious and social conflict between the godly and their enemies. Issues of conformity raised either by the clerical authorities or autonomously by alienated parishioners, claims of moral laxity and sexual incontinence, were all mobilised against the godly by their enemies. This was a local society in which the scandal of Barker's fall, while spectacular, was hardly unprecedented. When Thomas Sutton, vicar of Islip, was accused of fornication he replied from the pulpit, denouncing his accusers as 'the whore and the whoremaster'. When the case appeared before the church courts Sutton enlisted the help of six local clergymen to 'purge' him of the fame of his 'offence'. Francis Bradley of Towcester was said to have fathered a bastard by a local woman and then maintained the child for nine years with secret payments to the mother. Bradley also arrayed six local ministers to help him deny the charge and his accuser was excommunicated. Barker, of course, did not get off so lightly but the ministers attending him on the scaffold, if they could not attest to his innocence, could at least stand witness to his properly repentant and regenerate spiritual state, testimony clearly intended for a wider audience than that which attended the execution itself. The preceding account of his gallows performance is taken from a manuscript 'separate', designed to disseminate the puritan gloss on Barker's disgrace. The copy used here is from the Isham papers but the paper was clearly circulating quite widely, for a slightly reordered version was printed in 1652 under the typically lurid title *The Arraignment of Hypocrisy or a Looking Glass for Murderers and Adulterers.*[5]

We can eavesdrop a little on this local world of accusation and counter-accusation and trace its effects on puritan religiosity through the sermons of some of the local clergy. Here I want to concentrate on Robert Bolton the vicar of Boughton, until his death in 1631, and of his successor there, Joseph Bentham. Neither man was by any means a firebrand. Both were conformists and both were the protégés and chaplains of the eminently respectable Lord Montagu. Bentham took a moderate stand in relation to Laudian ceremonialism that was by no means typical of Northamptonshire puritanism, and ended up sequestered as a royalist. Their works with which we shall be concerned were all lectures given at the Kettering combination lecture in the 1620s and 1630s.[6] The Kettering lecture, at which Barker himself preached on occasion, took place under the aegis of Lord Montagu and has been identified by Fielding as one of the more moderate puritan exercises in the county. Through these books, therefore, we can listen to the local puritan community talking to itself in precisely the period of Barker's rise and fall.[7]

Here is the larger world view in defence of, and in terms of which, Barker framed his last dying speech. At its centre Bentham (like Barker) placed the divide between the godly and the ungodly, the puritans and the profane. The social world and the militant church were pictured as the stage for, indeed as in some sense constituted and structured by, the struggle between Christ and Satan. 'There have been and while the world stands there will be two sides in the church militant, the seed of the woman and the serpent's, twixt which there is constant enmity . . . And the true church upon earth hath always had and shall always have adversaries and enemies.'[8]

As that passage might be taken to imply, puritans tended to concentrate not so much on the visible church militant as a source of unifying grace and social cohesion as upon the true church of the elect, and its this-worldly concomitant the community of the godly, called into being and self-consciousness in and through the ordinances of the visible church, but in fact in open conflict with unregenerate members of that church and with the forces of the world, the flesh and the Devil that they represented. Thus puritan usage of the term 'the church' tended to slip and slide between these two poles, Bolton writing at one point of 'a mere civil man, or a formal professor at the best, whom the church never discovered or acknowledged to be any of hers' and at another of those who, finding themselves 'in the bosom of the church and civil men', erroneously assumed themselves to be saved.[9] In the first passage the church in question was clearly the invisible church of the elect, perhaps with a secondary reference implied to its embodiment on earth in the community of the godly; while in the second a more conventional reference to the visible church was presumably intended. In the same vein Bentham pointed out that while true professors were 'joined and compacted' to the visible church through visible ties (their 'profession of Christ, his doctrine, participation in the sacraments') they were in fact 'compacted and knit to the Lord Jesus' by other 'internal, invisible and indissoluble . . . ties and ligaments, to wit the band of their eternal election in Christ . . . and the band of the spirit of Christ and so of faith in him'.[10]

The notion of a visible community of the visibly godly, a sort of church within a church, provided both Bolton and Bentham with the focus for their religious style. This 'society of the saints' had ultimately predestinarian roots. It was based, as both men emphasised, on the objective fact of the immutable divine decree.[11] But in practice they both chose more often than not to describe the unity and growth of that community in intensely Christocentric terms. 'Christ was the foundation of foundations . . . of this society', Bentham explained, and he went on to employ a whole series of exaltedly Christocentric images to describe the godly's unity in Christ; the saints were all 'members of one and the self same body', 'all stones of the same building', 'all branches of the same vine', 'children of the same parents' and 'heirs of the same kingdom'.[12] The consistent use of such language was no accident since it was precisely the elect saint's membership of the mystical body of Christ that ensured his or her eventual salvation and provided the master image for that process of collective spiritual interchange and growth that characterised the life of the godly in this world and presaged the joys of the complete unity in Christ that awaited them in the next. 'Being thus incorporated into Christ he [the new convert] presently associates himself to the brotherhood, to the sect that is everywhere spoken against . . . I mean the people of God, professors of the truth and power of religion . . . the most excellent of the earth, the only true noble worthies of the world.' Bolton praised in the most extravagant terms the spiritual joys to be found in the company of the godly. 'Their comfortable fellowship in the gospel and mutual intercourse of godly conference, heavenly counsel, spiritual encouragement, consideration one of another, confirmation in grace and well grounded rectification of meeting together in heaven' were enough, he claimed, to convince the participants that 'they had the one foot in the porch of paradise already'.[13]

But just how visible was this community to be? Clearly, viewed from the inside out the godly were supposed to know who they were. Their inherently active faith in Christ, their consequently burgeoning sense of assurance of their own salvation, the mutual bonds of charity, love, admonition and advice that bound them one to another, all told them who they were.[14] But this was an identity confirmed from the outside as well by the natural hostility felt towards the godly by all those who were not members of the society of the saints. Here, therefore, was the basic polarity, the binary opposition, around which Bolton and Bentham arranged their view of the world.

The name puritan owed its origin to this antipathy. In Bentham, Bolton and Barker's lexicon it was an insult, but it was an insult that they were proud to own. Much like Barker, Bentham defined 'puritans' as 'practising Protestants; such men who daily read the scriptures, pray with their families, teach them the way to heaven, eschew lying, swearing, usury, oppression, time selling, defrauding and all known sins' and 'spend the Lord's day holily in hearing God's word, prayer, meditation, conference, singing of psalms, meditation of the creatures' and 'are merciful to the poor, diligent in their particular callings, frame their lives according to God's will revealed in his word etc.' Bolton agreed; the godly were to be distinguished from their fellows primarily through their 'reverent love and insatiable longing after the word preached and read, prayer, singing of psalms, meditation, conferences, vows, days of humiliation, use of good books, godly company, all God's ordinances and good means appointed and sanctified for our spiritual good'. It was the godly who kept the cause of true religion alive. These 'few neglected ones which truly serve God are the only men in all places where they live to make up the hedge and to stand in the gap against the threatened inundations of God's dreadful wrath'.[15]

Here were puritans, then, defined as the saints, 'true good fellows', a group of Christians marked out from their contemporaries by a round of religious observances and forms of ethical rigorism that transcended a merely formal attendance at the public congregation and the discharge of day-to-day social duty. But while such beliefs and practices might be distinctive, they were not, in Bentham's view, singular or divisive. Indeed, he went out of his way to emphasise that puritan values and practices worked with rather than against the grain of social and ecclesiastical order as it was conventionally conceived. Thus both Bolton and Bentham discussed the ethical values of the godly under the rubric of moderation. Bolton advocated 'moderation and conscionableness in getting' and Bentham waxed lyrical on the value of moderation in getting, spending, eating and dressing. This was the way to avoid sin and the judgements of sin 'as diseases of the body, beggary, infamy, security, sensuality, curse and condemnation'.[16] This was scarcely a radical social agenda but rather an appropriation of a set of ethical norms to which virtually all contemporaries would, in theory at least, have subscribed.

On the religious front Bentham emphasised that the central forms of puritan religion were similarly consensual, reflecting and strengthening rather than challenging or undermining the values of the national church and its leaders. Take, for instance, his discussion of sabbath observance. Of course by the 1630s this was becoming once again a rather controversial issue, but in his book of 1630 (which predated the reissue of the Book of Sports by three years) Bentham was able, by quoting the homilies, the sabbatarian statute of 1625 and the works of Bishop Babington, to claim that the church of England was a sabbatarian church.[17] Again, in his discussion of the role of fasting in heightening the godly self-consciousness of true professors, winning God's favour or averting or removing God's judgements from the land, he was able to cite national fasts decreed in the 1620s to aid the war effort or to avert the plague in order to show how the agenda and practices of the godly were in fact coterminous with those of the national church, the Christian prince and the parliament.[18]

These approving references to the exercise of public authority were followed by a warning to private men not to presume to call public fasts – that was a job for the magistrate – and a call on the godly to limit their fasting activities to their own individual households. While fasts called by the magistrate were, of course, compulsory and general, Bentham held that the fasts of the godly should be entirely voluntary (that is limited to the members of individual households, who of course were under the authority of a single *paterfamilias*) and intensely private, held behind closed doors, shunning the public display of piety and zeal that was a sure sign of pharisaical pride. And yet Bentham's proscriptions on this subject both fed off and in some sense invaded or took over the public exercises of the national church, as his concluding paragraph on the subject shows. 'Private persons' who either 'for their private or the public good' wanted to hold a fast should

> select and set apart such days which our church not only approves of but also appoints for the reading of the word and prayer: to which enjoined excellent exercises many preachers of good note do join exposition of some part of the scriptures, for by these

public ordinances they shall be much furthered and made more fervent and fertile in their intended service.[19]

Here, therefore, is a picture of the public observances of the national church being supplemented and subtly transformed by the godly, whose fasts, called privately but for public as well as private ends, and whose lectures, attached to the holy days of the church, remained formally voluntary and 'private' but in fact served to appropriate those holy days for their own distinctively zealous purposes. It was a vision reflected, too, in Bolton's thoroughly undifferentiated list of the public ordinances and private practices in and through which the godly lived their spiritual lives.

Bentham was similarly moderate and accommodating on the issue of conformity. 'In public assemblies and in the congregation' bodily worship was 'always needful', Bentham argued, and Christian professors should 'pray in public with unanimous uniformity in regard of our outward carriage and gesture, keeping, using and observing public gestures prescribed and practised as commendable and warrantable by our church, not breaking the bounds of comeliness and order'.[20] Here then is a very Collinsonian image of puritanism as a form of voluntary religion and ethical rigorism operating on the personal and interpersonal, the domestic and household levels, to supplement and extend rather than undermine or contest the norms and forms of the national church and the wider society.[21] Thus if the godly were 'singular', and Bolton admitted that they were, their 'singularity' resided not 'in respect of any fantasticalness of opinion, furiousness of zeal or turbulency of faction, truly so called, but in respect of abstinence from sin, purity of heart and holiness of life'.[22] In other words the godly were prodigious and peculiar only in their godliness. And yet all this was described without embarrassment by Barker, Bentham and Bolton as distinctively puritan and linked to what was an extraordinarily polarised view of the social world.

III   *The godly watch the ungodly hate the godly*

They were able to do this because the cause of any 'disorder' or disagreement that might attend puritan behaviour stemmed not from the godly or their values but from the hostile response to those values on the part of the ungodly. Bolton and Bentham externalised or evacuated the polarising, divisive and immoderate aspects of puritan religion, and projected them instead onto the ungodly, thus creating an image of 'the other' against which the godly could define themselves as paragons of peace, order and obedience.

For both men the enmity felt by the ungodly for the godly was natural and inevitable. It was built into the structure of post-lapsarian reality, based on a central ontological difference between the two groups who were as different as chalk and cheese. 'Can there be greater antipathy than betwixt God's saints and Satan's slaves? God's darlings and Satan's dross?' Bentham asked. It was true that both groups were drawn from the same sinful lump yet they were 'not cast in the same mould; some are vessels of honour, some of dishonour. Are there not contrary natures in them; grace working in one and sin in another ... Are there not contrary masters guiding and governing them, God in the good, Satan in the wicked?'[23] Bolton too described the differences between the two groups as visceral, basic, rooted in inherent differences of instinct and affinity. Just as the two groups were naturally drawn to their own kind, they were just as naturally repelled by each other. 'As the worldling cannot relish the sweet joys of gracious exercises, so neither can the Christian the frothy pleasures of good fellowship. You can as hardly draw the sound professor to a conventicle of swaggering companions as a good fellow to a day of humiliation.'[24] For Bolton and Bentham, it was axiomatic that those who hated and defamed the godly could not themselves be true professors. If the godly were 'the Lord's jewels' 'the apples of God's own eye', 'the Lord's own temples', then it followed with an inevitable logic that their enemies must be God's enemies, 'a serpentine brood', 'men of Belial'.[25]

The result of this inevitable cleavage in the social world was a stream of bile and vitriol directed steadily from the ungodly towards the godly. 'All earthly minded men', claimed Bolton, 'howsoever they may be outwardly restrained and reserved are secret deriders of the power of godliness, holy strictness of saints and mysteries of grace.'[26] To 'the men of Belial', Bentham explained, the practices of the godly would always appear as 'too unnecessary preciseness' and 'matter of unwarranted singularity'. He lamented the inevitability of the 'quipping taunts, scornful reproaches, slanderous backbitings, insolent mocking and flouting nicknames' deployed by the ungodly against the godly.[27] According to Bolton it was ever the lot of the saints to be 'trod upon with the feet of imperious contempt', to be treated as 'despised underlings whereas indeed they are God's jewels and the only excellent upon earth'. Bolton pictured the profane in their 'merry meetings and cursed conventicles', 'foaming out against God's chiefest favourites the foulest censures; that they are hypocrites, humorists, factionists, traitors, pestilent fellows and all that naught is'.[28] To the ungodly, Bentham explained, the godly were 'saints on Sunday, devils all the week after. Saint-seeming, bible-bearing, hypocritical puritans'. It was a commonplace amongst the profane that those they called 'scripture men, bible bearers, sermon haunters etc. are all notorious hypocrites and vile dissemblers'. The godly were 'proud, covetous, hypocritical, deceitful'. Such, at least, was the world's verdict.[29]

Their enemies dwelt lovingly on the perceived peccadilloes and lapses of the godly. 'If ever any heir of heaven' commit 'any notorious evil . . . he is sure to have . . . such exaggerating trumpeters and swift dromedaries of ale bench haunters.' The initial moral lapse may have been never so small but 'by their tossing and tumbling it amidst their drunken consorts and by their additions, forged in hell and hammered in their devilish hearts, it shall be made intolerable.' Then, having been exaggerated out of all proportion, the offence would be attributed to the godly as a whole to confirm the popular opinion 'that all these professors and puritans are stark nought. None so cruel, none so unconscionable as they'.[30]

If this failed and they could find no offences foul enough for their purposes amongst the godly, Bolton and Bentham explained that the ungodly would simply relabel the admirable traits of the godly as vices. Hence came their reputation for a hypocritical covetousness which was based on nothing more than their being 'so painful and laborious in their several callings', a trait prompted not by their love of money but by their desire to obey God and avoid idleness. The godly, who eschewed conspicuous consumption on 'new fangled attire or in good fellow meetings' the better to provide for their families and avoid profanity, also refused to give 'ostentatiously' and 'pharisaically' to every beggar who stopped them on the street. All these were admirable qualities but the profane persisted in presenting them as vices, thus revealing their presumptuous willingness to 'take upon you God's royal prerogative to enter into the secrets of men's hearts in accusing them of hypocrisy, covetousness and such like'.[31]

We know from a host of other sources that precisely such charges were levelled against the godly. Accusations of hypocrisy, self-righteousness, divisiveness, greed and lasciviousness were the common coin of anti-puritan insult. Such stereotyping achieved its most famous and funniest expression in certain literary texts, but more demotic versions of the same sort of charges can be found in altogether humbler and more obviously popular textual and social locales, in court cases, popular libels and poems. In 1606 members of the puritan clique in Dorchester were assailed in two anonymous libels distributed in the street as covetous, self-serving and lascivious hypocrites. Almost identical accusations were voiced against similar cliques in Stratford on Avon in 1619 and in Nottingham in 1617. In Northamptonshire in the aftermath of the Midlands rising of 1607 a number of JPs, Sir Edward Montagu amongst them, were libelled as puritans, and in Warwickshire Sir John Newdigate received an anonymous letter deriding his pretensions to godliness and harping on his hypocritical covetousness as an enclosing landlord. The 1628 parliament (led, in this instance at least, by the puritan John Pym) hauled a Mr Burgess, minister of Witney in Oxfordshire, over the coals for a series of diatribes against puritan hypocrisy, lasciviousness, greed, and divisive self-regard.[32] It seems, therefore, unlikely that we are dealing here with some sort of socio-cultural trickle-down whereby anti-puritan motifs and stereotypes were diffused from the plays and cheap print of the metropolis into the provinces, but rather with the stuff of local cultural and personal conflict. Here pompous, self-serving and self-important ministers, mayors, and magistrates were guyed for commonplace sins and peccadilloes: for greed, lust and pride, faults which in less self-consciously godly or overbearing persons might not have occasioned such sharp or derisive comment.

For the more exalted the moral and spiritual claims made by the godly, the more damaging even their minor moral lapses, petty vanities, pleasures and meannesses became. Hence, Bolton claimed, came the stress on puritan covetousness, and hypocrisy and (although interestingly enough, not in Bolton and Bentham's lectures) lasciviousness which were such central themes in the anti-puritan satires and libels of the day. As Bolton explained, covetousness and hypocrisy, perhaps more than any other sins, lay in the eye of the beholder. One man's meanness was another's prudence and sobriety, and puritan claims to an exalted sanctity could be easily undercut by examples of a common or garden attachment to the things of this world that in others might pass unremarked. Thus Bolton pictured the ungodly 'nibbling' at the good name of the godly 'with some such speeches as these: well, well though he be an excellent pulpit man or a forward professor yet . . . is not he as well given unto, and greedy of, the world as other men'. As Bolton protested such claims were *ipso facto* unfalsifiable.

> How is it possible or by what outward witnesses or compurgators may the Christian clear and discharge himself of the imputations of worldliness and hypocrisy, sith [since] the one lies in the greedy affections of the mind and the other lurks in the hidden corners of the heart.[33]

Bolton quoted Richard Greenham to the effect that, while the world would praise an ordinary civil professor for any isolated virtue while passing over his less than perfect behaviour in other spheres, it was precisely the opposite for puritans; be their general conversation never so godly, one lapse was enough to win them the opprobrium of the world. One might go further and observe that it is the fate of the bearers of any totalising ideology that deals in moral absolutes, as Christianity notoriously does, to condemn themselves, in their own eyes (and in those of at least some of their more jaundiced contemporaries) as in some sense moral failures and therefore, given their public stance *vis-à-vis* the public values of their faith, as hypocrites. We should view this sort of anti-puritan stereotyping as a structurally or logically necessary concomitant of, or response to, the sorts of Christian rigorism and ethical one-upmanship practised by the godly. Alienating their neighbours by their aggressively holier-than-thou self-image and rhetoric, the godly's pretensions to godliness and infractions of the norms of good neighbourhood and good fellowship positively invited the sort of inversionary libels and satires, the accusations of self-serving hypocrisy and faction described above.[34]

This situation was compounded for puritans by certain central characteristics of their own religious style. For the personal and interpersonal spiritual core of puritanism turned on the ability of the godly to see themselves as true believers, real saints. Much therefore was riding on their capacity to achieve a settled sense of their elect status, an assurance of their own salvation, through the observation of the workings of a saving faith and the holy spirit in their souls and outward conversation. In this search the capacity to tell the difference between a real and a temporary faith, a true and a hypocritical profession, was at a premium. It was doubly so since puritan piety oscillated violently between the inward and the outward, the objective and the subjective, the personal and the social. Faith without works was a dead faith but to rely on outward works was in itself deadly. Grace was ever active and sanctification a process which could and must lead to greater and greater levels of spiritual purity and godly works. Yet too great an obsession with such things led either to a pharisaical pride in mere externals, a potentially carnal security and self-satisfaction, on the one hand; or, on the other, to a desperate sense of the inadequacy, before the enormity of human sin and the majesty of divine justice, of one's own poor efforts towards salvation.[35]

Such themes were not only central to puritan divinity and piety in general, they echoed throughout the works under consideration here. Bolton's lectures in particular oscillated consistently between the internal spiritual dimensions of true faith and the outward forms that alone distinguished a true faith from a false or temporary one. His lectures were riven with warnings against pride and formality on the one hand, and a needless scrupulosity, self-criticism and desperation on the other. If it was possible to look inside the soul and see the operations of a saving faith, for Bolton too great a reliance on feeling and experience led to desperation and doubt. It was one thing to feel grace and quite another to possess it. Assurance of salvation was good, but an assurance untempered by doubt was false and the mark of a pharisaical hypocrite.[36]

Issues of formality, hypocrisy, pride and security were therefore central to the processes whereby puritans forged their image of themselves. It should come as no surprise, therefore, to find precisely those same issues at the centre of the puritan image of the ungodly and the anti-puritan. Bolton located the accusations of hypocrisy and sinfulness lodged by the ungodly against the godly in the latter's resentment of the minister's message and the saint's example. These consigned the ungodly to hell unless they mended their ways and they externalised their own anger and lurking sense of sin in a stream of accusations directed against the godly. 'It is a point of their hypocritical policy, cunningly and confidently to impute those sins unto others which are grossly predominant in themselves', claimed Bolton. Thus they hoped 'to procure some temporary ease to their hearts, against the checks and bitings of their guilty consciences'. If they could persuade themselves and others that the godly were in reality as sinful as they, there was no need for them to look to their own spiritual condition.[37] But if (as Bolton suggested) the profane externalised and expressed their own fears, anxieties and antipathies, and projected their own negative characteristics onto the godly, we can surely see the puritans doing the same thing themselves; projecting their own faults and foibles onto the ungodly and then invoking the resultant image of their enemies for precisely the same purposes of self-definition and defence.

For in the puritan view it was the ungodly who were the hypocrites and Pharisees who, placing all their spiritual eggs in the basket of external observance, divided the Christian community by attacking the godly. Of course that was not the view of themselves presented by the ungodly. In their own eyes they were the epitome of good fellowship and sociability, maintaining peace and good cheer in the face of the excessive austerity and hypocritical meanness of the godly.[38] 'They are men of good meaning,' Bentham ventriloquised:

> although they are not bookish they have a sure belief in God; they love God above all and their neighbour as themselves; God they hope did not make them to damn them; all men are sinners as well as themselves. They hope to be saved before or as soon as the strictest saint-seeming puritans of them.

Bolton imagined the reply of a mere civil honest man to the strenuous ministry of a puritan preacher, newly arrived on the scene:

> What tell you me of these high points or trouble me with this new learning? I was never asked thus much before in all my life, and yet the time is to come that ever our parson threatened to keep me from the communion. I do no man wrong; I pay every man his due: I am neither thief, nor drunkard, nor whoremaster: I live peaceably amongst my neighbours: I know as much as the preacher can teach me, though he preach out his heart: that I must love God above all and my neighbour as myself and that I hope I do.[39]

For both Bolton and Bentham, these were patently hypocritical and worryingly heterodox (because potentially pelagian or popish) claims, which in fact revealed that it was these men and not 'those who are called puritans by worldlings because they will not be profane' who were the real hypocrites. These were the 'unsanctified persons', the 'lewd companions', the 'civil honest men', the 'proud Pharisees' who defamed the godly for covetousness, but themselves 'seldom give except vaingloriously to some clamorous beggars, seldom or never pray in secret or in their families, only in public to be seen by men' and 'who by consequence avouch themselves to keep the law of God perfectly, for although they are sinners, as they say, yet they have kept the 1, 2, 3, 4 commandment etc.' They could believe this because when they looked at the moral law they saw only 'the gross acts' and 'the greatest transgressions' proscribed there and being themselves free from such dreadful sins concluded that since they were 'no image worshippers, no murderers, no adulterers' they had kept God's law and would therefore be saved. This of course was a grave mistake and showed that they had no true understanding of the nature of sin or the mystery of godliness. It was, therefore, the godly's enemies who were the true hypocrites and Pharisees, lodging their religion in mere outward forms and professions, habitually sinning and yet hoping to win salvation through their own puny efforts to keep the moral law and their equally empty attempts at death-bed repentance.[40]

Having thus constructed an image of the ungodly as pharisaical, hypocritical, proud and divisive, puritans could then invoke the hostility of the ungodly as a means to drive themselves away from some of their most characteristic faults and foibles. The godly, Bolton explained, were prone to be 'too austere, censorious, sour and imperious in their carriage towards those which are without'. They tended to place all *their* spiritual eggs into the basket of external forms; 'holding strict points, defending precise opinions, contesting against the corruptions of the times, [and], in the work wrought, external forms of religious exercises, set tasks of hearing, reading, conference and the like, in some solemn outward extraordinary abstinences and forebearances, censoring others.'[41] And they had a distressing propensity to carp competitively at one another's spiritual gifts, continually hunting after 'an opinion of precedency in graces and zeal by the disgrace of another'. All these vices were, of course, but the obverse side of some of the defining virtues of the godly, which elsewhere Bolton and Bentham pressed urgently upon their audiences. Thus they insisted on the saints' duty to advise, reprove and admonish one another and to take an even more negatively censorious attitude to the sins of the profane, a group which, with the godly, they more often than not defined in terms of their relationship to a series of external forms, observances and behaviours. But taken to excess not only was such behaviour a hallmark of 'vainglorious Pharisees', it played into the hands of the ungodly, giving them every encouragement and more material to use in their campaign to blackguard true religion and true professors.[42] Thus Bolton sought to use the 'raging and railing enemies of God's people' 'as scullions to scour the Lord's vessels of honour', constantly reminding the godly, through their accusations and hostility, of their own worst impulses and characteristics, their former sins and current lapses, and in so doing helping the true professor 'to a strict enquiry into his heart and life' and a consequent programme of repentance and reform.[43]

We can see, therefore, just how closely related the self-image of the godly was to their image of the ungodly. Here was a group onto whom the puritans could project many of the unwanted social, political and ideological consequences of their own position. Having distanced themselves from those tendencies, the godly could use the objective existence of the ungodly and their rooted hostility to the saints as a confirmation and prop for their own image of themselves. Most obviously since, as Bolton observed, the obloquy of the mob was ever the lot of the saints, the very enmity of the ungodly served to confirm that the godly were indeed elect saints, God's peculiar people. By accepting the term puritan as a description of forms of behaviour and belief that Bolton and Bentham both thought did indeed mark off true professors from real hypocrites and worldlings, both men gloried in it. Bolton told his auditory that 'scurrilities and scoffs, all spiteful speeches, odious trick names, lying imputations cast upon thee in this kind by tongues which cut like a sharp razor are in their due estimate and true account as so many honourable badges.'[44]

Secondly, having projected many of their own least likable characteristics and deviant tendencies onto the ungodly, the resulting image of their enemies could be invoked as an incentive to control and repress those same tendencies in themselves lest they give encouragement or polemical advantage to the ungodly in their unremitting campaign against true religion. The ungodly then were the *alter egos*, the evil twins, of the godly, through whom they could rid themselves of some of their least wanted characteristics and faults, and against whom they could define themselves as godly indeed, elect saints, God's peculiar people, an identity guaranteed by, indeed in some fundamental sense dependent upon, the image of the ungodly as their opposite.

Both puritan and anti-puritan identities were in this view integrally, indeed dialectically linked, the one implied, indeed needed and in part created, the other; and they were derived, not from the plays of Ben Jonson or the Marprelate controversy, but from myriad sets of local disputes and cultural clashes, and indeed from the very psychic struggles of the godly themselves. The origins of these very powerful negative and positive images were therefore neither merely literary, nor purely social; nor were they the simple projection outward of the atomised psychological stress of the godly. Rather all three of these causal levels were in play in the production of the identity of the godly and the image of the ungodly that went with it. By reading Barker's scaffold performance in the context of Bolton and Bentham's lectures and by setting both in the very polarised local context so brilliantly described by John Fielding, we can watch this process of identity formation at a crucial stage in the history of the English church.

IV   *The godly watch themselves hate the profane*

So much then for the puritans' account of the profane and their view of the godly, but how did this vision of the ungodly shape in turn the self-image of the godly? Put more crudely, given that the profane hated them, what were the godly, as true Christian professors, to do about it?

For both Bolton and Bentham the enemies of the godly were a polluting presence in the social world and Bentham stressed that the saints should not keep society with them any farther than was necessary. 'As it is altogether impossible for these to walk together, so is it extreme perilous to be sociable with wicked men, their society being dangerous and infectious'.[45] On this basis the godly should strictly monitor and regulate their contact with the ungodly. Here Bolton drew a crucial distinction between 'common' and 'special, dear, intimate' company with the profane. In a fallen world, he conceded, the former – involving 'bargaining, buying, selling, saluting, eating and drinking together', all the general 'intercourse of civil society' – was inevitable for even the godliest professor 'unless he will go out of the world'.[46] It was, therefore, lawful for the saints to be in 'company and conversant with the wicked . . . when they are of the same family, as parents and children, husbands and wives, masters and servants' or again when 'by plantation and cohabitation they be of the same particular church and congregation'. Again, when such social proximity was not desired or sought out by the godly, but either 'offered in courtesy . . . or enforced by authority, as in civil services, commissions, [as]sizes, sessions, imprisonments', contact was allowable. When a godly person met with a wicked person by accident on the road or at a market feast a minimum of social interaction was permissible. These, though, were enforced contacts, brought about by circumstances and often underwritten by divine precepts that, for instance, bound good subjects to bad princes or good wives to evil husbands or more generally godly persons to the exercise of certain social duties. But even 'voluntary' contact with the wicked was not completely off limits, if it was undertaken with the 'corrigible', in a desire 'to win him' to true religion. The godly person should, however, be careful not to enter into company with the ungodly ostensibly for their spiritual good but in reality to enjoy 'the unwarrantable delights of good fellowship', the 'pleasant passages of wit, idle and impertinent follies and familiarities which thou wast accustomed to exchange and enjoy with them in thy unregenerate time'. For here real danger lay. 'It is the voluntary society with the incorrigible sinner that is so sinful . . . and so dangerous . . . Namely if it be causeless, careless, comfortable and continual.'[47]

The godly, therefore, should order their social lives to minimise their contact with the ungodly. Godly masters should seek out and employ godly servants. Such, Bentham admitted, were hard to find, but that did not excuse the promiscuous employment of the ungodly and the profane.[48] Similarly, both Bolton and Bentham implied that the godly should concentrate their charitable donations and almsgiving on godly recipients. There was a duty to give to the poor in general, both conceded, and yet it was to 'our fellow members of Christ's body' that they should primarily give. It was 'the poor saints' who 'have right to our substance'. Both Bolton and Bentham praised those puritans who after 'mature deliberation' decided to use their limited resources discreetly to succour the godly rather than 'vaingloriously' casting 'away their right to every swinish beast, clamorous beggar and unworthy one'.[49] This was the preferred mode of giving of formal, pharisaical professors who, having amassed vast wealth through ungodly means, spent lavishly on hospitality and dole for the poor. They did so partly in the mistaken belief that their former sins could be bought off or compensated for by these charitable acts, and partly in the hope that by such ostentatious public giving they might gain a reputation in the world for charity. The godly, on the other hand, gave discreetly to poor Christians motivated by zeal towards the household of faith, not a desire for reputation in the world.[50] The result, Bentham claimed, was that 'over a whole country' there was scarcely anyone 'whom the world calls puritans so forsaken of God as to beg his bread' since nearly always the Lord stirred up 'some good Obadiahs to relieve them in secret'. The puritans, it would seem, at least claimed to look after their own.[51]

Indeed, Bentham doubted whether the godly should even pray for the wicked. Since, he observed:

> the desperate living [were] capable of some earthly corporal temporal favours, but of no heavenly, spiritual or eternal grace, we may not pray for any such in their behalf, but only for those others whereof they are capable: thus Moses for Pharoah, the prophet for Jeroboam, 1 King 13. 6. Moses was so far from praying for that he prayed against the cursed conspirators, Numb. 16. 15. The Lord forbids Samuel to mourn for Saul, I Sam. 16. 1. David prays against the wicked, Psal. 5. 10, 59. 5, and St John telleth us there are sinners for whom we should not pray.

At this point the elision between the 'society of saints' – or godly community as Bentham described it – and the elect members of Christ's mystical body, the church, seems to be complete, as does the equally direct identification of their enemies with Satan's brood, the reprobate. But here even Bentham was forced to draw back from the consequences of his own rhetoric, reminding himself and his readers that it was 'God's prerogative to know who are his, 2 Tim. 2. 19, and although they do oppose, God may give them repentance to the acknowledging of truth and to recover themselves etc.' For this reason, we ought to 'take heed that we pray not against, no not wicked men'. The godly could, of course, pray against 'the cause of wicked men', 'against the plots of private enemies', 'against the whole body of Satan' in general and even 'against some notorious members of Satan'. This last practice was allowable only if the objects of the godly's prayers were known to be incurable, the prayers were prompted by a concern for God's glory and the spiritual welfare of his children rather than by the pursuit of some private revenge, and if the petitions themselves were conditional. The godly should petition God, Bolton explained, as follows:

> if they [the persecutors in question] belong unto him, to humble them in their places and give them repentance but if he purpose to give them over finally to a reprobate mind . . . to cut them off and utterly confound them, that they be no longer a burden to the church and vexation to his people.

The position appears even more stark when we recall that the 'prayers of the saints poured out in the bitterness of their souls' were for Bolton 'means many times to bring persecutors to an untimely end'. The category of persecutor was in this context a wide one, including even those who insulted or 'look sour upon or browbeat a servant of Christ'. The consequent 'downfall of every raging incurable opposite' brought 'much glorious joy and heartiest songs of thanksgiving' to 'all good men and friends of the gospel' since thereby 'God's justice is glorified, his church delivered, Satan's kingdom weakened'.[52]

Of course, both Bolton and Bentham acknowledged that true professors had a duty to increase the size of the godly community, 'to conglutinate', as Bentham put it, 'others into this sweet society'. In pursuit of that aim both men envisaged the godly 'correcting our brethren', 'enlightening them with our knowledge, imparting God's graces to them and working grace in them'. Such a process presumably involved some spiritual trafficking with the profane and at times both Bolton and Bentham admitted that the ungodly were not all equally far gone in sin. Indeed, in one of his more charitable moments Bentham conceded that not all the critics of the godly were 'common drunkards, whoremongers, swearers' who died 'impenitent persons and are damned'. To assume that they were was 'false and uncharitable'. Here Bentham made a crucial distinction. The true professor, he explained, should always attempt to distinguish between the sin and the sinner. 'To hate the sin and love the person is a charitable Christian hatred; we ought to hate knowingly, loving the person, loathing his evil properties.' Such a distinction allowed the godly person to show 'such tokens of love to a son of Belial which may be beneficial unto him and not hurtful to thyself; advising, counselling, admonishing, reproving, correcting, relieving him in his distress and praying for his amendment', without joining 'with him in intimate fellowship' and thus commending 'him in his lewd conversation'.[53]

For all, therefore, that both Bolton and Bentham's thought normally organised itself around the binary opposition between the godly and the profane, the demands of a residual Christian charity, a certain Calvinist reluctance to decide finally on the identity of the sheep and the goats, together with the exigencies of ordinary social life, ensured that the godly must associate with the non-godly. In order to do that while yet avoiding the sort of polluting contacts with the wicked that both men proscribed, they had to be able to distinguish between different sorts of profane person. To facilitate that process, Bolton and Bentham provided a whole series of divisions and distinctions between the corrigible and the incorrigible, between the curable and the incurable, between the most overt and lewd sinners, 'Satan's revellers', and 'lukewarm or Laodicean Christians'. However uncompromising it might sound in theory, Bolton and Bentham's lexicon remained flexible enough to allow the godly, in practice, to avoid the sort of overt separation and systematic social shunning that would have rendered their daily lives impossible.

We can gain some sense of how this worked in practice from John Fielding's analysis of the diary of Robert Woodford, the puritan steward of Northampton. On his own account, Woodford did not consistently manage to avoid the company of the ungodly or the heterodox, or to resist the temptations of the ale-house and the loose company to be found there. Instead, he monitored his conduct and reproached himself for his lapses later, a practice foreshadowed in fact in Bolton's lectures.[54] For Bolton was well aware that the godly would inevitably sometimes fall into the sort of company where men will 'swear, blaspheme God's name, talk filthily, slander the ministry, rail against good men'. This put the true professor into a quandary; 'he dares not many times in such company for his heart hold his peace', and yet silence was so much the safest and most comfortable option. Accordingly, Bolton admitted that very often 'the omission of the discharge of this duty will sometimes very much vex the conscience and grieve the heart of the true-hearted professor when he is departed the place and considers that by his baseness and frailty he hath . . . been faint-hearted in the cause of God.' Bolton then proceeded to produce an elaborate casuistry on this subject. The duty to speak out had to be balanced against the scriptural injunction not to cast the spiritual pearls of true religion before swine. If the people in question were so sunk in sin as to count as such swine, then silence was allowable. It was, however, difficult to generalise or always to be sure whether one was dealing with genuine swine or not. Invariably to speak out in sharp rebuke smacked of that 'stoical sourness and commanding surliness' – that 'formal affectation of pharisaical severity' – of which the godly were always being accused by the ungodly. On the other hand, never to speak up smacked of cowardice 'in good causes' and treachery 'to the state of Christianity'.[55]

Thus, even if the actual shunning of the profane and the division of the social world undertaken by the godly took place as much in their own heads as it did in the open arena of social interaction, that did not render the basic oppositions that underpinned their practice any the less stark. Indeed Bolton and Bentham, rather than using these fine distinctions to soften the boundary between the godly and the rest, put considerable effort into assimilating the lukewarm Christian and the merely civil honest man into the more overtly sinful enemies of the gospel. If 'civil honest men', 'lukewarm Christians' and 'Laodicean gospellers' persisted in defaming the godly and in standing by when 'our glorious God and his divine truth' were blasphemed, then Bentham took them to be giving a very strong hint as to their real spiritual status.[56] Bolton went even further, arguing that 'God's children' were not, in practice, in much danger from 'notorious sinners' – after all 'who in his right wits will run upon a man which he clearly sees hath the plague sore running upon him?' The real threat came from

> merely civil men . . . who being more tolerable and plausible companions and yet disacquainted with the great mystery of godliness, unseasoned with the power of inward sanctification and unpractised in the ways of sincerity, do, secretly and insensibly, infuse, if not a notorious infection with some scandalous sin, yet many times a fearful defection of zeal, forwardness and fervency in the ways and services of God.

In the same spirit, Bolton claimed that when the godly heard a 'mere civil man or a formal professor at the best . . . commended for his religion, forwardness and the fear of God', they, knowing that he was 'utterly unacquainted with the mystery of godliness, family exercises, sanctification of the sabbaths, contributions to the saints, exercises of mortification, self-denial', owed it to the cause of true religion to denounce him, 'lest both the by-standers be heartened to come short of heaven and the power of Christianity be disparaged'.[57]

Bolton, in fact, was peculiarly severe on what he termed 'mere civil honesty' and habitually ran together 'lukewarmness, coldness in religion and good fellowship' as linked enemies to true religion. Too many Christians

> make moderation in religion a saint and undo their souls by adoring discretion as an idol. Moderation and discretion, truly so called and rightly defined by the rules of God, are blessed and beautifying ornaments of the best and most zealous Christians but being tempered with their coldness and edged with their eagerness against forwardness . . . become the very desperate cut throats to the power of godliness.

Many men take 'civil honesty', 'add a formal profession' and already in their own conceit they 'knock and bounce, as it were, at the gates of heaven for entrance'. This was a sad mistake for 'mere civil honesty never brought any into heaven and every lukewarm professor shall certainly be spewed out of the mouth of Christ'. Categories which, as Eamonn Duffy has shown, could in other hands be used to soften the impact of the master division between the godly and the profane were used for the most part to precisely opposite effect in these lectures by Bolton and Bentham.[58]

We can see this tendency even in Bentham's discussion of the spiritual transactions through which the godly community was to grow in size and purity. This was included in a section exclusively concerned with relations between the godly in which Bentham claimed that the processes of spiritual exchange whereby 'graces must be communicated' would inevitably appear ludicrous to 'the men of Belial'. Indeed, Bentham insisted that the affairs of the godly should in certain circumstances be kept a secret from the profane, whom, as we have seen with Bolton, he conceived as waiting to pounce on and recount with glee any moral failing committed by one of the saints. This led Bentham to the remarkable argument that the saints owed it to the cause of the gospel systematically to conceal their faults from the prying eyes of the ungodly, lest they be used to bring the whole profession of true religion into disrepute. 'The aberrations of your fellows', Bentham explained, 'should be hidden from the censorious eye of every worldling.' Citing Solomon and St Peter, he argued that ' "love covereth the multitude of sins" ' or, in other words, 'doth conceal, keep close or secret and doth not tell abroad the sins of the brethren'.[59]

At first sight this appears to be a veritable hypocrite's charter, but Bentham was able to resist this view of the matter because of what he took to be the basic ontological difference between the godly and the ungodly. As children of God, the godly had a completely different relationship to their sins than the profane. The latter made 'a trade of sinning, suffering it to reign and rage in them'. In so far as they shunned sin they did so for show. When they fell into sin they did not properly repent. The wicked man winked at his own petty sins, 'makes of mountains molehills, makes no scruple of petty oaths, . . . wanton dalliance, merry and officious lies, hurtful jests etc. Yea he is so ready not only to extenuate but to plead that they are small.'[60]

The godly, on the other hand, could not have been more different. They cared about the smallest sins, understanding that with respect to the party offended – God – there was no such thing as a small sin and that, given the 'insinuating, spreading and encroaching nature of sin', even the smallest lapse could be the first step on a slippery slope to depravity and damnation. Moreover, when they sinned they did not enjoy it, but loathed both their sinful act and the impulses that had produced it, using each lapse as the occasion for a renewed and more complete repentance. The godly man, claimed Bentham, 'beggeth pardon for his iniquity . . . he loathes his sin now more than ever . . . he becomes more nobly resolute against sin and its devilish occasions than he was before, so raising himself by true repentance.'

'Is there not great difference', asked Bentham quoting John Yates, 'betwixt touching sin and tumbling in it? Sipping of it and swallowing it up? Twixt sudden fallings into sin and carelessly lying in it?'[61] For Bentham that difference was obvious, confirmed daily by both the objective fact of the double decree – with the other orthodox Calvinists of the day Bolton and Bentham both held that elect saints *could not* fall totally or finally from grace – and the subjective experience of the godly. It was his certainty on this issue that enabled

Bentham to be so sure of the difference between hiding the 'impieties of disguised miscreants', which was very bad, and concealing 'the slips and frailties of true-hearted Nathaniels', which was entirely salutary. It was this same conviction that underlay Bolton's certainty that there could be no similarity between the puritans' denunciations of their enemies and their enemies' denunciations of them. The former were merely charitable Christian reproofs designed for the spiritual benefit of the recipient, the edification of the wider community and the vindication of the cause of religion; while the latter, properly understood, represented unprovoked attacks whereby he who 'is nothing but an accursed lump of sin and lust, damnation and hell' sought to load 'with censorious lies that happy soul which in the fountain of Christ's meritorious blood is made far whiter than the snow . . . though some spots and stains of infirmities and frailties still cleave unto it while it yet dwells in an house of flesh and tabernacle of clay.'[62]

Such emphasis on the inherent difference between the godly and the profane, such insistence on the relative freedom from sin that was conferred on the elect by the free grace of God, could lead to antinomianism – the claim that the godly were free not merely from the curse of the moral law but from the dictates of that law and thus from sin itself. Accusations that the sort of predestinarian Calvinism that passed for orthodox amongst the godly was indeed antinomian in its effects and logical consequences were becoming increasingly frequent in the 1620s and 1630s, and Bentham went out of his way to denounce such doctrines. The godly, he explained, had been freed by Christ from the yoke of the ceremonial law of the Jews, from the curse of the moral law, from the thraldom of the Devil and, through the process of sanctification worked in the soul of every elect saint by the holy spirit, from the domination of sin. They remained, however, subject both to the demands of the moral law and to sin, in the sense that they, along with the rest of fallen humanity, would remain prone to disobey God until they died.[63]

For all that Bentham might be able to see off the accusation of antinomianism at the level of formal theological argument, the puritan position as he expressed it was subject to other more practical and visceral falsifications and overthrows. And here we return to the figure of John Barker sweating on the scaffold. Here surely was proof positive that for all their expressions of piety and moral superiority, for all their religious observances and moral scruples, the godly were as sinful, indeed often a good deal more sinful, than the average Christian or 'good fellow'. Of course, as we have seen, Barker's whole performance on the scaffold was designed expressly to close down this interpretation of his fall.

Viewed from inside the parameters of the puritan world-view, Barker's very public journey from despair and fear via repentance to an assured sense of Christ's mercy and of his own eventual salvation, might well silence the other obvious reading of the proceedings as just another flagrant example of puritan sin, self-righteousness and hypocrisy. But viewed from outside the godly community that surely was just what the whole affair looked like.

V   *A bad death*

Of course, by the 1630s the sceptically anti-puritan view of these events had an audience considerably wider than the ale benches and taverns to which Bolton and Bentham attempted to consign their enemies. There were now those in power who, viewing the godly from Laudian and Arminian perspectives, would have been very unlikely to accept either Barker's self-presentation on the gallows or the view of the world that informed it. To gain some sense of what these events would have looked like from such a perspective we need to leave Northamptonshire and attend another execution, this time one held in Shrewsbury in August 1633. The victim was one Enoch ap Evan, a yeoman's son and allegedly a puritan, executed for killing his mother and his brother with an axe. His case became the subject of a number of pamphlets, the most important being by Peter Studley, a Shrewsbury minister who attended Enoch in prison and wrote up an extended account of his fate.[64] Studley, who emerges from his own text as an Arminian in theology and as a rabid anti-puritan, claimed that Enoch was a puritan who had fallen out with his family over his objections to kneeling to receive communion. In the course of the resulting argument he had done away with his brother and mother with the axe. According to Studley, the surrounding puritans knew this but, instead of attempting to convert Enoch to a true repentance and thus save his soul, they spent their whole time trying to convince anyone who would listen that he was mad and to persuade Enoch himself to suppress all mention of his puritanism in his account of the crime. Studley, or so he claimed, stood alone against this cover-up; pleading with Enoch to see the error of his puritan ways and, by laying aside all extenuating claims to elect status, to fly in true repentance to Christ and thus save his soul. Studley presented as virtual transcripts of his prison conversations what amounted to a form of anti-catechism, question-and-answer sessions, that proved Enoch's faulty view of the workings of divine grace and human free will and repentance. They showed (to Studley's satisfaction at least) that Enoch's view of himself as an elect saint, especially chosen by God for some central role in the process of reformation that would soon transform the church, had prompted both his dreadful matricide and his subsequent failure to achieve a true repentance. To the local puritans, of course, all this was nonsense. By their account, Enoch was no sort of puritan at all; he was simply deranged, and his act a meaningless tragedy with no wider religious consequences or resonances at all. Studley would have none of this, and in his pamphlet we have a precise negative image of the puritan account of Barker's death. There the damaging effects of Barker's sin and disgrace were mitigated, indeed cancelled, by the quality of his repentance and the emotional and religious resonance of his death. Here Enoch's initial offence was compounded by his failure to achieve a true repentance or to die a good death on the scaffold and all three lapses were taken to show the antinomian and subversive nature of puritan doctrine and practice.

Studley presented the case as but the culmination of the activities of the local puritans, in delineating which he reiterated many of the central features of the popular anti-puritan case as Bolton and Bentham had described it. He excoriated the 'formality' of the puritans' attitude to true religion. 'The intention of erecting private fasts and conventicles is, by the separation of a few from the community of God's people, to appropriate unto themselves the reputation of a higher strain of sanctity and sincerity than others . . . are endued withal.'[65] The godly were 'bold and busy scripturists', full of 'pride and folly'. Motivated by 'an itching desire to be accounted more zealous' than their neighbours, they were 'formal persons advancing themselves and despising others in matters of religion'.[66] But the forms which they devised to mark themselves off from ordinary Christians were mere outward observances devoid of the spiritual marrow of true piety. 'It was the easiest thing in all the world to be a formal sectary, such as men commonly call puritans',

claimed Studley. Following sermons 'without missing one on a week
day', using 'family prayers', keeping 'company and conventicles'
were all easily done. They were but outward actions containing
'neither marrow, spirit or power of true godliness which is placed in
piety, charity, unity.' To make such actions the basis for some sort
of separation between the godly and the ungodly, the wheat and the
chaff, the elect and the reprobate, to be effected in and through the
militant or visible church, as the puritans did, was, Studley claimed,
both incompatible with the unity of church and state and a usurpa-
tion of 'the prerogative royal of our saviour and Lord Jesus Christ'.[67]

In Studley's account, puritanism spread through this desire to be
considered more holy than the next person. 'They extol and advance
and thereby ensnare the hearts of credulous persons by praising them
for pious, virtuous, holy and good men when they once perceive in
them any inclination to adhere to their faction'. On the other hand,
all those who opposed them (like Studley who described himself as
'the known anti-puritan of the country') they 'traduce them with
obloquy and load them with defamation, secretly whispering against
them that they are dissolute, profane, boon companions, utterly
destitute of the power of godliness.'[68] Puritans, then, were divisive
and their religion inherently hypocritical. They were also covetous;
the origins of the puritan style amongst the clergy lay in clerical
poverty and a consequent desire to gain a following and an income
from the laity. This corrupt impulse was often reciprocated on the
lay side by rich men whose 'wealth hath begotten in them' a desire
'to please themselves and to be voiced abroad for religious persons
in giving entertainment to godly ministers'. The result was a mutual
admiration society in which the laity were assured through their
patronage of the godly clergy of their own holiness. Lay puritans
were then free 'to take some liberty to themselves to love the world
and worldly things under the names of frugality, good husbandry and
provident circumspection in all their affairs and also shall now and
then stretch their consciences for the enlargement of their temporal
estate, whereby they are made capable of dignities and precedencies
in the commonwealth.'[69] Having acquired a certain clout, these lay
puritans then abused it to confer honour, money and freedom from
episcopal oversight on their clerical clients. For their part, the
puritan clergy gloried in the patronage of the rich laity, creeping 'by
insinuation into the favour and esteem of great men and the richer
sort who are able to succour and support them and by obsequious

flattery to instill into their hearts an ill opinion of the present government'.[70]

It is not difficult to discern in Studley's description the central practices and pietistic forms of puritanism as Bentham had described them and as they have been identified by recent scholarship. Here were the conventicles, the private fasts, the lectures, the household worship proffered by Bentham as the positive characteristics of the godly. Here too was precisely the sort of patronage relationship between a rich and respectable patron (in Bentham's case Lord Montagu) and his tame puritan minister upon which Bentham's own career had been based.[71] Here too was an accurate reflection of Studley's own experience in Shrewsbury, where at or near the centre of the local establishment lay a clique of rich puritan merchants, connected with a network of other puritan ministers and gentry, which stretched up and down the Welsh borders from Lancashire and Cheshire into Warwickshire. These men, many of whom were overt nonconformists, supported their own stipendiary lecturer in Shrewsbury, the nonconformist and subsequent presbyterian Julines Herring.[72] While Studley's account of the central institutions and practices of puritan religion shared many central characteristics with Bentham's, Studley turned a positive into a negative image by simply inverting the labels attached by Bentham to what remained essentially the same practices and beliefs. Where Bentham presented the forms of puritan voluntary religion as the essence of true religion, crucial characteristics of that society of the saints that constituted the true church on earth, Studley presented them as the semi-separatist and factious means whereby a puritan clique hoped to take over the church and restructure the state. He did so by linking puritanism defined in terms of various forms of voluntary religion to nonconformity, crypto-presbyterianism and a strand of predestinarian antinomianism of the sort that had both underwritten Enoch ap Evan's matricide and produced his subsequent failure properly to repent. Here the popular inversionary anti-puritanism of the ale-house and the popular libel, which had been so reviled by Bolton and Bentham, joined company with the elite, theologically sophisticated anti-puritanism of the court sermon and the polemical tract in an alliance that Joseph Bentham had gone out of his way to disrupt with his scrupulous defence of conformity and fierce attack on antinomianism.[73] On this basis we can see why Studley was so attracted by the ap Evan case. Enoch's matricide prompted by his stiff-necked nonconformity and underwritten by his antinomian opinions on predestination stood as a perfect synecdoche for Studley's vision of the puritan threat to all order in church and state. Here, indeed, was a perfect 'looking glass of schism'.

VI *Puritans, anti-puritans and a touch of the other*

The very different verdicts on poor Barker and poor mad Enoch nicely encapsulate the widely divergent contemporary estimations of the ideological valence, the social and political significance, of puritanism. Comfortingly for historians, both views have a good many things in common; they are structured very similarly, and crucially they largely agree about the central characteristics of, and even the appropriate name for, the thing in question. All the authors under discussion here believed in puritanism and agreed on what they took to be the defining forms of puritan voluntary religion. In the light of this formidable contemporary consensus modern historians could, perhaps, be a little more confident in their attitude to puritanism, both name and thing, than some of them have of late allowed themselves to be.

Studley and Bentham might agree on the existence and appearance of puritanism but they certainly did not agree about what it meant. How are we to reconcile these wildly divergent interpretations? This question is all the more pressing since the interpretative choices offered to us by Studley and Bentham are in many ways replicated in much of the recent writing on this subject. Was puritanism merely the zealous face of orthodox reformed Protestantism, the leading edge of far wider bodies of reformed opinion in the struggle to evangelise the people and supplement and perfect the meagre proselytising resources of the national church?[74] Or was it an altogether more sinister phenomenon; a socially divisive, semi-separatist movement, the bearer of an inherently anti-hierarchical and divisive predestinarian ideology and a nonconformist and exclusivist set of religious practices that threatened 'order' as it was conventionally defined in both church and state?[75] Was 'puritanism' in this latter sense the mere invention of anti-puritans, caricaturing for profit on the stage or polemical advantage in the pamphlet wars of the period, what remained the largely harmless, merely prodigiously pious, forms of voluntary religion of the godly? Or was it more than that, a vivid, overdrawn but essentially accurate caricature of a dangerously divisive subculture?[76] These, of course, are perennial questions, but they have been (re)placed at the centre of the scholarly agenda by recent writing in the field. At first sight it might appear that we are doomed forever to choose between the interpretations of puritanism offered by Peter Studley on the one hand, and by Joseph Bentham on the other. The present chapter has argued that this was and is a false dichotomy and that perhaps the best way to escape it is the further investigation of the nature and origins of the dichotomy itself. The short answer to the question of which of these various versions of puritanism is 'true' is, of course, all of the above and none of the above. To begin with, they are all 'true' in the obvious relativist sense that many contemporaries believed them, that is to say that they allowed people to explain large chunks of their own social experience and of the behaviour and beliefs of their contemporaries in coherent and compelling ways. If therefore we accept that many contemporaries interpreted the world in terms of these images and acted on the basis of those interpretations we need to take these images very seriously if we want to understand what was happening in the early-Stuart church.

But the images in question were 'true' in another sense as well. Precisely because they purported to be pictures of reality, to incorporate many of the commonly observable features of the contemporary world into an explanation of why things were as they were, and how and why they could and should be different, they had to represent relatively faithfully many of the things that the people conventionally called puritans did – hence their remarkable agreement on that subject. The resulting images of the godly and the ungodly, of puritans and conformists, were constructed by people occupying particular ideological and subjective positions; in other words, all these authors had their different axes to grind, their different ideological and material interests to further and protect. This meant, of course, that their resulting accounts of puritanism were partial, accentuating certain aspects of the beast and playing down others. This process of accentuation, of the caricature of each side by the other, can provide historians with a useful counterweight against their consistent tendency, in the entirely honourable pursuit of historical empathy and heuristic good faith, to take the various parties to these disputes on their own valuation of themselves. Thus if we subject Bentham and Bolton's claims to represent moderation, true order and community to Studley's critique, various facets of their puritanism that their own accounts of themselves played down or suppressed, are thrown into relief.

Thus while Bentham's espousal of conformity and his subsequent career as a royalist is an important sign that not all puritan lecturers were nonconformists and crypto-presbyterians reliant on the protection of the laity against an increasingly suspicious episcopal authority, Julines Herring's career in Shrewsbury shows us that some were. Indeed, the Kettering lecture itself was the site during the 1630s of various acts of defiance against Laudian authority by, amongst others, John Barker and Daniel Cawdray, excesses which led to the eventual suppression of the lecture 'at some time prior to 1636'. Bentham's espousal of conformist principle is hidden away in a mere aside on page 264 of his *Christian Conflict* and his position was centred on a variety of tenets – scrupulous scripturalism and an intense concern with the integrity and purity of godly opinion – that while they may not have led him to nonconformity had precisely that effect on a good many other puritans.[77]

Again, Studley's critique of the antinomian tendencies within puritan predestinarianism, while almost certainly having nothing to do with the antics of poor mad Enoch, did speak to certain central features of Bolton and Bentham's style of religion. As we have seen, there were antinomian tendencies in their position, as the very intensity of Bentham's reaction to antinomianism shows. Indeed, Bentham admitted that this was a live issue amongst the Northamptonshire godly in the 1630s, with certain orthodox Calvinist ministers having been accused of not daring 'to preach the truth through fear of losing our livings', a monstrous suggestion that condemned at a stroke 'all the pious pastors and painful preachers of this our famous church' and which deserved 'sharp censure and severe scourge of the church'.[78]

The same sort of analysis can, of course, be applied to Studley's account of puritanism in Shrewsbury. The seditious semi-separatist cells and networks that he excoriated in *The Looking Glass of Schism* turn out on examination to be composed of precisely the sorts of godly ministers, substantial gentry and rich merchants who staffed local establishments all over early-Stuart England. Moreover their supposedly schismatic religious practices had clearly been allowed by Bishop Morton and his predecessors for decades. Enoch himself emerges, even from Studley's text and certainly from a later puritan reply, as simply mad and no sort of puritan at all. If there was a conspiracy against all order in church and state here, it clearly helped greatly to be a rabidly anti-puritan Arminian like Studley to be able to detect it. And yet of course, this puritanism had created local division and faction, of which Studley's own career and pamphlet were telling evidence.[79]

And this brings us to the last sense in which we might regard these visions of the other as 'true'. It has been argued here that the processes of accentuation or caricature at the heart of this image-making were in part a function of the projection onto the polemically defined other, of those aspects of the observer's own position and situation that he or she least wanted to face or own. This created a situation in which there were large gobs of the viewer left sticking onto or incorporated into the resulting image of the viewed. Thus if we want to interrogate the smooth self-image presented to the world by any of the participants in these debates the best place to start is with their picture of the 'other' against which they chose to define themselves.

If we want to gain a sense of Studley's insecurity about the material and ideological status of the ministry, if we want to capture his sacerdotalist and clericalist aggression in the face of what he took to be the lay domination of the post-Reformation English church, and if we want to grasp the divisive force of his attempt to redefine the doctrinal position of the English church in an Arminian direction, it is to his image of puritanism that we must turn. Having done so it is impossible to continue to accept at face value his presentation of himself as a simple son of the English church and a loyal subject of King Charles, merely defending an unproblematic notion of the status quo against a puritan conspiracy in church and state.

On the other side, anyone wanting critically to analyse the image of puritanism as a relatively anodyne form of voluntary religion and a simple reinforcement of the forces of social order and discipline (espoused by Bolton and Bentham and reproduced by a good many modern historians) need look no further than the puritan image of the ungodly. Let us start with a crucial silence or absence in the middle of Bentham and Bolton's rendition of the popular case against puritanism. John Fielding has shown that accusations of nonconformity bulked large in lay attacks on the puritans as these were recorded in the church courts. Indeed, by the 1630s they had all but drowned out the sort of assault on the moral probity of the godly envisaged by Barker, Bolton and Bentham.[80] But this aspect of popular anti-puritanism is completely omitted by Bolton and Bentham from their otherwise very vivid evocation of the popular image of the godly. Its absence is not hard to explain; as we have seen, Bentham and Bolton's purpose in mimicking so effectively the ungodly's critique of the godly was to reconfirm their own self-image as pillars of order, morality and obedience, and they naturally privileged those elements in popular anti-puritanism that served that purpose. Rehashing charges of nonconformity (even if only to refute them) merely served to remind the reader of an aspect of puritanism that might call those larger claims to moderation, orthodoxy and obedience into question, and adverted publicly to an increasingly controversial issue on which the godly were far from united. And so Bolton and Bentham simply left accusations of nonconformity out of their rendition of the discourse of popular anti-puritanism.

Bolton and Bentham's image of the profane sought to resolve many of the contradictions and instabilities at the heart of puritan piety. But in so doing it created an intensely polarised and polarising view of the world that must serve, if not to undercut, then at the least very seriously to modify, claims about the inherent moderation and orderliness of puritanism and about the psychic peace on offer within the safe haven of the godly community. For having externalised the divisive, pharisaical, hypocritical elements in puritan piety and projected them onto the ungodly, Bolton and Bentham then reintegrated and exacerbated them as they modified their position to respond to what they took to be the polluting presence and polemical aggression of the ungodly. The result was a view of the world so polarised and polarising, a vision of the community of the godly so exclusivist and aggressively self-righteous, that it was almost bound to create the division, controversy and conflict, the phariseeism and factionalism, that Bolton and Bentham's own rhetoric registered in the very act of evacuating them onto the profane.

Moreover, when we recall that the exchanges analysed here between puritan and anti-puritan were part of a long-standing dialectical debate or dialogue, conducted not merely on the London stage, but in myriad local conflicts and, at a higher level of abstraction, through a massive polemical literature over a period of decades, the notion of puritanism or indeed of its conformist opposite as entities with a stable ideological valence or identity becomes

doubly unlikely. Puritanism could be moderate, hierarchical, re-
pressive and orthodox, but it could also be divisive, extreme and
heterodox. Which aspect of this complex social and ideological
mixture predominated, which tendency came out on top, depended
on a whole series of social, political and doctrinal, local, national and
intellectual forces.[81] But it depended, too, on the complex dialectical
relationships between the puritan and anti-puritan images that this
chapter has sought to explicate and analyse.

I want to end where we began, with John Barker on the scaffold.
To the godly, no doubt, his fate confirmed the truths of puritan
religion. To other observers, less committed to the assumptions of
puritan piety, he was just another puritan hypocrite, telling proof
that for all their fuss and fury the godly were no better than the rest
of fallen humanity. Confronted with these variant readings of the
same event it is not the historian's job to usurp the prerogatives of
the Calvinist God and pronounce definitively on the state of John
Barker's soul. Nor should we seek to emulate some all-seeing *Times*
editorial, sonorously pronouncing on whether or not 'puritanism' *was*
in some essential sense 'radical' or 'moderate', a 'good' or a 'bad'
thing for 'the Church of England'. Rather we should attempt to
recover and listen to the alternative versions of and responses to
Barker's tragic end and, by comparing and collating the very
different visions of puritanism that they implied, come to a better
understanding of the complex and contested social and cultural
meanings that clustered around 'puritanism' in early-Stuart England.

6. A Road to Revolution: The Continuity of Puritanism, 1559–1642

JACQUELINE EALES

I

The royalist cleric Peter Heylyn in his *Aërius Redivivus* of 1670 described English presbyterianism, which he also termed puritanism, as part of an international Calvinist faction dedicated to raising rebellions against monarchical and episcopal government. Heylyn identified various phases in the history of English puritanism, describing the 1570s and 1580s as decades of expansion, followed by decline in the 1590s due to the deaths of prominent lay patrons and the successful efforts of the privy council in imprisoning and executing leading puritan agitators. At the accession of James I the puritans were, according to Heylyn, 'brought so low' that they might have been permanently suppressed, if the king had not been so taken with the pleasures of court life in England. His failure to act allowed puritanism to survive and eventually to overthrow royal power in the Civil War.[1]

Most subsequent historians have followed Heylyn's lead in tracing the fortunes of the puritan movement in relation to royal policies of accommodation or persecution. Such an interpretation tends to focus heavily on the changing nature of puritanism from the high-profile organisation of the presbyterian wing in the 1570s and 1580s, followed by decades of relative quiescence, until the effects of the Personal Rule and the 'Rise of Arminianism' in the 1630s once more drove puritans into militancy.[2] It ignores on the other hand the many continuities in puritan aspirations and activities between the Elizabethan Settlement and the 1640s. These are to be found in the various routes by which puritan culture was preserved and disseminated in the 80 years or so before the outbreak of the Civil War. Initially the patronage of puritan clergy by courtiers and gentry was of prime importance in the survival and growth of puritanism. Subsequently, the local influence of individual ministers, the impact of puritan authors on a national readership and the cultivation of religious traditions by individual family groups would also have important long-term effects on the nature and extent of puritanism in the 1640s.

This chapter will examine these developments in greater detail and will argue that despite the decline in organised presbyterian agitation after the early 1590s, puritan networks continued to flourish and to expand in many regions, affording protection to nonconformist clergy and keeping alive aspirations for plainer modes of worship and even more radical change in the form of the restriction or abolition of episcopacy. The favour shown by Charles I to Arminianism, with its emphasis on anti-predestinarian theology and elaborate liturgy and church decoration, created a state of tension in which puritans felt further repressed and isolated within a state of near independence from the established church. Although, as Nicholas Tyacke has shown, the religious policies of the 1630s forced many puritans into a more militant stance *vis-à-vis* the crown and the established church, it will be argued here that their opposition was more securely founded on long-term objectives. Puritans not only desired to remove recent religious 'innovations' such as Arminian theology, the altar policy and the Book of Sports, they also maintained the belief that older plans for reform dating back to Elizabeth's reign would eventually be reactivated.[3] From 1640 onwards the dense ties of patronage, kinship and religious sympathy which had been developed by the puritan gentry and clergy would be actively drawn upon in order to mobilise public opinion, to influence MPs and to shape the religious and social reforms undertaken by the Long Parliament. The puritan involvement in the parliamentarian cause was so central that it is still entirely legitimate to describe the English Civil War as a 'Puritan Revolution', even if it was ultimately unsuccessful.

II

The intellectual and social continuities between Elizabethan and early-Stuart puritanism are well illustrated by a proposal drawn up by the Shropshire curate William Voyle for the consideration of the Long Parliament in 1640.[4] Voyle's plea that no one should be branded as a 'puritan, precisian, schismatic or sectary', unless they had been officially admonished to conform, and 'after that continued unconformable', emphasises his own uneasy position in the Welsh borderland, an area which local puritans had long regarded as backward in religion. The curate's suggestions are worthy of detailed consideration, since they contain a conceptual blueprint for the reorganisation of the church and secular government to cater for puritan demands which had a lengthy history. Many of Voyle's demands are also contained, for example, in the Millenary Petition presented to James I by the puritan clergy in 1603 and supposedly supported by 'more than a thousand' petitioners.[5] Certainly Voyle urged the suppression of Arminianism as well as the reversal of the altar policy, which had resulted in the widespread erection of church altars with the sanction of Charles I from 1633 onwards. Beyond this, however, Voyle supported reforms which had been advocated by the puritan movement since the beginning of Elizabeth's reign, including the revocation of all ecclesiastical laws to be replaced by church laws established by parliament. Voyle was also in favour of more freedom for preachers, of private fasts, and of family prayers and religious exercises. He demanded the removal of what generations of puritans had seen as superstitious practices unwarranted by the Bible, such as the use of the surplice, bowing at the name of Jesus, kneeling during communion, the use of the sign of the cross in baptism and of the ring in the marriage ceremony, and the presence of godparents at baptism, who should be replaced by witnesses. Voyle also called for strict whole day observance of the sabbath and emphasised that the privy council should not sit on a Sunday, but instead should hear 'a good sermon'. He asked that no subscription should be required of ministers except 'against popery, Arminianism, socinianism and [to] certain of the thirty-nine articles, not . . . as now to the books of divine service, homilies, ordination and consecration'. Such easing of clerical subscription had also been demanded in Elizabeth's reign and had been raised in all early-Stuart parliaments except 1621 and 1624.[6]

Some 30 years later, in 1672, Voyle would be licensed as a presbyterian minister, but in this document he did not advocate the abolition of episcopacy, but argued that it might be best 'to yield in part' to the bishops. It should be stressed that the would-be revolutionaries of 1640 had no idea how far their plans would succeed nor what tactics would prove most advantageous and thus Voyle wrote that the purest path to reform would be to start with religion and the church, but the more 'politic way' would be to begin with matters of the 'commonwealth . . . for therein many would be easily won to be of one mouth, who being once joined together, would be the better kept together, even in matters of religion'. In an accompanying letter, Voyle cast a backward glance to Elizabeth's reign and argued that then caution had prevailed, but now 'we know not what invitations and encouragements [and] opportunities you may have beyond the common expectation'.[7] These plans were forwarded to Sir Robert Harley, senior knight of the shire for Herefordshire in the Long Parliament, whose reputation as an influential godly gentleman meant that he was the recipient of numerous communiqués from puritan clergy and gentry in the English marcher counties and the West Midlands in the 1640s.

In addressing his demands to such a prominent puritan gentleman, Voyle was also following earlier precedents. Individual MPs had pressed for religious reforms in Elizabethan parliaments and were regarded as spokesmen for the godly cause by widespread networks of clergy and laity. In 1571, for example, William Strickland had introduced a revision of the Prayer Book in the Commons and in 1587 Sir Anthony Cope had introduced a similar measure with draft legislation to revoke the existing ecclesiastical laws. In rejecting Sir John Neale's conclusion that there was an orchestrated puritan grouping in the Elizabethan House of Commons, Geoffrey Elton interpreted the actions of Strickland, Cope and others as isolated manoeuvres instigated by individuals with little support inside parliament and even less hope of success. Yet, as Patrick Collinson has pointed out, their efforts were part of a genuinely wider movement and coincided with organised campaigns to address parliament in print or through petitions.[8] During the 1580s the presbyterian wing of the puritan movement was at its zenith, having erected classes in Essex, Warwickshire, Northamptonshire, Suffolk, and elsewhere. Under the leadership of John Field, conferences of the clergy were summoned to London during sessions of parliaments and sophisticated methods of lobbying were developed. In the mid 1580s, for example, surveys of the sufficiency of the clergy were drawn up for presentation to parliament in a number of counties, including Essex, Cornwall, Warwickshire, Suffolk and Sussex.[9] Historians have largely overlooked the fact that this tactic was revived by puritan campaigners in 1640–1.[10] More attention has been given to the very successful outcome of this strategy, which resulted in the ejection of royalist or non-puritan clergy from their parishes on a mass scale in the 1640s.[11]

As a result of the work of Elton and Conrad Russell it is no longer feasible to write of a monolithic 'puritan opposition' in Elizabethan and early-Stuart Parliaments.[12] Instead puritan agitation surfaced in those parliaments over certain issues such as clerical subscription, sabbath observance, adequate stipends for the ministry and the ejection of scandalous ministers. Parliament was undoubtedly seen by the godly as the correct arena for reform in Elizabeth's reign, just as it would be in the early-Stuart period and during the Long Parliament. In 1602 Josias Nichols, rector of Eastwell in Kent, who had been suspended in 1584 for refusing to subscribe to Whitgift's articles and had been involved in the London presbyterian conference of 1587, explained that he and other ministers had petitioned parliament then 'because that is the place which by ancient custom of this realm serveth for the redress of all things to be reformed and the establishing of all matters in the state of this kingdom'.[13] Before the Civil War such agitation for radical change through parliament had failed because it did not have support from members with more moderate religious views nor from the wider gentry population outside parliament. Sir Walter Mildmay, Chancellor of the Exchequer and founder of the puritan seminary Emmanuel College, Cambridge, regarded the devisers of the 1587 bill presented by Cope as having 'small judgement, small experience'. He argued that their plans would throw down the existing church order without thought for financial provision for the clergy or other implications of the measure.[14] By the 1590s the deaths of powerful court patrons such as the earl of Leicester also meant that the leaders of the puritan movement were highly vulnerable. The imprisonment of prominent presbyterians such as Thomas Cartwright and Humphrey Fenn in 1590 and the execution of John Penry, Henry Barrow and John Greenwood in 1593 contributed to driving the more radical reformers underground or into exile.[15]

More specifically, the absence of organised pressure for a presbyterian system from the 1590s until the 1640s has led historians to see this as a period of discontinuity for puritanism. Such an interpretation places too much weight on the organisational activities of the clergy and ignores the importance of continued lay involvement in the puritan movement, which was sustained and developed in a variety of related ways. Not least among these were the activities of those lay men and women, whose patronage of ministers and encouragement of godliness within their own households and their local communities were crucial elements in the survival and expansion of puritanism into the seventeenth century.

III

Peter Heylyn certainly regarded patronage in high places as of central importance for the survival of the puritan threat against church and state.[16] Of the great courtiers named by Heylyn as sympathetic to the puritan cause, the earl of Leicester was the most prominent and stood at the centre of a family network of influential patrons, which included his brother the earl of Warwick and his brothers-in-law, the earl of Huntingdon and Sir Francis Walsingham. Leicester's commitment to the godly cause was, however, questioned by his political and religious opponents who decried him as a 'Machiavel', a calculating politician who used the militant Protestant clergy as it suited him, but with no real religious scruples. Unlike Leicester's critics, Patrick Collinson has detected a consistent religious policy in the earl's dealings with the godly, tracing his protection for the prophesying movement in the 1570s and 1580s and his patronage for radical preachers including Thomas Cartwright, John Knewstub, and Humphrey Fenn. Leicester strongly defended the Elizabethan Settlement and never openly endorsed a presbyterian system, but he consciously encouraged these ministers as a bulwark against Catholicism. Furthermore, he became more sympathetic to his puritan protégés as the threat from Spain increased in the 1580s and as the queen and bishops moved against nonconformity.[17]

Leicester's death in 1588 was a tremendous blow to the puritan movement, but attempts to reconstruct his patronage network under the earl of Essex ended in failure and the execution of Essex in 1601. Moreover, many of the first generation of godly Protestant patrons were also being lost in the final years of Elizabeth's reign, including Walsingham who died in 1590 and Huntingdon who died in 1595.[18] Nevertheless, we should not overlook the continuity of patronage that was sustained into the early-Stuart period. A notable contribution in this context was the foundation of Emmanuel College in 1584 by Sir Walter Mildmay, who endowed the college with the intention that its scholars would become preachers and spread their learning in the parishes. Under the first master, Laurence Chaderton, Emmanuel developed a reputation as a puritan stronghold which it retained into the Stuart period.[19] Amongst the college's clerical graduates were William Bradshaw, the nonconformist Thomas Pierson, who prepared some of the works of the famed puritan author William Perkins for the press, and John Cotton, who emigrated from Boston in Lincolnshire to New England in the 1630s.[20] In 1616 Samuel Clarke the martyrologist was placed by his father under the tutelage of another future exile, Thomas Hooker.[21] The activities of these and other graduates ensured that the influence of the college would be a continual thread in the fortunes of English and North American puritanism between the 1580s and the 1640s. As master, Chaderton also acted as an agent for promoting clerics to livings and it was on his recommendation to Sir Anthony Cope that the famous nonconformist preacher John Dod obtained his first benefice.[22]

Cope has already made a fleeting appearance in these pages as the promoter of the book and bill in 1587. His role as patron of the living of Hanwell in Oxfordshire illustrates the local dimensions of his godly influence, as well as the links between provincial puritan aspirations and their representation in parliaments in these years. Cope was responsible for supplying Hanwell with a succession of puritan ministers whose incumbencies spanned from 1584 to the outbreak of the Civil War. John Dod was the first but was suspended for nonconformity in 1606–7, whereupon he spent some time encouraging his successor before moving to Fenny Compton in Warwickshire and then Canons Ashby in Northamptonshire, where he was again silenced in 1611.[23] He was replaced at Hanwell by Robert Harris, whose views on ceremonies were conformist and differed markedly from his predecessor's. Nevertheless Harris epitomised the moderate puritan ideal of the evangelical minister. A godly life written after his death described him as having 'lived religion, whilst many only make it the subject of their discourse', in short, his 'life was a commentary upon his doctrine'. Harris remained at Hanwell until hounded out by royalist troopers in 1642 and ended his life as President of Trinity College, Oxford, where he died in 1658.[24]

Apart from furnishing a puritan ministry at Hanwell, Sir Anthony was also influential in godly circles in nearby Banbury, which he represented seven times in parliaments between 1571 and 1601. Under the aegis of Thomas Brasbridge, vicar from 1581–90, Banbury developed a national reputation as a puritan centre and in 1589 the sheriff of Oxfordshire accused Cope and others of the town of trying 'under the plea of religion' to abolish festive pastimes, including maypoles, morris dances and Whitsun Ales, to the 'great discontentment' of her Majesty's 'loving' subjects. Cope denied these charges and also that he had held any 'suspicious' religious meetings.[25] When Sir Anthony died in 1614 Robert Harris preached a funeral sermon in which he emphasised his patron's strong puritan consciousness of sin – 'he much respected and greatly countenanced every learned and unscandalous preacher, so most of all those that least favoured his corruptions, often blessing God for such teachers, as would not give him rest in sin.'[26]

A generation later Sir Robert Harley similarly brought a series of puritan ministers to the livings of Brampton Bryan, Wigmore and Leintwardine in the north-west corner of Herefordshire, where he was patron. At his funeral in 1656 the mourners were told that Sir Robert was 'the first that brought the gospel into' the region, he 'gave a great light to these parts . . . his planting of godly ministers, and then backing them with his authority, made religion famous in this little corner of the world'. Through Harley's influence 'profession began to grow and spread itself under his shade'. Here is a clear image of the puritan evangelisation of a former 'dark corner of the land'. Harley's own conviction that he was enlightening the locality is revealed in a draft letter of 1614 to the bishop of Hereford, in which he defended the nonconformity of the Emmanuel graduate Thomas Pierson, then rector at Brampton Bryan, by arguing that the parishioners 'never had any such settled preaching ministry here before'.[27]

Over a quarter of a century later many parishes in the locality still remained untouched by Protestant zeal according to puritan critics. In 1641 Stanley Gower, Pierson's successor at Brampton and a former chaplain to Archbishop Ussher of Armagh, asserted that in the whole county of Herefordshire there were only 'twenty constant and conscionable preachers & yet it is to be feared that there are more in this county than are to be found in all the thirteen shires of Wales upon which it bordereth'. Gower's concerns for preaching in

Wales were shared by leading Welsh puritan ministers, including William Wroth and William Erbury, who in a petition to parliament of 1641 also stressed the problems of the language barrier between the English clergy and their Welsh congregations.[28] Gower's own preaching at Brampton was on occasion Stakhanovite. It was his habit on private days of fasting to enter the pulpit between eight and nine in the morning to pray and preach '*extempore*, till past one of the clock following'. There followed a psalm, but Gower did not leave the pulpit until after five o'clock, 'if daylight continued so long'. It is not surprising that when the Harleys' eldest son, Edward, arrived at Oxford University in 1638 he complained that there he could not have the word of God preached 'in a right manner'.[29] There was no shortage of preaching at Oxford, but Gower's definition of edifying preaching was to preach 'against Arminianism, of predestination, faith, effectual vocation, regeneration etc.' and his sermons would have been very different in style from those encountered at the university.[30]

The patronage of powerful courtiers and gentry was supplemented by the concern of godly urban elites to furnish regular preaching in towns. Corporate patronage was responsible for establishing puritan lecturers in a large number of towns including Shrewsbury, Ipswich, Colchester, Coventry, Leicester, Norwich, Northampton and London amongst many others. London was also the headquarters of the feoffees for impropriations, a corporation of clergy, lawyers and merchants, including William Gouge, Richard Sibbes and John Davenport, set up in 1625 with the intention of augmenting clerical wages by buying up impropriated tithes. The feoffees were challenged in the courts in 1632 by the Attorney General and were disbanded, but during their brief years of activity they became a model for puritan reform and in 1640 the suppression of the corporation was one of the complaints in the 'Root and Branch' petition against episcopacy delivered to parliament from the City of London.[31]

IV

The stress on the need for preaching leads us to a consideration of the influence of individual puritan ministers, which was especially felt at parish level through the impact of their sermons. In the *Institutes* Calvin had singled out the pure preaching of the word as one of the marks of the true church and the puritan temperament placed great value on the efforts of edifying preachers.[32] The contrast to puritans between profitable and unprofitable preaching is exemplified by two entries in the diary of Lady Margaret Hoby for September 1599. On the 16th of that month she attended the Sunday service at her parish church of St Peter's, Hackness, in Yorkshire and on her return noted 'I praised God both for the enabling the minister so profitably to declare the word as he had, and myself to hear with that comfort and understanding I did'. A week later on a visit to her mother in York, Lady Hoby attended a service where she heard a Mr Palmer preach, but as she recorded 'to small profit to any'. Puritans did not simply demand frequent sermons, but sermons of a particular type, which they regarded as 'edifying'. Lady Hoby was thus a typically discriminating puritan auditor, who like so many others of her persuasion attended the sermons of Stephen Egerton at the parish of St Anne's, Blackfriars, when she was in London.[33] Under Egerton from 1598 and subsequently under William Gouge until his death in 1653, St Anne's developed a reputation as a centre of puritan sermonising, but not without attracting the animosity of less godly parishioners. In *The Alchemist*, first published in 1612, Ben Jonson satirised the playhouse's puritan neighbours in Blackfriars as 'sober, scurvy, precise . . . that scarce have smiled twice since the King came in'.[34]

At St Anne's the preachers could expect an attentive and searching audience, but elsewhere puritan ministers could find themselves faced by unresponsive congregations. Josias Nichols, looking back on his early ministry at Eastwell in Kent in the 1580s, wrote of his efforts to combat Catholic doctrines there and marvelled that his preaching had been 'so little regarded' by the people. He argued that where there was a non-resident, non-preaching ministry the parishioners would have no knowledge 'to tell what Christ is, or that we are saved by faith in him and not by works'.[35]

The influence of an individual minister could be long-lived and in some cases provided clear continuity between the early days of puritanism in Elizabeth's reign and the years immediately before or even during the Civil War. John Dod, for example, built up a national reputation as a godly guide. In 1601 the puritan zealot Job Throckmorton, having unsuccessfully sought 'comfortable assurance' of his salvation for many years, finally received it with Dod's help at the hour of his death. Throckmorton had been prominent in the puritan agitation of the late 1580s, when he had supported Sir Anthony Cope in the 1587 parliament and had been involved in the production of the Martin Marprelate tracts against the English bishops, which appeared in 1588 and 1589.[36] Dod was later summoned to provide similar solace in 1611 at the death-bed of Thomas Peacock, a fellow of Brasenose, Oxford, who was grievously troubled with the belief that there was 'no stamp of grace' in him and that he would be damned. In 1624 Dod was presented to the rectory of Fawsley in Northamptonshire by Sir Richard Knightley and remained there until his death in 1645. In 1639 he complained that his 'sight and hand' were both failing and at the close of 1642, when he calculated his own age as 95, he informed Lady Mary Vere that his own death could not be far off. Yet he was still actively dispensing spiritual guidance and offered if he 'might any way be helpful to your Ladyship to resolve you of any doubts or questions in your heart, I should be glad ere my departure, now at hand, to do you any service this way.'[37]

Another example of a lengthy and influential clerical career is provided by the life of Humphrey Fenn, whose reputation as a nonconformist dates from the late 1570s when he was in Northampton. In 1578 he became vicar of Holy Trinity, Coventry, where he was associated with Thomas Cartwright and the growing presbyterian movement. Like Josias Nichols in Kent, Fenn was suspended for refusing to subscribe to the articles of 1584, but was reinstated through the intervention of the earl of Leicester. He was imprisoned in 1590 for his role in the Warwickshire classes and released in 1592. As late as the mid 1620s we find him joining with the mayor and godly citizens of Coventry to invite Samuel Clarke to lecture in the town. When Fenn died in 1634 his will contained a sensational presbyterian preamble, which was sent at once to Archbishop Laud by the bishop of Coventry and Lichfield. It may also have been circulating in manuscript amongst the godly before its publication in 1641. In the preamble Fenn endorsed a presbyterian system of pastors, doctors, ruling elders and deacons as 'apostolical, universal and unchangeable' and argued that the churches in England 'do sin against their head and only monarch, in their violent opposition thereunto, for the upholding of an ambitious, pompous, worldly, prelacy, which being a human presumption . . . made way for Antichrist'. Episcopacy, he claimed, hindered the edification of the church and maintained a 'shameful schism' against all the reformed churches. In spite of these corruptions, Fenn argued that separation from the church of England was not lawful as long as 'a Christian may enjoy true doctrine with the sacraments from a minister able to teach the truth, and when a worshipper of God is not forced by a personal act to approve of these corruptions'.[38] Fenn's views had been forged during the debates about presbyterianism in Elizabeth's reign and his position was one which many puritans had subsequently adopted; it owed little, it must be stressed, to the religious 'innovations' of the 1630s.

Testimony to the powerful influence of individual ministers is further expressed in the funeral sermons and godly lives that were published after their deaths. Such publications were written primarily about the clergy, the aristocracy and the gentry as models of piety and provided a judicious blend of individual and idealised behaviour. They were part of an increasingly popular literary genre from late in Elizabeth's reign until well into the eighteenth century. In his funeral sermon we are told that Dod gave himself at Hanwell to 'much fasting and prayer and as his seed-time was painful, so his harvest was gainful, hundreds of souls being converted to his ministry'. In the life of Robert Harris we discover that while he was at Hanwell he also lectured at both Deddington and Stratford on Avon. At the latter lecture there was 'great resort of the chief gentry and choicest preachers and professors in those parts and among them Sir Thomas Lucy of Charlecote always had a great respect for him'. The vicar of Ashby-de-la-Zouch, Arthur Hildersham, a protégé of the earl of Huntingdon, preached at two 'famous exercises' with William Bradshaw at Burton-upon-Trent in Staffordshire and at Repton in Derbyshire, 'which were the means of great good to the souls of both ministers and private christians in the parts adjacent'. Hildersham was also an active manager of the Millenary Petition and was repeatedly suspended between 1590 and 1631 for nonconformity, including refusing to use the surplice.

As a result of John Cotton's ministry at Boston 'both the town and country thereabout' were 'much bettered, and reformed by his labours', while at the populous city parish of St Anne's, William Gouge was described as 'an aged father in Christ' and his funeral sermon tells us that 'thousands' were 'converted and built up by his ministry' there.[39] As has been noted, these descriptions and many like them are all to be found in printed contemporary sources and this leads us to a third route by which puritan culture was able to flourish in this period, namely through the book trade.

V

The importance of printing in spreading the doctrines of the Reformation and the Catholic Counter-Reformation has been the subject of numerous studies and unsurprisingly puritan culture was similarly disseminated in print.[40] Richard Baxter's autobiography published posthumously in 1696 gives us an insight into the religious influence exerted by printed books. He was born in 1615 and was raised in the Shropshire village of Eaton Constantine where there was 'but little preaching at all'. Baxter's father derived his religious convictions, which marked him as a puritan amongst his neighbours, almost entirely from reading the Bible and he passed on this instruction to his son. Richard believed that '(without any means, but books), was God pleased to resolve me for himself'. The influence of his reading is underscored by the fact that, as a relatively impoverished schoolboy, Baxter found it hard to get hold of many books. The few volumes that he obtained came into Baxter's hands in a haphazard way and had a tremendously forceful effect on him. He recalled that around the year 1630, at the age of 15, 'it pleased God to awaken my soul' as a result of reading Edmund Bunny's *A Book of Christian Exercise, Appertaining to Resolution*, but the copy he studied was an old torn one belonging to a local day-labourer. Baxter's father later bought Richard Sibbes's *Bruised Reed* from a pedlar and a family servant had 'a little piece of Mr Perkins' *Works*', the reading of which 'did further inform and confirm me' according to Baxter.[41]

The books of William Perkins, the Cambridge divine, were amongst the religious bestsellers of the late-sixteenth and early-seventeenth centuries. They were such a guaranteed success that his executors embarked on an ambitious programme of posthumous publication which continued for over three decades after Perkins's death in 1602. His writings provided a popular combination of Calvinist theology and practical puritan piety and outstripped sales of Calvin and Beza in England. Lady Hoby, for example, records in her diary how she obtained the latest work by Perkins in 1601. Her most frequent reading material was the Bible and Foxe's *Book of Martyrs*, but she also read practical works and sermons by puritan divines such as Richard Greenham and John Udall. Similarly, Lady Brilliana Harley's commonplace book dating from 1622 contains transcripts from the Bible, Calvin's *Institutes*, and William Perkins's *Cases of Conscience* and *Exposition of the Lord's Prayer*, as well as sermon notes.[42] The works of both Calvin and Perkins were instrumental in promoting the doctrine of assurance, which could give the individual a conviction of salvation, and Lady Harley's commonplace book is almost entirely devoted to analysing the behaviour displayed by the elect, those predestined to salvation.

Printed books also figured strongly in the moulding of the puritanism of Nehemiah Wallington, an artisan in London during the Civil War years, who claimed in 1650 to have read the Bible 'many times' and 'above two hundred other books', including works by Perkins, John Dod, Arthur Dent, Jeremiah Burroughes and John Brinsley. The works he read were mainly practical devotional works rather than works of systematic theology and, as with Lady Harley, his reading material was focused on predestination.[43]

Private libraries, particularly those of the clergy, could sometimes serve a wider population. In his will proved in 1633 Thomas Pierson provided for his library of over 400 books to be used by thirteen local puritan ministers 'while they continue in their several places'. Pierson's stepson, the minister Christopher Harvey, and three local godly gentlemen, Sir Robert Harley, Humphrey Walcot and Richard More, were to oversee the distribution of the books, some of which survive today as part of the parish library of More in Shropshire. Pierson also left his copies of the *Book of Martyrs*, and his *Works* of William Perkins, Robert Bolton and John Preston to his wife Helen.[44]

In considering the impact of the printing press, we should not neglect the influence of individual printers, publishers and booksellers, who were also involved in the process of moulding public tastes and opinions. Amongst the most prominent of the early Protestant members of the London Stationers Company was John Day, whose first imprints appeared in 1547. During Mary's reign he was briefly imprisoned along with John Rogers the martyr, but in Elizabeth's reign he was at the forefront of the production of Protestant literature and printed the first four editions of *Acts and Monuments of These Latter and Perillous Dayes*, more popularly known as Foxe's *Book of Martyrs*, as well as the *Works* of Thomas Becon. Day's epitaph at Little Bradley in Suffolk reveals his role in both encouraging and profiting from Foxe, who was assuredly his star author:

> Heere lies the Daye that darkness could not blynd
> when popish fogges had ouer cast the sunne:
> This Daye the cruell night did leave behynd
> To view and shew what bloudi Actes weare donne:
> he set a Fox to wright how Martyrs runne
> By death to lyte: Fox ventured paynes + health
> To give them light Daye spent in print his wealth
> But God with gayn retornd his wealth agayne.

Day's wealth was primarily derived from his licence to print the *Psalms in Metre* and the *ABC with the little catechism*, both of which were cheap to produce with large and dependable sales. He was operating very much within the confines of mainstream Protestant literature and in 1580 became Master of the Stationers Company. Given his commercial interests and his standing within the company it is not surprising to find that Day was zealous in hunting out unlicensed copies of the puritan *Second Admonition to the Parliament* in 1573.[45]

Robert Waldegrave on the other hand represents the clandestine end of the puritan publishing trade. In 1588 he printed an unlicensed anti-episcopal tract by John Udall and, in accordance with orders from Star Chamber, the Stationers Company secured the destruction of his press. Waldegrave subsequently set up a secret press in the house of Mrs Crane near Hampton Court, where he printed a series of attacks on episcopacy under the pseudonym of Martin Marprelate. After a brief imprisonment he moved the press to the house of Sir Richard Knightley at Fawsley and produced more Marprelate tracts, printing as many as 1000 copies of some of them. By 1590 he had fled to La Rochelle in France; he then made his way to Edinburgh and was appointed the king's printer, publishing works by James I including *Daemonologie* (1597), *The Trew Law of Free Monarchies* (1598) and *Basilikon Doron* (1603), as well as works by John Penry and Thomas Cartwright.[46]

The role of booksellers was also important to the circulation of puritan polemic. Philemon Stephens, whose first imprint appeared in 1622, combined the roles of London publisher and seller and traded mainly in works by Calvinist clergy, along with mathematical, medical and educational books. From 1625 until 1641 he was in partnership with Christopher Meredith, with whom he shared a shop at the Golden Lion in St Paul's Churchyard, which was a known meeting place for the godly. Thus on a brief visit to the capital in 1633 Richard Baxter 'fell into acquaintance with' Humphrey Blunden, 'a sober, godly, understanding apprentice of Mr Philemon Stephens the bookseller'. After Baxter returned home to Shropshire, Blunden supplied him with 'consolatory letters and directions for books'.[47]

Stephens and Meredith acted as publishers for a string of puritan ministers including Nicholas Byfield, Adam Harsnett, Thomas Hooker, Robert Horne, Thomas Gataker, John Downame, John Brinsley the elder, John Udall, William Hinde and Cornelius Burgess, as well as the more moderate puritan Robert Abbot, vicar of Cranbrook in Kent and the Calvinist bishops Joseph Hall and James Ussher. It is no surprise that Stephens and some of his stable of godly authors were troubled by the censorship of the 1630s. In 1633 he attempted to obtain a licence to print some sermons by Thomas Pierson, but was refused not because the work contained 'false doctrine; nor that it is any other than a very pious and good exhortation; and fit for the pulpit, but for the press (say they) there is no need of it'. Stephens persevered and obtained a licence from William Haywood, a domestic chaplain to Archbishop Laud, and the sermons appeared under the title *The Cure of Hurtful Cares and Fears . . .* in 1636.[48]

In the same year, however, Stephens was refused a licence to print *A True Relation of Ap Evan His Work* by the Shropshire JP Richard More of Linley. More's book was a riposte to a work by Peter Studley, vicar of St Chad's in Shrewsbury, entitled *The Looking Glass of Schism* (1634) in which he argued that Enoch ap Evan, a yeoman's son from Clun in Shropshire, had brutally murdered his brother and mother as a direct result of his puritan beliefs, which had led him, according to Studley, to fall out with them over his refusal to kneel in receiving the communion.[49] As Peter Lake demonstrates in his contribution to this volume, Studley explicitly set himself up as the chief 'anti-puritan' of the county and used the incident to attack the tight-knit circle of godly gentry and clergy that centred on Shrewsbury and the surrounding borderland between Shropshire and Herefordshire. Stephens was finally able to publish More's work in 1641, when printing restrictions against such material had been removed by the actions of the Long Parliament. The links that bound More's godly circle are further apparent in the production of his funeral sermon, *The Saints Gain by Assurance* which was preached by Humphrey Hardwick and was printed for sale by Philemon Stephens in 1644. It dwelt on the key puritan theme of assurance and was dedicated to More's fellow godly JP, Sir Robert Harley. The widespread influence of such godly networks brings us finally to a consideration of the importance of family traditions in strengthening and preserving puritanism.

VI

Thanks to the three volumes written by J. T. Cliffe on the puritan gentry in Stuart England, we know much about the transmission of godliness within families such as the Barnardistons and Springs in Suffolk, the Barringtons in Essex, and the Hampdens of Buckinghamshire.[50] It was not, of course, only gentry families who created and sustained puritan traditions. Less prominent families also transferred their puritan religious beliefs between the generations, as Baxter's description of his father's influence suggests. As we should expect, however, gentry families are by far the best documented sources for this type of enquiry. Some families, such as the Knightleys of Fawsley in Northamptonshire, could trace their puritan beginnings back into Elizabeth's reign. For others, such as the Harleys, puritanism was a relatively new phenomenon. Sir Robert Harley's grandfather, John, was a staunch Catholic who died excommunicate in 1582 and who read loudly from a 'Latin, popish primer' during divine service at the church at Brampton in the late 1570s, in order to demonstrate his disaffection from the Elizabethan church.[51]

It must be emphasised that there is nothing uniquely puritan about the creation of such family traditions. Catholicism was preserved in much the same way, but it survived as a clandestine religion on the margins of respectability, whereas moderate puritanism at least could be publicly acknowledged and celebrated. Such a celebration was contained for example in William Gurnall's funeral sermon for Lady Mary Vere who died in her ninetieth year in 1671 and whose 'zeal to the worship of God was eminent'. Both Lady Vere and her husband General Sir Horace Vere were renowned as patrons of godly ministers. Sir Horace was able to appoint puritan chaplains when he was on military campaign, while Lady Vere corresponded with numerous puritan clergy including John Dod, John Davenport, and two of her husband's chaplains, John Burgess and William Ames.[52]

In his sermon for Lady Vere, Gurnall also recorded how she self-consciously preserved a family tradition for radical Protestant piety. She 'took much delight in speaking of one of her ancestors, as one of the greatest honours to her family, (William Tracy of Toddington esquire) mentioned by Mr Foxe in his *Martyrology* ... who in the reign of King Henry the eighth, for the sound profession of his faith, set down by him in his last will and testament, was two years after his decease condemned to have his body taken up and burnt, which sentence was executed accordingly.'[53] To be able to claim a family connection with the early English Protestants was clearly regarded as a mark of special esteem. William Whateley described his wife's grandfather, John Hunt, as 'a blessed confessor, imprisoned, condemned to be burnt and prepared for the fire' who was saved by the death of Queen Mary. In his autobiography, dictated in the mid 1670s, the Quaker George Fox described his mother as 'an upright woman; her maiden name was Mary Lago, of the family of the Lagos and of the stock of the martyrs'.[54] Indirect family links with the martyrs were also celebrated into the latter half of the seventeenth century by the descendants of Mary Honeywood, who was born in 1527 at Lenham in Kent, and died in Markshall, Essex, in 1620. In his *Worthies*, first published in 1662, Thomas Fuller records that during Mary Tudor's reign, Mary Honeywood visited the prisons 'to comfort and relieve the confessors therein'. She was also present at the burning of John Bradford in Smithfield and 'resolved to see the end of his suffering', but in the great press of the crowd her shoes were trodden off and she was forced to walk barefoot from Smithfield to St Martin's before she could buy a new pair. Few individuals could have had such a large family audience for the appreciation and preservation of this story as did Mary Honeywood. According to Fuller her church monument recorded that she 'had at her decease lawfully descended from her, three hundred sixty seven children; sixteen of her own body, one hundred and fourteen grandchildren, two hundred twenty eight in the third generation, and nine in the fourth'. Amongst her many grandchildren was the puritan gentleman, Sir Thomas Honeywood, who made Markshall a stronghold for the parliamentarian cause in Essex in the 1640s.[55]

One respect in which puritan family traditions did clearly differ from Catholic experience was in the creation of clerical dynasties. After the Reformation there was a strong tendency for the Protestant clergy to marry the daughters, sisters or even widows of other clerics. The advantages of such marriages, where the wife was acquainted with the specific demands of the clergy's calling, are evident in Samuel Clarke's *Life* of his wife Katherine, who as the daughter of Valentine Overton, rector of Bedworth in Warwickshire, was 'brought up religiously' by her parents. Samuel Clarke regarded his marriage as a happy union and after his wife's death wrote that he 'looked upon this match as the greatest outward temporal blessing that ever God bestowed upon him; whereby he would experimentally say, that a prudent wife is the gift of God; and that in the enjoyment of her, he enjoyed more mercies than he could well enumerate'.[56] Katherine was a crucial link between three generations of ministers. Her brother William Overton was vicar of Eltham in Kent and her sons John and Samuel were both ejected from their livings in Nottinghamshire and Buckinghamshire in 1662.[57] Similarly William Whateley found great satisfaction in his marriage to Martha Hunt, daughter of George Hunt, minister at Collingbourne Dulcis in Wiltshire. In his famous handbook *A Bride-Bush: Or A Direction for Married Persons* (1619), Whateley declared: 'I have been better able to show what a good wife should do, by finding the full duty of a wife, in as exact completeness, as mortality can afford, daily and continually performed unto me in mine own house'.[58]

A Bride-Bush was one of a number of influential guides to family relationships written by puritan ministers before the Civil War. The stress which such books placed on religious observance within the family has led Christopher Hill amongst others to regard puritans as responsible for the 'spiritualisation of the household'.[59] This theory has received criticism from historians who have traced the emphasis on family devotions to the writings of pre-Reformation humanist and Catholic writers,[60] but despite such precedents the semi-separatist nature of puritanism before 1640 inevitably meant that household worship would play a particularly important practical role in the transmission of puritan ideals within family groups.

VII

The distinctiveness of puritan worship and aspirations was un-doubtedly sharpened by the religious policies of Charles I's regime. In particular the influence of Arminianism in the highest levels of the church and amongst some parish clergy combined with the policy of railing altars at the east end of churches aroused fears that the king was sympathetic to Catholic theology and practices. This in turn provoked militant puritans into increasingly overt opposition to the crown. The sustained meeting of the Long Parliament provided the arena in which opposition could be translated into practical action and the debates and deliberations of the members revealed the depth of their hostility to Caroline religious and secular policies. Many of the parliamentarian initiatives for godly reform in the Long Parlia-ment have, however, been interpreted as political responses to Scottish demands for religious advances in England.[61] This approach downplays the overwhelming evidence that such reforms often revived schemes that had been advocated in godly circles for many decades or had surfaced in earlier parliaments and were thus popular with puritans in the English and Welsh counties. In 1640 the puritan activitists looked far beyond a defensive reaction to the immediate religious policies of the 1630s and stressed the need to complete the work of reformation begun in Elizabeth's time. In a sermon to the House of Commons on November 17th, the anniversary of the queen's accession, Cornelius Burgess commented on the significance of the date and argued that 'the very memory of so blessed a work begun on this very day', should persuade the members to 'to go forward to perfect that happy Reformation, which yet in many parts lies unpolished and unperfected'.[62] Political tactics and programmes for religious reform dating from Elizabeth's reign were revived and during the summer of 1640 there is evidence that puritan clergy were organising meetings in London and the provinces in order to discuss reforms and promote petitioning campaigns. The first signs of such organisation came in response to the 'etcetera oath' contained in the church canons of 1640 binding all who took it to the approval of the doctrine and discipline of the Church of England and the mainten-ance of the church hierarchy of 'archbishops, bishops, deans and archdeacons etc'.[63] The oath triggered a spate of clerical meetings and petitioning which continued throughout the autumn and winter of that year.

Initially clergy from the diocese of London formulated an eight-point rebuttal of the oath, claiming additionally that convocation had no authority to formulate canons after the dissolution of the Short Parliament.[64] Their objections were circulated in the provinces and in Northamptonshire over 20 ministers met to discuss the arguments of the London ministers at Kettering, where the town lectureship had been disestablished in the mid 1630s, because of the nonconformity of some of the lecturers. These conferences soon provoked a more wide-ranging debate about the validity of episcopacy and the government of the church. Richard Baxter recorded that in Shropshire the ministers of the county met at Bridgnorth to discuss the oath, which was opposed by the majority present. Baxter later noted that the oath 'put me upon deeper thoughts of the point of episcopacy, and of the English frame of Church government, than ever I had before'. In November, 31 ministers in the diocese of Hereford petitioned parliament against both the canons and the oath, and Stanley Gower, one of the signatories of the Hereford petition, argued that it would make parliament 'take due notice of us and that it will be a good remonstrance against the corruption of that hierarchy, whose downfall we expect daily'.[65]

A nation-wide Petition and Remonstrance attacking *jure divino* claims for episcopal authority and carrying 'near upon a thousand ministers names' was delivered to the Commons on 23 January 1641. This tactic deliberately recalled the Millenary Petition, a similarly national document emanating from the clergy. The petitioners of 1641 also consciously drew attention to the situation following the failure of the Millenary Petition when 'many hundreds were deprived' for not conforming to the canons of 1604. Cross-questioning in the Commons of some of the key clerical promoters of the Petition and Remonstrance, including John White of Dorchester, Stephen Marshall, Edmund Calamy, Cornelius Burgess and George Downing revealed, however, that most of the signatories had not seen these documents, but had signed other similar petitions which had been centrally amalgamated and only 'some four score ministers' had heard the final versions read at a meeting in London. While the tactics employed appeared dubious, the spokesmen maintained that they had represented the sense of the discarded petitions accurately, and the evidence presented to the House further illustrates the active political involvement of possibly hundreds of puritan clergy outside the capital.[66]

Perhaps the most successful lobbying in these early stages was for the removal of non-godly clergy in the parishes, which recalled one of the demands of the Millenary Petition in 1603. Abortive legislation against scandalous and unworthy ministers had also been drawn up in the 1626 and 1628 sessions of parliament. Puritan pressure for the reform of the clergy was clearly expressed by Cornelius Burgess in his fast sermon of 17 November 1640 in which he urged parliament to promote preaching, which was now held in such contempt that to be an assiduous preacher had become 'the odious character of a Puritan'. Burgess called on the Commons to reform or cast out 'idle, unsound, unprofitable, and scandalous ministers' and to provide for a preaching ministry in every congregation. He was followed in the pulpit by Stephen Marshall, incumbent of an Essex parish, who also emphasised the importance of Elizabeth's accession. On this day 82 years earlier 'the Lord set up the Gospel among us and took us to be a nation in covenant with him'. Despite this the nation had fallen away and now hankered after idolatry and superstition. In order to check this decline Marshall too stressed the role of preaching and argued that of the 9000 or 10,000 parishes in England there were many thousands 'which these eighty years have not had the blessing to enjoy . . . a settled, faithful, preaching ministry'.[67]

In response to this and similar pressure the Commons resuscitated the idea of surveying the condition of the ministry, which had first been undertaken by puritan lobbyists in the mid 1580s. On December 19th the House ordered that all MPs should return information about the state of the ministry in their counties within six weeks.[68] In certain areas this work was undertaken with rapid enthusiasm by both laity and clergy, some of whom doubtless acted from personal animosity rather than godly principle. Sufficient documentation survives, however, to demonstrate the active involvement of the godly in preparing local returns. Uniquely, a complete manuscript 'survey of the ministry' drawn up by fourteen local puritans and covering 193 parishes has survived for Herefordshire.[69] Such evidence provided the basis for the proceedings of the committee for scandalous ministers, which undertook a massive investigation into these complaints and effected nothing less than a revolution in the personnel of the clergy in areas controlled by parliament in the 1640s. In 1643 John White, the London Lawyer and chairman of the committee appointed to consider these complaints, published an account of the first 100 investigations under the title *The First Century of Scandalous Malignant Priests*. His book illustrates the witch-hunt that was conducted against any clergyman who had accepted the altar policy and its associated church decorations in the 1630s or who had royalist leanings. The parliamentarians also pursued clergy who were regarded as morally lax and between 1641 and 1660 as many as a quarter of the parishes in England may have been under sequestration as a result of the work of White's committee and its successors.[70]

During the period leading up to the outbreak of the Civil War schemes for puritan reforms jostled with plans for political, military and legal reforms.[71] Amongst the many puritan measures that were discussed in committees were draft legislation against idolatry, which eventually emerged as a Commons' ordinance in September 1641, and draft legislation 'for the more free passage of the gospel', which would have allowed ministers to preach as often as they wished in their own parishes and parishioners to attend a Sunday sermon in other parishes, if they could not have one in their own.[72]

The most far-reaching religious measure to be discussed was undoubtedly the draft legislation for a Root and Branch bill drawn up in the summer of 1641, partly in order to appease parliament's Scottish allies, but also as a signal to puritan petitioners that their demands were being considered at Westminster. The subsequent shelving of this bill reflects its divisive nature even amongst parliamentarians, some of whom wanted total abolition whereas others would have preferred an episcopate with greatly reduced powers.[73] The removal of episcopacy would certainly have caused a tremendous backlash in favour of the crown and split the parliamentarians while the war was in progress, and this alone is sufficient to explain why abolition was not carried out until late in 1646, after the parliamentarian victory against the king. The subsequent erection of a presbyterian system was never achieved on a national basis and again reflects the lack of nation-wide popular support for such a system.[74]

The debate over religious reform was also seen by many MPs as a matter for the clergy as well as themselves and in August 1643 the Westminster Assembly of Divines was convened in order to present detailed proposals to parliament. Although the decision to call a clerical synod at this time has been interpreted as a manoeuvre to secure the support of the Scots,[75] it was also a proposal that had firm backing amongst English puritans in the provinces. In his plans discussed above William Voyle, for example, suggested that 'a free national synod' should approve all canons or orders concerning ecclesiastical affairs. The Herefordshire survey of the ministry of 1641 similarly advised that a synod 'of the best and learnedest divines' should 'treat and agree upon a settled platform of church government, to be ratified by Parliament'.[76] The Assembly drew up the Directory for Public Worship as a replacement for the Book of Common Prayer, although not all of its proposals were so readily accepted by parliament.

That religion was a mainspring to opposition against Charles I during the English Civil War was fully apparent to contemporaries caught in the unfolding events of the conflict in the early 1640s. Active supporters of the Long Parliament frequently defined themselves in terms of their puritan religious sympathies, as did Lady Brilliana Harley when writing to her husband about the activities of the local royalist party in Herefordshire in the late summer of 1642 to complain 'they say they maintain the true religion, but they shamefully use all that profess it'. Her voluminous correspondence provides ample testimony to the Harley family's staunch puritanism and to Lady Harley's own sense of religious as well as political isolation from her opponents in the county and beyond its borders.[77] In similar vein Oliver Cromwell wrote that the parliamentarian victory at Marston Moor in 1644 'had all the evidences of an absolute victory obtained by the Lord's blessing upon the godly party principally'.[78] The religious dimensions of the war were similarly emphasised by the king's supporters and during the course of 1642 royalist propaganda played upon the fears raised by religious radicalism and repeatedly branded the parliamentarian party as puritanical, heretical, schismatic and atheistic. Recent scholarship into the progress of the Civil War in the localities has also consistently demonstrated the links between religious belief and parliamentarianism in the 1640s. In Yorkshire J. T. Cliffe has found that the puritans represented 'by far the most important element' on the parliamentarian side, of Lancashire Dr Blackwood has observed that 'in few counties can puritans have formed such a large proportion of the parliamentarian gentry', and in Herefordshire the parliamentarian party centred on a godly clique headed by the Harley family.[79] National studies by Anthony Fletcher and John Morrill concur in their findings that many of the parliamentarians were religiously motivated.[80]

In the 1640s the more radical puritans were able to mount an effective political and military opposition to the crown because they could make common ground with moderate puritans and others who had been alienated by the Personal Rule of the 1630s. As with all revolutionaries the puritans would not stand united once they achieved victory and in time, as John Spurr shows later in this volume, the puritan movement would split permanently into moderate puritan opinion, presbyterianism and Independency. Before 1640, however, the difference between these groupings was not so obvious and, as has often been stated, what united them then was more important than what divided them.

The dynamic response of puritans to the political events of the early 1640s argues against any interpretation of puritanism as quiescent in the early-Stuart period. Far from being in retreat after Elizabeth's death puritanism continued as a growing cultural force, capable at any time of assuming a politically active form in response to challenge or opportunity. Between the 1590s and 1640 puritanism prospered in parishes and towns where lay patronage allowed the godly to operate in a state of near separation from the established church. The 1630s saw the creation of a number of *causes célèbres* with the prosecutions of William Prynne, Henry Burton and John Bastwick, and the suspension of ministers such as Thomas Wilson for not praying against the Scots and Richard Culmer for not reading the Book of Sports.[81] Both Wilson and Culmer were incumbents in the diocese of Canterbury where the archbishop's officials needed to appear to implement central policies effectively. Elsewhere, however, outside interference was often half-hearted or ineffectual in the face of powerful local interests such as those of the Harleys in the Herefordshire borderland or in Essex of Robert Rich, earl of Warwick, who was described in 1640 as 'the temporal head of the puritans'.[82] In 1640 the puritans did not look forward to the inevitable splits that lay ahead, they looked back to the reforms that should have been effected in Elizabeth's day and revived earlier tactics to achieve them. The parliamentarians implemented religious reforms with growing vigour as their military victory became assured after the battle of Naseby in 1645, though as Christopher Durston demonstrates below these reforms failed to gain popularity amongst the general population. The ultimate failure of the puritan revolution should not divert our attention either from the existence of an expanding puritan culture between 1559 and 1642 or from the central role which that culture undoubtedly played in creating a parliamentarian party in the 1640s.

7. Puritan Rule and the Failure of Cultural Revolution, 1645–1660

CHRISTOPHER DURSTON

In the summer of 1645, as parliament was gaining the decisive upper hand in the English Civil War, John Large the minister of Rother-field in Sussex was summoned to appear before Francis Cheynell, one of the most enthusiastic members of the Sussex Committee for Plundered Ministers. He was accused of two crimes: collecting his tithes on a Sunday and breaking a cake over the head of a bride during a wedding at which he had officiated. In his defence against the second charge, Large argued that the practice of cake-breaking at weddings was 'a custom which had long prevailed in his parish and which he thought might be inoffensive, in itself neither good nor bad, as many received customs were'. Cheynell, however, who was a staunch puritan, viewed such 'received customs' in a far more sinister light and promptly ordered that the cleric should be dismissed from the ministry.[1] This incident could perhaps be seen as the symbolic launching of the puritan attempt to bring about a cultural revolution in mid seventeenth-century England, for Large was one of the earliest casualties in a battle which the newly powerful English puritans would wage for the next 15 years in a bid to destroy the old pre-war popular culture of the English people and replace it with their own very different godly culture.

As has been shown in some of the preceding chapters, during the 80-year period that separated the Elizabethan Church Settlement from the outbreak of the Civil War puritans had been pressurising the leaders of the English church for the introduction of a pro-gramme of major liturgical and moral reform. Throughout this period they had spared no pains in the attempt both to purge the church of the remnants of an offensive 'popish' ritual and to improve

210

the morality of what they had increasingly come to regard as God's elect or chosen nation. When Archbishop Laud launched a highly successful counter-attack against such puritan agitation in the 1630s, the resultant tensions and divisions had led directly to the collapse of the state and the coming of civil war in 1642. As a result of the parliamentary victory in that war, the country fell under the control of a succession of godly regimes, and puritanism was presented with the perfect opportunity to use the full power of central government to impose its cultural values upon the English nation.

The attempt to do this began in earnest with the publication in early 1645 of the Directory for Public Worship. The product of long deliberation by the Westminster Assembly of Divines, the Directory contained the liturgy of a new presbyterian state church which the Long Parliament intended to impose on the country. The compilers of the Directory, who had made no secret of their hostility to some of the most cherished elements of popular religion, denounced many of the traditional celebrations of the old festive calendar and introduced a range of new pared-down and simplified ceremonies for some of the most important religious rites of passage. Before it was able to impose this new presbyterian establishment upon the country, however, the Long Parliament was purged and removed from power by the leaders of the Independent New Model Army. While the new military government that emerged in 1649 had no desire to preside over a compulsory national church, it fully shared the Long Parliament's commitment to core puritan values. As a result the Directory's liturgy remained in force throughout the Interregnum, and the assault on popular culture intensified and widened in scope.

One of the prime targets of the puritan reformers was the traditional festive calendar. In the century before the Civil War puritans had frequently attacked the popular celebrations associated with both the major Christian festivals, such as Christmas and Whitsun, and the remnants of the old pagan calendar, in particular the May Day fertility rites, and as soon as parliament had gained the upper hand in the Civil War they launched an all-out attack on these festivities. In April 1644 a parliamentary ordinance described may-poles as 'a Heathenish vanity, generally abused to superstition and wickedness' and declared that: 'no Maypole shall be hereafter set up, erected or suffered to be within this kingdom'.[2] In 1645 the Directory for Public Worship declared that: 'Festival days, vulgarly called holy days, having no Warrant in the Word of God, are not to be continued'.[3] Two years later in June 1647 a parliamentary ordinance summarily abolished the feasts of Christmas, Easter and Whitsun and 'all other Festival days, commonly called Holy-Days'.[4] The observance of Lent and the Shrove Tuesday rituals of misrule which preceded it was also discouraged.[5]

In place of these traditional festivals, the Long Parliament introduced its own new revolutionary calendar. To compensate scholars, servants and apprentices for the loss of the holidays associated with the major Christian feasts, in June 1647 parliament instituted a new secular holiday on the second Tuesday of every month. This new rest day was to be carefully regulated, for the authorities were insistent that they would not allow it to be misspent 'to the dishonour of God, scandal of Religion, and detriment of both Masters and Servants'. They thus ordered that all taverns and alehouses should be searched on the evening of the holiday to make sure that no apprentices remained in them after eight o'clock, and they threatened those who abused the day or joined in any 'riotous assembly' with the loss of their recreation.[6]

Another feature of the puritan calendar was the provision of a set of new religious holidays in the form of public days of fasting and humiliation and thanksgiving. Throughout the seven-year period between February 1642 and February 1649, the last Wednesday of every month was set aside as a day of national fasting and humiliation. Puritan opinion firmly believed that England's political and religious crisis was the product of divine anger, and that this would only be assuaged when the people acknowledged their sinfulness, unworthiness and insignificance in the face of their fearsome and imperious Calvinist God. The main purpose of the monthly fast-day, therefore, was to 'humble' the English people: to engender in them the deep sense of collective self-abasement which was a necessary precondition of their moral and spiritual reformation. The Long Parliament MPs observed the monthly fast-day by suspending normal business and attending two sermons at St Margaret's Church, Westminster. Elsewhere in the country, men and women were required to go without food, put aside their normal working activities, and attend their local parish churches for a round of prayer, readings and sermons which might last most of the day.

The 1645 Directory gave detailed instructions about how these fast-days were to be observed. Men and women were required to come to church early in the morning after preparing themselves in private beforehand and to spend 'so large a proportion of the day as conveniently may be' in public religious exercises. They were ordered to abstain not only from food 'but also from all worldly labour, discourses and thoughts, and from all bodily delights'.[7] Although the regular Wednesday fast-day was abolished in the spring of 1649, further occasional days of fasting and humiliation were called at frequent intervals throughout the Interregnum. The first, held by the Rump in April 1649, was aimed at improving the nation's morality, and further fasts for moral reformation were subsequently called by both Oliver and Richard Cromwell. Others were kept in the hope of ending visitations of plague or drought.[8]

On a number of occasions during the 1640s and 1650s puritan governments also called days of public thanksgiving in order that the nation could publicly display its gratitude to God, usually following some notable military victory or political success. While the authorities did not expect these holidays to be observed with quite the same degree of introspective gloom that was required on days of fasting and humiliation, they did believe they should be restrained and essentially religious events. Thus, the Directory stated that the people should attend their parish churches for morning and evening thanksgiving services and that they should 'spend the residue of that day in holy duties and testifications of Christian love and charity one towards another'. The one concession to secular celebration was the permitting of a communal midday meal, and this was clearly meant to be a sober and modest affair; indeed ministers were instructed to warn their congregations at the end of the morning service to 'beware of all excess and riot, tending to gluttony or drunkenness . . . and to take care that their mirth and rejoicing be not carnal, but spiritual'.[9]

A further distinctive feature of the new calendar was the imposition of the puritan Sunday. The belief that Sunday – the Christian sabbath – should be given over exclusively to a round of private and public religious exercises had been one of the core beliefs of early seventeenth-century puritans, and during the reigns of James I and Charles I they had reacted with intense anger to governmental initiatives like the publication in 1618 and 1633 of a Book of Sports which encouraged participation in a range of Sunday sports and leisure activities. Following the meeting of the Long Parliament, puritan MPs moved quickly to impose a strict sabbatarian discipline upon the country. In September 1641 they declared that 'the Lord's

Day should be duly observed and sanctified; that all dancing or other sports either before or after divine service be forborne and restrained; and that the preaching [of] God's word be promoted in the afternoon.'[10] In May 1643 they ordered that all copies of Charles I's Declaration of Sports should be burned, and in April 1644 they passed an ordinance for the better observation of the Lord's Day, which banned all sports and commercial activities on Sundays and stipulated that 'no person or persons shall hereafter upon the Lords-day use, exercise, keep, maintain, or be present at any wrestlings, Shooting, Bowling, Ringing of Bells for Pleasure or Pastime, Masque, Wake, otherwise called Feasts, Church-Ale, Dancing, Games, Sport or Pastime whatsoever.'[11] Nine months later the Directory declared that 'the whole day is to be celebrated as holy to the Lord, both in public and private, as being the Christian Sabbath', and ordered the population to attend morning and evening services and to spend the interim period 'in Reading, Meditation, Repetition of Sermons (especially by calling their families to an account of what they have heard) and catechizing of them, holy conferences, prayers for a blessing upon the Public Ordinance, singing of psalms, visiting the sick, relieving the poor, and such like duties of piety charity and mercy, accounting the Sabbath a delight.'[12] In 1650 and 1657 further legislation broadened the scope of the regulations and increased the penalties for infringement.[13] During the debates in parliament which preceded the passing of the 1657 act, some MPs even discussed at length whether people should be allowed to sit outside their homes on the sabbath.[14]

A second area where puritan governments introduced major change to traditional practice following their victory in the Civil War was that of the religious rites attached to the individual milestones of birth, marriage and death. Throughout the Christian era, newborn children had entered into the community of the church through the rite of infant baptism. Baptism had been one of the Roman Catholic church's most important sacraments, and following the Reformation crisis of the early sixteenth century, the vast majority of Protestant reformers had retained it as a sacrament. They had, however, rejected many of the ceremonial features of the old Catholic rite; in particular they had dispensed with the exorcising of the devil from the infant at the church door and with the anointing of the child's head with holy oil, or chrism.

The baptism ceremony used within the English church between 1560 and 1640 was laid out in the Elizabethan Book of Common

Prayer of 1559. Although it was modelled on that included in the 1552 English Prayer Book, which had been drawn up at the height of the Protestant reforms of Edward VI's reign, it was to prove the object of some considerable puritan hostility over the next 80 years. Many puritans believed that baptism should be administered at the front of the church before the entire congregation, rather than more privately at the font. They opposed the practice of making the sign of the cross over the infant and they objected to the choosing of godparents – or 'gossips' – for the child on the grounds that their involvement might lead to an abdication of parental responsibility. In line with these objections, in 1645 the Directory for Public Worship outlined a new baptism service, which was to take place in the front of the church and to dispense with the sign of the cross and a number of other 'popish' prayers. Ministers were now enjoined to sprinkle water on the child's head 'without adding any other ceremony', godparents were outlawed and parents were required to present their own children for baptism.[15] This Directory service remained the official form of public baptism until the Restoration.

An additional rite associated with childbirth was the churching of the new mother. A christianised version of the Jewish purification ceremony, this usually took place a few weeks after the birth of the child and marked the public re-entry of the mother into the religious and social community. Many Elizabethan and Jacobean puritans had been highly critical of what they regarded as this unnecessary relic of popery and numbers of godly women had refused to be churched in accordance with the Book of Common Prayer rite.[16] During the 1630s puritan opposition to the rite was further fuelled by the insistence of the Laudian bishops that women should wear veils and kneel during the ceremony.[17] Churching was thus another early target for the puritan reformers of the 1640s. In 1641 a Long Parliament committee suggested that the ceremony should be modified to include a new thanksgiving prayer. Several years later the question was considered by the Westminster Assembly of Divines, which decided to dispense with it altogether.[18] No churching ceremony was included in the Directory, and the rite was effectively banned for the next 15 years.

The years following the parliamentary victory in the Civil War also saw major changes in the way that marriages were solemnised in England. Puritan opinion had long been opposed to a number of features of the Book of Common Prayer marriage ceremony, in particular the use of the ring and the husband's promise to worship his wife with his body. It had also been greatly disturbed by the confusion surrounding matrimonial canon law, which allowed couples who married by licence to avoid having their banns read in church, and which still technically permitted couples to marry without setting foot in church through the public exchange of vows, or spousals. In 1645, therefore, the Directory laid out a new marriage service, which was much shorter and simpler than its predecessor, and dispensed with the ring and the promise of bodily worship.[19] Confusion and irregularity in marriage solemnisation nonetheless remained widespread, and in 1653 the fiercely anti-clerical members of Barebone's Parliament set out to remedy the problem by taking the radical step of redefining marriage as an entirely secular undertaking. Their 'Act touching marriages and the Registering thereof', which was passed in August 1653, outlawed church weddings and replaced them with civil ceremonies performed by justices of the peace. For the next three and a half years only these secular services were recognised as having legal validity. In April 1657, after much heated debate, the MPs of Cromwell's second protectorate parliament decided that religious weddings should once more be allowed and six months later the Civil Marriage Act was allowed to lapse. At the Restoration Charles II's government was faced with a desperately confused situation, and it responded by passing an act to legalise retrospectively all marriages 'had or solemnized in England since 1st May 1642 before any JP or pretended JP'.[20]

The final rite of passage reformed by the post-Civil War puritan authorities was that associated with the dying. Although the Protestant reformers of the sixteenth century had dispensed with many of the Roman Catholic death rites, in Elizabethan and early-Stuart England deaths had continued to be marked by a sequence of important consoling rituals. They were still traditionally announced to the community through the ringing of a death knell on the bells of the parish church; the deceased was still laid to rest in accordance with the elaborate ritual of the Book of Common Prayer burial service, and the burial was still normally followed by some form of funeral meal. Puritans had long regarded these rituals as both superstitious and uncomfortably similar to the death rites of the papists. In 1645, therefore, the Directory banned these traditional practices and ordered that henceforth the dead should be laid to rest 'without any ceremony'. All kneeling by, or praying over the corpse was forbidden, as was all 'praying, reading, and singing both in going to, and at the grave'. The presence of a minister at a burial was no longer thought to be essential or desirable, and the only activities considered appropriate for the mourners to engage in were private 'meditations' and 'conferences suitable to the occasion'.[21] By these measures, the compilers of the Directory attempted to secularise death, in much the same way as the members of Barebone's Parliament would later attempt to secularise marriage.

The third major area of puritan initiative was the campaign for moral reform. The vital importance of maintaining high standards of personal and public morality was a constant theme of puritan preaching and writing between 1560 and 1640; so too were godly denunciations of the English people for their addiction to 'cakes and ale'. Puritans were particularly scandalised by what they saw as widespread sexual promiscuity and excessive indulgence in drinking, gaming, dancing and swearing. Once they had seized the reins of power, they approached the daunting challenge of improving the moral calibre of the nation with a characteristic confidence and energy. While some moral initiatives – such as the 1642 ordinance which closed the London theatres – dated from the Civil War years, the campaign rapidly gathered pace in the early 1650s. In January 1650 the Rump Parliament passed an 'Act for the better prevention of prophane Swearing and Cursing', under which those caught swearing were fined on a sliding scale according to their social status; peers were to pay 30 shillings for a first offence, gentlemen 6s 8d, and those lower down the social scale 3s 4d. The fines were to be doubled for second transgressions and persistent offenders could be bound over for their good behaviour. Those who failed to pay their fines could be placed in the stocks, and children under the age of twelve could be whipped.[22] Five months later the Rump passed its notorious Adultery Act, which imposed the death penalty on those found guilty of adultery, and three months' imprisonment on convicted fornicators. Prostitutes and brothel-keepers were to be whipped, branded and imprisoned for a first offence, and to suffer the death penalty following any subsequent conviction.[23]

The pressure for moral reformation was maintained throughout the protectorate. In March 1654 Oliver Cromwell issued an ordinance prohibiting all cockfights, and several months later he placed a six months' ban on horse-race meetings.[24] In the autumn of 1655 he appointed a number of his army colleagues as major-generals and despatched them to the English localities with instructions to 'encourage and promote godliness, and discourage and discountenance all profaneness and ungodliness'. They were required to execute vigorously the laws against swearing, drunkenness and sabbath-breaking; to close down brothels, gaming-houses and illegal ale-houses; and to ensure that no horse-races, cockfights, bear-baitings or stage plays took place within their areas.[25] Although the major-generals' experiment was to prove short-lived, Cromwell and his colleagues remained firmly attached to their puritan moral vision. In June 1657, for example, acts were passed banning the performing of music in taverns and alehouses and outlawing all wagers and betting.[26]

The puritan reform initiatives described above – the frontal assault on the seasonal festivals that had traditionally marked the turning year, the transformation of the rites associated with the important stages in the lifecycle, and the sweeping measures to clamp down on popular leisure pursuits and moral laxity – constituted an ambitious and determined effort to change many of the English people's most deeply rooted customs. Taken together, they amount to nothing less than an attempt to bring about wholesale cultural revolution.

The repercussions of this attempted revolution were felt all over the country. In most English counties the magistrates felt obliged to take some account of the sustained pressure being exercised by the centre, and in counties as diverse as Devon, Somerset, Middlesex, Essex, Hertfordshire, Warwickshire, Northamptonshire, Norfolk and Yorkshire they responded by indicting offenders against puritan sensibilities, in particular those who kept or frequented unlicensed alehouses or failed to observe the sabbath regulations. The major-generals also approached their missions with energy and enthusiasm. Charles Worsley, for example, who controlled a large area in the north-west of the country, displayed what John Morrill has called 'exceptional zeal and thoroughness' in the work of moral reformation. He laboured tirelessly to prosecute sabbath breakers, drunkards and swearers, to eradicate the large numbers of unlicensed alehouses, and to punish those who participated in religious weddings.[27] Many urban corporations also took action. In Oxford parliamentary soldiers confiscated the garlands and musical instruments of those who attempted to celebrate May Day in 1648, and the town authorities subsequently banned the traditional college celebrations associated with All Saints' Day, Christmas, Candlemas and Shrove Tuesday.[28]

The campaign was particularly eagerly embraced by the puritan governors of those local communities where the battle to create godly New Jerusalems had already met with some measure of success before 1642. In Dorchester in Dorset – a town David Underdown has described as the most puritan place in England – the Interregnum authorities needed 'little encouragement when it came to moral reformation'. Throughout the 1650s they maintained a vigorous assault against swearers, drunkards, unlicensed ale-sellers and those who absented themselves from church. They also ensured that the Directory was employed in church services and that public fast-days were observed conscientiously.[29] In Coventry puritans within the municipal government made a similar concerted effort to impose the godly moral programme. Robert Beake, mayor of the town from 1655 to 1656, proceeded with vigour against drunkards, swearers and sabbath-breakers. He also imprisoned several couples for fornication, and took action against a man who had attempted to act as a godparent at a christening.[30] Puritan corporations were also very active in Rye and Lewes in Sussex.[31]

Within some communities the impetus for reform came from the local puritan minister, who could on occasions call on the help of his churchwardens and a small caucus of 'well affected' parishioners. Ralph Josselin, for example, made a concerted effort to change the cultural values of his Essex parishioners by denouncing their Christmas celebrations and vigorously promoting the new opportunities for public fasting.[32] Richard Baxter showed a similar dedication in his attempts to reform Kidderminster in the 1650s, where he introduced preaching, prayer meetings, cathechisings and monthly conferences on parish discipline.[33]

In some of these places puritan campaigning does appear to have achieved a limited degree of success. Josselin remarked in his diary in 1647 that he had 'weaned' many of his parishioners off the celebration of Christmas, and Richard Baxter claimed that his church in Kidderminster was full on Sundays and that by the end of the 1650s, 100 of the town's families spent the sabbath singing psalms and reading the Bible and other devotional works.[34] There is evidence from both Rye and Lewes of some genuine popular support among the townspeople for reforms such as civil marriage.[35] According to Anthony Wood, by 1660 the seasonal customs which had been such an important feature of college life in pre-war Oxford had been generally forgotten and they were not revived at the Restoration, and Ronald Hutton has recently confirmed that within a number of communities puritan reform did indeed deliver some 'serious blows to the old festival culture'.[36] But while there were a few localised success stories, with regard to the nation as a whole the campaign undoubtedly failed. This failure should be chiefly attributed to two distinct but closely linked reasons: the grudging and nominal response shown by a great many of those who were charged with implementing these puritan reforms at the local level, and the strong and defiant attachment of the great majority of the English people to their traditional pre-war culture.

Although victory in the Civil War had given English puritans control over the most important organs of central government, it had not delivered them a corresponding dominance over the various local jurisdictions of the English provinces. While there was a scattering of puritan justices of the peace who were more than willing to take up the lead given by Whitehall and Westminster, there were also many other JPs who were apathetic or openly hostile to the aspirations of the reformers. The result was that in many counties only a face-saving trickle of moral offenders was brought before the courts. In Warwickshire the level of indictment of those who broke the sabbath regulations or kept unlicensed alehouses was not markedly higher in the 1650s than it had been in the 1630s; throughout the entire decade only eight individuals were indicted for swearing, and only six for fornication.[37] In Essex, Devon, Hertfordshire, Somerset and Yorkshire, too, the justices dealt with only a handful of cases of drunkenness, swearing and sabbath-breaking each year.[38] Many JPs seem to have been especially reluctant to convict under the 1650 adultery legislation, with the result that probably no more than three women were executed for that crime.[39] In Essex seven people were indicted for adultery during the 1650s but none was hanged, while in Middlesex, of the 27 individuals brought before the justices for adultery, 25 were found not guilty.[40] The fact that the Middlesex JPs imprisoned some of those they had acquitted until they could provide sureties for their future good behaviour may suggest that they believed that they had in fact committed the offence, but did not wish to invoke the act's draconian penalty. Other magistrates took a similarly lenient attitude towards suspected fornicators; of the 30 individuals accused of fornication in Devon between 1655 and 1660, 27 were acquitted.[41]

Apathy or hostility to puritan aspirations was also widespread among more humble local officials. In 1652 a clergyman complained to the Somerset justices that the sabbath was regularly 'profaned' in West Chinnock in Somerset by those who engaged in sports and other pastimes, and that the local churchwardens and tithingmen 'do not only neglect but altogether refuse to do their duty in that behalf, whereby God is highly discouraged and the young people in licentiousness encouraged'.[42] During Whit week of 1653 the tithingmen of Alhampton in Somerset positively encouraged their neighbours to 'make merry with skimmington' and promised to provide beer for their Whitsun revels.[43] In November 1656 John Witcombe of Barton St David in Somerset was placed in his village stocks for persistent swearing. His local minister, who might have been expected to have approved of the punishment, in fact brought him beer to drink and publicly declared that the punishment was illegal and that he should be paid compensation. The next Sunday he further commented on the incident in his sermon, remarking that '[St] Paul was whipped and stocked and did not grieve it, neither should we'.[44] When two churchwardens raided the Black Lion Inn in Wincanton in Somerset late one evening in July 1657 and demanded to know why the landlord was still selling drink, they were told that they might as well join the company as it already included a number of the town's other officials.[45] In November 1658 John Morgan, a churchwarden from Cheadle in Cheshire, got into trouble for hiring out his bull 'to be baited from Alehouse to Alehouse on Cheadle Wake day'.[46]

Many puritans were well aware that the role of these local officers was crucial, and as the 1650s progressed they became increasingly frustrated by the failure of the great majority of them to embrace the reform work wholeheartedly. Cromwell's major-generals were frequently brought face-to-face with this problem. In November 1655 Edward Whalley, the major-general for a large area of the east Midlands, complained to Cromwell's secretary John Thurloe that 'what some justices in order to reformation do, others undo', and the following month he again protested that 'wicked magistrates by reason of their number overpower the godly magistrates'.[47] In January 1656 his colleague Charles Worsley told Thurloe that the lack of 'honest and sufficient men' to act as constables was a 'great evil to this nation', and in February another major-general, James

Berry, exclaimed in exasperation from Monmouth: 'I am much troubled with these market towns, everywhere vice abounding and magistrates fast asleep.'[48] In May 1656 William Goffe, major-general for Sussex, Hampshire and Berkshire, added his testimony by denouncing the 'wicked spirit' of the justices in Hampshire.[49] Later that year Richard Baxter commented in a letter to Edward Harley: 'It will never be well till we have either more zealous justices than most are, or else there be greater penalties on magistrates and constables for neglect of their duty.'[50] In June 1657 the Lord Chief Justice commented in parliament during the debate on the tightening of the sabbath regulations that constables and headboroughs were 'generally bad, all the nation over'.[51]

Writing to the Wiltshire justices in 1656 to request them to close down a number of unlicensed alehouses in his town, the puritan mayor of Salisbury, William Stone, subjected the bench to a stern lecture about its responsibilities and the consequences of any failure to act. He warned the JPs that:

> God hath honoured you in calling you to a place of power and trust, and he expects that you should be faithful in that trust. You are posting to the grave every day, you are dwelling upon the borders of eternity . . . therefore double and treble your resolutions to be zealous in a good thing. How dreadful will a dieing bed be to a negligent magistrate, what is the reward of a slothful servant, is it not to be punished with everlasting destruction from the presence of the Lord.[52]

Such dire warnings did not, however, cut much ice with those beyond the puritan fold. The attitude of most local officials remained at best lukewarm, and their lack of real support played a large part in the failure of puritan hopes for reform.

The second and perhaps more important reason for the failure of the puritan campaign was the fact that it proved impossible to impose it by force on a people who for the most part viewed it with a withering scorn and contempt, and defiantly refused to abandon their traditional practices.

A great many men and women clung tenaciously to the rituals of the old festive calendar. Official disapproval was not able to eradicate May Day celebrations, which clearly persisted in many parts of the country. A maypole was set up in Bury St Edmunds in 1648, and five years later in April 1653 the dissolution of the Rump was celebrated in Wolverhampton by the erecting of a maypole.[53] According to a contemporary newsbook report, May Day of 1654 was celebrated in Hyde Park by crowds of revellers and 'much sin was committed by wicked meetings with fiddlers, drunkenness, ribaldry and the like'.[54] Maypoles, may-bushes, morris dancing and 'other heathenish and unlawful customs' were still evident in Henley-in-Arden in Warwickshire in the mid 1650s and could still 'draw together a great concourse of loose people'.[55] Even in godly Coventry some individuals observed May Day in 1656 by playing cards and shovel board.[56] Not surprisingly, the fertility associations of the day had a particularly enduring appeal. Several pamphlets published in the late 1650s roundly denounced the sexual promiscuity of those who attended the annual May Day celebrations in Hyde Park, and in 1657 one William Morris of Duddington in Northamptonshire entered into the priapic spirit of the day by having sexual intercourse with his maidservant Anne Key.[57]

Christmas was even more resilient. While the government was able to keep most churches closed on Christmas Day, clandestine services were never totally eradicated and whenever they occurred they attracted a steady stream of worshippers. In 1657, for example, a number of services were held in and around London and the diarist John Evelyn joined a 'grand assembly' which celebrated the feast in Exeter House Chapel in the Strand.[58] While many others may not have been sufficiently motivated to risk punishment by attending church on Christmas Day, they nonetheless had no intention of allowing the government to rob them of their Christmas holiday. Despite a succession of orders to the contrary, the vast majority of shops and businesses remained closed on 25 December and most of the population continued to indulge in their traditional feasting and celebrating. In London in 1645 only a handful of shops opened on Christmas Day and several of these were forced to close after coming under attack from boys throwing stones.[59] In 1652 the newsbook *The Flying Eagle* observed that the 'taverns and taphouses' were full on Christmas Day and claimed that 'the poor will pawn all . . . to provide Christmas pies for their bellies and the broth of abominable things in their vessels, though they starve or pine for it all the year after'.[60]

On 25 December 1656 some of the most committed puritan members of Cromwell's second protectorate parliament ignored the

Christmas holiday and attempted to carry on with business as usual. They were unable, however, to insulate themselves entirely from the merrymaking that surrounded them. One MP complained bitterly that he had been kept awake the whole of the previous night by the preparations for 'this foolish day's solemnity', another exclaimed indignantly that the day was more solemnly observed than the sabbath, and a third commented that 'one may pass from the Tower to Westminster and not a shop open nor a creature stirring'.[61] A few days after Christmas 1657 Matthew Eyre of Frome in Somerset complained to the Somerset justices that he had been beaten up on Boxing Day by a crowd of carousing mummers who had been 'drinking, playing cards and fiddling all day in disguised habits'.[62]

On a number of occasions serious violence erupted when the authorities tried to curtail traditional Christmas pursuits. In 1646 several people were injured in Bury St Edmunds when scuffles broke out following a Christmas Day confrontation between some apprentices and the town corporation.[63] The following Christmas there were several more incidents; in London a mob attacked the mayor and his marshals as they attempted to remove Christmas decorations from the city conduit in Cornhill, and in Ipswich those who wished to observe the feast took part in a 'great mutiny', during the course of which a man was killed.[64] The most serious trouble, however, occurred in Canterbury, where Christmas Day rioters gained control of the city and retained it for more than a week; demanding a Christmas service and the closure of all the city shops, they decorated doorways with holly, attacked the mayor's house and assaulted a soldier.[65]

Although the central government maintained its opposition to Christmas until the very end of the Interregnum, by then some puritans in the provinces had been forced to acknowledge the deep and abiding appeal of the traditional Christmas customs. As early as Christmas 1647 Ralph Josselin had confessed that, despite all his reforming efforts, his Essex parishioners 'hanker after sports and pastimes that they were wonted to enjoy'.[66] Almost a decade later Ezekial Woodward, the puritan minister of Bray in Berkshire, complained in exasperation that Christmas was still widely observed and that 'the people go on holding fast to their heathenish customs and abominable idolatries and think they do well'.[67]

While the old calendar remained popular, the new one struggled for acceptance. From the early 1640s onwards puritan Sundays and fast-days were greeted with either apathy or hostility, with the result that, as Kenneth Parker has commented, 'the gap between regulation and enforcement remained quite wide'.[68] Throughout the 1640s the Long Parliament issued a stream of orders and ordinances in an attempt to encourage a more rigorous observance of these days, but in so doing they served only to publicise their inability to press the nation to a more committed approach. Preaching the fast sermon before parliament in March 1642, Cornelius Burgess complained that earlier fast-days had been totally ignored in some counties, and the following November the MPs admitted that 'many disorders have been and daily are seen in this Fast . . . as extraordinary eating, drinking, swearing, and diverse other abuses or absurdities, not fitting the time nor indeed not fitting any time.'[69] In 1643 another fast-day preacher, William Spurstowe, berated the MPs for their failure 'to vote our Churches full and the Taverns empty' on fast-days, and in 1644 a group of puritan ministers from Sussex complained to their local JPs that 'notwithstanding the just and pious ordinances of parliament for the strict observation of the Lord's Day and the monthly fast, the looser sort of people in this county do grossly profane the Lord's Day and refuse to observe the monthly fast.'[70] In September 1644 Matthew Newcomen commented on the widespread neglect of fast-days, in a sermon preached before the House of Commons. He confirmed that 'not only in the Country but here in the City and before your eyes, Sabbaths and Fasts are as much contemned as ever', and went on to declare bitterly: 'After two years of extraordinary judgements and three years of extraordinary Means and Days of Humiliation, we remain an unhumbled people.'[71]

Ralph Josselin was another puritan who became extremely despondent as a result of his parishioners' attitude to fast-days. In September 1644 he commented: 'it would make a man bleed to see how regardless people are of the same', and two years later in October 1646 he remarked that the fast-days were 'sadly neglected by people . . . custom makes us insensible'.[72] Nor were the public thanksgiving days always observed with the decorum and sobriety that Josselin and his fellow puritans expected. In April 1646, 500 inhabitants of Josselin's parish of Earls Colne and the surrounding area celebrated a thanksgiving day by attending a wrestling match.[73] Two years later the governors of puritan Dorchester had to postpone a thanksgiving day which coincided with the important Woodbury Hill Fair, because 'most of the town will be from home'.[74]

The execution of Charles I and the proclamation of the republic brought no noticeable improvement in the situation. In June 1649 the Middlesex justices of peace felt it necessary to instruct the constables under their jurisdiction to occupy themselves on Sundays and fast-days searching alehouses for drinkers and scouring the countryside for groups playing '9 pins, pigeon holes . . . or other games'.[75] A year later the Rump passed another act calling on JPs throughout the country to take action against all those who spent their Sundays and fast-days 'dancing, profanely singing, drinking or tippling'.[76] When, however, William Doble of Timberscombe in Somerset rebuked several inhabitants of neighbouring Wootton Courtenay for looking for lost sheep on a Sunday, he was told 'there were none but fools who published the late act'.[77] In May 1655 the fast-day called for the Protestant Vaudois of Savoy was ignored in some parts of the country, and in November 1656 the corporation of London admitted that fast-days were still 'very much neglected' in the capital and that many Londoners spent the day either at work, 'tippling and drinking' or indulging in 'unlawful Pastimes and Travelling'.[78]

The new puritan rites of passage were greeted with a similar lack of enthusiasm. A growing number of parents in the late 1640s and 1650s decided to avoid the Directory baptism ceremony by holding private baptisms in their own homes according to the Book of Common Prayer rite. The children of the London lawyer John Greene were baptised in private ceremonies in the family home at regular intervals during the late 1640s.[79] In 1647 Sir Ralph Verney wrote from France to his wife in London to discuss the arrangements for the baptism of the child she was carrying. He instructed her to 'have a Parson ready to christen the child', and advised her that 'the best way to prevent all danger and avoid all trouble will be to dispatch it as soon as it is born, and that as privately as may be'. In her reply, Lady Mary Verney expressed her distaste for the Directory service and strong opposition to the suppression of godparents. She agreed to find a minister to perform a private baptism 'in the old way', and concluded by exclaiming: 'Truly one lives like a heathen in this place.'[80] At regular intervals during the 1650s ejected clergymen conducted private baptisms for the children of the diarist John Evelyn and his wife at the family home of Sayes Court in Deptford. On each occasion the Book of Common Prayer was employed and godparents were chosen.[81]

The precise number of parents who adopted this course is necessarily difficult to assess, but by the mid 1650s such unauthorised private ceremonies were probably quite common, and some of the findings of the demographic historians Wrigley and Schofield appear to indicate that they produced a significant drop in the totals of recorded public baptisms. Within the 404 English parishes for which they have provided statistics, an annual average of 10,377 infants were baptised using the Book of Common Prayer during the period from 1630 to 1644. Following the return of the Prayer Book in 1662, a similar annual average of 10,230 baptisms took place during the remainder of the 1660s. By contrast, during the nine-year period between the introduction of the Directory in 1645 and the passing of the Civil Marriage Act in 1653 (when the injunction to record births rather than baptisms complicates the picture) an average of only 8192 public baptisms occurred each year. There may, of course, have been fewer babies born during this post-war period, but Wrigley and Schofield's calculations also indicate that, while the prayer-book baptism totals for the 1630s constitute about 93 per cent of estimated actual births and those for the 1660s about 95 per cent of estimated births, the baptism figures from the late 1640s and early 1650s constitute only about 82.5 per cent of estimated actual births.[82]

It is quite possible that popular aversion to the Directory ceremony was one of the main reasons for this 10 per cent drop in the level of public baptism. The fact that the reduction was not greater can be attributed to the refusal of many local ministers to comply with the government's orders and abandon the Prayer Book. John Morrill has suggested that fewer than one in four English parishes bothered to purchase a copy of the Directory in the late 1640s. It is likely that the retreat from public baptism was concentrated within the small minority of parishes which had obtained a copy and were using it regularly, and that within these communities it had a striking impact. Certainly in the parish of Earls Colne in Essex, where the minister Ralph Josselin consistently used the Directory after 1645, public baptisms had become very rare by the mid 1650s.[83]

Nor did the authorities manage to eradicate totally the churching ceremony. Although condemned by contemporary puritan opinion and some later historians for its suggestion of ritual purification, churching appears to have been viewed by the majority of seventeenth-century women both as an important thanksgiving ceremony which allowed them to express their gratitude to God for their safe delivery from childbirth, and as an enjoyable, largely female, social gathering marking their return to their circle of friends after their confinement. For these reasons many of them, including Lady Mary Verney, Mary Greene and Mary Evelyn, refused to give up the practice and continued to be churched privately at home by ejected clergymen.[84] So strong was the attachment of the women of Kidderminster to some form of public rite following childbirth that in the 1650s the town's puritan minister Richard Baxter was obliged to introduce a new thanksgiving ceremony as an alternative to the abandoned prayer-book service.[85]

The popular rejection of the new puritan marriage ceremonies was equally emphatic. Between 1645 and 1653 many couples ignored the Directory's service and continued to be married by the Book of Common Prayer.[86] When Barebone's Parliament passed its civil marriage legislation in August 1653, hundreds of couples deliberately avoided the new secular ceremony by marrying during the five-week period between the passing of the act and the date it came into force at the end of September. This sudden rush to marry was noted with some amusement by several London newsbooks. One reported that several London churches had witnessed more than 20 weddings a day.[87] Another claimed that there had been 500 marriages in London in one week, with the result that the capital's seamstresses had been unable to cope with the demand for bridal gowns and the goldsmiths had run out of gold to make the wedding rings, which many clearly still wished to exchange despite the 1645 ban on their use. This second commentator added that it was young girls who were particularly keen to wed in church 'because their tender consciences will not permit them to be married after the new way'.[88] Writing to his friend Sir Justinian Isham in September 1653, Brian Duppa, the ejected bishop of Salisbury, reminded him that 'when you did me the favour to see you last, you made haste away lest the Act for Marriage should overtake you and the Justice of the Peace become your Priest'.[89] According to Wrigley and Schofield, an estimated 9884 marriages were contracted in England during September 1653, as compared to 1401 in August and only 714 in October. This September 1653 figure was the highest total for any month during the 1650s; it was more than double the average monthly total for the decade, and three times greater than the figure for September 1652.[90]

Once the act had come into force, it was widely ignored and resisted. All over the country couples sought out conservative clergymen who were prepared to marry them either in church or according to a religious rite. Brian Duppa, for example, turned part of his house at Richmond in Surrey into an informal chapel for the solemnising of marriages, and religious marriages persisted even in conspicuously godly centres like Dorchester.[91] A great many couples grudgingly conformed and yet at the same time resisted by following their public civil marriage ceremony with a second private religious service.[92] During the debate in parliament in April 1657 which reinstated church weddings, Lord Broghill commented that the Barebone's legislation was 'never looked upon as a law', and several other members claimed that not one in a hundred marriages had been performed in accordance with its provisions.[93] Even allowing for some rhetorical exaggeration, it is clear that the civil marriage legislation had been decisively rejected by large numbers of men and women.

There is some evidence to suggest that puritan death rites were similarly repudiated. In 1646 the minister of Stretham near Ely in Cambridgeshire was threatened with violence when he tried to prevent some of his parishioners from singing over a corpse at his church-gate, and two years later an alderman in Ripon was indicted for assault and subsequently exiled from the town after he had tried to stop the burial of a child according to the Book of Common Prayer rite.[94] Death knells even continued to sound out over puritan Dorchester.[95]

Puritan efforts to eradicate ungodly leisure pursuits and improve the nation's moral standards also ended in dismal failure, as traditional sports and pastimes persisted and moral behaviour remained impervious to the pressure of the reformers. In May 1652 around 300 inhabitants from the Marlborough area gathered together on a Sunday with 'muskets, bandaleers and swords' and marched behind a drummer and a fiddler to Pewsey where 'they very disorderly danced the morris dance, drinking and tippling till many of them were drunk.'[96] Cudgel fights, cock whippings and fightings, and bull-baitings also remained regular occurrences in many parts of the country throughout the Interregnum. In August 1656 between three and four hundred people attended a cudgel fight at Timsbury in Somerset.[97] An illegal cockfight took place in Stepney in March 1656, and the following February the traditional Shrove Tuesday cock-running was held at Bethnal Green and 'a great multitude of people were unlawfully and riotously assembled'.[98] Bull-baitings were still taking place in Bath in 1648 and in London in 1654, where they regularly attracted 'a multitude of disorderly persons'.[99] Two years later a bull-baiting in Wincanton attracted another large crowd which refused to disperse when the authorities intervened.[100]

Drinking also remained the favourite pastime of large numbers of the population. The puritan Edward Curll was angered by the excessive drinking in Queen Camel in Somerset in the early 1650s, and one Wiltshire churchwarden complained in 1652 that his parishioners were addicted to drinking, that a great many of them sold illegal ale, and that one of them had even sold his shoes to buy drink.[101] In December 1656 a headborough from Shoreditch reported to the Middlesex justices that he had been threatened and abused by a group he had found 'ranting and singing in a disorderly and suspicious alehouse at an unseasonable hour in the night', and the following month those living around the Ship Inn in Glastonbury complained that they had been kept awake 'by people ranting, drinking and beating a drum'.[102] In April 1657 the Middlesex justices were told that one Christopher Waters was still travelling 'from Alehouse to Alehouse and from Tavern to Tavern to play upon organs and virginals . . . to delight persons that live loosely and ungodlily'.[103] The following October the Cheshire justices were informed that some men from the Bollington area spent most Sundays in an illegal alehouse in the village and that they came home 'in a drunken posture' to 'abuse their wives, terrify their children and trouble their neighbours, nothing at all mattering the breach of the Laws both of God and man'. Their informants added: 'Nor is there any hope of reformation unless it please your worships to take the matter into your grave consideration.'[104] The puritan assumption that the closure of alehouses would bring an automatic reduction in drunkenness may also have been flawed, for in June 1657 one MP argued that their suppression had merely led to an increase in the consumption of alcohol in private houses.[105] As for the attempt to reduce swearing, Keith Wrightson's work on the puritan reform campaigns in Essex and Lancashire led him to conclude that 'swearing was too deeply rooted in popular speech conventions to be easily eradicated'.[106]

A similar failure occurred in the sexual sphere. While England's puritan rulers may have made some fornicators and adulterers more careful during the Interregnum, there is no evidence that they were able to frighten them into abandoning their activities. Almost certainly the small number of sexual offences brought before the courts in the 1650s was only the tip of an iceberg of undetected illicit activity. In his study of seventeenth-century local government, Anthony Fletcher described the 1650s campaign against promiscuity as 'the most sustained magisterial effort of the century to . . . impose a sexual code based on the Christian doctrine of chastity outside marriage'. He concluded, however, that its implementation was 'never more than piecemeal', and that it 'undoubtedly left huge tracts of England untouched'.[107] Although the 1650s did see the lowest rate of recorded bastardy of any decade in the seventeenth century, Wrightson has argued convincingly that this was caused not by a reduction in fornication but by deficiencies in the registration system.[108] He has also suggested that the puritan attempt to improve the nation's sexual morality was seriously hampered by the abolition in the early 1640s of the extensive network of reasonably efficient local church courts.[109]

In 1660 the puritan rulers of Interregnum England fell from power and the Stuart monarchy was restored. Along with it returned the old festivals of the Christian calendar, the liturgy of the Book of Common Prayer, and official tolerance of the traditional pastimes of the English countryside. By that date, however, the puritan cultural revolution had already failed, and the Restoration merely delivered the *coup de grace* to a generally discredited experiment. In a few places the combined efforts of the central government and influential local puritans had brought some temporary alterations in cultural norms during the 1650s, but their efforts had at the same time often heightened municipal tensions and created deep splits within communities. In Coventry Robert Beake and his fellow puritans had encountered 'no small share of revilings' as they struggled to impose their reforms. They had also frequently been undermined by other officials. Alderman Joseph Chambers, for example, had encouraged the townspeople to resist them, mitigated the punishments they imposed on offenders, threatened the more zealous constables, and turned a blind eye to the existence of more than 50 unlicensed alehouses.[110] Richard Baxter, too, was forced to acknowledge after the Restoration that his proselytising had infuriated many of the inhabitants of Kidderminster and divided the town into two distinct godly and ungodly sectors. He admitted that, for all his efforts, at the

Restoration the town still contained many 'ignorant and ungodly people'.[111] As David Underdown has recently shown, even the formidable puritan governors of Dorchester had in the end been defeated by the 'obstinate tenacity of popular cultural traditions' and 'the chorus of mocking laughter' from the town's ungodly inhabitants.[112]

In many other less conspicuously godly communities, puritan campaigning failed to deliver even these modest, temporary gains. The unpalatable reality about the nation's attitude towards their reform aspirations had been brought home to some puritans during the election campaign for the second protectorate parliament in the summer of 1656, when all over the country the electorate had decisively rejected candidates associated with their cause. In August 1656 Hezekiah Haynes, the major-general for East Anglia, had written to Cromwell's secretary John Thurloe to inform him that 'such is the prevalency of that spirit which opposeth itself to the work of God . . . that the spirits of those that are otherwise minded have been much perplexed and discouraged from almost appearing at the election, seeing no visible way of balancing that interest'.[113] Several days after the election, he had written again to declare despondently that the result had been 'as bad as it could well have been made'. What had particularly upset him was that the voters of Norfolk had returned to parliament several 'common swearers' and a notorious scoffer at puritans.[114] Three years later in the spring of 1659 the MPs of Richard Cromwell's parliament acknowledged the failure of the puritan campaign by declaring that recent years had actually seen a growth in 'gross ignorance, atheism and profaneness of all sorts; such as vain swearing and cursing, profanation of the Lord's Day, drunkenness, uncleanness and other ungodly courses'.[115]

By now attachment to traditional popular culture had become a symbol of resistance to puritan rule. In February 1660 rioting apprentices in Bristol, who were angry about the refusal of the Rump to call fresh elections, turned the city's traditional Shrove Tuesday football and cock-running into a political demonstration.[116] On May Day 1660 some of the inhabitants of Oxford defiantly erected a maypole in the town and resisted the efforts of the university vice-chancellor to dismantle it; four weeks later on Ascension Day they celebrated Charles II's return to London with no fewer than twelve maypoles and several troupes of morris dancers.[117]

A few years before the outbreak of the English Civil War the poet George Herbert had given his fellow rural clergymen some sound advice. He had urged them to look indulgently upon their parishioners' 'old customs', on the grounds that: 'Country people are much addicted to them, so that to favour them therein is to win their hearts and to oppose them therein is to deject them.'[118] As we have seen, Interregnum puritans were unable to accept such advice; some simply could not see that there was a problem, and those who were aware that their attack on the people's traditional customs was alienating large sections of the nation from their rule, felt compelled to press on regardless. In a fast sermon delivered before the House of Lords in 1645 Anthony Burgess admitted: 'it is indeed a very hard thing to take men off from their religious usages', adding: 'this must be acknowledged, that people will generally startle and be astonished if an old custom be denied them'. He nonetheless concluded his sermon by declaring: 'God hath put an opportunity into our hands and we have all covenanted . . . to set upon this work.'[119] A decade later Richard Baxter similarly conceded that: 'Custom is the thing that sways much with the multitude; and they that first break a destructive custom must bear the brunt of their [the people's] indignation.' Again, however, he went on to comment: 'some body must do this.'[120] What such testimony makes clear is that for these men to have abandoned their efforts to achieve cultural revolution would have been to have given up their puritanism.

At one point in his study of the Interregnum published in the 1890s, Francis Inderwick declared:

> There was nothing in Puritanism itself which would specially commend itself to the English people. We are not and never were, notwithstanding the jibes of foreign jealousy, a melancholy people and the severity and asceticism of that section of the Puritans which appeared to spend one half of its time in finding out what people liked and the other half in endeavouring to deprive them of it, could never in itself have been grateful to the great body of our countrymen.[121]

This verdict, with its superior tones of self-righteous indignation, is typically and amusingly Victorian. It is, nonetheless, essentially correct.

8. From Puritanism to Dissent, 1660–1700

JOHN SPURR

What happened to English puritanism and its culture after the puritan revolution? One clue to puritanism's fate might lie in its change of name for, by the end of the century, those who had been called puritans were referred to as 'dissenters', a term which principally denoted their new legal status as dissidents from the re-established Church of England: 'puritan' was, as Bunyan observed, what 'the godly were called in times past'. The history of later seventeenth-century puritanism was a product of external pressures – most notably the church settlement of 1662, recurrent persecution and then, finally, toleration in 1689 – and internal evolution. The English Revolution had splintered 'the puritans' into Presbyterians, Independents, Baptists, Fifth-Monarchy Men, Quakers, Ranters, Muggletonians, Familists and many more competing sects. Some of these continued the struggle of earlier puritans for a reformed national church, while others sought only their own religious liberty. After 1662, however, these disparate, hostile groups all found themselves subject to persecution, with surprising results: 'its effect was to forge the corporate identity of dissent as all the parties in nonconformity shared together in the experience of exclusion and persecution they had hitherto in their history endured separately.'[1] As we shall see, there is indeed evidence that these mutually antagonistic groups discovered a community of interest, but there is also evidence of variety, tension and indifference. Life 'under the cross' brought the usual problems attendant on persecution – suffering, evasion, compromise – and, for the historian, the difficulties of demarcating one group from another and of distinguishing degrees of nonconformity.

I

The story of Restoration puritanism should begin in the 1640s and 1650s when the puritan tradition divided into two broad streams. One stream was that of separatism, a tradition based on the gathered church, a body made up of true believers, or 'professors', who had given the congregation an account of the work of grace in their souls and who had voluntarily agreed to abide by its rules. This congregation was self-governing, choosing its own members and pastor, and paying more heed to the action of the Holy Spirit on members and pastors than to external qualifications. Despite the exercise of discipline within the church, the emphasis on personal experience often made these congregations unstable, with members 'falling off' to discover other truths in groups like the Quakers or even in direct personal revelations from God.

The other stream of puritanism was more conservative. Taking its cue from the non-separating puritans of the Jacobean era, this tradition placed a high value on a reformed, parish-based, national church and a strong parish ministry; at least some set forms of worship were judged necessary, as was an educated and trained clergy; and any parishioner who seemed devout and respectable was eligible to attend the worship provided in the parish church. It seems that in the 1650s this position was named presbyterianism, despite the fact that full-blown presbyterianism had never taken root, and that some of those who held these principles were wary of all such labels – indeed 'a great number of ministers and people who had addicted themselves to no sect or party at all' were nevertheless dubbed presbyterians by 'the vulgar'.[2] As well as those who fought shy of labels, some Independent ministers and several Church of England clergy who had held on to their parishes (and who had probably been unsympathetic to the Laudian changes) shared this parish puritanism. Whether presbyterian, Independent or episcopalian, despite disagreements over indifferent ceremonial matters, they were all, said Sir William Waller, 'Israelites indeed', sharing a common detestation of separatism and the sects.[3]

The characterisation of these two traditions of puritan thinking as sectarianism and 'parish puritanism' should not obscure the fact that each was further divided into smaller sects and denominations by theological animosities, nor that the growing Quaker movement stood at odds to both. It is, however, a useful way of understanding events at the Restoration. As the Protectorate began to disintegrate in the late 1650s, religious moderation came into fashion and a strong clerical middle ground emerged which would have accepted a national religious settlement based on some form of moderate or 'reduced episcopacy'. This platform was designed to satisfy the parish puritans, whether presbyterian or episcopalian, and the royalist clergy, who would inevitably return with the monarchy. That 'presbyterians' could now accept government by bishops shows just how treacherous denominational labels had become: by 1660 it could be claimed that 'presbyterian' had come to mean 'any man that was for a spiritual serious way of worship (though he were for moderate episcopacy and liturgy) and lived according to his profession'. Such a man 'was called commonly a Presbyterian, as formerly he was called a Puritan, unless he joined himself to Independents, Anabaptists, or some other sect which might afford him a more odious name'.[4] Parish puritanism perhaps found its fullest elaboration in the Worcester House Declaration of October 1660. This scheme for a broad-based national church assumed that the parish minister would have a considerable degree of freedom in his use of the liturgy, his dress, his preaching and the exercise of discipline, especially in the vexed matter of which parishioners he admitted to the sacrament of the Lord's Supper. Yet in 1661–2 the movement towards this form of church settlement was stopped in its tracks. In a redefinition of what was acceptable or orthodox to the Church of England – a redefinition which was probably more far-reaching than that achieved by Archbishop Laud – the church settlement of 1662 excluded many of the parish puritans.

The Act of Uniformity imposed a single form of worship, outlawed other religious denominations, and set out the terms for those who wished to be clergymen of the Church of England. Puritan laity were no doubt most offended by the imposition of worship strictly according to the 1662 Book of Common Prayer; Pepys thought the degree of ceremony approached that in the Roman Church and Sir Edward Harley thought the surplice 'a proper massing garment'. The sects were aghast that despite royal promises there was to be no 'liberty for tender consciences' after all. Almost 200 congregationalist pastors who had enjoyed preferments in the church or universities left these posts rather than conform under the act; but, then, these sectarian divines had little interest in serving in a national church. A much larger number, approaching 2000, of the clergy who would in principle have continued to serve *a* national church refused to serve *this* church *on these terms*.[5] These ministers were 'ejected' from their parishes on the fateful 24 August, St Bartholomew's Day, 1662. The 'ejected divines' were to become the clerical backbone of dissent and their scruples are worth attention.

The terms of 1662 caused difficulties in four main areas. For those with presbyterian orders who had worked as ministers during the 1640s and 1650s the demand that they should submit to an ordination by a bishop was tantamount to 'reordination'. Although ministers would have been prepared to pursue their vocations under episcopacy, they could not repudiate their own ordinations and past ministries. Nonconformists also objected to declaring their 'unfeigned assent and consent' to the Prayer Book as if it had 'dropped immediately out of heaven, and that it is nothing else but a continued oracle from first to last'.[6] In reality its repetitions, obsolete words, implicit theological errors (especially in the baptism and burial services where all members of the church were presumed 'to be regenerated, converted, and in an actual state of grace'), and offensive rubrics requiring the wearing of the surplice, the sign of the cross at baptism and kneeling to receive the sacrament, fell far short of perfection. Ministers objected to a set form of worship which totally excluded the use of their own spiritual 'gifts' in extempore prayer and they were horrified by the authorities' insistence on such trivial matters despite the warning of the scriptures against offending the tender consciences of the 'weaker' or more scrupulous brethren.[7] The church's government was as imperfect as its liturgy: subscription to the Thirty-Nine Articles was repugnant because of the three and a half articles which dealt with ecclesiastical government; and the oath of canonical obedience was resented by those who felt that episcopal authority as it existed in the restored church contradicted the word of God. A fourth – and for many dissenters an insuperable – obstacle to conformity was the renunciation of the Solemn League and Covenant. Their difficulty was twofold. Many simply held that as a solemn oath before God the Covenant was inviolable. But the terms of the renunciation also required the conformist to forswear 'to endeavour any change or alteration of government either in church or state'.

So, while some puritans wanted no truck with the Church of England and others yearned for reunion with the national church, all were now dissenters. Separatist and parish puritans, Quakers,

Baptists, Independents and presbyterians, were all dissenters from the church as established by law. Although they might now all fall into the same legal category, they had little else in common: learned, university-educated and conservative presbyterian ministers shared nothing with Baptist ex-soldiers or wandering Quaker preachers. At the same time many of the parish puritans excluded from the ministry of the Church of England did have much in common with those who, thanks to chance, accident of birth, or lack of scruple, could serve as clergy of the restored church. An arbitrary line drawn across the spectrum of English religious life had severed a broad-based parish puritanism, leaving half of the ministers and their followers within the restored church and half outside. Those lumped together with Quakers and Baptists resented it: 'it is a palpable injury to burden us with the various parties with whom we are now herded by our ejection in the general state of dissenters.'[8] The author of this complaint saw himself as a 'nonconformist' – a subtle but significant distinction. For while their adversaries labelled them all as dissenters those, mainly the presbyterians, who could not bring themselves to conform to the church as it now stood, but who hoped that things might change, preferred to describe themselves as nonconformists; on the other hand those who had willingly separated from the state church, the Independents, Baptists and Quakers, were proud to adopt the label of dissenter. Perhaps it is now time to consider what was involved in being a dissenter or a nonconformist.

II

Members of separatist congregations were 'saints by calling, visibly manifesting and evidencing . . . their obedience unto that call of Christ, who being further known to each other by their confession of the faith wrought in them by the power of God, declared by themselves . . . do willingly consent to walk together according to the appointment of Christ.'[9] Once they had covenanted together these congregations called themselves simply 'this church of Christ' or 'the congregation of Christ in and about Bedford'. Admission often had several stages and some unfortunates had trouble progressing through them to full membership: Mrs Bevis, for instance, had desired full membership with the Bristol Broadmead church for two years, but she was hampered by 'a bad husband' whose presence cast doubt on 'her willingness to walk honestly and holy'. Eventually after professing her faith and repentance and describing her conversion, and in the hope that 'she was a Christian and regenerated', she was baptised, but she was still not allowed to take communion in the church.[10] Most congregational churches included an inner circle of full members and an outer circle of 'hearers'.

The congregation retained full authority over their affairs. No church hierarchy, nor minister, exercised powers beyond those of the church meeting; although in practice a small group within the church, often the 'elders' or 'deacons', tended to dominate affairs. The congregation chose the pastor on the grounds of the gift of the Holy Spirit rather than formal qualifications. Therefore their pastors were often laymen, many of whom continued to follow their trade or calling while exercising their pastoral duties.

What drew men and women to these churches was the chance to associate with similarly 'experienced' Christians and to shun the worldly. At heart their message was 'that truth of the Lord' that the godly should come out from among the ungodly and be separate (II Corinthians vi. 17). The congregation as a whole exercised discipline in the belief that members could be kept on the straight and narrow by admonition and exhortation, by fellowship and, if need be, by excommunication. The logic of their convictions led many separatist churches to adopt the practice of 'believers' baptism'. This meant that any who wished to join the church had to seal their 'covenant' with the congregation by undergoing baptism, often by total immersion in some chilly pond or river. It also meant a repudiation of the practice of automatically baptising babies into the universal church.

A handful of congregational churches left baptism as an open or undecided question, and admitted as members proponents of both infant and believers' baptism. Although described in 1674 as 'for the most part baptised', the Bristol Broadmead church regarded baptism as an open question, claiming that the pastor should instead 'promote that blessed principle of union among the saints, as saints, though of different persuasions'.[11] The church at Bedford did not find it easy to accommodate both principles: Bunyan complained bitterly in 1672 of an attempted takeover by Baptists.

Few of these congregational churches avoided internal divisions. They quarrelled among themselves not only about baptism, but about such issues as whether singing was permissible during worship or whether Sunday or Saturday was the sabbath. Neither separatist nor Baptist principles of church communion had any necessary correlation with the theologies of salvation which had been so controversial in the 1620s and 1630s. There were therefore both Calvinist and Arminian congregations: in 1660, for example, there were 110 Calvinist or 'Particular Baptist' congregations and 130 Arminian or 'General Baptist' churches. Some of these might be Particular and yet 'open' on the question of baptism, others might be Particular and 'Seventh-Day' (that is, believe that Saturday is the sabbath). Those who became disillusioned, especially with the varieties of Baptism, often drifted towards the more vaguely defined doctrines of the Quakers.

Autonomous though they were in such important matters as choice of pastors and admission of members, the separatist congregations did enjoy a loose affiliation with other churches and often had a sense of belonging to a certain tradition or denomination. The Baptists, in particular, were keen to establish local or national associations: they appointed 'messengers' to superintend groups of congregations and held General Assemblies in 1663 and 1668. The separate congregations were, however, clear about their distance from the established national church: the choice was between a faith 'bottomed . . . upon tradition, custom, example, etc, or [a faith based] upon the word of God, realized and imprinted upon our hearts through the Spirit'. They would have no truck with the Anglicans' 'superstitious and idolatrous worship, that with force and cruelty is maintained in opposition to the true worship and worshippers of God'.[12]

In short, then, the decision to join a separatist church was one which required effort, confidence, diligence and humility; the individual had to submit his or her spirituality and behaviour to the scrutiny of the brethren, and increasingly ran the risk of suffering financially and physically for the faith.

When we turn from separatist dissent to other types of nonconformity, and to presbyterianism especially, definitions are less easy. This form of nonconformity corresponds to part of the broad tradition of parish puritanism, a tradition in which the clergy played a leading role. Those clergymen who were to be found in the broad middle-ground of parish puritanism in the 1650s had several options at the Restoration. Quite a few, especially among the younger men, brought themselves to conform to the Church of England. With time, reluctant conformists like Isaac Archer could pronounce themselves 'more satisfied in the Church of England than ever', while divines like Tillotson, Fowler and Kidder eventually rose to bishoprics. Nor should we overlook the type of conformist epitomised by Ralph Josselin of Earls Colne or John Angier of Dedham, thoroughgoing puritans who by evasion, connivance and good luck managed to retain their livings without using the surplice or Prayer Book. All of these clergy presumably offered an element of puritanism, especially puritan preaching, within the established church. At the other extreme were those ministers who, much as they might dislike separatism, nevertheless cut themselves off from the national church and set up their own congregations. Thomas Jolly, ejected curate of Altham, Lancashire, and his congregation 'resolved that they could not comply with the way of worship used in public . . . [and] resolved rather to keep their meeting in private houses, though forbid by law': it was 'a matter of offence' when some members also attended the Church of England.[13]

Between the two extremes were many shades of conformity. As a leading dissenter later boasted, 'some of the most eminent of our ministers ever since 1662' had maintained communion with the Church of England 'with a design to show their charity towards that church'.[14] Thus the ejected presbyterian Thomas Manton went to St Paul's, Covent Garden, to hear the sermons of his successor, Simon Patrick. John Corbet 'joined in all the worship with the public assembly and had no sinful separating principles', according to his friend Richard Baxter, who himself attended his parish church. Philip Henry, another ejected minister, refused 'to overthrow our parish-order, which God hath owned' and attended Anglican services in Whitewell chapel for nearly 30 years. The position taken by these divines was that although *as clergy* they were personally excluded from the ministry by the unacceptable requirements of the Act of Uniformity, there was nothing to bar them or their lay followers from attending the worship of the Church of England or the sermons of the best Anglican preachers. They would lead their followers to the parish church and in print they would advise 'conjunction in church communion, and hearing such as taught the truth of the gospel in respect of the foundation, though in their worship and preaching some hay and stubble were superadded'.[15] Their reasoning was twofold. On the one hand they feared the dangers of division and separation, which could only end 'in some prodigious errors, or endless brawls' and confirm suspicions that all dissenters were quarrelsome, scandalous extremists. And on the other, they believed that the Church of England and her parishes were fundamentally sound. Their aim was to reunite with the church on broader terms of conformity than those of 1662; it was not to establish separate churches.

These persuasive divines touched a chord in their puritan followers. It is now clear that many puritans or nonconformists did attend their parish church, even if they attended for only part of the service or for only occasional services. The situation in Maidstone in the 1670s may have been common across the country: the local presbyterians 'usually come to church, and to divine service, one part of the day, and go to a conventicle the other, having a nonconformist teacher in the town, whom they maintain'. A few years earlier the puritanical Disney family had moved to Barkston in Lincolnshire 'for the sake of Mr Trott the minister of that town', but their pious son, Gervase, would also go into nearby Grantham 'to hear some nonconformist ministers'. Stalwarts of the puritan gentry like Sir John Gell would attend 'divine service and sermon constantly' despite also holding dissenting conventicles at their family homes. Those who went to both church and chapel in this way were aptly described by one Anglican cleric as 'neutralists between presbyterians and conformists'.[16]

The motives of these neutralists may become clearer if we look at what they actually did in their private meetings or conventicles. For all their recommendations of the worship of the parish church, most of the nonconformist clergy also sustained a godly flock of their own. They were, however, careful to make sure that their additional meetings were supplementing, rather than competing with, the parish church – 'only in due subordination to the public' and held at times which did not clash with church services. Richard Baxter, who described himself as a 'half-conformist', persuaded his neighbours 'to join in the public church, and help each other as private men . . . repeating sermons and praying and singing a psalm'. He drew to church the people 'that were averse' and 'sometimes I repeated the parson's sermon, and sometimes taught such as came to my house, between the sermons'. These and other private meetings 'were only spent in such actions as every Christian might do (to repeat a sermon and pray and propose his doubts to his pastor and sing psalms)'. The ejected minister Adam Martindale heard the sermons of his successor in the parish church, but then in the evening he repeated them 'to an houseful of parishioners of the devoutest sort, adding a discourse of mine own, and praying for a blessing upon all'. Roger Lowe, a Lancashire apprentice, described how 'after evening prayer there was a few went to Mr Wood's [the ejected curate] to spend the remaining part of the day, I repeated sermon and stayed [for] prayers'.[17] These nonconformists were performing those standard exercises of pious fellowship that puritans had been about for more than a century.

The nonconformist meetings provided a forum for godly fellowship and teaching, which was presumably felt to be lacking in the parish. This might be a matter of providing more inspiring worship than the 'dry stuff' of the Prayer Book. There were many complaints of 'the ineffectualness' of the liturgy: 'I have no hope of good by it,' complained one of the Gell family to John Angier, 'as having been bred up under its plenty, and tired with its emptiness, and yet surfeited of it.'[18] Yet it was also a conscious response to the organisational inadequacies of the national church. In large rural parishes, which contained several chapelries as well as the parish church, the Church of England simply did not provide services every Sunday: 'a man that [has] no preaching near him will take it where he can', observed John Birch the veteran presbyterian MP.[19] The city parishes fared no better. It was manifest to John Humfrey that the churches of London 'will not . . . hold their people; and the assemblies of presbyterians are upon this account nothing else but so many additions, helps, or supplies to the parish defect'.[20] The nonconformists might also be compensating for an insufficient or absent Anglican minister. John Quick, the ejected presbyterian minister of Brixton in Devon, waited a few months to see if he was replaced, 'but at length finding that no man was put in his stead and that the people went off, some to atheism and debauchery, others to sectar[ian]ism', he commenced preaching again. Even the cautious Philip Henry was prepared to say a few words from his seat in the chapel when the minister failed to appear one Sunday.[21]

Nonconformist clergy of this ilk clearly kept a foot in both camps. As laymen they maintained communion with the national church and as clergymen they exercised their own ministerial gifts in private meetings. They sensed the laity's need for preaching and catechising, and believed it to be as acute as it had been in the 1650s, and they also resented the restriction on their own right and duty as ministers to expound the word of God. Those lay people who came to the houses of men like Baxter seeking further instruction and worship were drawn by the reputation and charisma of these famous and now silenced divines, and by their dissatisfaction with the church. Beyond this their motives are murky. Even the many congregational churches which exercised strict control over admission, could not cut themselves off from the world. The congregation gathered around the presbyterian Oliver Heywood in Coley chapelry, Halifax, had a core of committed members who had subscribed a church covenant, but this did not prevent the maintenance of normal social relations with their neighbours.[22] In addition to the core members there was the usual wider circle of 'hearers' – and perhaps these were precisely the people who attended both church and meeting.

Those classed as dissenters by the legislation of 1662 ranged from committed separatists to 'neutralists between presbyterians and conformists'. But even the neutralists, perhaps *especially* the neutralists, covered a spectrum from church-goers supplementing their spiritual rations to nonconformists putting in an appearance at church as a sop to the authorities. When we consider the complexion of 'dissent', we are in the last resort asking what the harassed and persecuted members of the gathered church of Bristol Broadmead or Bedford had in common with a carefree fellow like Roger Lowe who attended both church and conventicle?

III

Historians of dissent tend to assume that the diverse groups of nonconformity were almost destined to end up in the same camp. Thus the Toleration Act of 1689 is seen as a long overdue recognition of the inescapable fact of religious pluralism. It is argued that while many presbyterians did not want to leave the national church at the Restoration – indeed they repeatedly sought a reunion or 'comprehension' within the church – yet they gradually accepted that their future lay with the sects and eventually all of the nonconformists came to think of themselves as willing separatists, as dissenters. In short, 1662 made them bedfellows and 1689 consummated the relationship. This view is, like all interpretations based on hindsight, both true and oversimplistic.

Contemporaries argued that there were 'two sorts of nonconformists . . . the one who do allow of a liturgy and our parochial churches, and these may be all comprehended upon very reasonable condescensions: the other who do not allow of either, and these must be indulged, or destroyed'.[23] In other words, the parish puritans might be reunited with the national church, but the sects must have religious toleration or be suppressed. A comprehension would require the lifting of various requirements for clerical subscription, but many of the 'moderate' nonconformist clergy would then return to the church as ministers and would bring their followers with them. Proposals for a comprehension were usually twinned with plans for a toleration or 'indulgence' of the irreconcilable minority. This was where the problems began. The difficulty was that all who desired a comprehension also welcomed an indulgence for others, but 'multitudes desire indulgence that most fervently oppose comprehension'. The congregationalists were suspicious of a comprehension because 'they thought that when the most considerable of the ministry were embodied with the conformists; their own exclusion and suppression would be unavoidable'.[24] Whether the congregationalists consciously sought to prevent comprehension is a matter of interpretation, but in practice their determination, under the leadership of the redoubtable John Owen, to achieve a toleration, repeatedly thwarted the delicate political negotiations for a comprehension. 'There will certainly now be room,' wrote one sympathiser with comprehension in 1668, 'if the Independents do not frustrate our hopes, by rejecting that which the old puritans would have leaped at'.[25]

Attempts at a legislated revision of the Act of Uniformity make a sorry tale. Comprehension and toleration were raised in parliament in 1663, in 1667 and 1668, in 1673 and 1674, and in 1680 when two bills were prepared which were to be dusted off and reintroduced in 1689. Political jockeying and mistakes in 1689 led to the shelving of the comprehension bill and the legislation of a toleration which covered far more non-anglican Protestants than had been intended.[26]

Yet a question mark hangs over the viability of the policy of comprehension, both on the part of the Church of England and of the nonconformists. The presbyterians were divided about their future. It is alleged that a 'major result' of 1662 for presbyterianism was 'the creation of two parties', often referred to as the 'dons' and the 'ducklings': the former tended to be older men, like Manton, Bates and Baxter, who remained wedded to the ideal of reunion with a wider national church and who accordingly rejected separation. The 'ducklings' were young men, like Samuel Annesley, Vincent Alsop, Thomas Watson and James Janeway, who had given up hope of a wider church and were prepared to exercise their ministry in separate congregations. For example, Alsop, pastor of the presbyterian congregation in Tothill Street, Westminster, roundly asserted that 'every particular church . . . has an inherent right to choose its own pastor, and every particular Christian the same power to choose his own church'.[27]

Such distinctions were not, however, set in concrete. These thoughtful ministers were used to weighing up the balance of interests and to making the best of their situation. The 1672 Declaration of Indulgence, for instance, posed a major dilemma for presbyterians: here was the offer of freedom of worship, but only at the price of acknowledging one's sectarian status. Oliver Heywood and others were 'desirous to enjoy the benefit of it, and yet to retain our principles of anti-separation or any appearance of it'.[28] While congregationalists and Baptists gladly took out licences, presbyterians agonised over whether they were committing the sin of schism, condoning arbitrary (rather than parliamentary) alteration of religion, or repudiating their aspirations for reunion. Yet many of them did take out a licence; even those who had constantly taught that it was a duty to attend the parish church, such as Corbet, Baxter or Philip Henry. Indeed Henry's congregation was loyal in politics 'and not rigid or schismatical in their separation, but willing to attend . . . upon those administrations which they found most lively and edifying, and most helpful to them, in the great business of working out their salvation.'[29]

This was second best to reunion with the national church. The ministers took into account not only their principles of church communion, but whether by taking out a licence they could prevent the godly from straying to rival congregations, exercise discipline over them, and hearten them against further persecution. Nor should we be too quick to think that for a presbyterian minister to take out a licence was an irreversible step towards sectarianism. Heywood gave up preaching when his licence under the declaration was withdrawn. Philip Henry was clearly attempting to keep his congregation in a relationship with the parish church. The same is true of his attitude in the 1680s: in 1687 Henry joined in an address of thanks to James II for his Declaration of Indulgence, but in 1689 he was full of plans for a comprehension.[30] Of course, some presbyterians did join with other dissenters to welcome toleration under James II, but that does not mean that all hopes of comprehension were at an end: Roger Morrice thought it 'would be yet attained' if the Anglicans were prepared to bend. It would, moreover, be most unwise to trust the self-interested Anglican view that 'of all the various sects and parties among us, none but the presbyterian is capable of being comprehended and they are but few now, most of them being run into Independency.'[31] Those presbyterians who took advantage of toleration in 1672, 1687 or 1689 did have scruples over separation, over the surrender of their principles of parish puritanism, but they were prepared to see that for the time being at least immediate pastoral duty must come before unattainable ecclesiological purity. This is also true of the question of presbyterian ordination. Although it was a momentous step to ordain ministers, as happened in Exeter in 1666 or Lancashire in 1672, it did not amount to the perpetuation of a separate church. After all, one of the aims of comprehension negotiations was to win some recognition of the validity of presbyterian ordination from the church.

It is, then, in my view, premature to say that presbyterianism had wholeheartedly embraced a sectarian future at any time before 1689. Presbyterian clergy may well have been more reluctant than their lay adherents to accept a separate existence. But, as we have seen, some of the laity were less than consistent in their church-going. While the prevailing political circumstances were largely beyond the control of dissenters, they could only react to events, and most could only react at the local level. And in practice, at the grass-roots, theological principle frequently had to bend before common experience.

IV

Neil Keeble has argued that it was a shared experience of persecution which 'created Dissent out of the various nonconformities of 1660'. Religious dissidents were harried under several laws, some dating back to Elizabeth I and others, known as the 'Clarendon Code', passed in the 1660s. Yet the enforcement of this legislation waxed and waned according to the political fears of the day. When the papist threat loomed, dissenters could worship in peace. Even when persecution was visited on Protestant dissenters, it did not touch all equally; when Quakers and Baptists were being harried, the ejected ministers might escape lightly. The local authorities, mainly the JPs and the mayors, who had to apply the laws, were not always efficient or enthusiastic: there were complaints that the mayors of Newcastle, Coventry and Bristol were prepared to 'wink' at conventicles, while Yarmouth was a notorious safe haven for Independents. The lack of prosecutions under the 1664 Conventicle Act in some areas was blamed on the unwillingness of constables and JPs to prosecute their neighbours. The next Conventicle Act, in 1670, moved the initiative for prosecution to informers who received a part of the fines imposed.

Persecution ranged from minor harassment, through disruption and rough handling by constables, soldiers or mob, personal injury and wanton destruction, to mass imprisonment; on several occasions whole congregations were carted off to gaol. The phases of persecution were discernible: the Somerset Quaker John Whiting counted seven great persecutions of the Quakers and the Broadmead church had suffered eight by 1674. The early 1680s seem to have been particularly hard: 'many persons in trouble up and down the nation, meetings disturbed, divers imprisoned . . . O Lord God, cease I beseech you', prayed Philip Henry; disturbed by 'the tribe of persecutors, enemies of all righteousness', the dissenters of Rye were 'forced to meet in several parcels in our own families with three or four besides' to escape the penalties of the Conventicle Act. Alsop's Tothill Street congregation began to meet in private for the sacrament; while several of the leading ejected ministers found themselves prosecuted under the Five Mile Act for living within cities or boroughs; and in January 1684 the nonconformist ministers were presented to the Middlesex Grand Jury 'as the cause of all the dangers to the government and of the disorders among us'.[32]

The imposition of fines on convicted dissenters was often vindictive and even ruinous, for when the dissenter could not pay, his or her goods were seized, even down to the tools of a trade or a family cow, leaving the family destitute: in Shropshire in 1681, Mr Berry was distrained of his bed, sheets, books and dishes, and the sale of his goods was announced in local churches.[33] Those who ended up in gaol, either awaiting trial or as punishment, suffered appalling conditions and frequently succumbed to gaol-fever, plague or small-pox. Although it was the Quakers who suffered most in this way – perhaps 450 died – many other dissenters found themselves in prison. William Dewsbury spent 19 years in Warwick gaol and Isaac Pennington was imprisoned six times between 1662 and 1679. John Bunyan's long imprisonment between 1660 and 1672 seems, how-ever, to have been lax; he was permitted to leave gaol and even to travel to London. Yet for every prisoner who was treated well or allowed out to attend church meetings, there were more whose health suffered. During Charles II's reign 215 ejected clergy were imprisoned and seven died there of natural causes, including William Jenkins whose mourning rings bore the inscription 'murdered in Newgate'.[34]

Dissenters were not only persecuted, they suffered discrimination. One point of the Clarendon Code was to exclude them from positions of local government, while the penalties of excommunica-tion by the national church included curtailment of their civil and parochial rights. Once again, however, this discrimination was not consistent. Dissenters served as parish constables and churchwar-dens, aldermen and mayors, and even as MPs.[35] Although the congregationalist churches usually sought to provide for their own poor, when they could not raise sufficient funds, they along with the presbyterians were prepared to accept parochial poor relief – to which, after all, they had contributed through the parish rates. Religious tests had been established to bar dissenters from member-ship of the universities, but this did not stop them from spending some time at Oxford, Cambridge or the Inns of Court, as well as at one of the dissenting academies which offered a very similar educa-tion.[36]

The response of dissent to this persecution was mixed. Some gloried in their persecution in this world as 'a manifestation of our predestination to the ease and peace of another world'. 'Dear brethren,' announced a London church exultantly in 1669, 'many trials may yet attend us, we have not yet resisted unto blood . . . the Lord's winnowing and sifting may yet be more general, and more sharp.' The chance to witness to the faith should be embraced: the Bristol Quakers decided that 'in times of persecution' they should meet publicly, while a Baptist church in Kent ejected members who sought 'to make our knees feeble . . . by creeping into corners, and meeting by fours'. But other churches were more prudent; the

Norwich congregational church agreed to meet in 'small parcels' so as not to infringe the Conventicle Act.[37] The braver spirits exhorted the weaker to trust in the Lord and pointed out his providence at work in the escapes of various saints and the divine judgements delivered against informers and persecutors.

There are, however, always some who buckle under pressure. In January 1665, the Broadmead church ejected 'some for neglecting their duty of assembling through fear'; in the 'troublous times' of 1668 'many of the friends' of the Bedford congregation had 'withdrawn themselves from close walking with the church'. Some were eventually persuaded back, but others, like Humphrey Merrill, had turned coat for good: Merrill recanted his profession of faith before the Quarter Sessions and railed against the Bedford church, saying that they had the king's blood on their hands and were disobedient to government and 'despising also the gifts of, and doctrines of God in the congregation'.[38]

Dissenters were not simply passive before the persecution, however, they organised to withstand or combat it. The Baptists held national assemblies, and even the Quakers had local monthly and quarterly Meetings in the 1660s, and central Morning Meetings by the 1670s; in their 'public friends', they also had the beginnings of a ministry. Although the Quakers and some other sects disdained to protect themselves against the attentions of the informers and constables, many nonconformist congregations adopted ruses such as meeting under the guise of a banquet or at the boundaries of two or three counties to enable escape. They met in secret, in caves and in woods, set lookouts, blocked the stairs of their halls or provided a backstairs escape route for the preacher. To evade the purpose of the law, some ministers paid attention to its letter, never preaching to more than four besides the biggest family, and as many under 16 years as would come, or dividing the hearers into small groups and preaching the same sermon four or five times a day. This legalism shades into legal tactics. Some dissenters, such as Philip Henry or Vavasour Powell, became formidable legal opponents of the authorities and the Quakers especially became adept at questioning the minutiae of the law and of legal procedure. Several dissenters were able to avoid prosecution by exposing clerical errors in the writs issued against them – and some kept their first names secret to foil the authorities. When they did get into court, however, dissenters often relished the opportunity to witness for the truth. Many a courtroom became a stage for a fine performance, which would immediately be written up and published.[39]

A political strategy against persecution was also open to dissenters. They had perhaps 50 sympathisers in the Cavalier Parliament's House of Commons and some in the Lords, while there were almost 100 dissenting MPs returned to the three Exclusion parliaments. Just as important was persistent lobbying of the king through contacts with the royal court. The Bristol dissenters were able to enlist the help of James, duke of York, who later, as king, had several dissenting courtiers, such as William Penn the Quaker. But all dissenters did not pull in the same direction: Penn was suspicious of comprehension, while others disliked religious liberty granted at royal whim and extended to Roman Catholics. The politically radical wing of dissent believed that the Stuarts were never to be trusted with the good old cause and so preferred exile or conspiracy: Fifth-Monarchy Men did rebel in 1661 and presbyterians were suspected of involvement in the 1663 Yorkshire rising, but it seems to have been Baptists who were most deeply implicated in the Rye House plot and the Monmouth rebellion.[40]

Most dissenters were not seeking a traitor's death on the scaffold, but simply a way of pursuing their own spiritual goals and surviving the persecution. There was strength in unity. Predictably in the borrowed houses and rented halls where conventicles met and dissenting clergy preached and taught, theological and denominational differences often counted for little. In Bristol a presbyterian, a congregationalist and two Baptist churches were forced by legal persecution 'to join together and unite in counsel and charge, as poor sheep driven together by wolves'; later they met together for prayer and timetabled their meetings to accommodate each other.[41] Presbyterians and congregationalists co-operated to raise funds and for worship in Yarmouth and in Heywood's North Owram; while in London they met together to mark the anniversary of the ejections or to establish special lectures as at Hackney in 1669 or Pinners' Hall in 1672. Such co-operation began to blur the meaning of names: certainly the labels of presbyterian and Independent become confused; and the denominational names applied in the licences issued in 1672 are notoriously unreliable. Someone like Bunyan, who in 1672 was licensed as a 'congregationalist', called himself a Baptist, but recognised some fundamental differences between himself and other Baptists about the doctrine of baptism; and he is for theological purposes best labelled a Calvinist. One of the Rye House plotters, William Hone, 'heard sometimes Baptists, sometimes Independents, and sometimes presbyterians'.[42] The abortive plans drawn up for 'an accommodation' between the presbyterian and 'congregational' ministers in the late 1670s certainly suggests that 'common sufferings had made them ready to co-operate in the practical work of maintaining the ministry and serving conventicles'.[43]

V

Nonconformist life 'under the cross' was one of rich diversity as well as common suffering. The churches of Restoration dissent were frequently as different as the communities from which they sprang: a rural conventicle held in a draughty barn to which the saints had tramped many miles through the mud was a far cry from the large, wealthy, city congregations 'consisting of many hundreds' which had established meeting places 'whereto the people did resort as common as to the ... [parish] churches'.[44] In the countryside, especially, dissenters were often scattered widely, a family or a few individuals in each parish: the church at Rothwell, Northamptonshire, drew members from 16 distinct places. Some communities boasted several congregations. The Cambridgeshire village of Over had Baptists, Quakers, a congregational conventicle and visits from the 'prophet Ludowick Muggleton', while the city of Bristol could claim the Broadmead church, Andrew Gifford's Particular Baptist, Mr Kitchen's General Baptist, Mr Week's presbyterian and two Independent churches led by William Troughton and John Thompson, in addition to a Quaker Meeting.[45] A detailed account of the Broadmead church, compiled by Edward Terrill, an elder, shows that in 1671, when the entire church invited Mr Hardcastle to be their pastor, the congregation was made up of 72 women and only 28 men. The predominance of women was characteristic of dissenting churches: Heywood's congregation had almost twice as many women as men. Yet despite this, women had neither power nor equality in the church; for all the talk of 'brother' and 'sister', men and women sat apart at the meeting; women had no role in the public duties of prayer, prophesying or giving thanks: many women only spoke when giving testimony of their faith. The Broadmead church's pastor, deacons and other officials were men: only 'Sister West, a widow woman, was set apart to the office or work of widow or deaconess in the church'. Although Quaker women had more freedom to preach and from the 1670s held a separate Women's Meeting, they were firmly excluded from decision-making. In some ways this situation represents a step backwards from the Interregnum when women had played a prominent role in the congregations. Of course, we cannot know what informal role was played by the 'gracious women' who figure largely in the private visits, counselling and correspondence of ministers like Heywood and Baxter. But it is plain that the aspirations of women to exercise congregational authority or even serve in the ministry were as far from realisation as ever. Sheltering behind the figure of St Paul, the male leaders of dissent were adamant that women must play a subordinate role: Bunyan argued against separate women's prayer meetings and that women should 'keep their places'; and Richard Baxter may have regarded it as a fault in his wife 'that she busied her head so much about churches, and works of charity, and was not content to live quietly and privately'.[46] Eloquent testimony of both the male perception of godly women and an essential female contribution to puritanism is afforded by the tombstone of Abigail Hickes in the chancel of St Thomas à Becket, Portsmouth: 'here grandchild, daughter, sister, niece and wife of several preachers lies'.

Wherever dissent flourished, in towns like Hull, Newcastle, Yarmouth, Coventry, Reading, Norwich and Bristol, the proportions of the rich, the well-off and the poor within the congregation generally matched those within the surrounding community.[47] Each congregation had its share of widows and journeymen and its prosperous elders like Terrill, merchant in the sugar trade and second husband to a wealthy widow. Gentry and aristocrats were also to be counted among the supporters of dissent. The puritan gentry who had been the backbone of early-Stuart puritanism continued to keep up godly households and patronise the godly cause: Lady Mary Armyne, Samuel Dunch and Richard Knightley offered annuities for ejected ministers or employed them in their households; Baxter was sustained by the Ashurst, Foley and Hampden families; Heywood preached in the Rodes family chapel at Great Houghton Hall. The roll-call of puritan patrons also includes the Gell, Duckenfield, Hobart, Swinfen, Harley, Younge, Duke, Mansell, Hoby and Trevor families. Upper-class support was most forthcoming from the ladies:

Dr Jacombe became chaplain to the dowager countess of Exeter; the countess of Bedford was arrested at Manton's conventicle and the countess of Anglesey at Owen's. Owen's church at Leadenhall Street not only included ex- Cromwellian grandees but some of the cream of fashionable society: there were 67 carriages of the nobility and gentry at his funeral in 1683. Aristocratic sympathisers with dissent included the earls of Anglesey and Denbigh, Lord Holles and Lord Delamere, and most prominently, Phillip, Lord Wharton. However, most of these upper-class sympathisers with dissent were also conformists to the Church of England: although Sir Edward Harley 'was a favourer of such as dissented from the church for conscience's sake . . . yet he constantly attended the church'.[48] The days of the puritan gentry were, however, slowly passing, and it was the urban middle class who were succeeding to their role as sponsors of dissent: during the Restoration dissent became ever more identified with the manufacturing and 'trading part of England'.[49]

The dissenting clergy were a mixed bunch. Some were no more than part-time lay preachers – but then consider what such an individual could achieve if he had the talents of John Bunyan. Among those who had been trained for the ministry, but found themselves ejected or excluded from the church, some became the pensioners, chaplains or tutors to gentle families, while others eked a living from school-teaching or medicine or by their pens. Giles Firmin had little of his own, but got 'somewhat by the practice of physic' and received £12 a year in subscriptions. Collections were made among the godly of London 'to stave off with gifts, those who for poverty are likely to conform'. Some were tempted and fell, but others remained resolute. The scrupulous congregationalist divine Thomas Gilbert turned down the prospect of the presidency of Harvard, preferring 'to suffer in Old, than to reign in New England'; although reduced to barley bread, he refused Lord Wharton's offer of a Westmorland curacy rather than administer the sacraments to all parishioners 'promiscuously'. In Dorset Thomas More refused the same living three times 'because unsatisfied with the terms of conformity'.[50] Some had private means. William Bagshaw of Derbyshire inherited money, while Stephen Hughes of Swansea married into it, and John Owen did both. The wealthy Philip Henry spent 12 pence of every pound he received in rents on 'my dear fellow ministers and the poor'. Several of the Baptist ministers, like Hanserd

Knollys and William Kiffin, were successful in business, and ploughed their profits back into God's work.

The physical distribution of dissenters followed a predictable pattern. Dissent was strong where there was a tradition of puritanism, as in the North-West or the West Country, and particularly strong where dissenting clergy had gathered, in towns like Exeter, where 22 ejected ministers were living in 1664, or London suburbs like St Giles, Cripplegate. Towns acted as a magnet for the surrounding region: in 1672 there were seven buildings licensed for presbyterian worship in Norwich and four for the Independents. But rural dissent was also sustained by the ejected divines. In 1669, seven ejected Derbyshire ministers were taking turns to serve a Sunday meeting of between 200 and 400 at Colonel Saunders's house in Little Ireton, Derbyshire.

These pockets of dissent were linked not only by the nonconforming clergy, but also by a lay 'spiritual and familial cousinage'.[51] The shared experience of persecution, the meetings in prisons and boarding houses, the clandestine preaching and printing, the network of friendships and correspondence, visits, recommendations, and gifts, wove a community. This was a community in which members were never forgotten. In 1669 the Bedford church appointed the elders to write letters of 'comfort and edification,' to members who lived at some distance or who, like brother Harrington, had been driven from hearth and home by the prospect of arrest. The Broadmead church decided to write to former members 'to inquire into the state of their souls, and to know whether they did keep close to their duty in walking with some church'. One woman had left Bristol 14 years before, but dutifully reported her progress in London, which had included major surgery and two spells in Bedlam 'bereaved of my senses'.[52] The sense of belonging to a community was profound. When Gervase Disney and his new wife decided to move to Nottingham in 1672 'we soon then enquired, and found out (by the help of Mr Reyner) a religious family to table in'.[53] A godly set of lodgings almost provided a surrogate family. To many dissenters the church was a family and their family was a church: their ideal was to marry into the faith, and those who went outside the people of God for a partner risked chastisement, if not ostracism.[54]

The saints corresponded with each other, courted and married each other, aided and encouraged each other, in good times and in bad. But they did not achieve complete harmony. Against the inspiring picture of unity growing out of common suffering, we must place the equally true fact that dissenters were   prey to mutual animosity and intolerance. In many ways dissent bred dissent. The pursuit of purity and truth, the love of debate and controversy, even on the most arcane matters, kept the different groups at one another's throats. Formal public debates between the denominations were common in London, and even in rural backwaters like Cambridgeshire, and inevitably contention spilled over into daily life, with Baptists haranguing their presbyterian neighbours in the shops of Dover or Roger Lowe quarrelling with episcopalians in the alehouse at Ashton. Such wrangling doomed many of the attempts at co-operation. The Pinners' Hall lecture in London was intended as a common platform for presbyterian and Independents, but by 1674, Baxter was being attacked by Independents for his 'Arminian' theology and he, in turn, portrayed their Calvinism as antinomian and anti-rational.

Theology not only divided the denominations from each other, it split the same denomination. The presbyterians were divided as to whether they were 'Arminians' or old-style Calvinists; moreover there is at least a good *prima facie* case for seeing the lines drawn on this question as following the battle-lines between the dons and ducklings over separation. The older dons were moving towards Arminianism and reluctant to jettison their ideal of a national church, while the ducklings shared the Calvinism of their congregationalist allies. Baptists, who were already divided on the question of Calvinism, struggled with the problem of maintaining open congregations. Congregations would split and split again over these weighty theological issues, but dissent was also divided over apparently more trivial questions of worship. At the Islington funeral of John Burgess, a nonconformist minister, Philip Henry was 'grieved' to see half of the 120 ministers leave the church rather than hear the Anglican burial service.[55] Richard Baxter and his assistant Stephen Lobb disagreed over the reading of the Creed, Lord's Prayer and Ten Commandments in a congregation meeting in Swallow Street. When Baxter withdrew from preaching there in deference to Lobb's scruples about these readings, he was accused by Lobb of 'separation and not bearing with others' tolerable weaknesses'. Where would all this end, asked Baxter, if a congregation scrupled the singing of the psalms were they to have their way?[56]

Nevertheless congregations insisted on their autonomy. They were, for example, extremely careful in transferring a member to another congregation or, as the Bedford church expressed it, 'giving up to you our beloved brother . . . to fellowship with you for your mutual edification and joy of faith'. Although they might seek 'the assistance and advice of the other churches' in difficult cases, the Bedford church could be touchy about interference. When chastised by the Cambridgeshire congregationalist Francis Holcroft for admitting to their communion a man who had been excommunicated from Holcroft's church, they responded angrily, asking 'if in such weighty cases you would have us refuse the use of our own judgements in the word, and be governed by the wills and opinions of others?'[57] What mattered was the church's own experience of that individual, of his or her testimony of grace, repentance and godly life.

If the congregational churches deeply resented being told what to think, so too did godly individuals. William Whitbread withdrew from the Bedford church because he disapproved of the pastor and of his administration of the Lord's Supper. Whitbread was 'persuaded from scripture grounds, of the consonancy of the congregational way with the rule', and was happy still to assemble with them, but he insisted upon his right to 'dissent from you' in anything 'wherein I am doubtful'. The church, however, would not budge and eventually a repentant Whitbread rejoined them 'without any reservation'. Ironically perhaps, the same church took comfort in the obstinate conscience of those who withstood the persecutors: they admired brother Harrington 'who prizest good conscience above thine own enjoyments' – he left everything to avoid arrest.[58] This, in the last resort, was what nonconformity was all about, giving precedence to the regenerate conscience, refusing to truckle to the profane world, following the exhortation of St Paul, 'be ye not conformed to this world; but be ye transformed by the renewing of your mind' (Romans xii. 2). 'Nonconformists value themselves,' wrote Marvell, 'on their conscience, not their numbers.'[59] The privileged role accorded to the individual conscience brings us close to the puritan bedrock of late seventeenth-century dissent.

VI

The piety of dissenters was recognisably that of earlier saints: 'God's graces are much the same in all his holy ones . . . when we describe their humility, piety, soundness of judgement, fidelity, peaceableness, concord, secret and open holiness, sobriety, etc., we must speak over the same thing of all.'[60] The puritan lifestyle was one of austerity and self-denial, but it should not be caricatured: many ministers disliked, for example, popular pastimes and superstitions, but their followers, especially the younger high spirits, would not be denied. The apprentice Roger Lowe is often cited as an example of a dissenter who enjoyed music, courting, drinking and other worldly pleasures. However his diary also shows that this godly young man travelled miles to hear sermons and to attend conventicles; he joined pious associations of young men and stood up for his religious convictions not only against neighbours in the alehouse but also against Anglican clergymen. Despite occasionally being bored by his dissenting elders, Lowe did his duty by them and lapped up their stories of the sufferings of the ejected ministers; in private, he read pious works and wrote religious verses; and he was prepared, even in matters of romance, to trust in the Lord. There is little here that would have been out of place in the puritanism of the 1560s.

The godly household lived on among dissenters: Hopton Hall, Derbyshire, home of the Gell family, was 'a Bethel, a house of God', while the servants of Sir Edward Harley each 'had a bible and were instructed in what was read [at family prayers], and in the principles of the Christian faith from the poor postboy to the waiting gentlemen'.[61] John Angier's household repeated sermons and the Westminster Assembly catechisms during the week, while Sunday was given over to private, family and public devotions, which included hearing two sermons and then repeating them in the family.[62] The dissenters generally disapproved of superstitious celebrations, including Christmas, which they rejected 'as a day to be kept holy, for want of divine institution' or kept 'in mourning for the sin of the time privately and in prayer'. Braver, perhaps, were those many Quaker shop-keepers who deliberately opened their shops on 25 December only to have them attacked by mobs.[63]

The dissenter was rarely without a godly book. Where the reading of dissenters can be traced in detail, we find them saturating themselves in the works of the great puritan divines of the first half of the seventeenth century.[64] Dissenters built upon their puritan heritage: Baxter's *Christian Directory* (1673) was in the tradition of William Gouge, while Bunyan's stories of judgements against sinners were part of a genre going back to John Foxe; but *The Pilgrim's*

Progress (1678), *Paradise Lost* (1667) and George Fox's *Journal* (written *c.* 1675, published 1694) took puritan literature to new heights.[65] Whether in the form of Bunyan's realistic prose or Milton's soaring poetry, this was a literature written with the simple purpose 'that all may know the dealings of the Lord with me' and with his people.[66]

Personal dealings with the Lord were at the heart of puritan piety. Devotional manuals and broadsheets designed to be pinned to the wall provided a list of questions with which the earnest, introspective puritans assessed their performance: 'wherein have I denied myself this day for God? Have I been diligent in the duties of my calling? Am I a mourner for the sins of the land?'[67] Puritan devotional life made 'a conscience' of this 'closet piety'. Even a busy man like Sir John Gell observed 'his hours of retirement that he might maintain his converse with God, in the exercise of closet religion'.[68] Prayer and meditation alone, with the family, or in private gatherings of 'professors', was a constant feature of dissenting life. In the privacy of the closet, or bedroom, the Christian wrestled with the Lord in prayer, dwelling upon his own sins and inadequacies. Diary after diary tells us that this was generally difficult, unrewarding work – described as 'restrained' or 'hard' – and only occasionally do we get a sense of prayer flowing easily and of its immense rewards.

The godly also set days apart 'to seek the Lord by prayer' in personal, church or national matters – the tradition of fasts was long established: many were deeply personal as when Henry Maurice of Llyn visited his cousin John Williams in 1672; 'we discoursed together very earnestly and seriously about his long silence, and neglecting the Lord's work in that country, insomuch that it drew tears from us both'. A fast could serve private and public ends: Henry and friends 'mourned and prayed before the Lord at W. Ben's house' on 24 August 1663, the anniversary of the ejections and also Henry's birthday: 'this day thirty two years I was born, this day twelvemonth I died'.[69] Heywood kept an average of 35 fasts a year. The many public fasts held by dissenters were in addition, of course, to their weekly or monthly meetings for worship. Prayer, Bible-reading, preaching and psalm-singing were the staples of the dissenting meeting. Although sectaries had always opposed set forms of prayer, preferring to extemporise prayers with the aid of the Holy Spirit, presbyterians had little against prescribed forms as such, but took exception to those of the Prayer Book. Preaching was something which increasingly became the preserve of ministers and other appointed preachers: the spirit of prophesying by which any moved member of the congregation could get up and deliver his message was restricted, even in the sects, to special evening or weekday meetings, and often suppressed altogether; only among the Quakers did it remain a vital part of worship. Many dissenting congregations routinely celebrated the communion or 'broke bread' once a month, which was far more frequently than in the established church.

This puritan piety was underpinned by puritan habits of thought. Some argue that puritanism appealed to and reinforced a mixture of arrogance and anxiety. The morally censorious attitude of dissenters was well known: 'it is the guise and property of too many of you that think you are assured you are the Lord's, to question whether others be so, that dissent from you'.[70] But the reverse of this assurance was a profound fear that one might not be saved, that the experience of conversion was delusory. Eleanor Stockton was plagued by doubts as to 'whether I was still in the state of nature or in a lapsed and back-sliding condition'.[71] And just like earlier saints, such as Nehemiah Wallington, the dissenters committed their spiritual hopes and doubts to paper. It was the 'custom' of Hannah Allen 'to write in a book I kept for that purpose in shorthand, the promises, together with my afflictions, and my experiences how God delivered me out of them, mixing therewith prayer and praises.'[72] Thus the dissenters, like their puritan forbears, recorded in detail how they came to Christ, the progress of their sanctification or regeneration, and the divine providences, or 'catalogue of mercies', which confirmed their conversion and faith.

Justification by faith alone was an axiom of dissent. Justification is the imputation of Christ's righteousness to the sinful believer: God 'showed me I was lost if I had not Christ, because I had been a sinner,' wrote Bunyan, 'I saw that I wanted a perfect righteousness to present me without fault before God, and this righteousness was nowhere to be found, but in the person of Jesus Christ.' The Christian's faith is what grasps Christ's righteousness. And faith is more than a simple intellectual belief in Christ, it is an affectionate, emotional commitment to Christ – in the words of Thomas Manton, 'trust is not a bare opinion of Christ's fidelity, but a dependence upon his word.'[73] God deals with men in a variety of ways. And while it was to be hoped that experience of faith would come as a conversion, that it would bring assurance of salvation, if it did not, then one trusted Christ: 'the point being thus,' explained Bunyan, 'I

am for going on, and venturing my eternal state with Christ, whether
I have comfort here or no; if God doth not come in, thought I, I will
leap off the ladder even blindfold into eternity, sink or swim, come
heaven, come hell, Lord Jesus, if thou wilt catch me, do; if not, I will
venture for thy name.'[74]

Bunyan was a committed Calvinist and so believed that those who
were justified by faith had been chosen or 'elected' by God. These
'saints' were predestined for salvation from eternity, just as others
were predestined to damnation. Not all dissenters, however, subscribed to this Calvinist doctrine of a 'double decree' of predestination. The Civil War had released the theological log-jam created by
the Calvinist–Arminian debates of the 1620s and 1630s and suddenly
new interpretations of the Reformed Protestant doctrine of salvation
became permissible. Inspired by meeting 'new notions' of grace
among parliamentary troops, Richard Baxter began to grope his way
towards a refinement of an earlier position known as 'hypothetical
universalism'. Baxter suggested that rather than Christ dying only for
the elect, he died for all, but the Holy Spirit conveys a special saving
grace only to the elect. This 'middle way' won followers and was
taken up by Edmund Calamy and other dissenters in the 1690s. But
to orthodox Calvinists, of course, any deviation from the pure
teaching of the Westminster Assembly was a descent into Arminianism. Baxterian theology was not Arminian, either in the sense of
Arminius or of Archbishop Laud, but there is some truth in G. R.
Cragg's remark that such mediating positions were 'in line with
Arminianism' simply because they were conditional, moderate and
eirenic.[75] Baxter aspired to drive doctrinal controversies out of the
world, but they may have been dying anyway: he admitted that the
dissenting clergy were too poor to buy books and too busy 'with mere
preaching to the people' to study controversy, and he alleged that
the Anglicans were uninterested. In practice predestinarian Calvinism was being undermined by two related factors. One was the
distaste felt by many educated people for a theological system which
was highly speculative, peering into the hidden decrees of God, and
yet dismissive of human reason and free will and sternly determinist
about salvation. The other factor was pastoral. Sinners were reluctant to respond to a message which seemed to assert their inability
to influence their own eternal fate; and alarmingly, a few of those
who did embrace predestinarianism used it to justify a total neglect
of outward piety and even morality. In the eyes of Calvinism's critics,

too much preaching had concentrated on divine grace to the neglect of human effort. Baxter simply believed himself to be redressing this imbalance when he taught 'that men might have Christ and Life if they were truly willing, though grace must make them willing'.[76] It is likely that many of the dissenting laity, too, felt the need for a religion which allowed some role to their own efforts. The evidence of dissenters' wills and of the more popular forms of religious tract suggests that they preferred a simple moralising message to the abstruse doctrines of Calvinism.[77]

Dissent had also inherited from puritanism a deeply providential and apocalyptic mentality. Every blow, from the Great Plague to the renewal of persecution, from personal illness to children's disobedience, was interpreted by dissenters as God working out his purpose. However, although divine providence ruled the world, it no longer seemed to many dissenters that God was about to bring about the rule of the saints on earth. The millenarianism which had been such a feature of puritanism was transmuted into a more introspective, politically passive conviction that only through the personal transformation of sinners would the world be remade.

Puritanism was a Bible religion and the Bible coloured all of the dissenters' thinking: it supplied the images and metaphors by which they interpreted not only their spiritual lives, but also the wider world around them, the world of politics and persecution. They made a literal application of the scriptures to their lives and worship, judging such issues as marriage within the sect, the role of women in the church, or going to law, by direct reference to scripture and, especially, St Paul. The Pauline ideal of 'edification', or spiritual self-improvement, was a powerful motive for separation from the formality of the national church. Yet the dissenters carried the same imperative with them into the dissenting churches: it was this impulse which lay behind such apparently trivial disputes as whether the Ten Commandments should be read in conventicles or whether individuals could 'dissent' from the congregation in anything 'wherein I am doubtful'.

Puritan habits of piety and thought connected Restoration dissenters with their puritan predecessors, but so too did more personal associations. Many of the leaders of dissent had been leading figures of the puritan revolution: John Owen, leader of Cromwellian Independency, lived until 1683; George Griffiths had been a trier and ejector in the 1650s and survived to be a protagonist in the antinomian controversies of the 1690s. Puritanism was spread through families: John Dunton the dissenting whig bookseller was the son of a puritan minister. John Angier had been trained by John Rogers and John Cotton, the great Jacobean puritans, before beginning his ministry in the 1630s; his son, Samuel, lived with John Owen before becoming assistant to his own father in 1667. John Angier was ordained in the Church of England, but was an Interregnum presbyterian and licensed as such in 1672; his son was ordained as a presbyterian in 1672, but may have been serving a congregational church by 1680 when he described himself simply as 'preacher of God's word at Duckinfield'. The lesson of such family histories is surely that a common puritanism transcends the denominationalism of dissent.

VII

'Now we were freed from the fears of persecution,' wrote the diarist Samuel Jeake on hearing of the Toleration Act in 1689.[78] The legislated freedom of worship which followed the 1688 revolution offered the dissenters far greater security than the indulgences of 1672 or 1687, but it also posed them greater challenges. They had to organise themselves for freedom and to sustain a zeal hitherto honed by persecution.

Erecting the central institutions to co-ordinate and unite separate congregations into communions or denominations, to train and pay ministers, to decide creeds and controversies, was not easy. First item on the agenda when the General Baptists held a national assembly in May 1689 was whether such a general meeting trespassed on the rights of the individual congregations. The Particular Baptists' assembly disclaimed 'all manner of superiority . . . over the churches' and the authority to prescribe anything upon their faith and practice. Yet practical needs dictated co-operation. The presbyterians and Independents established the 'Common Fund' in 1690 to pay ministers and then, in 1691, attempted a closer alliance, known as the 'Happy Union'. But during the years of persecution congregations and ministers had not simply become used to their independence, they had elevated it to a principle. This divisive, self-destructive force within dissent had been held in check before 1689; but once persecution had been lifted, there was no restraint. The Happy Union had collapsed by 1695 when the congregationalists seceded from the Common Fund, taking umbrage at its attempt to control the heterodox minister Richard Davis.

Davis's offence had been to teach 'antinomianism' which, along with the Trinity, was one of the most controversial religious issues in the 1690s and after. The antinomian debate turned on the difference between an educated faith and an emotional conversion. Expressed in terms of the role of 'reason' and reflecting the drift of many presbyterians towards Arminianism, this difference was also one of tone: the presbyterians taught that assurance of salvation depended on 'the divine truth of the promise of salvation' while congregationalists relied on 'the blood and righteousness of Christ'.[79] The trinitarian dispute culminated in a national conference at Salters' Hall, London, on whether the scriptures were a sufficient guide or men should subscribe to some human definition of the Trinity. The conference's failure to resolve the issue left the ball in the congregations' court and accelerated the trend among presbyterian churches towards Arminianism and Unitarianism. Once again the real decisions were being made at the local, congregational level where many presbyterian and Independent congregations still worshipped together, baptised each other's children, or shared chapels.

The heroic age of dissent was passing, however. John Bunyan had died in 1688 and was soon followed by Baxter, Knollys and Fox. Something of English puritanism's zeal seemed to pass away with this generation. The piety of the next, of men like Defoe or John Dunton or Samuel Jeake, was more worldly, more complacent, in tone: providences were invariably benevolent to a man like Jeake; while many dissenters were happy to co-operate with Anglicans in the campaign for reformation of manners, a utilitarian drive to clean up society. Indeed, dissenters were often as wary of enthusiasm and fanaticism, as keen to be polite, rational and metropolitan, as their church-going neighbours. To assert that dissenters were interested in commerce, journalism and politics, in the coffee-houses and the Exchange, is simply to say that they were susceptible to the social and cultural trends sweeping Augustan England. The loss of spiritual energy in some quarters was undeniable: the number of presbyterian congregations was soon dwindling, and even the Bedford church fasted in 1697 that 'the work of God might be revived among us'. Yet if one attempted to characterise dissent at the beginning of the new century, then one might stress its growing political confidence, its wealth and commercial prominence, and perhaps the narrowing of its social base, as gentry and aristocratic support fell away. The habits and values of puritanism were still embodied in dissent, and were to be spread further into the polite and commercial society of Hanoverian England as dissenters became less distinguishable from their neighbours. That said, however, another major reconfiguration and reinvigoration of the tradition of English puritanism was already on the horizon. In the 1730s the dissent created out of puritanism would find itself rudely shouldered aside by the Evangelical Revival.

Bibliography

The place of publication for books is London unless otherwise stated.

INTRODUCTION: THE PURITAN ETHOS, 1560–1700
Christopher Durston and Jacqueline Eales

The historiography of puritanism is addressed in C. H. George, 'Puritanism as History and Historiography', *Past and Present*, 41 (1968) and in R. L. Greaves, 'The Puritan Non-Conformist Tradition in England, 1560–1700: Historiographical Reflections', *Albion*, 17 (1985).

Any consideration of the corpus of modern research into the history and cultural expression of puritanism must start with the work of Patrick Collinson, who has dominated the field since the publication of *The Elizabethan Puritan Movement* (1967). Subsequent contributions by Collinson include *The Religion of Protestants: The Church in English Society, 1559–1625* (Oxford, 1982) and *The Birthpangs of Protestant England: Religious and Cultural Change in the Sixteenth and Seventeenth Centuries* (1988). Many of his stimulating essays are to be found in *Godly People: Essays on English Protestantism and Puritanism* (1983) and *Elizabethan Essays* (1994). A useful introduction to Collinson's thought and work is contained in his essay *English Puritanism*, Historical Association General Series, 106 (1983).

Collinson's work is complemented by a number of local studies; for example, W. J. Sheils, *The Puritans in the Diocese of Peterborough, 1558–1610* Northamptonshire Record Society, 30 (1979) and R. C. Richardson, *Puritanism in North-West England: a Regional Study of the Diocese of Chester to 1642* (1972).

An important starting point for considering contemporary concepts of puritanism is B. Hall, 'Puritanism: the Problem of Definition' in G. J. Cuming (ed.), *Studies in Church History*, vol. 2 (1965), which argues for the exclusion of separatism from the definition of puritanism. This theme is further explored in P. Collinson, 'A Comment: Concerning the Name Puritan', *Journal of Ecclesiastical History*, 31 (1980), which emphasises the importance of anti-puritanism in the process of definition. An important source of information on this latter point is to be found in W. Holden, *Anti-Puritan Satire, 1572–1642* (1954).

R. T. Kendall eschews the term 'puritan' in favour of 'experimental predestinarians' thus highlighting the importance of predestinarian theology to individual puritans in *Calvin and English Calvinism to 1649* (Oxford, 1979). The intellectual and theological basis of the puritan world-view is also the subject of Peter Lake, *Moderate Puritans and the Elizabethan Church* (Cambridge, 1982) and *Anglicans and Puritans? Presbyterianism and English Conformist Thought from Whitgift to Hooker* (Cambridge, 1988). For the tensions between Calvinism and the Arminian wing of the English church before the Civil War see Nicholas Tyacke, *Anti-Calvinists: the Rise of English Arminianism, c. 1590–1640* (Oxford, 1987), which argues for the existence of a Calvinist consensus which was shattered by the growth of Arminianism from the mid 1620s.

Many aspects of puritan culture are addressed in Christopher Hill's *Society and Puritanism in Pre-Revolutionary England* (1965), which has stimulated a lively debate about the originality of puritan theology and practical piety. The connections between social control and puritanism suggested by Hill are drawn in local contexts in K. Wrightson and D. Levine, *Poverty and Piety in an English Village* (New York, 1979) and William Hunt, *The Puritan Moment: The Coming of Revolution in an English County* (Cambridge, Mass., 1982), but are questioned by Margaret Spufford, 'Puritanism and Social Control?' in Anthony Fletcher and John Stevenson (eds), *Order and Disorder in Early Modern England* (1985) and Martin Ingram, 'The Reform of Popular Culture? Sex and Marriage in Early Modern England', in Barry Reay (ed.), *Popular Culture in Seventeenth Century England* (1985). Puritan reactions to popular culture are discussed in Jeremy Goring, *Godly Exercises or the Devil's Dance? Puritanism and Popular Culture in pre-Civil War England*, Dr Williams's Library Lecture (1983).

The puritan responses to the years of Civil War are considered by W. Lamont, *Godly Rule, Politics and Religion, 1603–1660* (1969), and W. Haller, *Liberty and Reformation in the Puritan Revolution* (New York, 1955). For the fate of puritanism after the Civil War see the wide-ranging collection of essays in O. P. Grell, J. I. Israel and N. Tyacke (eds), *From Persecution to Toleration: the Glorious Revolution and Religion in England* (Oxford, 1991) and M. R. Watts, *The Dissenters: from the Reformation to the French Revolution* (Oxford, 1978).

1. ELIZABETHAN AND JACOBEAN PURITANISM AS FORMS OF POPULAR RELIGIOUS CULTURE *Patrick Collinson*

For all aspects of the onslaught on traditional rituals, pastimes and festivity, puritan or otherwise, see Ronald Hutton, *The Rise and Fall of Merry England: the Ritual Year 1400–1700* (Oxford, 1994). The local politics of this repression can be investigated in David Underdown's two books, *Revel, Riot, and Rebellion: Popular Politics and Culture in England 1603–1660* (Oxford, 1985), and *Fire From Heaven: Life in an English Town in the Seventeenth Century* (1992). See also Patrick Collinson, *The Birthpangs of Protestant England: Religious and Cultural Change in the Sixteenth and Seventeenth Centuries* (1988); and C. J. Sisson, *Lost Plays of Shakespeare's Age* (1936). The fullest and most recent account of the sabbatarianism of the period is Kenneth Parker, *The English Sabbath: A Study of Doctrine and Discipline from the Reformation to the Civil War* (Cambridge, 1988). Parker is perhaps excessively 'revisionist' in minimising what was distinctively puritan about the hard-line sabbatarian position. The original source materials to be found in the many volumes of the great (and continuing) Toronto series *Records of Early English Drama* are very accessible to students at all stages and levels and deserve to be better known among historians.

The definitive account of the new, Protestant calendar and ritual festivities of Elizabethan and post-Elizabethan England is David Cressy, *Bonfires and Bells: National Memory and the Protestant Calendar in Elizabethan and Stuart England* (Berkeley and Los Angeles, 1989).

The Protestant and puritan sermon as (in Clifford Geertzian terms) a cultural institution is so far a neglected topic, although one shortly to be addressed by Arnold Hunt of Trinity College, Cambridge. But see Patrick Collinson, *The Elizabethan Puritan Movement* (London and Berkeley, 1967, and Oxford, 1989). For a more extensive account of puritan fasts than *The Elizabethan Puritan Movement* furnishes (including a very fully documented account of the Stamford fast of 1580), see Patrick Collinson's unpublished London PhD thesis of 1957, 'The Puritan Classical Movement in the Reign of Elizabeth I'. Puritan fasts as exorcism can be investigated in Keith Thomas, *Religion and the Decline of Magic* (1971) and *Witchcraft and Hysteria in Elizabethan London: Edward Jorden and the Mary Glover Case*, ed. Michael MacDonald (1990). Some aspects of puritan culture neglected in this essay, particularly those having to do with language, will be found in the pioneering study by the German Shakespearean, Levin L. Schücking, *The Puritan Family: A Social Study from the Literary Sources* (originally published in 1929), trs. B. Battershaw (1969). Two books on Scottish-Irish-American religious culture have wider horizons than any English studies yet attempted. They are Leigh Eric Schmidt, *Holy Fairs: Scottish Communions and American Revivals in the Early Modern Period* (Princeton, NJ, 1989); and David Hall, *Worlds of Wonder, Days of Judgment: Popular Religious Belief in Early New England* (Cambridge, Mass., 1990).

2. PURITANS AND THE CHURCH COURTS, 1560–1640
Martin Ingram

Older views on the relationship between puritans and the church courts, based in an adverse assessment of ecclesiastical justice, are best illustrated by Christopher Hill, *Society and Puritanism in Pre-Revolutionary England* (1964), esp. chs 8–10. For more recent assessments of the church courts see Ronald A. Marchant, *The Church under the Law: Justice, Administration and Discipline in the Diocese of York, 1560–1640* (Cambridge, 1969); Ralph Houlbrooke, *Church Courts and the People during the English Reformation, 1520–1570* (Oxford, 1979); and Martin Ingram, *Church Courts, Sex and Marriage in England, 1570–1640* (Cambridge, 1987). Consistory courts and ecclesiastical visitations are help-fully located in the wider context of episcopal activities in Kenneth Fincham, *Prelate as Pastor: the Episcopate of James I* (Oxford, 1990). The relationship between the courts and puritans has been explored in detail, and with varying emphases, in a number of local or regional studies: see in particular Ronald Marchant, *The Puritans and the Church Courts in the Diocese of York, 1560–1642* (1960); Roger B. Manning, *Religion and Society in Elizabethan*

Sussex: a Study of the Enforcement of the Religious Settlement, 1558–1603 (Leicester, 1969); R. C. Richardson, *Puritanism in North-West England: a Regional Study of the Diocese of Chester to 1642* (Manchester, 1972); Richardson, 'Puritanism and the Ecclesiastical Authorities: the Case of the Diocese of Chester', in Brian Manning (ed.), *Politics, Religion and the English Civil War* (1973), pp. 3–33; W. J. Sheils (ed.), *The Puritans in the Diocese of Peterborough, 1558–1610,* Northamptonshire Record Society, XXX (Northampton, 1979); Sheils, 'Some Problems of Government in a New Diocese: the Bishop and the Puritans in the Diocese of Peterborough, 1560–1630', in Rosemary O'Day and Felicity Heal (eds), *Continuity and Change: Personnel and Administration in the Church of England, 1500–1642* (Leicester, 1976), pp. 145–66; John Fielding, 'Arminianism in the Localities: Peterborough Diocese, 1603–1642', in Kenneth Fincham (ed.), *The Early Stuart Church* (1993), pp. 93–113, 262–4. These studies tend to focus on conflict between the courts and puritan ministers and lay people. For recognition of the ways in which puritans might themselves exploit the machinery of the courts, see Keith Wrightson and David Levine, *Poverty and Piety in an English Village: Terling, 1525–1700* (New York, San Francisco and London, 1979), esp. ch. 5, and David Underdown, *Revel, Riot and Rebellion: Popular Politics and Culture in England, 1603–1660* (Oxford, 1985). For the general context, see the indispensable Patrick Collinson, *The Elizabethan Puritan Movement* (London, 1967) and Collinson, *The Religion of Protestants: the Church in English Society, 1559–1625* (Oxford, 1982).

3. PURITANS AND ICONOCLASM, 1560–1660
Margaret Aston

Iconoclasm, and attitudes towards visual imagery in England, have received increasing attention since the useful survey by John Phillips, *The Reformation of Images: Destruction of Art in England, 1535–1660* (Berkeley, CA, and London, 1973), which includes a chapter on 'The Puritan Reaction' to the 'New Anglicanism' of the Laudians. M. Aston, *England's Iconoclasts*, I (Oxford 1988), *Faith and Fire* (1993), and *The King's Bedpost* (Cambridge, 1994), consider the critical theological base of Reformation iconoclasm and some of its manifestations, including developments under Elizabeth I. Tessa Watt, *Cheap Print and Popular Piety, 1550–1640* (Cambridge, 1991) is important for attitudes towards religious images, including woodcuts and wall paintings. Eamon Duffy, *The Stripping of the Altars* (New Haven, CT, and London, 1992), considers the impact of Tudor iconoclasm up to *c*.1580, but is not concerned with puritans.

More specifically related to puritans are studies of some seventeenth-century iconoclasts. Paul Slack, 'Religious Protest and Urban Authority: the Case of Henry Sherfield, Iconoclast, 1633', in *Studies in Church History*, vol. 9 (1972), pp. 295–302; Slack, 'The Public Conscience of Henry Sherfield', in John Morrill, Paul Slack and Daniel Woolf (eds), *Public Duty and Private Conscience in Seventeenth-Century England* (Oxford, 1993), pp. 151–71; in the same volume, pp. 173–203, is John Morrill, 'William Dowsing, the

Bureaucratic Puritan'; on Robert Harley see Jacqueline Eales, *Puritans and Roundheads. The Harleys of Brampton Bryan and the Outbreak of the English Civil War* (Cambridge, 1990), and also see J. Eales, 'Iconoclasm, Iconography, and the Altar in the English Civil War', in *Studies in Church History*, vol. 28 (1992), pp. 313–27. This volume also includes Brett Usher, 'The Silent Community: Early Puritans and the Patronage of the Arts', pp. 287–302, and K. A. Newman, 'Holiness in Beauty? Roman Catholics, Arminians, and the Aesthetics of Religion in early Caroline England', pp. 303–12.

Among the numerous writings on puritanism which reflect on the phenomenon of iconoclasm, only a few can be mentioned: Patrick Collinson's illuminating pages on this topic include his lecture, *From Iconoclasm to Iconophobia; the Cultural Impact of the Second English Reformation* (Reading, 1986); the chapter on 'Protestant Culture and the Cultural Revolution' in *The Birthpangs of Protestant England* (New York, 1988); *Archbishop Grindal, 1519–1583* (1979); and more recently ch. 4 of *Elizabethan Essays* (1994). Also useful – since purification is allied to iconoclasm – is Jeremy Goring's lecture *Godly Exercises or the Devil's Dance? Puritanism and Popular Culture in pre-Civil War England* (1983). John Morrill's investigations of iconoclasm in the context of the Civil War are now gathered in his *The Nature of the English Revolution* (1993). Illuminating examples of 1640s iconoclasm are to be found in Brian Manning, *The English People and the English Revolution 1640–1649* (1976); William Hunt, *The Puritan Moment; The Coming of Revolution in an English County* (Cambridge, Mass., 1983); and David Underdown, *Revel, Riot and Rebellion; Popular Politics and Culture in England 1603–1660* (Oxford, 1985).

4. THE PURITAN DEATH-BED, c.1560–c.1660
Ralph Houlbrooke

Despite the abundance of available source materials, the puritans' approach to the business of dying has been relatively little studied. The two monographs devoted to *ars moriendi* writings in England, Sister Mary Catharine O'Connor's *The Art of Dying Well: The Development of the Ars Moriendi* (New York, 1942), and Nancy Lee Beaty's *The Craft of Dying. A Study in the Literary Tradition of the Ars Moriendi in England* (New Haven, CT, and London, 1970), are indispensable guides. But they say curiously little about William Perkins's *A Salve for a Sicke Man*, probably the most important single work in the corpus of puritan writings on the 'craft of dying'. David E. Stannard's *The Puritan Way of Death: A Study in Religion, Culture and Social Change* (New York, 1977), is a valuable pioneer study of all aspects of the New England way of death during the colonial period which offers the student of English puritanism some thought-provoking comparisons. His picture of puritan death-bed experiences is, however, considerably darker then the one painted here. Neither of them will fit very easily into the stimulating yet sometimes tantalisingly vague schema presented by Philippe Ariès, *Western Attitudes towards Death from the Middle Ages to the Present*, trans. P. M. Ranum (Baltimore,

MD, 1974) and *The Hour of Our Death*, trans. H. Weaver (1981). M. Claire Cross has edited one of the fullest accounts of a puritan's death with a useful introduction in 'The Third Earl of Huntingdon's Death-bed: A Calvinist Example of the *Ars Moriendi*', *Northern History*, XXI (1985), 80–107. 'The Good Death in Seventeenth-Century England' has been discussed by Lucinda McCray Beier in Ralph Houlbrooke (ed.), *Death, Ritual and Bereavement* (London and New York, 1989), pp. 43–61.

5 'A CHARITABLE CHRISTIAN HATRED': THE GODLY AND THEIR ENEMIES IN THE 1630s *Peter Lake*

For the best and most influential statement of the view of puritanism as but the leading edge of a broader body of reformed opinion, and of the godly as the shock troops of a reformed yet consensual English church, see Patrick Collinson's *The Religion of Protestants* (Oxford, 1982). The position taken there should be read against Collinson's brilliant analysis of the cultural and ideological tensions engendered by 'perfect protestantism' in the last two chapters of his *The Birthpangs of Protestant England* (1989) and in his article on 'The English Conventicle' in D. Wood and W. Sheils (eds), *Voluntary Religion* (Oxford, 1986), *Studies in Church History*, vol. 24. Also see Peter Lake, *Moderate Puritans and the Elizabethan Church* (Cambridge, 1982) and Lake 'Defining puritanism – again?' in F. Bremer (ed.), *Puritanism: Transatlantic Perspectives on a Seventeenth Century Anglo-American Faith* (Boston, 1993). For the best analysis of anti-puritanism see three articles by Patrick Collinson: *The Puritan Character: Polemics and Polarities* (Los Angeles, 1989); 'Ecclesiastical Vitriol: Religious Satire in the 1590s and the Invention of Puritanism', in J. Guy (ed.), *The Reign of Elizabeth I* (Cambridge, 1995); and 'Jonson's *Bartholomew Fair* and the Theatrical Construction of Puritanism' in D. Bevington, D. Smith and R. Strier (eds), *The Theatrical City* (Cambridge, 1995). On the tensions between the godly and the profane also see Collinson's 'The cohabitation of the faithful with the unfaithful', in O. P. Grell, J. I. Israel and N. Tyacke (eds), *From Persecution to Toleration: the Glorious Revolution and Religion in England* (Oxford, 1991). For a rather different approach see J. Fielding, 'Opposition to the Personal Rule of Charles I: the diary of Robert Woodford, 1637–41', *Historical Journal*, 31 (1988); and P. Lake, 'Puritanism, Arminianism and a Shropshire axe murder' *Midland History*, 15 (1990). For local tensions between the godly and their enemies even in a town under puritan control see D. Underdown, *Fire from Heaven* (1992), and the brilliant article by A. L. Hughes, 'Religion and Society in Stratford upon Avon, 1619–38' *Midland History* (1994), 19. Of the greatest relevance to the present study is J. Fielding, 'Arminianism in the Localities: Peterborough Diocese, 1603–42', in K. Fincham (ed.), *The Early Stuart Church* (1993). On the inner tensions within 'the puritan self' compare John Stachniewski, *The Persecutory Imagination* (Oxford, 1991) with P. Lake, *Moderate Puritans and the Elizabethan Church* (Cambridge, 1982), ch. 7, and Charles Cohen, *God's Caress* (New York, 1986).

6. A ROAD TO REVOLUTION: THE CONTINUITY OF
PURITANISM, 1559–1642 *Jacqueline Eales*

Patrick Collinson's *The Elizabethan Puritan Movement* (1967) is still the standard work on the initial history of the puritan movement. The early-Stuart period still awaits, however, a similar in-depth treatment, although Nicholas Tyacke has provided a preliminary but selective sketch in his 1990 Dr William's Library Lecture, *The Fortunes of English Puritanism, 1603–1640*. R. A. Marchant, *The Puritans and the Church Courts in the Diocese of York, 1560–1642* (1960) and R. C. Richardson, *Puritanism in North-West England: a Regional Study of the Diocese of Chester to 1642* (Manchester, 1972) are both exemplary local studies providing an overview of the longer period. John Fielding, 'Arminianism in the Localities: Peterborough Diocese, 1603–1642' in K. Fincham (ed.), *The Early Stuart Church, 1603–1642* (1993) provides an introduction to his forthcoming study on conformists and puritans in the diocese in the early-Stuart period. H. C. Porter, *Puritanism in Tudor England* (1970) provides extracts from key documents with a lucid commentary. Peter Lake, *Moderate Puritans and the Elizabethan Church* (Cambridge, 1982) and *Anglicans and Puritans? Presbyterianism and English Conformist Thought from Whitgift to Hooker* (Cambridge, 1988) both consider the intellectual development of puritan thought. For the 1630s see Julian Davies, *The Caroline Captivity of the Church: Charles I and the Remoulding of Anglicanism* (Oxford, 1992); for an alternative interpretation see Jacqueline Eales, 'Iconoclasm, Iconography and the Altar in the English Civil War', in Diana Wood (ed.), *Studies in Church History*, vol. 28 (Oxford, 1992), pp. 313–27. Older studies still have much to offer in illustrating the puritan religious and social milieu before the Civil War, for example Horton Davies, *The Worship of the English Puritans* (1948), and the classic work by Christopher Hill, *Society and Puritanism in Pre-Revolutionary England* (1964). An account of an influential puritan courtier is to be found in Claire Cross, *The Puritan Earl: the Life of Henry Hastings, third Earl of Huntingdon, 1536–95* (1966). P. Seaver, *The Puritan Lectureships: The Politics of Religious Dissent, 1560–1662* (1970) although largely focused on London, traces the importance of puritan sermons through a study of urban lectureships. William Haller, *The Rise of Puritanism: Or the Way to the New Jerusalem as Set Forth in Pulpit and Press from Thomas Cartwright to John Lilburne and John Milton* (New York, 1938) contains many useful insights and references on the subjects of sermons and the press. J. T. Cliffe has written an unrivalled trilogy on the transmission of puritanism within gentry family groups in the seventeenth century, see *The Puritan Gentry: The Great Puritan Families of Early Stuart England* (1984), *Puritans in Conflict: The Puritan Gentry During and After the Civil Wars* (1988) and *The Puritan Gentry Besieged, 1650–1700* (1993). Jacqueline Eales, *Puritans and Roundheads: the Harleys of Brampton Bryan and the Outbreak of the English Civil War* (Cambridge, 1990) is a detailed case study of the regional and national influence of a puritan family in the early-Stuart period, and David Underdown, *Fire From Heaven: Life in an English Town in the Seventeenth Century* (1992) provides a rich study of the puritan town of Dorchester.

7. PURITAN RULE AND THE FAILURE OF CULTURAL
   REVOLUTION, 1645–1660 *Christopher Durston*

The effect of puritan rule upon traditional festive culture is superbly dealt with in Ronald Hutton's magisterial *The Rise and Fall of Merry England: The Ritual Year 1400–1700* (Oxford, 1994), where the author puts the period 1640–60 in the context of changes across the early-modern period as a whole. This book complements David Cressy's *Bells and Bonfires: National Memory and the Protestant Calendar in Elizabethan and Stuart England* (1989). Kenneth Parker, *The English Sabbath* (Cambridge, 1988) is a useful study of early-modern sabbatarianism, but its contention that this was not distinctively puritan is controversial. The present author has touched on aspects of calendar reform in earlier work; in particular Chris Durston, 'Lords of Misrule: The Puritan War on Christmas 1642–60', *History Today*, 35 (Dec., 1985); and Christopher Durston, ' "For the Better Humiliation of the People": Public Days of Fasting and Thanksgiving during the English Revolution', *The Seventeenth Century*, 7 (1992).

For puritan changes to the way the personal milestones of birth, marriage and death were marked see two important pieces by John Morrill: 'The Church in England 1642–9', in John Morrill (ed.), *Reactions to the English Civil War* (1982); and 'The Impact of Puritanism', in John Morrill (ed.), *The Impact of the English Civil War* (1991). Further material on baptism, churching and marriage is given in Christopher Durston, *The Family in the English Revolution* (Oxford, 1989). For the churching ceremony see also David Cressy, 'Purification, Thanksgiving and the Churching of Women in post-Reformation England', *Past and Present*, 141 (1993).

The best recent work on the attack on popular sports and pastimes is contained in Hutton's *Merry England*; David Underdown's *Revel, Riot and Rebellion: Popular Politics and Culture in England 1603–1660* (Oxford, 1985); and Anthony Fletcher's *Reform in the Provinces* (New Haven, CT, and London, 1986). Helpful material on the pre-1640 background can be found in Jeremy Goring's article, *Godly Exercises or the Devil's Dance: Puritanism and Popular Culture in pre-Civil War England* (1983). Keith Wrightson's doctoral study, 'The Puritan Reformation of Manners with special reference to the counties of Lancashire and Cheshire', University of Cambridge PhD thesis (1974), is a seminal work in the field; it unfortunately remains unpublished, but is available for consultation on microfilm. On the specific question of sexual misconduct, see the important article by Sir Keith Thomas, 'The Puritans and Adultery: The Act of 1650 Reconsidered', in D. H. Pennington and K. V. Thomas (eds), *Puritans and Revolutionaries* (Oxford, 1978); Stephen Roberts, 'Fornication and Bastardy in Mid Seventeenth-Century Devon: How was the act of 1650 Enforced?', in J. Rule (ed.), *Outside the Law: Studies in Crime and Order 1650–1850* (Exeter, 1982); and Durston, *The Family in the English Revolution*, ch. 7.

Interesting case studies of puritan reform efforts in specific local communities during the Civil War period are given in John Morrill, *Cheshire 1630–1660: County Government and Society during the English Revolution* (Oxford,

1974); Anthony Fletcher, *A County Community in Peace and War: Sussex 1600–1660* (1975); and David Underdown, *Fire from Heaven: The Life of an English Town in the Seventeenth Century* (1992), which deals with the conspicuous puritan centre of Dorchester in Dorset.

8. FROM PURITANISM TO DISSENT, 1660–1700 *John Spurr*

The best introduction to Restoration dissent is contained in M. R. Watts, *The Dissenters – From the Reformation to the French Revolution* (Oxford, 1978; pbk, 1985). Valuable monographs include N. H. Keeble, *The Literary Culture of Nonconformity in Later Seventeenth-Century England* (Leicester, 1987); J. T. Cliffe, *The Puritan Gentry Besieged, 1650–1700* (1993); G. R. Cragg, *Puritanism in the Period of the Great Persecution 1660–1688* (Cambridge, 1957); G. H. Jenkins, *Protestant Dissenters in Wales, 1639–1689* (Cardiff, 1992). C. G. Bolam, J. Goring, H. L. Short and Roger Thomas, *The English Presbyterians – From Elizabethan Puritanism to Modern Unitarianism* (1968), G. F. Nuttall and O. Chadwick (eds), *From Uniformity to Unity* (1962), O. P. Grell, J. I. Israel and N. Tyacke (eds), *From Persecution to Toleration – The Glorious Revolution and Religion in England* (Oxford, 1991), and Richard Greaves, *John Bunyan and English Nonconformity* (1992) are valuable essay collections. Among older works C. E. Whiting, *Studies in English Puritanism from the Restoration to the Revolution, 1660–1688* (1931; 2nd imp. 1968) is particularly useful.

The plentiful sources for the history of later seventeenth-century dissent include congregational records, spiritual autobiographies, clerical diaries, exemplary biographies (often contained in funeral sermons), and testimonies of harassment and persecution. M. Mullett, *Sources for the History of English Nonconformity 1660–1830* (British Records Association, Archives and the User 8, 1991) provides an introduction. A. G. Matthews's monumental biographical dictionary of the ejected ministers, *Calamy Revised* (Oxford, 1934; reprinted 1991), repays browsing. But the spirit of dissent may best be appreciated in works like John Bunyan's *Grace Abounding to the Chief of Sinners* (1666: Everyman pbk, 1976) or *The Autobiography of Richard Baxter*, abridged by J. M. Lloyd Thomas and ed. N. H. Keeble (1974). Those with access to N. H. Keeble and G. F. Nuttall (eds), *Calendar of the Correspondence of Richard Baxter*, 2 vols (Oxford, 1991) will find it rewarding. Among the many good biographies of dissenters are G. F. Nuttall, *Richard Baxter* (1965); W. Lamont, *Richard Baxter and the Millenium* (1979); P. Toon, *God's Statesman – The Life of John Owen* (1971); and C. Hill, *A Turbulent, Seditious, and Factious People – John Bunyan and his Church 1628–1680* (Oxford, 1989).

Recently there have been attempts to study dissent in the context of the broader life of a particular community. By using the records of the Church of England, of the parish and the town, historians can produce a 'horizontal' picture of dissent in its context which often modifies the older, 'vertical', denominational histories. The trailblazer here was M. Spufford, *Contrasting Communities – English Villagers in the Sixteenth and Seventeenth Centuries* (Cambridge, 1974), followed by much valuable work which remains in the form of unpublished dissertations; but see J. D. Ramsbottom, 'Presbyterians and

"Partial Conformity" in the Restoration Church of England', *Journal of Ecclesiastical History*, 43 (1992); and J. J. Hurwich, 'Dissent and Catholicism in English Society: a Study of Warwickshire, 1660–1720', *Journal of British Studies*, 16 (1976).

Among the more specialised works on Dissent are C. W. Horle, *The Quakers and the English Legal System 1660–1688* (Philadelphia 1988); D. R. Lacey, *Dissent and Parliamentary Politics in England 1661–1689* (New Brunswick, NJ, 1969). The involvement of radical puritans in plotting has been chronicled in R. L. Greaves's trilogy: *Deliver Us from Evil: The Radical Underground in Britain, 1660–1663* (Oxford, 1986); *Enemies Under His Feet: Radicals and Nonconformists in Britain, 1664–1677* (Stanford, Cal. 1990); and *Secrets of the Kingdom: British Radicals from the Popish Plot to the Revolution of 1688–89* (Stanford, Cal. 1992).

Notes and References

The place of publication for books is London, unless otherwise stated.

INTRODUCTION: THE PURITAN ETHOS, 1560–1700
Christopher Durston and Jacqueline Eales

We should like to thank Susan Doran, Ralph Houlbrooke, Martin Ingram and Peter Lake for their helpful comments on earlier drafts of this introduction.

1. Patrick Collinson, 'A Comment: Concerning the Name Puritan', *Journal of Ecclesiastical History*, 31 (1980), 484; Richard L. Greaves, 'The Puritan Non-Conformist Tradition in England, 1560–1700: Historiographical Reflections', *Albion*, 17 (1985), 449–86.

2. Giles Widdowes, *The Schismatical Puritan* (Oxford, 1631), unpaginated; Henry Parker, *A Discourse Concerning Puritans* (1641), p. 9; Fuller is quoted by Patrick Collinson in *English Puritanism* (1983), p. 6.

3. Christopher Hill, *The Economic Problems of the Church, from Whitgift to the Long Parliament* (1956), p. xii; Christopher Hill, *Society and Puritanism in Pre-Revolutionary England* (1964), p. 13.

4. Basil Hall, 'Puritanism: the Problem of Definition', in *Studies in Church History*, vol. 2 (1965), 287; Elton's comment is quoted by W. J. Sheils in *Puritans in the Diocese of Peterborough 1558–1610*, Northants Record Society, XXX (1979), 2.

5. C. H. George, 'Puritanism as History and Historiography', *Past and Present*, 41 (1968), 104.

6. William Hunt, *The Puritan Moment: The Coming of Revolution in an English County* (Cambridge, Mass., and London, 1983), pp. 145–6.

7. Leonard J. Trinterud, *Elizabethan Puritanism* (New York, 1971), p. 7.

8. Samuel Ward, *A Coal from the altar to kindle the holy fire of zeal in a sermon preached at a general visitation at Ipswich* (1615), p. 41.

9. William Prynne, *A quench-Coal . . .* (1637), p. 14.

10. Jacqueline Eales, 'Sir Robert Harley, K. B. (1579–1656) and the "Character" of a Puritan', *The British Library Journal*, 15 (1989), 134–57.

11. F. Rogers, *A Visitation sermon preached at the Lord Archbishops triennial ordinary visitation* (1633), sig. C3r.

12. Collinson, *English Puritanism*, p. 10.

13. Patrick Collinson, *The Birthpangs of Protestant England* (1988), p. 143.

276

14. Collinson, 'A Comment: Concerning the Name Puritan', p. 488.

15. Quoted by Collinson in *English Puritanism*, p. 39.

16. Parker, *Discourse Concerning Puritans*, p. 55.

17. Sheils, *Puritans in the Diocese of Peterborough*, p. 2. In the present volume, Patrick Collinson adds to this bestiary of puritanism by comparing the movement to an okapi.

18. J. F. H. New, *Anglicans and Puritans: the Basis of their Opposition 1558–1640* (1964); J. Sears McGee, *The Godly Man in Stuart England: Anglicans, Puritans, and the Two Tables* (New Haven, CT, 1976); Richard L. Greaves, *Society and Religion in Elizabethan England* (Minneapolis, 1981); Peter White, *Predestination, Policy and Polemic: Conflict and Consensus in the English Church from the Reformation to the Civil War* (Cambridge, 1992).

19. Nicholas Tyacke, *Anti-Calvinists: The Rise of English Arminianism c. 1590–1640* (Oxford, 1987); R. T. Kendall, *Calvin and English Calvinism to 1649* (Oxford, 1979); Peter Lake, *Anglicans and Puritans? Presbyterianism and English Conformist Thought from Whitgift to Hooker* (1988); and Peter Lake, 'Calvinism and the English Church 1570–1635', *Past and Present*, 114 (1987).

20. Josias Nichols, *The Plea of the Innocent . . .* (1602), pp. 84–5.

21. W. Barlow, *The summe and substance of the conference . . . at Hampton Court* (1604), p. 29.

22. Eales, 'Sir Robert Harley and the "Character" of a Puritan', pp. 150–2.

23. Conrad Russell, *Parliaments and English Politics, 1621–1629* (Oxford, 1979), p. 435; Russell identifies some 30 anti-Arminian speakers in the parliaments of the 1620s.

24. Hall, 'Puritanism: the Problem of Definition', p. 296.

25. Peter Burke, *Popular Culture in Early Modern Europe* (New York, 1978), prologue.

26. For more details of this controversy see Kaspar von Greyerz's introduction to K. von Greyerz (ed.), *Religion and Society in Early Modern Europe 1500–1800* (1984); Richard C. Trexler, 'Reverence and Profanity in the Study of Early Modern Religion', in Greyerz, *Religion and Society*, pp. 252–3; Keith Thomas, *Religion and the Decline of Magic: Studies in Popular Beliefs in Sixteenth and Seventeenth Century England* (1971), passim; and the debate between Hildred Geertz and Keith Thomas entitled 'An Anthropology of Religion and Magic, Two Views', in *Journal of Interdisciplinary History*, 6 (1975), 71–110.

27. John Calvin, *Institutes of the Christian Religion*, ed. J. T. McNeill, 2 vols (Philadelphia, 1960), 1, 191; Mary Potter Engel, *John Calvin's Perspectival Anthropology* (Georgia, 1988), pp. 8–10; T. F. Torrance, *Calvin's Doctrine of Man* (1949), pp. 87–8.

28. Ferdinando Nicholls, *The Life and Death of M. Ignatius Jordan . . .* (1654), p. 7.

29. R. H. Tawney, *Religion and the Rise of Capitalism* (1926), passim; Hill, *Society and Puritanism*, passim.

30. A. G. Dickens, *The English Reformation* (1964), p. 319.

31. Nicholls, *Ignatius Jordan*, p. 2.

32. Richard Baxter, *A Breviate of the Life of Margaret, the daughter of Francis Charlton of Appleby in Shropshire esquire* . . . (1681), p. 4.

33. John Morrill, 'The Making of Oliver Cromwell', in John Morrill (ed.), *Oliver Cromwell and the English Revolution* (1990), pp. 19–48; T. T. Lewis (ed.), *The Letters of Lady Brilliana Harley*, Camden Society, 58 (1854), 94.

34. Barlow, *The summe and substance of the conference* . . . *at Hampton Court*, p. 37; Collinson, *English Puritanism*, p. 9.

35. For more details on Wallington see Paul S. Seaver, *Wallington's World: A Puritan Artisan in Seventeenth Century London* (Stanford, Cal., 1985), passim, but especially ch. 2; the quotes are from pp. 6 and 26.

36. Alan Macfarlane (ed.), *The Diary of Ralph Josselin 1616–83* (1976), passim; these examples are from pp. 51, 64, 88, 90–1.

37. Ibid., p. 348.

38. Nichols, *The Plea of The Innocent*, p. 12.

39. Parker, *Discourse Concerning Puritans*, passim, but especially pp. 8–9, 53.

40. John Geree, *The Character of an Old English Puritane or Non-Conformist* (1646), passim.

41. William Bradshaw, *English Puritanisme* (1605), p. 1; Eales, 'Sir Robert Harley and the "Character" of a Puritan', pp. 150–2; Bradshaw, *English Puritanisme*, pp. 1–2.

42. Quoted by Collinson in *English Puritanism*, p. 10.

43. Eales, 'Sir Robert Harley and the "Character" of a Puritan', pp. 150–2; Bradshaw, *English Puritanisme*, pp. 1–2.

44. Collinson, *English Puritanism*, p. 16.

45. For baptism see Christopher Durston, *The Family in the English Revolution* (Oxford, 1989), pp. 115–21; for churching, David Cressy, 'Purification, Thanksgiving and the Churching of Women in Post-Reformation England', *Past and Present*, 141 (1993), 106–46.

46. Jacqueline Eales, 'Iconoclasm, Iconography, and the Altar in the English Civil War', in D. Woods and W. Sheils (eds), *The Church and the Arts, Studies in Church History*, vol. 28 (1992), 313–27.

47. J. S. Coolidge, *The Pauline Renaissance in England* (Oxford, 1970), p. 147.

48. Seaver, *Wallington's World*, p. 37.

49. For more details see Christopher Durston, ' "For the Better Humiliation of the People": Public Days of Fasting and Thanksgiving During the English Revolution', *The Seventeenth Century*, 7 (1992), 129–49.

50. Ibid., p. 132.

51. Ibid., pp. 133–4.

52. Macfarlane, *Josselin Diary*, pp. 8–474; Josselin regularly participated in private fasts at Earls Colne throughout the 1640s and 1650s.

53. This phrase is John Geree's; see *Character of an Old English Puritane*, pp. 2–3.

54. Patrick Collinson, 'The Beginnings of English Sabbatarianism', in *Studies in Church History*, Vol. 1 (1964), 207–21.

55. Kenneth Parker, *The English Sabbath* (Cambridge, 1988), passim.

56. Nicholas Tyacke, 'Popular Puritan Mentality in Late Elizabethan England', in Peter Clark, A. G. R. Smith and N. Tyacke (eds), *The English Commonwealth 1547–1640* (Leicester 1979), pp. 77–92.

57. K. Wrightson and D. Levine, *Poverty and Piety in an English Village: Terling 1525–1700* (New York, 1979), passim.

58. Hunt, *Puritan Moment*, p. 140.

59. M. Spufford, 'Puritanism and Social Control?', in Anthony Fletcher and John Stevenson (eds), *Order and Disorder in Early Modern England* (Cambridge, 1985), p. 57.

60. Martin Ingram, *Church Courts, Sex and Marriage in England 1570–1640* (Cambridge, 1988), passim.

61. Martin Ingram, 'Religious Communities and Moral Discipline in Late Sixteenth and Early Seventeenth England' in K. von Greyerz (ed.), *Religion and Society*, pp. 177–93.

62. Ronald Hutton, *The Rise and Fall of Merry England: the Ritual Year 1400–1700* (Oxford, 1994), pp. 111–13, 130, 144, and chs 3, 4 and 5 passim.

63. Hunt, *Puritan Moment*, p. 146.

64. Patrick Collinson, *The Religion of Protestants* (Oxford, 1982), p. 230.

65. For details see Seaver, *Wallington's World*, passim; and Macfarlane, *Josselin Diary*, passim.

66. Jacqueline Eales, *Puritans and Roundheads: The Harleys of Brampton Bryan and the Outbreak of the English Civil War* (Cambridge, 1990), pp. 58–9.

67. Ibid., pp. 24–9.

68. For more details see Jacqueline Eales, 'Samuel Clarke and the "Lives" of Godly Women in Seventeenth-Century England', in D. Wood and W. Sheils (eds), *Women in the Church, Studies in Church History*, vol. 27 (1990), 365–76.

69. William Perkins, *Christian OEconomie* (1609) and *How to Live, and That Well* (1601); Thomas Gataker, *Marriage Duties briefly couched togither* (1620); Robert Cleaver and John Dod, *A Plaine and Familiar Exposition of the Ten Commandments* (1604); William Gouge, *Of Domesticall Duties* (1622); William Whately, *A Bride-Bush* (1619) and *A Care-Cloth* (1624).

70. British Library Additional Manuscripts 70001, William Gouge to Harley, 24 June 1613, unfoliated between ff. 131 and 135.

71. Hunt, *Puritan Moment*, pp. 87, 90, 94, 97–8, 104, 132, 149, 153, 175–6, 260–2, 276–7, 284, 293–4, 296–7, 302; see also M. S. Byford, 'The Price of Protestantism: Assessing the Impact of Religious Change on Elizabethan Essex: The Cases of Heydon and Colchester, 1558–1594', Unpublished University of Oxford DPhil thesis (1988), passim.

72. *Victoria County History of Oxfordshire*, vol. 2, edited by W. Page (1907), p. 46; vol. 10, edited by A. Crossley (1972), p. 8.

73. David Underdown, *Fire from Heaven: Life in an English Town in the Seventeenth Century* (1992), passim.

74. David Underdown, *Revel, Riot and Rebellion: Popular Politics and Culture in England 1603–1660* (Oxford, 1985), passim.

75. G. F. Nuttall, *The Holy Spirit in Puritan Faith and Experience* (Oxford, 1946), p. 9.

76. S. Gardiner (ed.), *Documents of the Puritan Revolution*, third edn (Oxford, 1906), p. 416.

77. William Haller, *The Rise of Puritanism* (New York, 1938), p. 9.

1. ELIZABETHAN AND JACOBEAN PURITANISM AS FORMS OF POPULAR RELIGIOUS CULTURE   *Patrick Collinson*

1. Clifford Geertz, *The Interpretation of Cultures* (1975), Part III, Ch. 4, 'Religion as a Cultural System'.

2. David Underdown, *Revel, Riot, and Rebellion: Popular Politics and Culture in England 1603–1660* (Oxford, 1985), especially ch. 3, 'Cultural Conflict'; David Underdown, *Fire from Heaven: Life in an English Town in the Seventeenth Century* (1992); Patrick Collinson, *The Birthpangs of Protestant England: Religious and Cultural Change in the Sixteenth and Seventeenth Centuries* (1988), especially chs 4 and 5, 'Protestant Culture and the Cultural Revolution' and 'Wars of Religion'.

3. Kenneth Parker, *The English Sabbath: A study of doctrine and discipline from the Reformation to the Civil War* (Cambridge, 1988), p. 158.

4. *The Commission for Ecclesiastical Causes Within the Dioceses of Bristol and Gloucester*, ed. F. D. Price, Publications of the Bristol and Gloucestershire Archaeological Society: Records Section 10 (1972), pp. 49, 52, 60, 62, 78, 84, 101–2. The liberal use of the word 'puritan', and the application of the term 'recusant' to 'puritans', is unusual in a formal act book, and is probably indicative of the conservative, even crypto-Catholic, views of Bishop Richard Cheyney of Gloucester and Bristol. See Caroline Litzenberger, 'Responses of the Laity to Changes in Official Religious Policy in Gloucestershire (1541–1580)', unpublished Cambridge PhD thesis (1993), pp. 154–61, 197–205. I am grateful to Caroline Litzenberger for a copy of her dissertation and for permission to cite it.

5. M. S. Byford, 'The Price of Protestantism: Assessing the Impact of Religious Change on Elizabethan Essex: the Cases of Heydon and Colchester, 1558–1594', unpublished Oxford DPhil thesis (1988), p. 5. I am grateful to M. S. Byford for a copy of his dissertation and for permission to cite and quote from it.

6. See, most recently, Underdown, *Revel, Riot, and Rebellion*, p. 48: 'the Puritan Philip Stubbes'.

7. 'I beseech the Lord that we may all agree together in one truth, and not to divide our selves, one from another, for trifles, making schisms, ruptures, breaches and factions in the Church of God . . .' (*The second part*, Sigs P6ᵛ–7ʳ).

8. The devil's advocate in Stubbes's dialogue complains: 'You will be deemed too stoical, if you should restrain men from these exercises upon the Sabbath . . .' (*The Anatomie of Abuses*, Sig. L2ᵛ.)

9. See my two forthcoming essays: 'Ecclesiastical Vitriol: Religious Satire in the 1590s and the Invention of Puritanism', in *The Reign of Elizabeth I*, ed. John Guy (Cambridge); and '*Bartholomew Fair*: Theatre Invents Puritans', in *The Theatrical City: London's Culture, Theatre and Literature, 1576–1649*, ed. David Bevington, David Smith and Richard Strier (Cambridge, 1995).

10. *Records of Early English Drama* (Toronto): *Chester*, ed. Lawrence M. Clopper (1979); *York*, 2 vols, ed. Alexander F. Johnston and Margaret Rogerson (1979); *Coventry*, ed. R.W. Ingram (1981); *Norwich 1540–1642*, ed.

David Galloway (1984); *Cumberland, Westmorland, Gloucestershire*, ed. Audrey Douglas and Peter Greenfield (1986); *Devon*, ed. John M. Wasson (1986); *Cambridge*, 2 vols, ed. Alan H. Nelson (1989); *Herefordshire, Worcestershire*, ed. David N. Klauser (1990).

11. Humphrey Roberts, *An earnest complaint of divers vain, wicked and abused exercises, practised on the Sabbath day* (1572), Sigs Di^v–2^r D5^v–6^r. In 1564–5, the Norwich magistrates licensed 'certain games of silver' to be 'showed' at Pulham Market, south of Norwich. In 1576, 'certain silver games', to be shown and played within the liberties of Norwich itself, were licensed, 'so that it be not on the Sabbath day' (*REED, Norwich 1540–1642*, pp. 52, 57, 393). Cf. payments at Carlisle 'for silver playgames upon shrovetuesday' (*REED, Cumberland, Westmorland, Gloucestershire*, pp. 65, 115).

12. In addition to the writers quoted here, see the anonymously published *A treatise of daunses, wherein it is shewed, that they are accessories to whoredome* (1581), Thomas Lovell, *A dialogue between custom and veritie concerning the use and abuse of daunsing and minstrelsie* (1581), and Christopher Fetherston, *A dialogue agaynst light, lewde, and lascivious dauncing* (1582). This crescendo of anxiety about dancing in 1581–2 is very striking.

13. Roberts, *An earnest complaint*, Sig. E8.

14. Stubbes, *Anatomie of Abuses*, Sigs. Pvi^r–Vii^r There was nothing especially 'puritan' about the objection to football. The conservatively minded Sir John Elyot had written of the game in 1531: 'Wherein is nothing but beastly fury and extreme violence: whereon proceedeth hurt . . .' (*The boke named the governor*, fol. 99^v). Elyot's review of 'sundry forms of exercise necessary for every gentilman' (fols 62^v–103^r) was rather less 'stoical' than that of Stubbes ('I am not of that opinion that all dancing generally is repugnant unto virtue', fol. 74^r) but was written in a similar literary tradition and spirit, which it is misleading to call 'puritan'.

15. Stubbes, *Anatomie of Abuses*, Sigs Mvii^v–Nii^r.

16. John Northbrooke, *Spiritus, est vicarius Christi in terra: a treatise wherein dicing, dauncing, vaine playes or enterludes with other idle pastimes etc. commonly used on the Sabboth day, are reproved* (1577?) (1579 edn), p. 171.

17. Patrick Collinson, *The Religion of Protestants: the Church in English Society 1559–1625* (Oxford, 1982), pp. 205–7, 224–30.

18. Stubbes, *Anatomie of Abuses*, Sigs. M3^r–4^v; T. F. Thistleton Dyer, *Popular Customs, Present and Past* (1876), pp. 217–18.

19. The report of 17 Lancashire preachers, 1587; Bodleian Library, MS Tanner 144, fol. 28, printed *REED, Lancashire*, p. 219. In 1589, 16 Lancashire JPs headed certain orders for sabbath observance with 'The Enormities of the Sabbath are these': 'Wakes, fairs, markets, bearbait, Bullbait, Ales, maygames, Resorting to Alehouses in time of divine service, Piping and dancing, Hunting and all manner of unlawful gaming.' (Huntington Library, MS EL 6299, 6300; *REED, Lancashire*, p. 220.) A letter of Edward Fleetwood, vicar of Wigan, which can be dated between 7 September and 10 December 1589, gives a slightly different list (ibid., p. 226).

20. Ibid., pp. 27–8, 228.

21. Ibid., p. 228; *Proceedings of the Lancashire Justices of the Peace at the Sheriff's Table During Assizes Week, 1578–1694*, ed. B. W. Quintrell, Record Society

of Lancashire and Cheshire, cxxi (1981), 41–2, 72–3; Parker, *The English Sabbath*, pp. 139–49; *REED, Devon*, pp. 293–300.

22. Parker, *The English Sabbath*, pp. 128–33; *Proceedings of the Lancashire Justices*, 41–2, 72–3; *REED, Lancashire*, pp. xxiv–xxv, 229–34, 369; *Visitation Articles and Injunctions of the Early Stuart Church*, 1, ed. Kenneth Fincham, Church of England Record Society, i (1994), 149–51; L. A. Govatt, *The King's Book of Sports* (1890); James Tait, 'The Declaration of Sports for Lancashire (1617)', *English Historical Review*, XXXII (1917), 561–8.

23. Parker, *The English Sabbath*, pp. 178–216; Collinson, *Religion of Protestants*, p. 147.

24. Parker, *The English Sabbath*, pp. 129–33, 154–60.

25. Ibid., pp. 117, 62, 118; *Visitation Articles and Injunctions*, 1, 11, 35, 70, 195, 165, 207, 152. For an example of a minister unseasonably prolonging evening prayer until it was too dark to dance, see Underdown, *Revel, Riot and Rebellion*, p. 67.

26. Jacqueline Eales, *Puritans and Roundheads: the Harleys of Brampton Bryan and the Outbreak of the English Civil War* (Cambridge, 1990). For a penetrating and evocative account of this region in the seventeenth century, emphasising its significance as a crucible of modernising rather than those conservative cultural tendencies (and with nothing at all about sport and dances), see David Rollinson, *The Origins of Modern Society: Gloucestershire 1500–1700* (1992).

27. *REED, Herefordshire, Worcestershire*, pp. 125–36, 280–2.

28. *Old Meg of Herefordshire, and a Mayd-Marian* (*STC* 12032) was published anonymously in 1609. According to Archbishop Sancroft's notes on the pamphlet (see n. 30 below), the author was 'Old Hopkins', by whom 'this Morris 'tis said was contrived'. If so, Hopkins, presumably a local, was a man of some wit and erudition.

29. *Kemps nine daies wonder. Performed in a daunce from London to Norwich* (*STC* 14923) (1600). See *REED, Norwich 1540–1642*, pp. 331–8.

30. Bodleian Library, MS Sancroft 28, pp. 28–31. *Old Meg* had a lengthy afterlife. The event was noted by Francis Bacon in his *Historia vitae et mortis* (1623), English edn, *History naturall and experimentall of life and death* (1638), p. 135; and by James Easton in *Human Longevity* (1799), p. 6. I owe these references to Peter Laslett.

31. *REED, Herefordshire, Worcestershire*, pp. 125–6, 150, 157, 168, 169, 174, 175–7, 180.

32. Ibid., pp. 382–3.

33. Ibid., pp. 74–94. Defendants in the case denied that the plaintiff, Philpot, held the office of constable in the township of the parish where the affray occurred. Cf. a Star Chamber case from the village of Rangeworthy, north of Bristol. In this 1611 case it was the parish constable, John Parker, who took the puritan part, opposing a revel and standing accused of 'arrogating to himself a singularity of sanctity and religion' (Underdown, *Revel, Riot, and Rebellion*, pp. 61–2).

34. *REED, Cumberland, Westmorland, Gloucestershire*, pp. 368–86 (Latin text), 402–19 (translation). Note this footnote to Windle's treatise (p. 386): 'Remember at the pulling down of 2. poles in Barkley so 1. in St Nicolas

parish in Gloucester. some say at the Judges commandment, at the Instigation of the Mayor & prior that puritan Minister. & thomas cherics a precisian.'

35. *Robert Dover and the Cotswold Games: Annalia Dubrensia*, ed. Christopher Whitfield (1962); *REED, Cumberland, Westmorland, Gloucestershire*, p. 257.

36. Drayton's accompanying map of Gloucestershire shows a group of dancers around a flag (or maypole?) on a Cotswold hilltop. Since this portion of *Poly-Olbion* was published in 1612, the year in which Dover seems to have taken over the games, the representation may precede his intervention.

37. G. O. and P. Jones (eds) (Exeter, 1845).

38. *REED, Cambridge*, pp. 269–72, 291–3, 395–7, 570–2.

39. J. H. Marsden, *College Life in the Time of James the First As Illustrated by an Unpublished Diary of Sir Symonds D'Ewes* (1851), pp. 109–10.

40. *Robert Dover and the Cotswold Games*, pp. 105–6. 'Whirlings' refers to the custom of distributing 'whirlin-cakes' on the fifth Sunday in Lent.

41. *Robert Dover and the Cotswold Games*, p. 134.

42. *Pasquils Palinodia, and his progresse to the taverne* (1619), Sig. B3.

43. This paragraph is based on first-hand observation at Bolsover. But see Timothy Mowl, *Elizabethan-Jacobean Style* (1993), pp. 117–23. There are clear references to the decorative scheme of the castle, including the mechanical music of 'Heaven', in *Loves Wel-Come*, Ben Jonson's masque performed before the king and queen at Bolsover in 1634. See also Patricia Fumerton, 'Consuming the Void: Jacobean Banquets and Masques', in her *Cultural Aesthetics: Renaissance Literature and the Practice of Social Ornament* (Chicago and London, 1991). I owe these latter references to Jeremy Maule.

44. Collinson, *Birthpangs of Protestant England*, especially chs 2 and 4, 'The Protestant Town' and 'Protestant Culture and the Cultural Revolution'.

45. For some late references to the Kendal play, one of the last survivors, see *REED, Cumberland, Westmorland, Gloucestershire*, pp. 171–213, 218–19.

46. *REED, Devon*, pp. 51–2, 265.

47. *REED, Chester*, p. 184.

48. *REED, Norwich 1540–1642*, pp. 198–9.

49. Collinson, *Birthpangs of Protestant England*, p. 137.

50. Edgar I. Fripp, *Shakespeare, Man and Artist* (Oxford, 1938), II, 838–45. For the widespread use of libellous ballads in the political culture of the early-modern town, see C. J. Sisson, *Lost Plays of Shakespeare's Age* (1936), and Adam Fox, 'Aspects of Oral Culture and its Development in Early Modern England', unpublished Cambridge PhD thesis, 1993.

51. Byford, 'The Price of Protestantism', especially ch. 5, 'Windows Into Men's Souls: Popular Culture, Protestant Piety, and the Punishment of Sin in Colchester 1569–94'. The best accounts of the English skimmington and related cultural forms are Martin Ingram's two essays, 'Ridings, Rough Music and the "Reform of Popular Culture" in Early Modern England', *Past and Present*, 105 (1984), 79–113, 'Ridings, Rough Music and Mocking Rhymes in Early Modern England', in *Popular Culture in Seventeenth-Century England*, ed. Barry Reay (1985), pp. 166–97.

52. The fullest account of this 'symbiosis' will be found in Alexandra Walsham's forthcoming Cambridge doctoral thesis on aspects of

'providentialism' in late sixteenth-and early seventeenth-century England. See also Peter Lake, 'Deeds Against Nature: Cheap Print, Protestantism and Murder in Early Seventeenth-Century England', in *Culture and Politics in Early Stuart England*, ed. Kevin Sharpe and Peter Lake (1994), pp. 257–83; and Tessa Watt, *Cheap Print and Popular Piety, 1550–1640* (Cambridge, 1991).

53. *REED, Norwich 1540–1642*, pp. 15, 47. The best and most tangible evidence of the afterlife of 'Old Snap' will be found in the Castle Museum, Norwich.

54. *REED, Newcastle Upon Tyne*, p. xv. At Plymouth, 'Gogmagog' was cut out on the turf of the Hoe (*REED, Devon*, pp. 221–2).

55. *REED, Chester*, pp. 198, 234–6, 251–3, 354, 434–5, 526.

56. *REED, Cumberland, Westmorland, Gloucestershire*, pp. 91–2, 112, 115, 158.

57. *REED, Devon*, pp. 245, 261, 262, 264, 268, 451.

58. *REED, Coventry*, pp. 364–5.

59. Underdown, *Revel, Riot, and Rebellion*, p. 51.

60. *REED, York*, pp. 407, 434–5, 441, 445, 452–3, 458–9, 468–9.

61. Collinson, '*Bartholomew Fair*: Theatre Invents Puritans'.

62. David Cressy, *Bonfires and Bells: National Memory and the Protestant Calendar in Elizabethan and Stuart England* (Berkeley and Los Angeles, 1989), pp. xi–xii.

63. Cressy, *Bonfires and Bells*, passim; Thomas Cogswell, *The Blessed Revolution: English Politics and the Coming of War, 1621–1624* (Cambridge, 1989); Thomas Cogswell, 'England and the Spanish Match', in *Conflict in Early Stuart England*, ed. Richard Cust and Ann Hughes (1989), pp. 107–33; Alexandra Walsham, ' "The Fatall Vesper": Providentialism and Anti-Popery in Late Jacobean London', *Past and Present*, 144 (1994).

64. Cressy, *Bonfires and Bells*, p. 97.

65. Ibid., p. xiii.

66. Christopher Haigh, *English Reformations: Religion, Politics and Society Under the Tudors* (Oxford, 1993), pp. 279–81.

67. A good example is the sermons preached at the Kettering combination lecture by Robert Bolton, conventionally regarded as a Puritan, but, within the locality of the Mountagus' Northamptonshire, an establishment figure. See his *Workes* (1641), and especially *Some generall directions for a comfortable walking with God* (1624) and *Mr Boltons last and learned worke of the foure last things* (1632). See Patrick Collinson, 'The Cohabitation of the Faithful with the Unfaithful', in *From Persecution to Toleration: the Glorious Revolution and Religion in England*, ed. O. P. Grell, J. I. Israel and N. Tyacke (Oxford, 1991), pp. 66–7.

68. Collinson, *Birthpangs of Protestant England*, especially chs 1 and 5, 'The Protestant Nation' and 'Wars of Religion'; Patrick Collinson, 'Biblical Rhetoric: the English Nation in the Prophetic Mode', in *Books in Chains, Bodies in Flames: Religion and Culture in the English Renaissance*, ed. Debora Shuger and Claire McEachern (forthcoming).

69. Rich was the father of Nathaniel Rich, a leading figure in the Virginia Company and the Providence Island Company, and himself (in all probability) a member of the Virginia voyage of 1609, one of the victims of

the famous shipwreck in the Bermudas (without which there would have been no *Tempest*), and the very same Richard Rich who wrote *Newes from Virginia, the lost flock triumphant* (1610).

70. Cambridgeshire Record Office, MS M32/8/13/15.

71. I refer, by implication, to the forthcoming Cambridge doctoral thesis of Arnold Hunt, which will address these issues.

72. Christopher Haigh, 'Puritan Evangelism in the Reign of Elizabeth I', *English Historical Review*, XCII (1977), 30–58; Christopher Haigh, 'The Church of England, the Catholics and the People', in *The Reign of Elizabeth I*, ed. C. Haigh (1984), pp. 195–219. In 'Evangelists in Action', ch. 16 of *English Reformations*, Haigh is more willing to concede that Protestant reformers had their successes, while still insisting (p. 282) that they set 'awesome, and perhaps unachievable standards'.

73. Collinson, *Religion of Protestants*, pp. 243–5.

74. Here, again, I refer to the forthcoming work of Arnold Hunt.

75. Quoted in Jeffrey Knapp, 'Preachers and Players in Shakespeare's England', *Representations*, 44 (1993), 31.

76. Ibid., 29–59.

77. *REED, Cumberland, Westmorland, Gloucestershire*, pp. 415–16.

78. Ibid., p. 365.

79. Collinson, *Religion of Protestants*, pp. 201–2.

80. See, for example, the case of the three sermon-goers of Canterbury who (in the 1560s) dropped into the pub for a pot of beer, only to be asked by the company: 'Where have you been you three good husbands, not at the sermon I trust?' (Collinson, *Birthpangs of Protestant England*, p. 38). The Suffolk preacher Bartimaeus Andrewes admitted that the godly man who courteously invited his neighbours to accompany him to the sermon risked 'intolerable contempt'. 'Oh say the scorning railers, now this holy man will go to heaven in a hay barn, now these *Puritans* flocke together . . .' (Collinson, *Religion of Protestants*, p. 242).

81. Byford, 'The Price of Protestantism', p. 413.

82. Mrs Whetcombe and Mrs Grace Brewer of Sherborne are coming away from a sermon in the Dorset parish of Lillingstone in about 1593. Mrs Brewer says 'that they were happy that they had so good a minister'. When a drunken serving man who had attached himself to their company suggests that the preacher might have made his sermon shorter, Mrs Whetcombe replies: 'If you love to hear the word of God you cannot be weary hearing it' (BL, MS Harl. 6849, fol. 189ᵛ).

83. Patrick Collinson, 'The English Conventicle', in *Voluntary Religion, Studies in Church History*, vol. 23, ed. W. J. Sheils and Diana Wood (Oxford, 1986), 223–59.

84. Patrick Collinson, 'Towards a Broader Understanding of the Early Dissenting Tradition', in Patrick Collinson, *Godly People: Essays on English Protestantism and Puritanism* (1983), pp. 547–8.

85. Ibid.

86. Ibid., p. 521 n. 98; Collinson, 'The English Conventicle', 234–5.

87. *The Rev. Oliver Heywood, B. A. 1630–1702: His Autobiography Diaries, Anecdotes and Event-Books*, ed. J. Horsfall Turner, 4 vols (Brighouse, 1881–5);

W. J. Sheils, 'Oliver Heywood and his Congregation', in *Voluntary Religion*, 261–77.

88. John Earle, *The Autograph Manuscript of the Microcosmographie* (Leeds, 1966), pp. 115–21. The character identified in Earle's MS as the 'She-Puritan' is renamed 'A She-precise Hypocrite' in the published *Microcosmographie* (1628).

89. Cressy, *Bonfires and Bells*, p. 22. But see Underdown, *Revel, Riot, and Rebellion*, ch. 4, 'Regional Cultures' and the somewhat less broad brush of D. P. Dymond in 'Place-Names as Evidence for Recreation', *The English Place-Name Society Journal* 25 (1992–3), 12–18, and 'A Lost Social Institution: the Camping Close', *Rural History*, 1 (1990), 165–92.

90. John Fielding, 'Conformists, Puritans and the Church Courts: the Diocese of Peterborough, 1603–1642', unpublished Birmingham PhD thesis (1989), Map 2 (between pp. 147 and 148). The seven combination lectures were held at Brackley, Daventry, Kettering, Northampton, Oakham, Peterborough and Wellingborough, adding two (Northampton and Peterborough) to my 'Gazetteer of Combination Lectures', Collinson, *Godly People*, p. 563. I am grateful to John Fielding for the loan of his dissertation.

91. The interlocutor Atheos in George Gifford's Essex dialogue *The Countrie Divinitie* (1581) complained: 'I could like the better if the preaching might be only upon the Sabbath day, but now they run in the week days and leave their business and beggar themselves. They go to other towns also, which is a pity that it is suffered; it is a great disorder.' In the same county, a group of sermon gadders was told by the archdeacon's official: 'If you can trot to sermons, we will make you trot to the courts' (Patrick Collinson, *The Elizabethan Puritan Movement* (1967), p. 373).

92. 'Necessary causes of humiliation at this present' (1587/88?), BL, MS Add. 38492 (papers of Edward Lewkenor, JP, MP, of Denham, Suffolk), no. 55, fol. 98.

93. *The Holy Exercise of a True Fast* (1580), ascribed to Thomas Cartwright, and included in *Cartwrightiana*, ed. Albert Peel and Leland H. Carlson, Elizabethan Nonconformist Texts, I (1951), 127–42.

94. A full account of the Stamford fast will be found in my unpublished London PhD thesis (1957), 'The Puritan Classical Movement in the Reign of Elizabeth I', pp. 330–7; and a shorter account in my *Elizabethan Puritan Movement*, pp. 216–17.

95. Norfolk and Norwich Record Office, Norfolk and Norwich Archaeological Society, MS Frere, Box K.12a.

96. At a fast held at Erwarton in Suffolk in 1589, 20s was collected for the French Church (in France, or the French congregation in London?) (*The Presbyterian Movement in the Reign of Queen Elizabeth, as Illustrated by the Minute Book of the Dedham Classis, 1582–1589*, ed. R. G. Usher, Camden 3rd ser. VIII (1905), 59). The future Archbishop Bancroft reported that collections were made at puritan fasts 'for their brethren that travel for them beyond the seas', the proceeds being sent to the preacher John Field in London (*Tracts Ascribed to Richard Bancroft*, ed. Albert Peel (Cambridge, 1953), p. xxix).

97. BL, MS Lansdowne 83, no. 34, fol. 98.

98. Archbishop Edwain Sandys to Bishop William Chaderton of Chester, 2 May 1581; Francis Peck, *Desiderata Curiosa* (1732), I, Book III, 29.

99. *The State of the Church in the Reigns of Elizabeth and James I as Illustrated by Documents Relating to the Diocese of Lincoln*, I, ed. C. W. Foster, Lincoln Record Society, XXIII (Horncastle, 1926), cxvi.

100. Hertfordshire Record Office, ASA 5/5/291.

101. Keith Thomas, *Religion and the Decline of Magic* (1971), pp. 483–6; Collinson, *Elizabethan Puritan Movement*, pp. 437–8.

102. *Witchcraft and Hysteria in Elizabethan London: Edward Jorden and the Mary Glover Case*, ed. Michael MacDonald (1990).

103. Canon 72, with its particular and somewhat bizarre reference to exorcism, was regularly made the basis of an article of enquiry in the early-Stuart church (Fincham, *Visitation Articles and Injunctions*).

104. Collinson, *Elizabethan Puritan Movement*, pp. 373–4.

105. Robert Whiting, *The Blind Devotion of the People: Popular Religion and the English Reformation* (Cambridge, 1989), pp. 54, 66.

106. George M. Doe, 'North Devon in Elizabethan Times', *Transactions of the Devonshire Association*, LVIII (Plymouth, 1927), 241. This account of the Pilton fast is not without its problems. 'They called it an exercise or holy fast' has a puritan ring to it. But 'to the admiration [scil., 'surprise'] of all Protestants' may seem to imply that the participants were Catholics, which is David Cressy's impression (*Bonfires and Bells*, p. 9). 'Trental' is a Catholic term, but the Barnstaple town clerk may have used it parodically.

107. Leigh Eric Schmidt, *Holy Fairs: Scottish Communions and American Revivals in the Early Modern Period* (Princeton, NJ, 1989).

108. The correspondence of Anthony Gilby, preacher of Ashby-de-la-Zouch; Cambridge University Library, MS Mm.1.43, pp. 436–7.

109. *Acts of the Privy Council*, ed. J. R. Dasent, XI, 74, 77, 132.

110. *The Life of William Weston, S. J.*, in *The Troubles of Our Catholic Forefathers Related by Themselves*, ed. John Morris, SJ (2nd ser. 1875), I, 240–1. Another translation will be found in *The Autobiography of an Elizabethan*, tr. Philip Caraman (1955), pp. 164–5. There were 'walking communions' at Northampton in the early 1570s, part of the regime of the radical preacher Percival Wiburn, a protégé of Carleton (Collinson, *Elizabethan Puritan Movement*, p. 369). In support of Weston's allegations about 'discussions', 'quarrels' and 'fights', see the remarks of the anti-puritan Suffolk preacher Thomas Rogers about the reception of a sermon he had preached at Bury St Edmunds: 'Are all the people of one mind? And are the people, think we, so ignorant that they perceive not unto what side the discreetest among you do incline? Do all the people favour that part? Assure your selves so many of their auditors as in the matter of discipline dissented from them were their adversaries, and moved questions about discipline . . .' (Chicago University Library, MS Codex 109, fol. 266ᵛ. I owe this reference to the kindness of Dr John Craig).

111. Schmidt, *Holy Fairs*, p. 218.

112. *The Diary of Roger Lowe of Ashton-in-Makerfield, Lancashire 1603–1674*, ed. William L. Sachse (1938), pp. 1, 16, 26, 52.

113. Schmidt, *Holy Fairs*, p. 3.

114. David Hall, *Worlds of Wonder, Days of Judgment: Popular Religious Belief in Early New England* (Cambridge, Mass., 1990).

115. Schmidt, *Holy Fairs*, pp. 23, 28–9.

116. The reference is to a pejorative account of a sermon at Bury St Edmunds in 1636: 'The deep, passionate, trembling, quavering, singultive twang, which crept into the breasts of the thirsty auditory and was received *bibulis auribus*; the womens sighs and the mens hawkings showed it' (quoted, Collinson, *Godly People*, p. 493).

117. *Oliver Heywood's Life of John Angier of Denton*, ed. Ernest Axon, Chetham Society n.s. XCVII (1937), 50–1.

118. Schmidt, *Holy Fairs*, p. 97.

119. *State of the Church*, p. cxvi. Richard Rich, the second Lord Rich's bastard brother, was accused in 1582 of having organised unauthorised fasts in Essex which included 'at these feasts' the singing of psalms, 'not set out as allowed by the said book of common prayer'; and with having insisted that psalms must be sung, not read antiphonally by minister and people, which may have been common practice in parish churches which had no choir and where there was no puritanical, congregational spirit present to express itself in metrical psalm singing.

120. Levin L. Schücking, *The Puritan Family: A Social Study from the Literary Sources*, tr. B. Battershaw (1969). *Die Puritanische Familie* was published in Leipzig in 1929.

2. PURITANS AND THE CHURCH COURTS, 1560–1640
Martin Ingram

1. W. H. Frere and C. E. Douglas (eds), *Puritan Manifestoes: A Study of the Origin of the Puritan Revolt* (1954), pp. 32–4; on the language of John Field's share of the *Admonition*, see Patrick Collinson, *The Elizabethan Puritan Movement* (1967), p. 120.

2. E.g. F. D. Price, 'The Abuses of Excommunication and the Decline of Ecclesiastical Discipline under Queen Elizabeth', *English Historical Review*, LVII (1942), 106–15; Collinson, *Elizabethan Puritan Movement*, pp. 38–41; Christopher Hill, *Society and Puritanism in Pre-Revolutionary England* (1964), chs 8–11.

3. For the major themes and variations, see Ronald Marchant, *The Puritans and the Church Courts in the Diocese of York, 1560–1642* (1960); Roger B. Manning, *Religion and Society in Elizabethan Sussex: a Study of the Enforcement of the Religious Settlement, 1558–1603* (Leicester, 1969); R. C. Richardson, *Puritanism in North-West England: a Regional Study of the Diocese of Chester to 1642* (Manchester, 1972); Richardson, 'Puritanism and the Ecclesiastical Authorities: the Case of the Diocese of Chester', in Brian Manning (ed.), *Politics, Religion and the English Civil War* (1973), pp. 3–33; W. J. Sheils (ed.), *The Puritans in the Diocese of Peterborough, 1558–1610*, Northamptonshire Record Society, XXX (Northampton, 1979); Sheils, 'Some Problems of Government in a New Diocese: the Bishop and the Puritans in the Diocese of Peterborough, 1560–1630', in Rosemary O'Day and Felicity Heal (eds), *Continuity*

and *Change: Personnel and Administration in the Church of England, 1500–1642* (Leicester, 1976), pp. 145–66; John Fielding, 'Arminianism in the Localities: Peterborough Diocese, 1603–1642', in Kenneth Fincham (ed.), *The Early Stuart Church* (1993), pp. 93–113, 262–4; and, more generally, Collinson, *Elizabethan Puritan Movement*. My conclusions are based also on my own researches in the archives of the dioceses of Oxford, Peterborough and Salisbury and of the archdeaconries of Buckingham and Leicester, respectively located at the Oxon, Northants, Wilts, Bucks and Leics R[ecord] O[ffices].

4. For the jurisdiction and relevant surviving records of the Dean of Salisbury, see Pamela Stewart, *Diocese of Salisbury, Guide to the Records of the Bishop, the Archdeacons of Salisbury and Wiltshire, and Other Archidiaconal and Peculiar Jurisdictions* (Wiltshire County Council, Guide to the Record Offices, Part IV, n.p., 1973), pp. 71, 75–83, 88–90, 137–40. The returns of 1603 are in Wilts RO, D5/28/3. For the deans of Salisbury, see William Henry Jones, *Fasti Ecclesiae Sarisberiensis, or a Calendar of the Bishops, Deans, Archdeacons, and Members of the Cathedral Body at Salisbury*, 2 parts in 1 vol. (London and Salisbury, 1879–81), pp. 321–2, and (for Bridges, Gordon, Williams and Bowle) *Dictionary of National Biography*, s.n. The following Wiltshire places mentioned in the text were *not* within the jurisdiction of the dean of Salisbury: Aldbourne, Box, Marlborough, Melksham, Salisbury, Slaughterford, Stockton, Upton Scudamore, Wylye.

5. The best guides to the post-Reformation church courts in England are Ronald A. Marchant, *The Church under the Law: Justice, Administration and Discipline in the Diocese of York, 1560–1640* (Cambridge, 1969); Ralph Houlbrooke, *Church Courts and the People during the English Reformation, 1520–1570* (Oxford, 1979); and Martin Ingram, *Church Courts, Sex and Marriage in England, 1570–1640* (Cambridge, 1987).

6. R. H. Helmholz, *Roman Canon Law in Reformation England* (Cambridge, 1990).

7. Helmholz, *Roman Canon Law*, pp. 156–7; Marchant, *Church under the Law*, pp. 4–9; cf. Mary H. Maguire, 'Attack of the Common Lawyers on the Oath *Ex Officio* as Administered in the Ecclesiastical Courts in England', in *Essays in History and Political Theory in Honour of Charles Howard McIlwain* (Cambridge, MA, 1936), pp. 199–229.

8. J. P. Kenyon (ed.), *The Stuart Constitution, 1603–1688*, 2nd edn (Cambridge, 1986), pp. 118–19; Ingram, *Church Courts, Sex and Marriage*, pp. 49–50 and the references there cited.

9. Houlbrooke, *Church Courts and the People*, pp. 50–3, 271; Ingram, *Church Courts, Sex and Marriage*, pp. 9–10, 65–6, 212. On Gloucester diocese, see F. D. Price, 'An Elizabethan Church Official – Thomas Powell, Chancellor of Gloucester Diocese', *Church Quarterly Review*, CXXVII (1939), 94–112; Price, 'Abuses of Excommunication'; Price, 'Elizabethan Apparitors in the Diocese of Gloucester', *Church Quarterly Review*, CXXXIV (1942), 37–55; Price, 'Bishop Bullingham and Chancellor Blackleech: a Diocese Divided', *Transactions of the Bristol and Gloucestershire Archaeological Society*, XCI (1972), 175–98.

10. Marchant, *Church under the Law*, pp. 19, 141–6, 243–4; Ingram, *Church Courts, Sex and Marriage*, pp. 55–8.

11. Frere and Douglas (eds), *Puritan Manifestoes*, pp. 20, 34; Ingram, *Church Courts, Sex and Marriage*, pp. 58–67; Marchant, *Church under the Law*, p. 31 and passim; J. A. Fisher (ed.), 'The State of England Anno Dom. 1600 by Thomas Wilson', in *Camden Miscellany*, vol. XVI, Camden Society, 3rd ser., LII (1936), p. 25.

12. Frere and Douglas (eds), *Puritan Manifestoes*, pp. 16, 118–23; cf. Albert Peel (ed.), *The Seconde Part of a Register*, 2 vols (Cambridge, 1915), vol. I, 258, vol. II, 1–4, 42. For some less radical proposals for reform, see Collinson, *Elizabethan Puritan Movement*, pp. 180–3.

13. Frere and Douglas (eds), *Puritan Manifestoes*, p. 17; Price, 'Abuses of Excommunication', but cf. Ingram, *Church Courts, Sex and Marriage*, pp. 14, 52–3, 340–62.

14. For puritan criticisms of penance, see Frere and Douglas (eds), *Puritan Manifestoes*, pp. 17–18; Frederick J. Furnivall (ed.), *Phillip Stubbes's Anatomy of the Abuses in England in Shakspere's Youth, A. D. 1583*, 2 parts in 3, New Shakspere Society, series VI, nos. 4, 6, 12 (1877–82), part I, pp. 98–9; Sir Keith Thomas, 'The Puritans and Adultery: the Act of 1650 Reconsidered', in Donald Pennington and Keith Thomas (eds), *Puritans and Revolutionaries: Essays in Seventeenth-Century History Presented to Christopher Hill* (Oxford, 1978), pp. 263–4, 269–71. On the practice of penance, see Ingram, *Church Courts, Sex and Marriage*, pp. 53–4, 334–8.

15. Edward Cardwell (ed.), *The Reformation of the Ecclesiastical Laws* (Oxford, 1850), and for the background see Houlbrooke, *Church Courts and the People*, pp. 17–18; Edward Cardwell (ed.), *Synodalia: a Collection of Articles of Religion. Canons and Proceedings of Convocations in the Province of Canterbury, from the Year 1547 to the Year 1717*, 2 vols, consecutively paginated (Oxford, 1842), vol. II, pp. 513–14; cf. John Ayre (ed.), *The Sermons of Edwin Sandys* (Parker Society, Cambridge, 1841), pp. 40–54; Thomas, 'Puritans and Adultery', p. 264.

16. Peel, (ed.), *Seconde Part of a Register*, vol. I, p. 258, cf. vol. II, pp. 1–4.

17. Ingram, *Church Courts, Sex and Marriage*, pp. 31, 125, 199, 262–3; Laura Gowing, 'Language, Power and the Law: Women's Slander Litigation in Early Modern London', in Jenny Kermode and Garthine Walker (eds), *Women, Crime and the Courts in Early Modern England* (1994), pp. 30–3; for the Highworth case, see Wilts RO, D5/28/7, no. 56.

18. Wilts RO, D5/28/6, no. 21 (the minister and the parish are unnamed, but it is clear from internal evidence and from comparison with no. 80 that it was Francis Scarlett of Sherborne).

19. Examples are discussed in Patrick Collinson, *De Republica Anglorum: or, History with the Politics Put Back, Inaugural Lecture Delivered 9 November 1989* (Cambridge, 1990), pp. 30–2; Richardson, *Puritanism in North-West England*, pp. 15–17.

20. Thomas, 'Puritans and Adultery', pp. 266–7; Martin Ingram, 'Reformation of Manners in Early Modern England', in Adam Fox, Paul Griffiths and Steven Hindle (eds), *The Experience of Authority in Early Modern England* (in press).

21. W. J. Sheils, 'Erecting the Discipline in Provincial England: the Order of Northampton, 1571', in James Kirk (ed.), *Humanism and Reform: the Church*

in Europe, England, and Scotland, 1400–1643. Essays in Honour of James B. Cameron, Studies in Church History, Subsidia, vol. 8 (Oxford, 1991), pp. 331–45; Elliot Rose, *Cases of Conscience: Alternatives Open to Recusants and Puritans under Elizabeth I and James I* (Cambridge, 1975), pp. 158–68; Patrick Collinson, *The Religion of Protestants: the Church in English Society, 1559–1625* (Oxford, 1982), pp. 158–61.

22. Cardwell (ed.), *Synodalia*, vol. I, pp. 117–19, 130–1, 137–8, 142–6, 152–63, 216–43, 298–327. See also Ingram, *Church Courts, Sex and Marriage*, ch. 1 passim; Kenneth Fincham, 'Ramifications of the Hampton Court Conference in the Dioceses, 1603–1609', *Journal of Ecclesiastical History*, XXXVI (1985), 208–27.

23. Kenneth Fincham, *Prelate as Pastor: the Episcopate of James I* (Oxford, 1990), esp. chs 4–6; Ingram, *Church Courts, Sex and Marriage*, ch. 3 and passim. On the crucial role of deputies in forwarding or frustrating episcopal policy, see Kenneth L. Parker, *The English Sabbath: a Study of Doctrine and Discipline from the Reformation to the Civil War* (Cambridge, 1988), pp. 64–7.

24. Rosemary O'Day, *The English Clergy: the Emergence and Consolidation of a Profession, 1558–1642* (Leicester, 1979), chs 2, 10; Collinson, *Religion of Protestants*, ch. 3; Fincham, *Prelate as Pastor*, ch. 6; Ingram, *Church Courts, Sex and Marriage*, pp. 86–90.

25. These are contentious issues. For a variety of viewpoints on the state of popular religion and the relationship between Christian beliefs and magical practices, see Sir Keith Thomas, *Religion and the Decline of Magic: Studies in Popular Beliefs in Sixteenth and Sevententh Century England* (1971), esp. ch. 6; Imogen Luxton, 'The Reformation and Popular Culture', in Felicity Heal and Rosemary O'Day, *Church and Society in England: Henry VIII to James I* (1977), pp. 57–77; Christopher Haigh, *English Reformations: Religion, Politics and Society under the Tudors* (Oxford, 1993), pp. 288–91 and chs 14–16. For the term 'post-Reformation' and its utility, see Tessa Watt, *Cheap Print and Popular Piety, 1550–1640* (Cambridge, 1991), p. 327 and passim.

26. Penry Williams, *The Tudor Regime* (Oxford, 1979), pp. 269–72; Ingram, *Church Courts, Sex and Marriage*, pp. 85–6. For a less positive view, see Christopher Haigh, 'The Church of England, the Catholics and the People', in Haigh (ed.), *The Reign of Elizabeth I* (1984), pp. 195–219; Haigh, *English Reformations*, chs 14–15.

27. Ingram, *Church Courts, Sex and Marriage*, ch. 3 passim; Jeremy Boulton, 'The Limits of Formal Religion: the Administration of Holy Communion in Late Elizabethan and Early Stuart London', *London Journal*, X (1984), 135–54, but cf. Ian Archer, *The Pursuit of Stability: Social Relations in Elizabethan London* (Cambridge, 1991), pp. 90–1; Nick Aldridge, 'Loyalty and Identity in Chester Parishes, 1540–1640', in S.J. Wright (ed.), *Parish, Church and People: Local Studies in Lay Religion, 1350–1750* (1988), pp. 97–9; Parker, *English Sabbath*, passim.

28. Ingram, *Church Courts, Sex and Marriage*, passim; Ingram, 'Spousals Litigation in the English Ecclesiastical Courts, c.1350–c.1640', in R. B. Outhwaite (ed.), *Marriage and Society: Studies in the Social History of Marriage* (1981), pp. 35–57; Ingram, 'The Reform of Popular Culture? Sex and Marriage in Early Modern England', in Barry Reay (ed.), *Popular Culture in*

Seventeenth-Century England (1985), pp. 129–65; Keith Wrightson and David Levine, *Poverty and Piety in an English Village: Terling, 1525–1700* (New York, San Francisco and London, 1979), ch. 5; for the demographic perspective, see Peter Laslett, Karla Oosterveen and Richard M. Smith (eds), *Bastardy and Its Comparative History* (1980), pt 1, passim; and for a rather different view from that presented in the text, see John R. Gillis, *For Better, For Worse: British Marriages, 1600 to the Present* (Oxford, 1985), pt 1.

29. Houlbrooke, *Church Courts and the People*, pp. 43–4, 46, 271; Ingram, *Church Courts, Sex and Marriage*, pp. 50, 317–18; Richard M. Wunderli, *London Church Courts and Society on the Eve of the Reformation*, Medieval Academy of America, Speculum Anniversary Monographs, no. 7 (Cambridge, MA, 1981), pp. 55–60.

30. *The Works of George Herbert*, ed. F. E. Hutchinson (Oxford, 1941), pp. 236, 259–60; Ingram, *Church Courts, Sex and Marriage*, pp. 110–11, 294; 5 Edw. VI c. 4. More generally see Ian Green, ' "Reformed Pastors" and *Bons Curés*: the Changing Role of the Parish Clergy in Early Modern Europe', in W. J. Sheils and Diana Wood (eds), *The Ministry: Clerical and Lay, Studies in Church History*, vol. 26 (Oxford, 1989), p. 274 and passim, and John Bossy, *Christianity in the West, 1400–1700* (Oxford, 1985), ch. 4.

31. Paul L. Hughes and James F. Larkin (eds), *Tudor Royal Proclamations*, 3 vols (New Haven, CT, and London, 1964–9), vol. I, pp. 432–3, vol. II, pp. 122–3, 128.

32. Peel (ed.), *Seconde Parte of a Register*, vol. I, pp. 230–1, 238–41, 292, 297, vol. II, pp. 30, 32.

33. E.g. Sheils, *Puritans in the Diocese of Peterborough*, pp. 29, 32, 74n; Peel (ed.), *Seconde Parte of a Register*, vol. I, pp. 291–6; Ian W. Gowers, 'Puritanism in the County of Devon between 1570 and 1641', University of Exeter MA thesis (1970), pp. 26–31; Wilts RO, D1/43/6, fol. 15v; see also Anne Whiteman, 'The Church of England, 1542–1837', in *The Victoria History of the Counties of England: Wiltshire*, 14 vols, in progress (London and Oxford, 1953–), vol. III, pp. 34–5.

34. Wilts RO, D5/28/5, no. 95; D5/28/6, no. 62, cf. nos. 5, 163; D5/28/7, nos. 2, 25–6, 28–9, 100; D5/28/10, no. 100, fol. 2.

35. Christopher Haigh, *Reformation and Resistance in Tudor Lancashire* (Cambridge, 1975), pp. 306–7; Haigh, 'The Church of England, the Catholics and the People', pp. 217–18; Haigh, *English Reformations*, pp. 289–90; Judith Maltby, ' "By this Book": Parishioners, the Prayer Book and the Established Church', in Fincham (ed.), *Early Stuart Church*, pp. 118–28; cf. for a later period, John Morrill, 'The Church in England, 1642–9', in Morrill (ed.), *Reactions to the English Civil War* (1982), pp. 103–14.

36. Wilts RO, D5/28/7, no. 2; D5/28/6, no. 21 (the minister and the parish are unnamed but it is clear from internal evidence and from comparison with no. 80 that Francis Scarlett of Sherborne is meant); D1/39/1/26, fol. 226v–7.

37. Wilts RO, D5/28/7, nos 2, 28–9; cf. Northants RO, Peterborough Diocesan Records, X608/15, fol. 124v, cf. fol. 125v; Gowers, 'Puritanism in the County of Devon', pp. 279–80.

38. Collinson, *Elizabethan Puritan Movement*, pp. 68–9; William Pierce (ed.), *The Marprelate Tracts, 1588, 1589* (1911); cf. John Bale, *Yet a Course at the Romyshe Foxe* ([Zurich, 1543]) and Bale, *The Actes of Englysh Votaries* ([Wesel, 1546]) (I am grateful to Helen Parish for drawing these works to my attention).

39. Wilts RO, D1/39/1/26, fol. 227; D5/28/7, no. 29; D5/28/10, no. 30, cf. no. 62. Cf. Richard. Bauman, *Let Your Words Be Few: Symbolism of Speaking and Silence among Seventeenth-Century Quakers* (Cambridge, 1983), chs 5–6.

40. Wilts RO, D5/28/5, no. 95; D1/43/6, fol. 15; D5/28/7, no. 2.

41. Wilts RO, D5/28/7, no. 28; D5/19/11, fols 93–4v, 99; for deprivations in other dioceses, see Collinson, *Elizabethan Puritan Movement*, pp. 243–72; Fincham, *Prelate as Pastor*, pp. 212–31.

42. Wilts RO, D5/19/11, fols 93v–4; D5/19/8, fols 31, 109v; D5/19/15, fols 21, 26, 81, 102v; cf. D1/39/2/1, fol. 8v; D1/42/9, fols 85–6.

43. Wilts RO, D5/28/15, no. 31, cf. D5/28/10, no. 98; D5/28/22, no. 32; G. D. Squibb, *Dorset Incumbents, 1542–1731* (n.p., n.d.), p. 61; more generally see Fincham, *Prelate as Pastor*, ch. 7, but cf. Fielding, 'Arminianism in the Localities', pp. 98–103.

44. Keith Wrightson and David Levine, *Poverty and Piety in an English Village: Terling, 1525–1700*, esp. chs 5–6; but cf. Keith Wrightson, *English Society, 1580–1680* (1982), pp. 206–14; Martin Ingram, 'Religion, Communities and Moral Discipline in Late Sixteenth- and Early Seventeenth-Century England: Case Studies', in Kaspar von Greyerz (ed.), *Religion and Society in Early Modern Europe, 1500–1800* (1984), pp. 177–93; Margaret Spufford, 'Puritanism and Social Control?', in Anthony Fletcher and John Stevenson (eds), *Order and Disorder in Early Modern England* (Cambridge, 1985), pp. 41–57; David Underdown, *Revel, Riot and Rebellion: Popular Politics and Culture in England, 1603–1660* (Oxford, 1985), chs 1–5 passim.

45. Wilts RO, D5/28/11, no. 24; D5/28/17, no. 96; D5/28/25, no. 72; D5/28/26, no. 38; D5/28/28, no. 81; D5/28/30, no. 17; D5/28/31, no. 83; D5/28/35, no. 73; D5/28/38, no. 2; Underdown, *Revel, Riot and Rebellion*, pp. 57–8.

46. Wilts RO, D1/39/2/11, fol. 42; cf. Bucks RO, MS Oxford Archdeaconry Papers, *Bucks*, c. 290, fol. 86. For cases of feuding, see Ingram, *Church Courts, Sex and Marriage*, pp. 112–23.

47. E.g. Wilts RO, D5/28/30, no. 17; D5/28/35, no. 51; D5/28/38, no. 18. (Note, however, that these complaints arose partly from problems with small prebendal jurisdictions, over which the dean of Salisbury and his officers had only partial control.)

48. Wilts RO, D5/28/10, nos 40–1, 44; D5/28/28, nos 66–7; and for other cases of ceremonial and liturgical nonconformity see D5/28/17, nos 32, 88, 94. For a different situation in Peterborough diocese, see Fielding, 'Arminianism in the Localities', p. 99.

49. Collinson, *Elizabethan Puritan Movement*, ch. 4.

50. Wilts RO, A1/110/1604E, no. 148; for further information on the background, see Ingram, *Church Courts, Sex and Mariage*, p. 91 and the references there cited.

51. Wilts RO, D5/28/17, no. 46; D4/10/1, nos. 48, 81, 83, 91, 93 and passim; D2/4/1/13, fols 143, 144, 151v–2v.

52. Wilts RO, A1/110/1603E, no. 121; the document has been abstracted in *HMC, Report on Manuscripts in Various Collections*, 8 vols (1901–14), vol. I, pp. 71–2. For further information on the background, see Ingram, *Church Courts, Sex and Marriage*, pp. 110–11. On the Millenary Petition, see Patrick Collinson, 'The Jacobean Religious Settlement: the Hampton Court Conference', in Howard Tomlinson (ed.), *Before the English Civil War: Essays on Early Stuart Politics and Government* (1983), pp. 30–2.

53. Wilts RO, D5/19/15, fols 170, 174; for another striking case, see H. C. Johnson (ed.), *Wiltshire County Records: Minutes of Proceedings in Sessions, 1563 and 1574 to 1592*, Wiltshire Archaeological and Natural History Society: Records Branch, 4 (Devizes, 1949), p. 123.

54. Wilts RO, D5/28/8, no. 151; D5/28/17, no. 16; D5/28/25, no. 93; D5/19/28, fols 164–5; cf. Ingram, *Church Courts, Sex and Marriage*, p. 94. See also Patrick Collinson, *Godly People: Essays on English Protestantism and Puritanism* (1983), pp. 10–11, and on 'conventicles' more generally, Collinson, 'The English Conventicle', in W. J. Sheils and Diana Wood (eds), *Voluntary Religion, Studies in Church History*, vol. 23 (Oxford, 1986), pp. 223–59.

55. E.g. Johnson (ed.), *Minutes of Proceedings in Sessions*, p. 123; cf. Buckinghamshire RO, MS Oxford Archdeaconry Papers, *Bucks*. c. 290, fol. 37v; Oxfordshire RO, MS Oxford Archdeaconry Papers, *Oxon*. c. 13, fo. 159v. On churching more generally and the controversies surrounding it, see David Cressy, 'Purification, Thanksgiving and the Churching of Women in Post-Reformation England', *Past and Present*, 141 (Nov. 1993), pp. 106–46.

56. Wilts RO, D5/28/15, no. 43; D5/28/17, no. 35; D5/28/18, no. 15; D5/28/21, no. 26; D5/28/22, no. 51; cf. Collinson, *Elizabethan Puritan Movement*, pp. 367–9; Richardson, *Puritanism in North-West England*, pp. 76–9.

57. Wilts RO, D5/28/15, no. 46, cf. no. 47; Oxon RO, MS Oxford Archdeaconry Papers, *Oxon*, c. 12, fol. 81v.

58. E.g. Wilts RO, D5/28/8, no. 148; D5/28/17, nos 22, 74; D5/28/20, no. 58. See also Collinson, *Godly People*, pp. 7–10; Collinson, *Religion of Protestants*, pp. 249–50, 257–64.

59. Northants RO, X614/41, p. 412; Wilts RO, D1/39/2/8, fol. 121. The Northampton case has been several times quoted: see E. J. I. Allen, 'The State of the Church in the Diocese of Peterborough, 1601–1642', Oxford University B. Litt. thesis (1972), p. 121; Fielding, 'Arminianism in the Localities', p. 101 (quoting what the woman was *accused* of saying, not what she confessed).

60. Wilts RO, D5/28/34, no. 34; Oxon RO, MS Oxford Archdeaconry Papers *Oxon*. c. 12, fol. 279; for some other inflamatory cases, see John Bruce (ed.), *Calendar of State Papers, Domestic . . . 1633–1634* (London, 1863), p. 540.

61. Julian Davies, *The Caroline Captivity of the Church: Charles I and the Remoulding of Anglicanism, 1625–1641* (Oxford, 1992), ch. 5.

62. Wilts RO, D3/4/7, fols 57v, 64v; D5/28/34, nos 34–7, D5/28/35, no. 56. On prosecutions for Sunday and holy day work see Ingram, *Church Courts, Sex and Marriage*, pp. 371–2. For evidence on other areas and broader discussion of Laudian policies, see Anthony Fletcher, *A County Community in Peace and War: Sussex, 1600–1660* (London and New York, 1975), ch. 4; Davies, *Caroline Captivity of the Church*, passim; Kevin Sharpe, *The Personal Rule of Charles I* (New Haven CT, and London, 1992), ch. 6. Inter alia Davies and Sharpe debate the appropriateness or otherwise of terms such as 'Laudian' and 'Arminian', on which see also the contrasting views of Nicholas Tyacke, *Anti-Calvinists: the Rise of English Arminianism, c. 1590–1640* (Oxford, 1987), and Peter White, *Predestination, Policy and Polemic: Conflict and Consensus in the English Church from the Reformation to the Civil War* (Cambridge, 1992).

63. Wilts RO, D1/41/1/5, no. 9. On the increase in venality and slackness and the diminishing social role of the church courts in Salisbury diocese, see Ingram, *Church Courts, Sex and Marriage*, pp. 67, 69, 369–72.

64. Samuel Rawson Gardiner (ed.), *The Constitutional Documents of the Puritan Revolution, 1625–1660*, 3rd edn (Oxford, 1906), pp. 137–44. On the background to the fall of the ecclesiastical courts, see Anthony Fletcher, *The Outbreak of the English Civil War* (1981), esp. chs 3, 9.

3. PURITANS AND ICONOCLASM   *Margaret Aston*

1. Ben Jonson, *Bartholomew Fair*, III, vi; cf. V, v, for the 'good Banbury vapours' of Busy's outburst against stage-players; *Works of Ben Jonson*, ed. C. H. Herford, P. and E. Simpson, 11 vols (Oxford, 1925–52), VI, pp. 84–5, 133.

2. *Visitation Articles and Injunctions of the Period of the Reformation*, ed. W. H. Frere and W. M. Kennedy (Alcuin Club Collections, XIV–XVI, 1910), III, pp. 8, 16 (my italics); cf. II, p. 126; M. Aston, *England's Iconoclasts*, I (Oxford, 1988), pp. 298–300.

3. *The Political Works of James I*, ed. C. H. McIlwain (Cambridge, MA, and London, 1918), p. 125, from 'A Premonition to all Most Mightie Monarches, Kings, Free Princes, and States of Christendome'. James makes clear the important distinction between crucifix and plain cross, with not even 'resemblance or representation of eyes or ears'.

4. C. L. Kingsford, 'Essex House, formerly Leicester House and Exeter Inn', *Archaeologia*, LXXIII (1923), 46; *Statutes of the Realm*, IV, ii, p. 1082 (3 Jac. I, c. 5; xv); R. Parker, *A Scholasticall Discourse* (1607), pp. 7, 10, 11. On Parker and his ambiguous position between orthodoxy and dissent see the *Dictionary of National Biography* (*DNB*), and P. Collinson, *Godly People: Essays on English Protestantism and Puritanism* (1983), p. 531.

5. Exod. 33: 20; Deut. 4:12; J. Calvin, *Institutes of the Christian Religion*, ed. J. T. McNeill, trans. F. L. Battles, 2 vols (1961), I, p. 112, cf. pp. 99–103 (Bk I, ch. xi, 1–3 and 12); W. Perkins, *A Warning against the Idolatrie of the last times* (Cambridge, 1601), pp. 21–2, 24–5; *Political Works of James I*, p. 125.

6. *Certain Sermons or Homilies* (Oxford, 1844), pp. 196, 199, 239; Aston, *England's Iconoclasts*, pp. 322–3.

7. P. Collinson, *Archbishop Grindal 1519–1583: The Struggle for a Reformed Church* (1979), pp. 190, 198–9, 201, 203; *The Life of Adam Martindale, written by himself*, ed. R. Parkinson (Chetham Society, IV, 1845), pp. 156–8; R. C. Richardson, *Puritanism in North-West England: A Regional Study of the Diocese of Chester to 1642* (Manchester, 1972), p. 158; Jeremy Goring, *Godly Exercises or the Devil's Dance? Puritanism and Popular Culture in pre-Civil War England* (1983).

8. W. Harrison, *The Description of England*, ed. G. Edelen (Ithaca, NY, 1968), pp. 35–6.

9. [A. Gilby], *A Pleasaunt Dialogue* (Middelburg? 1581), sigs. D1^r, L7^r, M2^v–3^r; *The Seconde Parte of a Register*, ed. A. Peel, 2 vols (Cambridge, 1915), I, pp. 74–5; *The Reformation of Religion by Josiah* (1590?), sig B2^v. .

10. *Correspondence of Matthew Parker*, ed. J. Bruce (Parker Society, Cambridge, 1853), pp. 234, 236, 238; H. C. Porter, *Reformation and Reaction in Tudor Cambridge* (Cambridge, 1958), pp. 110, 114.

11. W. Hinde, *A Faithfull Remonstrance of . . . John Bruen* (1641), pp. 18, 28, 47, 128–9; G. Ormerod, *The History of the County Palatine and City of Chester*, 3 vols (1882), II, p. 314.

12. Hinde, *Remonstance*, p. 78–9. On William Hinde, *c.*1569–1629, see *DNB*. Bunbury, where he was perpetual curate from 1603 until his death, is only a few hours' ride from Tarvin and Bruen Stapleford, and Hinde was a personal friend of Bruen's and at his deathbed.

13. Hinde, *Remonstrance*, pp. 79–80.

14. BL Harl. MS 2151, ff. 37^r–38^r, at 37^v; Ormerod, *County Palatine*, II, pp. 306–14. What seems to have been a simple wall monument, with a 'table of arms', was erected for John Bruen (d. Jan. 1625) on the south side of Tarvin church.

15. BL Harl. MS 6607, 'A Godly Profitable Collection of Divers Sentences out of Holy Scripture', ff. 24^r, 25^v, 40^r.

16. John Jewel, *An Apology of the Church of England*, ed. J. E. Booty (Ithaca, NY, 1963), p. 115; M. Aston, *Faith and Fire* (1993), pp. 296–7 ('commandeth' a misprint for 'commendeth'); *Homilies*, p. 165 on Deut. 7:5.

17. Edward Peacock (ed.), *English Church Furniture, Ornaments and Decorations, at the Period of the Reformation* (1866), p. 142n; Richardson, *Puritanism*, pp. 122–3.

18. *Rites of Durham*, ed. J. T. Fowler (Surtees Society, CVII, 1903), p. 28; P. D. A. Harvey, 'Where was Banbury Cross?' *Oxoniensia*, XXXI (1966), 83–106, at 101–6.

19. H. Peacham, *The Art of Drawing* (1606), pp. 63–5; Peacham, *The Gentlemans Exercise* (1612), pp. 11–12.

20. W. Perkins, *A Reformed Catholike* (Cambridge, 1598), p. 172; Perkins, *Warning against Idolatrie*, pp. 106–7.

21. *Visitation Articles and Injunctions of the Early Stuart Church*, ed. Kenneth Fincham (Church of England Rec. Soc., Woodbridge, 1994), I, pp. 37, 39, 45, 48, 50, 105, 110, 114, 194; cf. 113, 161, and on Montagu, p. xviii; *Articles of Enquiry and Direction for the Diocese of Norwich* (Cambridge, 1638), Tit. 2.14.

22. BL Harl. MS 6607, f. 15ᵛ.

23. *Political Works of James I*, p. 124; BL Harl. MS 159, f. 136ʳ⁻ᵛ (my punctuation). On this source see Conrad Russell, *Parliaments and English Politics 1621–1629* (Oxford, 1982), p. xx; K. Fincham and P. Lake, 'The Ecclesiastical Policy of King James I', *Journal of British Studies*, 24 (1985), 170.

24. W. Prynne, *Histrio-Mastix. The Players Scourge* (1633), p. 865, marginal note.

25. G. I. Soden, *Godfrey Goodman, Bishop of Gloucester, 1583–1656* (1953), pp. 236–42 (cited at 239); *Calendar of State Papers Domestic*, 1650, p. 261 (31 July 1650, orders for demolition of royal statues at St Paul's and the Royal Exchange, London).

26. M. Archer, 'English Painted Glass in the Seventeenth Century: The early work of Abraham van Linge', *Apollo*, CI (Jan. 1975), 26–31; T. G. Jackson. *The Church of St. Mary the Virgin, Oxford* (Oxford, 1897), pp. 61, 63, 127–8.

27. Paul Slack, 'The Public Conscience of Henry Sherfield', in J. Morrill, P. Slack and D. Woolf (eds), *Public Duty and Private Conscience in Seventeenth-Century England* (Oxford, 1993), pp. 151–71; Paul Slack, 'Religious protest and urban authority: the case of Henry Sherfield, iconoclast, 1633', in *Studies in Church History*, vol. 9 (1972), 295–302; *Complete Collection of State Trials*, ed. W. Cobbett and T. B. Howell, 33 vols (London, 1809–26), III, cols 519, 521, 537, 543, 550, 554; *Churchwardens' Accounts of S. Edmund and S. Thomas, Sarum*, ed. H. J. F. Swayne (Salisbury, 1896), p. 294; *Rites of Durham*, pp. 76–7; *Visitation Articles*, ed. Frere and Kennedy, III, p. 323, cf. p. 104.

28. *State Trials*, III, col. 522; *Churchwardens' Accounts, Sarum*, p. 190.

29. *State Trials*, III, cols 525, 539, 543, 545, 546–7.

30. *State Trials*, III, cols 541, 547.

31. Jacqueline Eales, *Puritans and Roundheads: The Harleys of Brampton Bryan and the Outbreak of the English Civil War* (Cambridge, 1990), pp. 47, 54, 78.

32. BL MS Harl. 165, ff. 21ᵛ, 22ᵛ.

33. BL MS Harl. 165, ff. 21ʳ–23ʳ; [W. Prynne], *A New Discovery of the Prelates Tyranny* (London, 1641), pp. 91–109, 218–26; W. Prynne, *The Antipathie of the English Lordly Prelacie* (1641), I, p. 223, II, pp. 290–1. On *Sions Plea* and Leighton's case see Stephen Foster, *Notes from the Caroline Underground* (Hamden, CT, 1978), pp. 30–9.

34. [W. Prynne], *Newes from Ipswich* ([Edinburgh and ?London, 1636]), title and sigs. A3ᵛ–A4ᵛ; Prynne, *Antipathie of the Prelacie*, II, p. 291; R. V. H. Burne, 'The History of Chester Cathedral', *Journal of the Chester and North Wales Archit., Archaeol., and Hist. Soc.*, XXXIX (1952), 82–5. According to Prynne 'fear of questioning' led Bridgeman to reinter the altar after the meeting of the Long Parliament. Some substance is lent to Prynne's charge by John Ley, parson of Great Budworth, Cheshire, in *A Letter (Against the erection of an Altar)*, addressed to the bishop of Chester in June 1635, and published at the end of the author's *Defensive Doubts* (1641). According to the bishop's reported reply (pp. 24–5) 'the materials (whereof it [the altar] was made) were found ready for such a purpose' when seats were removed from the upper end of the chancel to the west end of the cathedral. Bridgeman said that 'hearing great offence was taken at it' he had the altar taken down.

35. J. S. Morrill, *Cheshire 1630–1660: County Government and Society during the English Revolution* (Oxford, 1974), p.36; *Lords Journal*, 4, p. 225; BL Harl. MS 165, f. 23ʳ (Matth. 18:17).

36. BL Add. MS 70002, ff. 206ʳ, 213ʳ; Eales, *Puritans and Roundheads*, p. 47.

37. Exod. 32:20; Eales, *Puritans and Roundheads*, p. 49.

38. William Hunt, *The Puritan Moment: The Coming of Revolution in an English County* (Cambridge, MA, 1983), p. 288; Aston, *Faith and Fire*, p. 298.

39. *Commons Journal* II, p. 72; *The Orders from the House of Commons* (BL, E. 171 (8), p. 4); John Morrill, *The Nature of the English Revolution* (1993), pp. 73–4.

40. *Constitutional Documents of the Puritan Revolution*, ed. S. R. Gardiner (Oxford, 1951), pp. 197–8; 8 Sept. 1641 order (BL 669.f.3(14)); Morrill, *English Revolution*, pp. 75–7; Aston, *England's Iconoclasts*, I, pp. 75–6.

41. E. Dering, *A Collection of Speeches . . . in matter of Religion* (1642), pp. 3, 5–6, 50, 81, 84–6; N. Tyacke, *The Fortunes of English Puritanism, 1603–1640* (1989), p. 21.

42. T. P. S. Woods, *Prelude to Civil War 1642: Mr. Justice Malet and the Kentish Petition* (Salisbury, 1980), p. 142; Alan Everitt, *The Community of Kent and the Great Rebellion 1640–60* (Leicester, 1966), pp. 95–107.

43. Lucy Hutchinson, *Memoirs of the Life of Colonel Hutchinson*, ed. J. Sutherland (1973), p. 54; Morrill, *Cheshire*, p. 36; J. Morrill, 'Sir William Brereton and England's Wars of Religion', *Journal of British Studies*, XXIV (1985), 311–32; [B.Ryves], *Mercurius Rusticus* ([Oxford] 1646), pp.22–3; Christopher Woodforde, *English Stained and Painted Glass* (Oxford, 1954), pp. 45–6.

44. BL Add MS 70003, ff. 158ʳ⁻ᵛ, 161ʳ, 162ʳ (draft of Leominster letter); Eales, *Puritans and Roundheads*, pp. 32, 115–16.

45. J. Vicars, *The Sinfulness and Unlawfulness, of having or making the Picture of Christs Humanity* (1641), p. 38; C. H. Firth and R. S. Rait (eds), *Acts and Ordinances of the Interregnum*, 3 vols (1911), I, pp. 265–6, 425–6.

46. J. Morrill, 'William Dowsing, the Bureacratic Puritan', in Morrill, Slack and Woolf (eds), *Public Duty*, pp. 173–203.

47. BL Add. MS 70005 (not foliated); Culmer receipt dated 14 June 1645; Richard Culmer, *Cathedrall Newes from Canterbury* (1644), pp. 2, 6; Eales, *Puritans and Roundheads*, p. 183.

48. Paul S. Seaver, *Wallington's World: A Puritan Artisan in Seventeenth-Century London* (1985), p. 151; Morrill, *English Revolution*, p. 76; *The Petition of the Weamen of Middlesex* (1641), sig. A2ʳ; *Commons Journal*, II, p. 35.

49. H. Dixon, 'Original Account of the Springett Family', *Gentleman's Magazine*, October, 1851, p. 372, cited Everitt, *Community of Kent*, p. 148.

50. *The Inventories and Valuations of the King's Goods 1649–1651*, ed. Oliver Millar, *Walpole Society*, 43 (1970–2), xi, xiii, n. 5; Claude Phillips, *The Picture Gallery of Charles I* (1896), p. 47; C. Thomas-Stanford, *Sussex in the Great Civil War and the Interregnum 1642–1660* (1910), pp. 153–4, cited P. Collinson, *From Iconoclasm to Iconophobia* (Reading, 1986), p. 28; Eales, *Puritans and Roundheads*, p. 184. On executioners' roles in the ritual punishment of idols see S. Michalski, *The Reformation and the Visual Arts* (1993), pp. 90–1.

51. *Inventories,* ed. Millar, xxii, 205, 257–8, 299, 310, 315; W. L. F. Nuttall, 'King Charles I's Pictures and the Commonwealth Sale', *Apollo,* LXXXII (Oct. 1965), 306; Dering, *Collection of Speeches,* p. 10.

52. G. E. Aylmer and R.Cant (eds), *A History of York Minster* (Oxford, 1977), p. 315.

4. THE PURITAN DEATH-BED, *c.*1560–*c.*1660 *Ralph Houlbrooke*

The author wishes to acknowledge the grant of a British Academy/Leverhulme Trust Senior Research Fellowship which made possible the research on which this chapter is based.

First references to books printed before 1700 are usually given in the form in which they appear in the *Short Title Catalogue of Books Printed in England, Scotland, & Ireland* (1991). 'He' and 'his' will, for the sake of conciseness, normally be employed in general statements in this chapter which apply to both sexes.

1. Charles Fitz-Geffrey, *Death's sermon unto the living* (1620), sig. A3, p. 29.

2. George Ferebe, *Lifes farewell. Or a funerall sermon. At the funerall of John Drew gentleman* (1615), p. 27.

3. A. J. Collins (ed.), *Manuale ad vsum percelebris ecclesie Sarisburiensis,* Henry Bradshaw Society, XCI (1958), 97–118; F. E. Brightman, *The English Rite,* 2 vols (1915), vol. II, 818–47; R. Whiting, *The Blind Devotion of the People. Popular religion and the English Reformation* (Cambridge, 1989), p. 126.

4. M. C. O'Connor, *The Art of Dying Well: The Development of the Ars Moriendi* (New York, 1942), pp. 1–60; N. L. Beaty, *The Craft of Dying. A Study in the Literary Tradition of the Ars Moriendi in England* (New Haven CT, and London, 1970), pp. 1–53; *The boke of the craft of dying,* in C. Horstmann (ed.), *Yorkshire Writers: Richard Rolle of Hampole and his Followers* (1896), vol. II, pp. 406–20.

5. Brightman, *The English Rite,* vol. II, 828–9, 834–5, 842–3.

6. D. S. Bailey, *Thomas Becon and the Reformation of the Church in England* (Edinburgh and London, 1952), p. 144; T. Becon, *The Sicke Mannes Salue,* in J. Ayre (ed.), *Prayers and other Pieces of Thomas Becon STP,* Parker Society (1844), 87–91.

7. W. Perkins, *A salve for a sicke man: or a treatise containing the nature, differences, and kindes of death; as also the right manner of dying Well* (?1610), pp. 84–94.

8. *Ibid.,* pp. 95–108, 140–52.

9. *Ibid.,* pp. 153–71, 191–4.

10. C. J. Stranks, *Anglican Devotion: Studies in the Spiritual Life of the Church of England between the Reformation and the Oxford Movement* (1961), pp. 36–7, 59–60.

11. *A directory for the publique worship of God throughout the three kingdoms* (1645), pp. 64–72.

12. P. Collinson, ' "A magazine of religious patterns": an Erasmian topic transposed in English Protestantism', in his *Godly People: Essays on English Protestantism and Puritanism* (1983), pp. 499–525; J. Eales, 'Samuel Clarke and

the "Lives" of Godly Women in Seventeenth-Century England', in *Studies in Church History*, vol. 27 (1990), 365–76.

13. S. Clarke, *The Lives of sundry eminent persons* (1683), Part 2, p. 140.

14. P. Stubbes, *A Christal Glasse for Christian women. Contayning An excellent Discourse of the godly life and Christian death of Mistrese Katherine Stubbes . . .*, reprinted with some omissions in F. J. Furnivall (ed.), *Philip Stubbes's Anatomy of Abuses in England in Shakspere's Youth A. D. 1583* (1877–82), Part I, pp. 195–208.

15. J. O. Halliwell (ed.), *The Autobiography and Correspondence of Sir Simonds D'Ewes, Bart.* (1845), vol. II, pp. 275–82.

16. R. Spalding (ed.), *The Diary of Bulstrode Whitelocke 1605–1675*, Records of Social and Economic History, new ser., vol. XIII (1990), pp. 62–3, 65–6.

17. M. C. Cross, 'The Third Earl of Huntingdon's Death-bed: A Calvinist Example of the *Ars Moriendi*', *Northern History*, XXI (1985), 80–107.

18. I. F., *A sermon preached at Ashby De-la-zouch at the funerall of the lady Elizabeth Stanley late wife to Henrie earle of Huntingdon* (1635), pp. 37–40.

19. T. Oldmayne, *Lifes brevitie and deaths debility* (1636), p. 34; Perkins, *Salve for a Sicke Man*, p. 168; G. Hickes, *The life and death of David* (1645), pp. 23–4.

20. Stubbes, *A Christal Glasse*, p. 200; Oldmayne, *Lifes brevitie*, p. 28; S. Clarke, *The marrow of ecclesiastical history* (3rd edn, 1675), Part I, p. 417; B. Potter, *The baronets buriall* (Oxford, 1613), pp. 31–2; C. Fitz-Geffrey, *Elisha his lamentation, for his losse* (1622), p. 50.

21. *Diary of Whitelocke*, p. 66.

22. F. R. Raines (ed.), *The Journal of Nicholas Assheton of Downham, in the County of Lancaster, Esq.*, Chetham Society, old ser., XIV (1848), p. 131; J. Preston, *A Sermon preached at the funeral of Arthur Upton* (1619), p. 35; S. Ashe, *Gray hayres crowned with Grace* (1654), pp. 60–1; S. Clarke, *A collection of the lives of ten eminent divines* (1662), p. 19; Clarke, *The marrow*, Part I, p. 462.

23. Stubbes, *A Christal Glasse*, pp. 202, 207; C. Cross (ed.), *The Letters of Sir Francis Hastings. 1574–1609*, Somerset Record Society, LXIX (1969), p. 63; J. Horsfall Turner (ed.), *The Rev. Oliver Heywood, B. A., 1603–1702: his Autobiography, Diaries, Anecdote and Event Books*, 4 vols (Brighouse, 1882–5), vol. I, p. 72; *Diary of Whitelocke*, p. 62.

24. Perkins, *Salve for a sicke man*, pp. 100, 155–67; Clarke, *The marrow*, Part I, pp. 354–5, 458.

25. J. Chardon, *A comfortable sermon for all such as thirst to be joined with Jesus Christ* (Oxford, 1586), sig. C7^v; Cross, 'Huntingdon's Death-bed', 99, 101.

26. Stubbes, *A Christal Glasse*, pp. 203–5 (passages in the confession of faith omitted from this edition can be found in *A Christall Glasse* (1591), sig. B1^v–C1^v; T. Gataker, *Certaine sermons now gathered together into one volume* (1637), p. 215.

27. R. Kilbie, *A sermon preached . . . in Oxford at the funeral of Thomas Holland* (Oxford, 1613), p. 19; Stubbes, *A Christal Glasse*, p. 201; Ashe, *Gray hayres*, p. 60 (actually the day before Gataker's death).

28. Perkins, *Salve for a sicke man*, pp. 97–8; Preston, *Sermon at the funeral of Arthur Upton*, p. 35; Oldmayne, *Lifes brevitie*, pp. 27, 32–3, 35.

29. S. Clarke, *The second part of the marrow of ecclesiastical history* (1675), Book II, pp. 54–5.

30. Ibid., p. 55; Perkins, *Salve for a sicke man*, p. 194; Stubbes, *A Christal Glasse*, pp. 205–7; I. F., *A Sermon preached at Ashby-De-la-zouch*, p. 42, I owe the point about Eve to Jacqueline Eales.

31. Stubbes, *A Christal Glasse*, pp. 207–8; S. Clarke, *The lives of sundry eminent persons* (1683) *I. Of divines*, pp. 67, 76.

32. Cross, 'Huntingdon's Death-bed', p. 103; Gataker, *Certaine sermons*, p. 216.

33. Cross, 'Huntingdon's Death-bed', pp. 94–103; J. Chadwich, *A sermon preached at Snarford at the funeral of Sir George Sanct-Paule* (1614), pp. 24–5, 27; Oldmayne, *Lifes brevitie*, p. 34; *Autobiography and Correspondence of D'Ewes*, vol. I, p. 111; *Journal of Assheton*, p. 133.

34. *Diary of Whitelocke*, pp. 62–3, 66.

35. Perkins, *Salve for a sicke man*, pp. 104–5; Clarke, *Lives of eminent persons. II Of nobility and gentry*, p. 139; *I Of divines*, p. 67.

36. *Rev. Oliver Heywood*, vol. I, p. 73; Clarke, *The marrow*, Part 1, p. 383; *Diary of Whitelocke*, p. 66.

37. *Journal of Assheton*, p. 133; Kilbie, *A sermon preached*, p. 20; Elizabeth Jocelin, *The Mothers Legacie, to her unborne childe* (1624), sig. A5r; Perkins. *A salve for a sicke man*, sig. A1.

38. *Rev. Oliver Heywood*, vol. I, pp. 66–8.

39. J. Janeway, *A token for children: being an exact account of the conversion, holy and exemplary lives, and joyful deaths, of seveal young children* (1676), sig. A3v–A4r, pp. 43–9, part II, pp. 14–22. Janeway's significance is discussed by C. John Sommerville, *The Discovery of Childhood in Puritan England* (Athens, GA, and London, 1992), esp. pp. 55–7.

40. Alan Macfarlane (ed.), *The Diary of Josselin 1616–83* (1976), pp. 200–4, 335.

41. R. Parkinson (ed.), *The Autobiography of Henry Newcome, M.A.*, 2 vols, Chetham Society, old Ser., XXVI, XXVII (1852), vol. I, p. 53. My italics.

42. L. Andrewes, *A Manual of Directions for the Sick. With many Sweet Meditations and Devotions of the Right Reverend Father in God, Lancelot Andrews, late L. Bishop of Winchester*, in *Two Answers to Cardinal Perron and other Miscellaneous Works by Lancelot Andrewes*, Library of Anglo-Catholic Theology (Oxford, 1854), 169–221.

43. J. Taylor, *The Rule and Exercises of Holy Dying* (1929 edn), pp. 178–220.

5. 'A CHARITABLE CHRISTIAN HATRED': THE GODLY AND THEIR ENEMIES IN THE 1630S   *Peter Lake*

I should like to thank Patrick Collinson, David Como, Richard Cust, Jacqui Eales, Ken Fincham, Ann Hughes and Bill Jordan for reading and commenting on various drafts of this paper.

1. See Northamptonshire Record Office Isham (Lamport) Mss 2570, a manuscript separate account of Barker's death. I owe my knowledge of this document to the kindness of John Fielding. A slightly rearranged version was printed in 1652 as *The arraignment of hypocrisy or a looking glass for murderers and adulterers* (Thomason tract E. 1290 (3)). I owe my knowledge of this tract to

Alistair Bellany. The account of these events which follows proceeds on the assumption that the description given in the separate bears a relatively close relationship to what actually happened on the scaffold. In the absence of other sources this can be no more than an assumption, albeit a rather probable one, since the purposes of puritan damage limitation would have been ill served by the circulation in the county of a largely fictional account of what must have been a local *cause célèbre*. As Brad Gregory's massive researches on the history of martyrdom are showing, confessional disputes about the scaffold seldom revolved around what happened – neither side would take the risk of lying about such notorious events – but were centred much more on the meanings of commonly agreed narratives. That seems reason enough for the minimal suspension of disbelief necessary to legitimate the account given here. Certainly, both separate and pamphlet were written within and structured by certain theological and generic conventions and there must always remain the tantalising possibility that these conventions were used to obscure a different and altogether more desperate and unresolved death. Ultimately we cannot know *for sure* how Barker died. However, for the wider purposes of my argument the literal truth of this account is a side-issue; what really matters is the nature of the story that was told about Barker's end by the local puritan community and the other, anti-puritan purposes to which that story could be put, and for those questions the separate represents rather good first hand evidence.

2. J. Sharpe, ' "Last dying Speeches": Religion, Ideology and Public Execution in Seventeenth Century England' *Past and Present*, 107 (1985); P. Lake, 'Deeds against Nature: Cheap Print, Protestantism and Murder in early Seventeenth Century England' in K. Sharpe and P. Lake (eds), *Culture and Politics in early Stuart England* (1994).

3. For these general points made by a local preacher see R. Bolton, *Some General directions for a comfortable walking with God* (1626), pp. 33–5, 38–9, 322–3, 330, 387–8 and R. Bolton, *Instructions for a right comforting afflicted consciences* (1635), pp. 130–5, 227–9, 292, 352, 363, 371, 508–9, 512–15; J. Bentham, *The Christian Conflict* (1635), p. 175.

4. See for instance Patrick Collinson's famous remark that 'there is little point constructing elaborate statements defining what, in ontological terms, Puritanism was and what it was not, when it was not a thing definable in itself but only one half of a stressful relationship'; Collinson, *The Birthpangs of Protestant England* (1988) p. 143. Collinson has also sought to flesh out that remark in a number of other studies, most notably in chs 4 and 5 of *The Birthpangs* and in his 'The Cohabitation of the Faithful with the Unfaithful' in O. P. Grell, J. I. Israel and N. Tyacke (eds), *From Persecution to Toleration: the Glorious Revolution and Religion in England* (Oxford, 1991), an article which might be taken as the jumping-off point for the present chapter's investigation of what Collinson has memorably termed 'the malign reciprocities of religious identity formation'.

5. J. Fielding, 'Conformists, Puritans and the Church Courts: the Diocese of Peterborough, 1603–1642', unpublished University of Birmingham PhD thesis (1989), especially chs 3–6; for Sutton and Bradley see pp. 69–70. Also see John Fielding's article, 'Arminianism in the Localities: Peterborough Diocese, 1603–1642' in K. Fincham (ed.), *The Early Stuart Church* (1993).

6. R. Bolton, *Directions* and *Instructions* and J. Bentham, *The Society of the Saints* (1630) and *The Christian Conflict*.

7. Fielding, 'Conformists, Puritans and the Church Courts', pp. 150–1, where Fielding notes that conformists like John Williams and his chaplain John Fosbrooke preached at Kettering too; for Montagu see E. Cope, *The Life of a Public Man: Edward, First Baron Montagu of Boughton, 1562–1644* (Philadelphia, 1981).

8. Bentham, *Christian Conflict*, p. 6.

9. Bolton, *Directions*, pp. 145, 305.

10. Bentham, *Society of the Saints*, p. 215.

11. Ibid., pp. 78, 118–21; Bentham, *Christian Conflict*, pp. 93, 95–6; Bolton, *Directions*, pp. 9–10, 18, 24; Bolton, *Instructions*, pp. 505–6, 535–6, 541–2.

12. Bentham, *Society of Saints*, pp. 219, 3. Also see ibid., p. 233 and Bolton, *Directions*, p. 23.

13. Bolton, *Directions*, pp. 191–2, 87 and Bolton, *Instructions*, pp. 342–6.

14. Hence the title of Bentham's book 'the Society of the Saints'. For one of many passages linking the collective activities and spiritual exchanges of the godly and the individual believer's sense of assurance see Bolton, *Directions*, pp. 332–3.

15. Bentham, *Society of the Saints*, p. 29; Bolton, *Directions*, p. 333 and *Instructions*, p. 156. For Bolton's rather more subtle appropriation of the term puritan see his references to 'puritan Lot' and 'precise' David, *Directions*, p. 352; also see Bolton, *Instructions*, pp. 47, 207, for references to the 'puritan fathers' and the claim 'that some of the ancient fathers do puritanise'. For a description of the sins of the ungodly as the precise observe of the virtues of the godly see ibid., p. 93.

16. Bentham, *Christian Conflict*, p. 152; Bolton, *Directions*, p. 293, Moderation was a social virtue but not, for Bolton in particular, a religious or spiritual one. See below at notes 56 and 57. On the interplay within puritanism of the imperatives of zeal and moderation see P. Collinson, ' "A Magazine of Religious Patterns": an Erasmian topic transposed in English Protestantism' in his *Godly People* (1983) and P. Lake, *Moderate Puritans and the Elizabethan Church* (Cambridge, 1982), pp. 145–50.

17. Bentham, *Society of the Saints*, pp. 149–77; for the re-emergence of sabbatarianism as a controversial issue in the 1630s see K. Parker, *The English Sabbath* (Cambridge, 1988) ch. 7; on the broader issue of the puritan provenance of sabbatarianism compare Parker's position with J. H. Primus, *Holy Time: Moderate Puritanism and the Sabbath* (Macon, GA, 1989).

18. For fasting see Bentham, *Christian Conflict*, pp. 265–79; for the public fasts of the 1620s see p. 272.

19. Ibid., p. 279. In reality, as John Fielding has shown, the voluntary religion of the godly was not always or even very often so elaborately respectful of the norms and forms of the national church. Tampering with the prayer book, extempore prayer, private fasts and exercises attended by a good deal more than the members of one family, and sermon gadding were all central to the life of the godly in Northamptonshire during this period. The point is that even such activities could be glossed as Bentham

was here glossing them as supplements to rather than replacements for the practices of the national church. The extent to which such practices were seen as subversive of the integrity and unity of the national church depended (and depends), in large part, on the observer's view of that church. By the 1630s, of course, power lay with those (the Laudians) to whom such activities were indeed subversive – hence perhaps the care with which Bentham sought to explain how the central forms of puritan religion could operate acceptably within the structures of the national church. On all this see Fielding, 'Conformists, Puritans and the Church Courts', passim but especially chs 3, 5, 7, 10. The tensions at play here are beautifully summarised in P. Collinson, 'The English Conventicle' in D. Wood and W. Sheils (eds), *Voluntary Religion* (Oxford, 1986) *Studies in Church History*, vol. 24.

20. Bolton, *Christian Conflict*, p. 264; for more general admonitions that over things in themselves indifferent 'we should have peace' and thus fall in with the church's customs and orders see Bentham, *The Society of the Saints*, pp. 36–7, where Bentham told his audience that 'we may yield to some things inconvenient for the peace of this society' before telling the story of Luke accepting a false but publicly accepted translation of the Bible to avoid offence, thus tolerating 'a public error to prevent a greater evil'. The application of such sentiments to puritan scruples about ceremonial conformity, while left tactfully implicit, is obvious.

21. For this view of puritan religion see P. Collinson, *The Religion of Protestants* (Oxford, 1982).

22. Bolton, *Directions*, p. 2.

23. Bentham, *Society of the Saints*, p. 6.

24. Bolton, *Directions*, pp. 28, 30; also see Bolton, *Instructions*, p. 47.

25. Bentham, *Society of the Saints*, pp. 126–8.

26. Bolton, *Directions*, p. 60.

27. Bentham, *Society of the Saints*, p. 18; *Christian Conflict*, p. 55.

28. Bolton, *Directions*, pp. 7, 131; also see Bolton, *Instructions*, pp. 15, 49, 64–5, 303, 356.

29. Bentham, *Society of the Saints*, pp. 29, 213–14, 24.

30. Ibid., pp. 28–9; also see Bolton, *Directions*, pp. 272–3, 350–1.

31. Bentham, *Society of the Saints*, pp. 24–5; for essentially the same points see Bolton, *Directions*, pp. 282–8.

32. See, for example, Ben Jonson's *The Alchemist* and *Bartholomew Fair*; W. P. Holden, *Anti-puritan Satire* (New Haven, CT, 1954). B. Capp, *The World of John Taylor the Water-poet, 1578–1653*, (Oxford, 1994), chs 6, 8. Underdown, *Fire from Heaven* (1992), pp. 28–9, 148–50; A. L. Hughes, 'Religion and Society in Stratford upon Avon, 1619–38' *Midland History* (1994), vol. 19, pp. 62–3; for Nottingham see C. J. Sisson *The Lost Plays of Shakespeare's Age* (Cambridge, 1936), pp. 201–3. For the Northamptonshire JPs see Public Record Office (PRO) Stac 8/205/20. For Newdigate see Warwickshire Record Office CR136 B/22. For Burgess see R. C. Johnson, M. F. Keeler, M. J. Cole and W. B. Bidwell (eds), *Proceedings in Parliament 1628*, 6 vols (New Haven, CT, 1977–83), vol. III, pp. 131–2, 135. I owe these last references to the kindness of Richard Cust and Ann Hughes and would like to thank both of them for discussions on this point.

33. Bolton, *Directions*, p. 277. This might help to explain Bentham and Bolton's virtual obsession with enclosure and usury. Both were common enough practices; indeed, as Bolton conceded, in the economic conditions of the time, they were almost essential activities for those contemporaries who wanted to maximise the return on their wealth, but they were also both conventionally regarded as sins, signs of covetousness indeed. For Bentham they were sins which, when the godly committed them, seemed merely to confirm the suspicion of the profane that the high religious and moral tone maintained by puritans was a mere cover for self-interest. See Bentham, *Society of the Saints*, pp. 26–7, 67–8, 98–100 and his *Christian Conflict*, pp. 317–26, and on usury, ibid., pp. 329–60. Also see R. Bolton, *A short and private discourse between Mr Bolton and one M. S. concerning usury* (1637).

34. Bolton, *Directions*, pp. 286–7; also see Bolton, *Instructions*, p. 155. For more on this point see F. Nietzsche, *On the Genealogy of Morals*, trans. and ed. Walter Kaufmann (New York, 1989). On the potential significance of puritan infractions of the norms of good neighbourhood in alienating their contemporaries see Collinson, 'The Cohabitation of the Faithful with the Unfaithful'.

35. For these points in general see P. Lake, *Moderate Puritans*, ch. 7. For a rather different account of puritan spirituality see J. Stachniewski, *The Persecutory Imagination* (Oxford, 1991).

36. Bolton, *Directions*, pp. 57–8, 307, 317–18, 320, 325, 333–5, 352–4, 381. Also see Bolton, *Instructions*, pp. 74, 299.

37. Bolton, *Directions*, pp. 276, 127, 135–6; Bolton, *Instructions*, p. 321, 369–71.

38. Bentham, *Society of the Saints*, pp. 278, 19; also see Bolton, *Instructions*, pp. 97–9 for a vivid listing of the collective festivities – 'taverns, ale houses, play houses, whore houses, gaming houses, may games, morris dances, church ales, cards, dice, dancing, feasts, wakes, misrules, drinking matches, fooleries and good fellow meetings' – which held the profane together and kept them from godliness.

39. Bentham, *Society of the Saints*, p. 131; Bolton, *Directions*, pp. 300–1, also see p. 298.

40. Bentham, *Society of the Saints*, pp. 56–7; Bolton, *Instructions*, pp. 72, 219–21; for the falsity of most death-bed repentance see ibid., pp. 231–2, 249–50.

41. Ibid., pp. 348, 57.

42. Ibid., pp. 138–40.

43. Ibid., pp. 270–2; also see Bolton *Instructions*, pp. 356–7 where the perennial accusation of puritan hypocrisy is rejected but also used to urge the godly to 'search more thoroughly and walk more warily'.

44. Bolton, *Directions*, p. 369; also see Bolton, *Instructions*, pp. 67–8.

45. Bentham, *Society of the Saints*, pp. 6–7.

46. Bolton, *Directions*, pp. 73–4.

47. Bentham, *Society of the Saints*, pp. 7–8; Bolton, *Directions*, p. 86.

48. Bentham, *Christian Conflict*, pp. 312–13.

49. Bentham, *The Society of the Saints*, pp. 13–15, 26; also see Bolton, *Directions*, p. 151, pp. 286–7, where Bolton delivered himself of the opinion

that 'Christian distresses are the principal object of the Christian's compassion and bounty', and p. 278 where he described the Christian's primary obligation to every 'true-hearted Nathaniel and the whole household of faith' and only then not to be 'any ways wanting . . . in other charitable passages with spiritual discretion to any truly distressed and miserable'. Also see pp. 267–8.

50. Ibid. pp. 278–83.

51. Bentham, *Society of the Saints*, p. 70–1.

52. Bentham, *Christian Conflict*, pp. 233–4; Bolton, *Directions*, pp. 144–5; Bolton *Instructions*, pp. 68–70.

53. Bentham, *The Society of the Saints*, pp. 20–1, 31, 10.

54. J. Fielding, 'Opposition to the Personal Rule of Charles I: the diary of Robert Woodford, 1637–41', *Historical Journal*, 31 (1988).

55. Bolton, *Directions*, pp. 113–19.

56. Bentham, *The Society of the Saints*, p. 33.

57. Bolton, *Directions*, pp. 75–6, 145–6. Also see Bolton, *Instructions*, p. 71.

58. Ibid., pp. 303, 305–6, 50–1, also see pp. 295, 330–1 and Bolton, *Instructions*, pp. 169, 182, 194, 196, 234, 243–4, 321–2, 330; E. Duffy, 'The godly and the multitude in Stuart England' in *The Seventeenth Century*, 1 (1986).

59. Bentham, *Society of the Saints*, pp. 18–20, 26–8.

60. Ibid. pp. 57–60; for essentially the same point see Bolton, *Directions*, pp. 352–3.

61. Bentham, *Society of the Saints*, pp. 57–60. Also see Bolton, *Directions*, p. 352.

62. Ibid., pp. 26–7; Bolton *Directions*, pp. 132–3; also see Bolton, *Instructions*, pp. 288–93 for the countervailing claim that even after conversion and repentance the professor must continue to feel sorrow for the sins he or she would inevitably commit; 'in a leaking ship there must be continual pumping'.

63. Bentham, *Society of Saints*, pp. 242–53, and 178–89; also see Bentham, *Christian Conflict*, pp. 135–49, a section written 'against the anti-nomists'.

64. Peter Studley, *The Looking Glass of Schism* (1634) which was followed in 1635 by an expanded second addition replying to a puritan reply by a local gentleman and JP Richard More that was not published until 1641 as *A true relation of the murders committed in the parish of Clune in the county of salop by Enoch ap Evan* (1641). Quotations below are from Studley's second edition. On the whole affair see P. Lake, 'Puritanism, Arminianism and a Shropshire Axe-murder' *Midland History*, 15 (1990) upon which the account below is based.

65. Studley, *Looking Glass*, from the separately paginated refutation of More, p. 73.

66. Studley, *Looking Glass*, pp. 12, 24, from the 'Epistle to the Christian Reader' of the refutation of More.

67. Ibid., p. 85 and from the refutation of More pp. 74–5.

68. Ibid., pp. 244–5

69. Ibid., pp. 201–5, quotation at pp. 204–5.

70. Ibid., pp. 224–5.

71. For this see Bentham's obsequious manuscript life of Montagu, Northamptonshire Record Office Montagu Mss 186, a reference I owe to Richard Cust.

72. Lake, 'Puritanism, Arminianism and a Shropshire Axe- murder', pp. 44–50, for the Shrewsbury background to Studley's pamphlet.

73. Ibid., pp. 41–2.

74. See Collinson, *Religion of Protestants*.

75. This vision of puritanism has recently been revived by Kevin Sharpe in his massive study of *The Personal Rule of Charles I* (1992), especially in chs 6 and 12; also see A. Zakai, *Exile and Kingdom* (Cambridge, 1992) and P. White, *Predestination, Policy and Polemic* (Cambridge, 1992).

76. The former position represents a perforce rather crude rendition of what I take to be the dominant interpretative strand in three recent articles by Patrick Collinson: *The Puritan Character: Polemics and Polarities* (Los Angeles, 1989), 'Ecclesiastical Vitriol: Religious Satire in the 1590s and the Invention of Puritanism' in J. Guy (ed.), *The Reign of Elizabeth I* (Cambridge, 1995) and *'Bartholomew Fair*: Theatre Invents Puritans' in D. Bevington, D. Smith and R. Strier (eds), *The Theatrical City* (Cambridge, 1995). I should like to thank Patrick Collinson for allowing me to see both pieces in typescript. As always his position is complex and subtle; there are elements in all three articles which anticipate and are certainly entirely compatible with the arguments advanced here. The latter position underpins much of the argument of Sharpe's *Personal Rule*.

77. Fielding, 'Conformists, Puritans and the Church Courts', pp. 122–5.

78. Bentham, *Christian Conflict*, p. 142.

79. Lake, 'Puritanism, Arminianism and a Shropshire Axe-murder'.

80. Fielding, 'Conformists, Puritans and the Church Courts', ch. 6, especially p. 173.

81. See P. Lake, 'Defining puritanism – again?' in F. Bremer (ed.), *Puritanism: Transatlantic Perspectives on a Seventeenth Century Anglo-American Faith* (Boston, 1993); Hughes, 'Religion and society in Stratford upon Avon'.

6. A ROAD TO REVOLUTION: THE CONTINUITY OF PURITANISM, 1559–1642 *Jacqueline Eales*

1. P. Heylyn, *Aërius Redivivus: or the History of the Presbyterians* (1670). I am grateful to Sheila Hingley and Sarah Gray of Canterbury Cathedral Library and to Charlotte Hodgson and Michael Stansfield of Canterbury Cathedral Archives for their unflagging responses to my various requests for information. I would like to thank Christopher Durston for his comments on an earlier draft of this paper, Peter Lake for a number of helpful discussions on the general issues it contains and Richard Eales for his comments during the final stages of writing.

2. See for example P. Collinson, *The Elizabethan Puritan Movement* (1967) p. 466 and N. Tyacke, 'Puritanism, Arminianism and Counter-Revolution' in C. Russell (ed.), *The Origins of the English Civil War* (1973), pp. 119–43.

3. Nicholas Tyacke, *Anti-Calvinists: The Rise of English Arminianism c.* 1590–1640, (Oxford, 1987), passim; for the policies of the 1630s see also Julian Davies, *The Caroline Captivity of the Church: Charles I and the Remoulding of Anglicanism* (Oxford, 1992). For the puritan response to these policies see Jacqueline Eales, 'Iconoclasm, Iconography and the Altar in the English Civil War' in Diana Wood (ed.), *Studies in Church History*, vol. 28 (Oxford, 1992), 313–27.

4. For Voyle's paper see B[ritish] L[ibrary], Add[itional] Manuscripts 70002 ff. 363r–7v.

5. J. P. Kenyon, *The Stuart Constitution, 1603–1688: Documents and Commentary* (Cambridge, 1966), pp. 132–4.

6. Conrad Russell, *Parliaments and English Politics, 1621–1629* (Oxford, 1979), pp. 231, 307; Jacqueline Eales, *Puritans and Roundheads: the Harleys of Brampton Bryan and the Outbreak of the English Civil War* (Cambridge, 1990), p. 53.

7. For Voyle see A. G. Matthews, *Calamy Revised: Being a Revision of Edmund Calamy's Account of the Ministers and Others Ejected and Silenced, 1660–2* (Oxford, 1934), p. 504; BL Add Mss 70002, ff. 363r, 315r.

8. John Neale, *Elizabeth I and Her Parliaments, 1559–1581* (1953), pp. 193–200, *Elizabeth I and Her Parliaments, 1584–1601* (1957), pp. 148–50; Geoffrey Elton, *The Parliament of England, 1559–1581* (Cambridge, 1986), pp. 208–9; Patrick Collinson, 'Puritans, Men of Business and Elizabethan Parliaments', in Collinson, *Elizabethan Essays* (1994), pp. 84–5.

9. Collinson, *Elizabethan Puritan Movement*, pp. 291–382; Collinson, 'John Field and Elizabethan Puritanism' in Collinson, *Godly People: Essays on English Protestantism and Puritanism* (1983), pp. 335–70; Collinson, *Elizabethan Puritan Movement*, pp. 280–1.

10. Although see Eales, *Puritans and Roundheads*, pp. 108–10.

11. Ian Green, 'The Persecution of "Scandalous" and "Malignant" Parish Clergy during the English Civil War', *English Historical Review*, 94 (1979). For biographical information on the ejected clergy see A. G. Matthews, *Walker Revised: Being a Revision of John Walker's Sufferings of the Clergy during the Grand Rebellion, 1642–60* (Oxford, 1988), and for the careers of many of the puritan clergy who were intruded into parishes by Parliament see Matthews, *Calamy Revised*.

12. Elton, *The Parliament of England, 1559–1581*, p. 216; Conrad Russell, 'Parliamentary History in Perspective', *History*, LXI (1976), 18; Russell, *Parliaments and English Politics*, p. 26.

13. Josias Nichols, *The Plea of the Innocent* (1602), p. 119.

14. Stanford E. Lehmberg, *Sir Walter Mildmay and Tudor Government* (Austin, Texas, 1964), pp. 286–90.

15. Collinson, *Elizabethan Puritan Movement*, pp. 403–47.

16. Heylyn, *Aërius Redivivus*, p. 231.

17. Patrick Collinson, 'Letters of Thomas Wood, Puritan, 1566–1577', in Collinson, *Godly People*, pp. 58–82.

18. See D[ictionary] of N[ational] B[iography] under Walsingham, Sir Francis (1530?–90) and Hastings, Henry, third Earl of Huntingdon (1535–95).

19. Lehmberg, *Sir Walter Mildmay and Tudor Government*, pp. 223–33.

20. *DNB* under Bradshaw, William (1571–1618), for Pierson see Eales, *Puritans and Roundheads*, pp. 53–4, for Cotton see Lehmberg, *Sir Walter Mildmay and Tudor Government*, p. 233. Lehmberg notes that 'Emmanuel supplied a disproportionate number of the early immigrants to New England. Thirty-three Emmanuel men – about a third of the Cambridge graduates, and more than the entire number from Oxford – fled from the personal rule of Charles and Laud between 1629–40.'

21. Samuel Clarke, *The Lives of Sundry Eminent Persons in this Later Age* (1683), p. 3.

22. Peter Lake, *Moderate Puritans and the Elizabethan Church* (Cambridge, 1982), p. 39.

23. *DNB* under Dod, John (1549?–1645).

24. Samuel Clarke, *The Lives of Thirty Two English Divines* (1677), pp. 314–28.

25. Cope also represented Oxfordshire in the Parliaments of 1604 and 1614, P. W. Hasler, *The House of Commons, 1558–1603*, 1 (1981), pp. 648–9; PRO SP12/224/58, 66.

26. The links between Sir Anthony and Brasbridge are reflected in the 1592 edition of a treatise on the plague which the minister dedicated to Cope and his wife, Frances; Thomas Brasbridge, *The Poor Man's Jewel . . .* (1592); Robert Harris, *Samuel's Funeral: or, a Sermon Preached at the Funeral of Sir Anthonie Cope Knight and Baronet* (1626) Leaf A3r.

27. Thomas Froysell, *The Beloved Disciple: or a Sermon Preached at the Funeral of the Honourable Sir Robert Harley . . .* (1658), pp. 98–109; Sir Robert Harley to Bishop Bennet, 25 January 1613/14, BL Add Mss 70108/39b.

28. BL Add Mss 70109/69 'petition from many in the principality of Wales'.

29. Corpus Christi, Oxford, Ms. 206, f. 9r; PRO SP16/381/92; BL Add Mss 70002 ff. 211r, 216r, 232r.

30. Corpus Christi, Oxford, Ms. 206, f. 10v.

31. I. M. Calder, *Activities of the Puritan Faction of the Church of England, 1625–1633* (1957); Samuel Rawson Gardiner, *The Constitutional Documents of the Puritan Revolution, 1625–1660*, 3rd edn revised (Oxford, 1912), pp. 138–9.

32. Henry Beveridge (trans.), *The Institutes of the Christian Religion by John Calvin*, vol 2, pp. 289–90.

33. Dorothy M. Meads (ed.), *Diary of Lady Margaret Hoby, 1599–1605* (1930), pp. 72, 73, 150, 151, 153, 154, 156, 157, 158, 159, 162.

34. *DNB* under Egerton, Stephen (1555?–1621?) and Gouge, William (1578–1653); Ben Jonson, *The Alchemist* (1612), leaf B3r.

35. Josias Nichols, *Plea of the Innocent*, p. 213.

36. *DNB* under Throckmorton, Job (1545–1601).

37. Robert Bolton, *A Narration of the Grievous Visitation and Dreadfull Desertion of Mr Peacock in His Last Sicknesse* (1641), pp. 9, 47, 48, 57; *DNB* under Dod, John (1549?–1645); BL Add Mss 4275 f. 185r, a reference I owe to Peter Lake, who also kindly allowed me to make use of his transcripts of Lady Vere's correspondence.

38. *DNB* under Fenn, Humphrey (d 1634); PRO SP16/260/83; BL Add Mss 70002 f. 75r–v.

39. S. Clarke, *The Lives of Thirty Two English Divines*, pp. 169, 320, 117, 220, 106.

40. See for example Elizabeth Eisenstein, *The Printing Revolution in Early Modern Europe* (Cambridge, 1993), pp. 148–86.

41. Matthew Sylvester (ed.), *Reliquiae Baxterianae, or Mr Richard Baxter's Narration of the Most Memorable Passages of His Life and Times* (1696), pp. 1–6.

42. Meads (ed.), *The Diary of Lady Margaret Hoby*, pp. 170, 63, 65, 69, 163; Nottingham University Library, Portland Manuscripts, Commonplace Book of Brilliana Conway, 1622, passim.

43. Paul S. Seaver, *Wallington's World: A Puritan Artisan in Seventeenth Century London* (1985), p. 5.

44. PRO PCC/Probate 11/164 f. 358r–v; for a more detailed account of the influence of clerical libraries see Jacqueline Eales, 'The Mendham Collection: the Contents and their Historical Context' in *Catalogue of the Law Society's Mendham Collection* (1994), pp. lxxv–cxxviii.

45. C. L. Oastler, *John Day, the Elizabethan Printer* (Oxford, 1975); see also *DNB* under Day, John (1522–84).

46. *DNB* under Waldegrave, Robert (1554?–1604).

47. *Short-Title Catalogue of Books Printed in England, Scotland, & Ireland and of English Books Printed Abroad, 1475–1640*, vol. 3 (1991), pp. 164–5; Sylvester, *Reliquiae Baxterianae*, p. 11.

48. BL, Add Mss 70002 f. 81r.

49. Lambert B. Larking (ed.), *Proceedings Principally in the County of Kent* Camden Society, Old Ser., vol. 80 (1861), pp. 86, 87; Peter Lake, 'Puritanism, Arminianism and a Shropshire Axe-Murder', *Midland History*, vol. xv (1990), pp. 37–64.

50. J. T. Cliffe, *The Puritan Gentry: The Great Puritan Families of Early Stuart England* (1984), *Puritans in Conflict: The Puritan Gentry During and After the Civil Wars* (1988), *The Puritan Gentry Besieged, 1650–1700* (1993).

51. PRO SP12/118/7(i); I owe this reference to Janet Hammond.

52. William Gurnall, *The Christian's Labour and Reward* (1672); for Lady Vere's correspondence see BL Add Mss 4274, 4275 passim.

53. Gurnall, *The Christian's Labour and Reward*, pp. 126–7.

54. William Whateley, *A Bride-Bush: Or a Direction for Married Persons* (1619), leaf Alv; John L. Nickalls (ed.), *The Journal of George Fox* (Cambridge, 1952), p. 1.

55. Thomas Fuller, *The History of the Worthies of England* (1662), II, pp. 85–6; *DNB* under Honywood, Sir Thomas (1586–1666).

56. Samuel Clarke, *A Looking-Glass for Good Women to Dress Themselves by* .. (1677), pp. 4, 13.

57. Matthews, *Calamy Revised*, pp. 376, 117, 119–20.

58. Whateley, *A Bride-Bush*, leaves Alr–A2v.

59. Christopher Hill, *Society and Puritanism in Pre-Revolutionary England* (1964), pp. 429–66.

60. See for Example M. Todd, 'Humanists, Puritans and the Spiritualised Household', *Church History*, 49 (1980), 18–34.

61. See for example Conrad Russell, *The Fall of the British Monarchies, 1637–1642* (Oxford, 1991).

62. C. Burgess, *The First Sermon Preached to the Honourable House of Commons now assembled in Parliament at their Publique Fast* (1641), p. 66.

63. Kenyon, *The Stuart Constitution*, p. 169.

64. *Thirteenth Report of the Royal Commission on Historical Manuscripts* Appendix, Part 1 (1892), pp. 4–6.

65. PRO SP16/465/8; Sylvester (ed.), *Reliquiae Baxterianae*, p. 16; BL Add Mss 70002 ff. 309r, 346r. For the Kettering lecture see John Fielding, 'Arminianism in the Localities: Peterborough Diocese, 1603–1642' in K. Fincham (ed.), *The Early Stuart Church, 1603–1642* (1993), p. -107.

66. Wallace Notestein (ed.), *The Journal of Sir Simonds D'Ewes from the Beginning of the Long Parliament to the Opening of the Trial of the Earl of Strafford* (New Haven, CT, 1923), pp. 277, 313–14. The central demands of the Petition and Remonstrance can be reconstructed from the debates recorded by D'Ewes and in the papers of the Committee of 30 set up to consider church government and printed in John Bruce (ed.), *Verney Papers. Notes on the Proceedings of the Long Parliament*, Camden Society, Old Ser. (1845), pp. 4–14.

67. Burgess, *The First Sermon*, pp. 72, 78; S. Marshall, *A Sermon Preached before the House of Commons, now assembled in Parliament at their Publike Fast . . .* (1641) pp. 35, 48.

68. *Commons Journals*, vol. II, 54.

69. Larking (ed.), *Proceedings Principally in the County of Kent*, pp. 101–240; Bodleian Library, Carte Mss 103 f. 50, I am grateful to Conrad Russell for drawing this reference to my attention; *A Certificate from Northamptonshire . . . As there is an Order lately Printed and Published concerning Ministers, by a Committee of the High Court of Parliament* (1641); Corpus Christi College, Oxford, Ms. 206.

70. Matthews, *Walker Revised*, pp. xiii–xxi.

71. Kenyon, *Stuart Constitution*, pp. 216–17.

72. William Shaw, *A History of the English Church During the Civil Wars and Under the Commonwealth, 1640–1660*, vol. 1 (1900), pp. 104–8, 114.

73. The fullest discussion of this issue is to be found in W. M. Abbott, 'The Issue of Episcopacy in the Long Parliament, 1640–48', Oxford DPhil thesis (1982).

74. For the extent of the presbyterian system after 1646 see Shaw, *A History of the English Church*, vol. 2, pp. 373–440.

75. Russell, *Fall of the British Monarchies*, p. 492.

76. BL Add Mss 70002 f. 363r; Corpus Christi, Oxford, Ms. 206 f. 13v.

77. BL Add Mss 70004 f. 301r, for Lady Harley see Eales, *Puritans and Roundheads*, passim.

78. W. C. Abbott, *The Letters and Speeches of Oliver Cromwell* (Cambridge, Mass., 1937–47), vol. 3, p. 586.

79. J. T. Cliffe, *The Yorkshire Gentry from the Reformation to the Civil War* (1969), p. 361; B. G. Blackwood, *The Lancashire Gentry and the Great Rebellion, 1640–1660* (Manchester, 1978), pp. 65–6.

80. J. Morrill, *The Revolt of the Provinces: Conservatives and Radicals in the English Civil War, 1630–1650* (1976), p. 50; A. J. Fletcher, *The Outbreak of the English Civil War* (1981), p. 405.

81. W. Prynne, *Canterburies Doome* . . . (1646), pp. 110–14, 488–97, 199, 146, 505, 506.

82. *Calendar of State Papers Domestic,* . . . *1640* (1880) p. 278; for Warwick's patronage of puritan clerics see K. W. Shipps, 'Lay Patronage of East Anglian Clerics in Pre-Revolutionary England' University of Yale PhD thesis (1971), pp. 167 ff.

7. PURITAN RULE AND THE FAILURE OF CULTURAL
    REVOLUTION, 1645–1660   *Christopher Durston*

I should like to thank Margaret Aston, Susan Doran, Jacqueline Eales, Ralph Houlbrooke and Ronald Hutton, all of whom read earlier versions of this article, for their helpful comments and advice.

1. F. 'E. Sawyer (ed.), 'Proceedings of the Committee of Plundered Ministers relating to Sussex', *Sussex Archaeological Society*, 31 (1881), 178; for more detail on pre-1640 puritan campaigning see Jeremy Goring, *Godly Exercises or the Devil's Dance; Puritanism and Popular Culture in pre-Civil War England* (1983), passim.

2. C. H. Firth and R. S. Rait (eds), *Acts and Ordinances of the Interregnum,* 3 vols (1911), vol. 1, p. 421.

3. Ibid., vol. 1, p. 607.

4. Ibid., vol. 1, p. 954.

5. The puritan neglect of Lent during the Interregnum was referred to after the Restoration by Charles II's government, which made an attempt to reintroduce this period of collective penance; see B[ritish] L[ibrary, Thomason Tracts], 669 f. 26. 49; E. 1084.3.

6. *Acts and Ordinances*, vol. 1, pp. 985–6.

7. Ibid., vol. 1, pp. 604–7.

8. For more details of these Civil War and Interregnum fast-days, see Christopher Durston, ' "For the Better Humiliation of the People": Public Days of Fasting and Thanksgiving during the English Revolution', *The Seventeenth Century*, 7 (1992), 129–49.

9. *Acts and Ordinances*, vol. 1, pp. 604–7.

10. K. L. Parker, *The English Sabbath* (Cambridge, 1988), p. 218.

11. Ibid., p. 218; *Acts and Ordinances*, vol. 1, pp. 420–2.

12. *Acts and Ordinances*, vol. 1, pp. 598–9.

13. Ibid., vol. 2, pp. 383–7, 1162–70.

14. J. S. Rutt (ed.), *The Diary of Thomas Burton Esq.*, 4 vols (1828), vol. 2, pp. 264–5.

15. *Acts and Ordinances*, vol. 1, pp. 594–6.

16. David Cressy, 'Purification, Thanksgiving and the Churching of Women in Post-Reformation England', *Past and Present*, 141 (1993), 106–46; see also Keith Thomas, *Religion and the Decline of Magic: Studies in Popular Beliefs in Sixteenth and Seventeenth Century England* (1971), pp. 59–61, and John Milton's 1642 tract, *An Apology Against a Pamphlet Called a Modest Confutation* in D. Wolfe et al. (eds), *The Complete Prose Works of John Milton* (New Haven, CT, and London, 1953–82), vol. 1, p. 939.

17. Cressy, 'Purification, Thanksgiving and the Churching of Women', pp. 135–40.

18. Christopher Durston, *The Family in the English Revolution* (Oxford, 1989), pp. 121–2.

19. *Acts and Ordinances*, vol. 1, pp. 599–601.

20. For more details, see Chris Durston, ' "Unhallowed Wedlocks": The Regulation of Marriage during the English Revolution', *Historical Journal*, 31 (1988), 45–59; and Durston, *The Family in the English Revolution*, pp. 57–86.

21. *Acts and Ordinances*, vol. 1, p. 604.

22. Ibid., vol. 2, pp. 393–6.

23. Ibid., vol. 2, pp. 387–9.

24. Ibid., vol. 2, pp. 861, 941–2.

25. W. C. Abbott (ed.), *The Writings and Speeches of Oliver Cromwell*, 4 vols (Cambridge, Mass., 1937–47), vol. 3, pp. 844–8.

26. *Acts and Ordinances*, vol. 2, pp. 1098, 1249–50.

27. J. S. Morrill, *Cheshire 1630–1660: County Government and Society during the English Revolution* (Oxford, 1974), pp. 276–87.

28. David Underdown, *Revel, Riot and Rebellion: Popular Politics and Culture in England 1603–1660* (Oxford, 1985), p. 269; A. Clark (ed.), *The Life and Times of Anthony Wood*, Oxford Historical Society, 19 (1891), 138–40.

29. David Underdown, *Fire from Heaven: The Life of an English Town in the Seventeenth Century* (1992), pp. ix, 216–18.

30. L. Fox (ed.), 'The Diary of Robert Beake, Mayor of Coventry 1655–6', *Dugdale Society*, 31 (1977), 114–37.

31. Anthony Fletcher, *A County Community in Peace and War: Sussex 1600–1660* (1975), pp. 111–13; Derek Hirst, 'The Failure of Godly Rule in the English Republic', *Past and Present*, 132 (1991), 53.

32. Alan Macfarlane (ed.), *The Diary of Ralph Josselin 1616–83* (1976), pp. 14, 15, 17, 24–5, 28, 30, 42, 64, 99, 100, 125, 131, 138, 141, 163; See also Durston, 'Public Days of Fasting and Thanksgiving', pp. 137–9.

33. Matthew Sylvester (ed.), *Reliquiae Baxterianae* (1696), pp. 84–5.

34. Macfarlane, *Diary of Ralph Josselin*, p. 108; Sylvester, *Reliquiae Baxterianae*, pp. 84–5.

35. Fletcher, *Sussex*, p. 113.

36. Clark, *Life and Times of Anthony Wood*, pp. 138–40; Ronald Hutton, *The Rise and Fall of Merry England: The Ritual Year 1400–1700* (Oxford, 1994), p. 221.

37. S. C. Ratcliff and H. C. Johnson (eds), *Quarter Sessions Indictment Book 1631–1674*, Warwick County Records (Warwick, 1941), vol. 6, passim.

38. Hirst, 'Failure of Godly Rule', p. 52.

39. Keith Thomas, 'The Puritans and Adultery: The Act of 1650 Reconsidered', in D. H. Pennington and K. V. Thomas (eds), *Puritans and Revolutionaries* (Oxford, 1978), p. 258.

40. Anthony Fletcher, *Reform in the Provinces* (New Haven, CT, and London, 1986), p. 259; J. C. Jeaffreson (ed.), *Middlesex County Records* (1974), Old Ser., vol. 3, passim.

41. Stephen Roberts, 'Fornication and Bastardy in Mid Seventeenth-Century Devon: How was the Act of 1650 Enforced?', in J. Rule (ed.), *Outside the Law: Studies in Crime and Order, 1650–1850* (Exeter, 1982), pp. 13–15.

42. E. H. Bates-Harbin (ed.), *Quarter Sessions Records for the County of Somerset*, vol. 3, Somerset Records Society, 28 (1912), p. xlvii.

43. Underdown, *Revel, Riot and Rebellion*, p. 264.

44. Bates-Harbin, *Quarter Sessions Somerset*, p. 342.

45. Ibid., p. 338.

46. J. H. E. Bennett and J. C. Dewhurst (eds), *Quarter Sessions Records . . . for the County Palatine of Chester 1559–1760*, Records Society of Lancashire and Cheshire, 94 (1940), 166.

47. T. Birch (ed.), *A Collection of the State Papers of John Thurloe Esq.* (1742), 7 vols, vol. 4, pp. 241, 273.

48. Ibid., vol. 4, pp. 473, 545.

49. Ibid., p. 764.

50. Quoted by Anthony Fletcher in 'Oliver Cromwell and the Problem of Consent', in C. Jones, M. Newitt and S. Roberts (eds), *Politics and People in Revolutionary England* (Oxford, 1986), p. 200.

51. Rutt, *Diary of Thomas Burton*, vol. 2, p. 265.

52. B. H. Cunnington (ed.), *Records of the County of Wilts* (Devizes, 1932), p. 230.

53. Underdown, *Revel, Riot and Rebellion*, p. 269.

54. F. A. Inderwick, *The Interregnum* (1891), p. 56.

55. S. C. Ratcliff and H. C. Johnson (eds), *Quarter Sessions Order Book 1650–1657*, Warwick County Records (Warwick, 1937), vol. 3, pp. 271–2.

56. Fox, 'Diary of Robert Beake', pp. 136–7.

57. BL E. 878. 1, W. B. *The Yellow Book* (1656), passim and BL E. 878.2, W. B., *The Trial of the Ladies* (1656), passim; J. Wake (ed.), *Quarter Sessions Records of the County of Northampton*, Northants Records Society, 1 (1924), 212–13.

58. E. S. De Beer (ed.), *The Diary of John Evelyn* (Oxford, 1955), vol. 3, pp. 203–4; see also BL E. 747.18, *The Public Intelligencer*, 21–28 Dec. 1657; for more details on the Christmas during the Civil War and Interregnum see Chris Durston, 'Lords of Misrule: the Puritan War on Christmas 1642–60', *History Today*, 35 (Dec. 1985), 7–14.

59. E. M. Symonds (ed.), 'The Diary of John Greene', *English Historical Review*, 43 (1928), 604.

60. BL E. 684.18, *The Flying Eagle*, 25 Dec. 1652–1 Jan. 1653.

61. Rutt, *Diary of Thomas Burton*, vol. 1, p. 229.

62. Bates-Harbin, *Quarter Sessions Somerset*, p. 324.

63. BL E. 370.8, *A Perfect Relation of the Horrible plot and Bloody Conspiracy of the Malignant party at Edmondbury in Suffolk* (London, 1647), passim.

64. BL E. 421.15, *Mercurius Pragmaticus*, 21–28 Dec. 1647; BL E. 422. 1, *The Kingdom's Weekly Post*, 29 Dec. 1647–5 Jan. 1648; BL E. 421.30, *The Kingdom's Weekly Intelligencer*, 28 Dec. 1647–4 Jan. 1648.

65. BL E. 421.22, *A Canterbury Christmas*, 1 Jan. 1648; BL E. 421. 23, *A Declaration of Many Thousands of the City of Canterbury*, 5 Jan. 1648; BL E. 421.29, *Mercurius Pragmaticus*, 28 Dec. 1647–4 Jan. 1648; BL E. 421.30, *The Kingdom's Weekly Intelligencer*, 28 Dec. 1647–4 Jan. 1648.

66. Macfarlane, *Diary of Ralph Josselin*, p. 108.

67. BL E. 868.3, Ezekial Woodward, *Christmas Day, the Old Heathen's Feasting Day* (1656), p. 18.

68. Parker, *English Sabbath*, p. 218.

69. Cornelius Burgess, *Two Sermons Preached to the Honourable House of Commons at Two Publicke Fasts* (1645), p. 33; for more details on the response to the fast-days, see Durston, 'Public Days of Fasting and Thanksgiving', pp. 139–46.

70. William Spurstowe, *England's Patterne and Duty in its Monthly Fasts* (1643), p. 17; Fletcher, *Sussex*, pp. 113–14.

71. Matthew Newcomen, *A Sermon Tending to Set Forth the Right Use of Disasters* (1644), pp. 11, 39.

72. Macfarlane, *Diary of Ralph Josselin*, pp. 22, 74.

73. Ibid., p. 58.

74. Underdown, *Fire From Heaven*, p. 226.

75. Jeaffreson, *Middlesex County Records*, Old Ser., vol. 3, pp. 189–90.

76. *Acts and Ordinances*, vol. 2, pp. 383–7.

77. Bates-Harbin, *Quarter Sessions Somerset*, pp. xlvii–xlviii.

78. *Calendar of State Papers Domestic 1655*, p. 239; BL 669 f. 20. 33.

79. E. M. Symonds (ed.), 'The Diary of John Greene', *English Historical Review*, 43 (1928), 599, 603; 44 (1929), 109, 115.

80. F. P. Verney and M. M. Verney, *Memoirs of the Verney Family during the Seventeenth Century* (1904), vol. 1, p. 355.

81. De Beer, *Diary of John Evelyn*, vol. 2, pp. 78, 544, 567; vol. 3, pp. 19, 63, 75, 89, 147, 166–7, 194, 218.

82. E. A. Wrigley and R. S. Schofield, *The Population History of England 1541–1871* (1981), pp. 28, 540. The average annual figures are my calculations from their yearly totals. The figures on the percentages of actual births recorded in the registers are also mine compiled from their raw data.

83. John Morrill, 'The Church in England 1642–9', in John Morrill (ed.), *Reactions to the English Civil War 1642–1649* (1982), p. 104; Macfarlane, *Diary of Ralph Josselin*, p. 382.

84. Cressy, 'Purification, Thanksgiving and the Churching of Women', pp. 140–1.

85. Durston, *The Family in the English Revolution*, p. 122.

86. F. W. Bennitt (ed.), 'The Diary of Isabella, wife of Sir Roger Twysden, bart', *Archaelogia Cantiana*, 51 (1939), 123.

87. BL E. 714.2, *The Kingdom's Weekly Intelligencer*, 20–27 Sept. 1653.

88. BL E. 713.10, E. 714.5, E. 714.13, *Mercurius Democritus*, 14 Sept.–5 Oct. 1653.

89. G. Isham (ed.), *The Correspondence of Bishop Brian Duppa and Sir Justinian Isham 1650–1660*, Northants Records Society, 17 (1955), 67.

90. Wrigley and Schofield, *Population History*, p. 521.

91. Isham, *Correspondence of Duppa and Isham*, pp. xxvi, 108; Underdown, *Fire from Heaven*, p. 218.

92. For more details, see Durston, *The Family in the English Revolution*, pp. 80–4.

93. Rutt, *Diary of Thomas Burton*, vol. 2, pp. 38, 44, 67–74.

94. John Morrill, 'The Impact of Puritanism', in Morrill (ed.), *The Impact of the English Civil War* (1991), p. 59; Morrill, 'The Church in England 1642–9', p. 108.

95. Underdown, *Fire From Heaven*, p. 218.

96. *Historic Manuscripts Commission, Various Collections*, vol. 1, p. 126.

97. Bates-Harbin, *Quarter Sessions Somerset*, p. 285.

98. Jeaffreson, *Middlesex County Records*, Old Ser., vol. 3, pp. 247, 257–8.

99. Underdown, *Revel, Riot and Rebellion*, p. 266; Jeaffreson, *Middlesex County Records*, Old Ser., vol. 3, p. 231.

100. Underdown, *Revel, Riot and Rebellion*, p. 264.

101. Ibid., p. 264; Cunnington, *Records of the County of Wilts*, p. 222.

102. Jeaffreson, *Middlesex County Records*, Old Ser., vol. 3, p. 256; Bates-Harbin, *Quarter Sessions Somerset*, p. 347.

103. Jeaffreson, *Middlesex County Records*, Old Ser., vol. 3, p. 258.

104. Bennett and Dewhurst, *Quarter Sessions Chester*, p. 165.

105. Rutt, *Diary of Thomas Burton*, vol. 2, pp. 264–5.

106. K. E. Wrightson, 'The Puritan Reformation of Manners with special reference to the counties of Lancashire and Essex 1640–1660', unpublished University of Cambridge PhD thesis (1974), p. 213.

107. Fletcher, *Reform in the Provinces*, p. 260.

108. Keith Wrightson, 'The Nadir of English Illegitimacy in the Seventeenth Century', in P. Laslett, K. Osterveen and R. Smith (eds), *Bastardy and its Comparative History* (1980).

109. Ibid.

110. Birch, *State Papers of John Thurloe*, vol. 4, pp. 273–4.

111. Sylvester, *Reliquiae Baxterianae*, pp. 84–5.

112. Underdown, *Fire From Heaven*, pp. 264–5.

113. Birch, *State Papers of John Thurloe*, vol. 4, pp. 312.

114. Ibid., pp. 328, 371.

115. Rutt, *Diary of Thomas Burton*, vol. 4, p. 328.

116. Jonathan Barry, 'Popular Culture in Seventeenth Century Bristol', in Barry Reay (ed.), *Popular Culture in Seventeenth Century England* (1985), p. 70.

117. Clark, *Life and Times of Anthony Wood*, pp. 314, 317.

118. George Herbert, *A Priest to the Temple or the Countury Parson* (1652), in F. E. Hutchinson, *The Works of George Herbert* (Oxford, 1941), pp. 283–4; quoted by Eamon Duffy in 'The Godly and the Multitude in Stuart England', *The Seventeenth Century*, 1 (1986), 38.

119. Anthony Burgess, *The Reformation of the Church to be Endeavoured more than that of the Commonwealth* (1645), pp. 18, 27.

120. Richard Baxter, *Gildas Salvianus; The Reformed Pastor* (1656) p. 332.

121. Inderwick, *The Interregnum*, p. 55.

8.   FROM PURITANISM TO DISSENT, 1660–1700   *John Spurr*

1. N. H. Keeble, *The Literary Culture of Nonconformity in Later Seventeenth-century England* (Leicester, 1987), p. 47.

2. M. Sylvester (ed.), *Reliquiae Baxterianae* (1696), part II, p. 146.

3. Quoted in J. T. Cliffe, *The Puritan Gentry Besieged, 1650–1700* (1993), p. 39.

4. *Reliquiae Baxterianae*, II, 278.

5. See A. G. Matthews (ed.), *Calamy Revised* (Oxford, 1934), p. xiii; John Spurr, *The Restoration Church of England, 1646–1689* (New Haven, and London, 1991), pp. 42–5.

6. A. B., *A Letter from a Minister to a Person of Quality, shewing some Reasons for his Non-Conformity* (1679), p. 1.

7. See [George Gould (ed.)], *Documents Relating to the Settlement of the Church of England by the Act of Uniformity of 1662* (1862), p. 117, and 111–46 passim.

8. John Corbet, *An Account Given of the Principles and Practices of Several Nonconformists* (1680), p. 27.

9. A. G. Matthews (ed.), *The Savoy Declaration of Faith and Order 1658* (1959), p. 122.

10. E. B. Underhill (ed.), *The Records of a Church of Christ Meeting in Broadmead Bristol*, Hanserd Knollys Society, 1847, p. 211.

11. Ibid., pp. 213, 211.

12. Ibid., p. 124; H. G. Tibbutt (ed.), *The Minutes of the First Independent Church (now Bunyan Meeting) at Bedford, 1656–1776*, Bedfordshire Historical Record Society, 55 (1976), p. 62.

13. See H. Fishwick (ed.), *The Note Book of the Rev. Thomas Jolly*, Chetham Society, XXXIII, 1895.

14. Quoted in D. L. Wykes, 'Religious Dissent and the Penal Laws: An Explanation of Business Success?', *History*, 75 (1990), 53.

15. John Tombes, *Theodulia* (1667), sig. A6r.

16. Anne Whiteman (ed.), *The Compton Census of 1676: A Critical Edition* (1986), p. xxxix; Gervase Disney, *Some Remarkable Passages in the Holy Life and Death of Gervase Disney* (1692), p. 49; Cliffe, *Puritan Gentry Besieged*, p. 88.

17. N. H. Keeble and G. F. Nuttall (eds), *Calendar of the Correspondence of Richard Baxter*, 2 vols (Oxford, 1991), vol. II, pp. 156, 188; R. Parkinson (ed.), *The Life of Adam Martindale*, Chetham Society, IV, 1845, pp. 173–4; W. L. Sachse (ed.), *The Diary of Roger Lowe* (1938), p. 16.

18. E. Axon (ed.), *Oliver Heywood's Life of John Angier of Denton*, Chetham Society XCVII, 1937, p. 107.

19. Quoted in A. Fletcher, 'The Enforcement of the Conventicle Acts 1664–1679', *Studies in Church History*, vol. 21 (1984), p. 237.

20. John Humfrey, *Answer to Stillingfleet* (1680), p. 6. For the problems of one London parish see M. A. Goldie and J. Spurr, 'Politics and the Restoration Parish: Edward Fowler and the Struggle for St Giles Cripplegate', *English Historical Review*, CIX (1994).

21. Matthews, *Calamy Revised*, pp. 401–2; M. H. Lee (ed.), *The Diaries and Letters of Philip Henry* (1882), p. 133.

22. See W. J. Sheils, 'Oliver Heywood and his congregation', *Studies in Churd History*, vol. 23 (1986).

23. [Edward Polhill], *The Samaritan* (1682), p. 114.

24. Dr Williams's Library, MS Morrice Entering Book P, fo. 288; *Reliquiae Baxterianae*, II, 433–5.

25. Joseph Hunter, *The Rise of the Old Dissent Exemplified in the Life of Oliver Heywood* (1842), p. 200.

26. See R. Thomas, 'Comprehension and Indulgence', in G. F. Nuttall and O. Chadwick (eds), *From Uniformity to Unity* (1962); J. Spurr, 'The Church of England, Comprehension and the Toleration Act of 1689', *English Historical Review*, CIV (1989).

27. See C. G. Bolam, J. Goring, H. L. Short and R. Thomas, *The English Presbyterians* (1968), p. 87; R. Beddard, 'Vincent Alsop and the Emancipation of Restoration Dissent', *Journal of Ecclesiastical History*, 24 (1973), 166.

28. Hunter, *Heywood*, p. 225.

29. Matthew Henry, *The Life of the Rev. Philip Henry* (ed. by J. B. Williams, 1825; reprint 1974), p. 133.

30. Hunter, *Heywood*, p. 268; Lee, *Henry Diaries*, p. 327; *Life of Philip Henry*, appendix xviii.

31. BL Egerton MS 3337, fo. 2v.

32. Lee, *Henry Diaries*, p. 313; M. Hunter and A. Gregory (eds), *An Astrological Diary of the Seventeenth Century – Samuel Jeake of Rye 1652–1699* (Oxford, 1988), p. 148; Beddard, 'Alsop', 171–3.

33. Lee, *Henry Diaries*, p. 301.

34. See G. R. Cragg, *Puritanism in the Period of the Great Persecution 1660–1688* (Cambridge, 1957), ch. 4; M. R. Watts, *The Dissenters* (Oxford, 1978), pp. 234–6.

35. Among many other examples see Hunter, *Heywood*, p. 257; Sheils, 'Heywood', 273–4; Hunter and Gregory, *Jeake*, p. 34.

36. On charity and education see Watts, *Dissenters*, pp. 336–41 and 366–71 respectively.

37. Tibbutt, *Bedford*, p. 60; Underhill, *Broadmead*, p. 103; R. Mortimer (ed.), *Minute Book of the Men's Meeting of the Society of Friends in Bristol 1667–1686*, Bristol Record Society, XXVI, 1971, pp. 130–1; Watts, *Dissenters*, p. 228.

38. Underhill, *Broadmead*, p. 86; Tibbutt, *Bedford*, pp. 39–42.

39. See Keeble, *Literary Culture*, pp. 50–5; C. W. Horle, *The Quakers and the English Legal System 1660–1688* (Philadelphia, 1988).

40. See R. L. Greaves's trilogy on the plotting of the period: *Deliver Us from Evil* (Oxford, 1986); *Enemies Under His Feet* (Stanford, Cal. 1990); and *Secrets of the Kingdom* (Stanford, Cal., 1992).

41. Underhill, *Broadmead*, p. 218.

42. See C. E. Whiting, *Studies in English Puritanism from the Restoration to the Revolution, 1660–1688* (1931), pp. 62–3, 75, 118; Cliffe, *Puritan Gentry Besieged*, p. 115; R. Greaves, *John Bunyan and English Nonconformity* (1992), p. 5.

43. Bolam et al., *English Presbyterians*, p. 90.

44. Underhill, *Broadmead*, p. 214.

45. M. Spufford, *Contrasting Communities – English Villagers in the Sixteenth and Seventeenth Centuries* (Cambridge, 1974), p. 295; Underhill, *Broadmead*, pp. 213–14.

46. Greaves, *Bunyan and Nonconformity*, p. 67; Jacqueline Eales, 'Samuel Clarke and the "Lives" of Godly Women in Seventeenth-century England', *Studies in Church History*, vol. 27 (1990), p. 367; for the Interregnum see A.

Laurence, 'A Priesthood of She-believers: Women and Congregations in Mid-seventeenth-century England', *Studies in Church History*, vol. 27 (1990).

47. Watts, *Dissenters*, pp. 346–66 is the best introduction to the social constitution of dissent; also see Spufford, *Contrasting Communities*, pp. 301–3.

48. Cliffe, *Puritan Gentry Besieged*, p. 84.

49. On this affinity with commerce and manufacture see Watts, *Dissenters*, p. 360; Wykes, 'Religious Dissent'; D. H. Sacks, *The Widening Gate – Bristol and the Atlantic Economy, 1450–1700* (Berkeley, Cal., and Los Angeles, 1991), ch. 10, pp. 323–6 especially; Greaves, *Bunyan and Nonconformity*, pp. 2–3.

50. Matthews, *Calamy Revised*, pp. 197, 221–2; Cliffe, *Puritan Gentry Besieged*, p. 108.

51. Sheils, 'Heywood', 262–3.

52. Tibbutt, *Bedford*, p. 69; Underhill, *Broadmead*, pp. 166, 186–7.

53. *Disney*, p. 55.

54. See Keeble, *Literary Culture*, pp. 74–5; Cragg, *Puritanism*, pp. 172–3; and, for exceptions to this rule, Sheils, 'Heywood', 270–1.

55. Lee, *Henry Diaries*, p. 242.

56. *Calendar of Baxter Correspondence*, II, 202–4.

57. Tibbutt, *Bedford*, pp. 81–2, 32, 54.

58. Ibid., pp. 45–6, 70, 56.

59. Keeble, *Literary Culture*, pp. 285, 137.

60. Richard Baxter's preface to Samuel Clarke, *The Lives of Sundry Eminent Persons* (1683), sig. a3v–a4r.

61. Cliffe, *Puritan Gentry Besieged*, pp. 71, 138.

62. Axon, *Heywood's Life of Angier*, p. 85–6.

63. Lee, *Henry Diaries*, pp. 153–4; Watts, *Dissenters*, p. 313.

64. See Hunter and Gregory, *Jeake*, p. 44; Cliffe, *Puritan Gentry Besieged*, pp. 142–3, 203.

65. See Keeble, *Literary Culture*, and his *Richard Baxter – Puritan Man of Letters* (Oxford, 1982).

66. *The Journal of George Fox*, revised by N. Penney (Everyman edn, 1924), p. 1.

67. Alleine quoted by Greaves, *Bunyan and Nonconformity*, p. 23.

68. *Life of Philip Henry*, p. 69; Cliffe, *Puritan Gentry Besieged*, p. 71.

69. G. H. Jenkins, *Protestant Dissenters in Wales, 1639–1689* (Cardiff, 1992), pp. 97–8; Lee, *Henry Diaries*, p. 145.

70. John Bryan, *Dwelling with God* (1670), p. 323.

71. Quoted by Greaves, *Bunyan and Nonconformity*, p. 24.

72. Hannah Allen, *Satan His Methods and Malice Baffled* (1683), p. 12.

73. John Bunyan, *Grace Abounding* (Everyman edn, 1976), p. 28; Manton is quoted by Keeble, *Literary Culture*, p. 178.

74. Bunyan, *Grace Abounding*, p. 100.

75. G. R. Cragg, *From Puritanism to the Age of Reason* (Cambridge, 1950; pbk reprint 1966), p. 29.

76. Bolam et al., *English Presbyterians*, p. 105; *Calendar of Baxter Correspondence*, II, 148, 172.

77. See Spufford, *Contrasting Communities*, pp. 332, 343; and the forthcoming work of I. M. Green on religious instruction.

78. Hunter and Gregory, *Jeake*, p. 197.
79. See B. R. White, 'The Twilight of Puritanism in the Years Before and After 1688', in O. P. Grell, J. I. Israel and N. Tyacke (eds), *From Persecution to Toleration* (Oxford, 1991), pp. 327–8.

Notes on Contributors

MARGARET ASTON, now an independent historian, taught at St Anne's College, Oxford, Newnham College, Cambridge, and the Catholic University of America, Washington DC. Her publications include *The Fifteenth Century* (reprinted 1994), *Lollards and Reformers, Faith and Fire, England's Iconoclasts*, and most recently *The King's Bedpost*.

PATRICK COLLINSON is Regius Professor of Modern History in the University of Cambridge, having previously held chairs at the universities of Sydney, Kent at Canterbury, and Sheffield. He is a Commander of the British Empire and a Fellow of the British Academy. His best known book is *The Elizabethan Puritan Movement* (1967, pbk edn 1989), and his latest *Elizabethan Essays* (1994), to be followed by *From Cranmer to Sancroft: Essays on English Religion in the Age of the Reformation*.

CHRISTOPHER DURSTON is Reader in History at St Mary's University College, Strawberry Hill. His publications include *The Family in the English Revolution* (1989), *Princes, Pastors and People: The Church and Religion in England 1529–1689* (1991 with S. Doran), and *James I* (1993). He has also published a number of articles on the religious and cultural impact of the English Revolution.

JACQUELINE EALES is Senior Lecturer in History at Christ Church College, Canterbury. Her first book *Puritans and Roundheads: the Harleys of Brampton Bryan and the Outbreak of the English Civil War* (1990) was runner-up for the 1991 Whitfield Prize awarded by the Royal Historical Society. She is currently working on the history of women in early-modern England.

RALPH HOULBROOKE is Reader in History at the University of Reading. His publications include *Church Courts and the People during the English Reformation, 1520–1570* (1979), *The English Family, 1450–1700* (1984), and *English Family Life, 1576–1716: An Anthology from Diaries* (1989). He also edited the volume *Death, Ritual and Bereavement* (1989). He is currently working on a book provisionally entitled *Death, Religion and the Family, 1480–1750*.

MARTIN INGRAM is a Fellow, Tutor and University Lecturer in Modern History at Brasenose College, Oxford. His publications include *Church Courts, Sex and Marriage in England, 1570–1640* (1987) and a number of articles on crime and the law, sex and marriage, and popular customs. He has also published on the history of climate.

PETER LAKE is Professor of History at Princeton University. He is the author of a number of studies of religion, politics and culture in late sixteenth- and early seventeenth-century England, and is currently working on a study on conformist thought from Hooker to Laud.

JOHN SPURR was educated at St Edmund Hall, Oxford, and now teaches history at University College, Swansea. He has published *The Restoration Church of England, 1649–1689*, and is completing a study of *English Puritanism, 1603–1689*.

Index